*Gender, Race, and Ethnicity
in the Workplace*

Gender, Race, and Ethnicity in the Workplace

Issues and Challenges for Today's Organizations

VOLUME 3

Organizational Practices and Individual Strategies for Women and Minorities

EDITED BY
Margaret Foegen Karsten

PRAEGER PERSPECTIVES

Westport, Connecticut
London

Library of Congress Cataloging-in-Publication Data

Gender, race, and ethnicity in the workplace: issues and challenges for today's
organizations / edited by Margaret Foegen Karsten.
   p. cm.
   Includes bibliographical references and index.
   ISBN 0-275-98802-3 (set: alk. paper)—ISBN 0-275-98803-1 (v. 1: alk. paper)—
   ISBN 0-275-98804-X (v. 2: alk. paper)—ISBN 0-275-98805-8 (v. 3: alk. paper)
     1. Diversity in the workplace—United States.   I. Karsten, Margaret Foegen
HF5549.5.M5G46   2006
658.3008—dc22   2006010950

British Library Cataloguing in Publication Data is available.

This book is included in the African American Experience database from
Greenwood Electronic Media. For more information,
visit www.africanamericanexperience.com.

Library of Congress Catalog Card Number: 2006010950
ISBN: 0-275-98802-3 (set)
     0-275-98803-1 (vol. 1)
     0-275-98804-X (vol. 2)
     0-275-98805-8 (vol. 3)

First published in 2006

Praeger Publishers, 88 Post Road West, Westport, CT 06881
An imprint of Greenwood Publishing Group, Inc.
www.praeger.com

Printed in the United States of America

The paper used in this book complies with the
Permanent Paper Standard issued by the National
Information Standards Organization (Z39.48-1984).

10 9 8 7 6 5 4 3 2 1

Ideas and opinions expressed in the chapters of volumes 1, 2, and 3 of
Gender, Race, and Ethnicity in the Workplace are those of the authors and
do not necessarily reflect views of the set editor or the publisher.

In gratitude to all the women of strength—colleagues, relatives,
and friends both living and deceased—who have
influenced my life.

Contents

Acknowledgments

I gratefully acknowledge the University of Wisconsin-Platteville for granting a sabbatical leave that ultimately led to this project and Nicholas Philipson, senior editor, Business and Economics at Praeger, for all his assistance. Furthermore, I thank the contributors for the ideas and insights they shared in their chapters. Dealing with them to complete this set has been a pleasure. Finally, I want to express appreciation to Mary Christoph Foegen for her counsel; J. H. Foegen for instilling in me the desire to write; and my immediate family: children in their birth order, John, Kathryn, and Amy, and my husband, Randy, for their support as I completed two major writing projects in eighteen months.

Margaret Foegen Karsten
March 2006

Introduction

Two generations have grown to adulthood since sweeping federal laws were passed to end employment discrimination based on race, color, religion, sex, and national origin and to ensure that women and men were paid equally for doing the same or substantially similar jobs. Why, then, is it still necessary—even compelling—to have a diverse group of practitioners, academics, and theorists in business, psychology, and related disciplines address issues related to gender, race, and ethnicity in the workplace?

Three reasons, *not* in order of importance, are money, power, and ethics. Women in management and the professions supposedly experience a $2 million lifetime income disparity vis-à-vis their male counterparts.[1] Economists indicate that white women experience a 7 percent wage penalty for *each child* they have.[2] Though no wage penalty is attached to motherhood for black women, they unfortunately tend to be paid significantly less than whites.

Though the sexes have reached numerical parity in management overall, scarcely more than a handful of women lead the powerful Fortune 500 firms in the United States. As of this writing, only one is a woman of color. And 95 percent of top executives in U.S. corporations are white males, though no appreciable difference exists in the percent of women and men who aspire to become chief executives.[3]

If those facts are not persuasive enough, consider that from 2000 through the first half of 2001, twenty-five cases filed with the Equal Employment Opportunity Commission involved egregious racial harassment—the use of nooses reminiscent of lynching.[4] Not in out-of-the way rural areas, the sites of such despicable incidents were cities such as San Francisco and Detroit. Those are only the overt acts; columnist Leonard Pitts commenting on the death of civil rights advocate Rosa Parks in 2005 said, "Racism that was once brazen enough to demand a black woman's bus seat is covert now, a throw-the-rock-and-hide-your-hand charade, its effects as visible as ever, its workings mostly hidden."[5]

How long will it take before repugnant incidents and effects—blatant and subtle—are abolished? When will future U.S. citizens wonder why publications in the early twenty-first century found it necessary to create lists of the top fifty women or blacks in major firms? Those from cultures characterized by extreme time consciousness, a strong streak of individualism, and a desire to pursue promotions into the pinnacles of power have become impatient with the slow pace of change. Incrementalists might urge them to learn from those of other cultural traditions that social change occurs slowly and that forty to fifty years, though a large portion of any person's life, is very little time in the context of social institutions that have existed for centuries. Others are not convinced that change must be slow. They argue that any additional time is too long to wait for those who have been deprived of full participation in and equal benefits of their work in this society.

Corporate downsizing notwithstanding, the United States may again face a shortage of highly skilled professionals. Baby Boomers, born between 1946 and 1964, are starting to retire in record numbers and will be replaced by the much smaller Baby Bust and Generations X and Y. Record numbers of women are in the labor force already, so they will not be a ready supply of additional labor, but women and people of color who are currently marginalized and underutilized may be.[6]

Twenty-five percent of U.S. firms do not have diversity programs.[7] Of those that do, only about one-third succeed; 20 percent fail.[8] This abysmal track record does not promote positive relations among people of various races and ethnicities. The road to a multicultural workplace is uneven and full of potholes; temporary spikes in dysfunctional conflict are to be expected. Miscommunication and misunderstanding even among people of similar backgrounds can result in serious organizational problems. Without honest, open face-to-face dialogue, which presupposes self knowledge such that people can explain who they are, their worldviews, and the factors, including ethnicity and race, that have shaped them, U.S. firms face trying times. Progressing from different starting points on the continuum ranging from monolithic to pluralistic to multicultural organizations will be challenging.

Stereotypes and the debate over the extent to which gender differences in behavior exist and their causes affect the enthusiasm with which workplace diversity is embraced. A 2005 Catalyst study showed that although few managerially relevant behavioral differences exist between the sexes, men are still viewed as more likely to "take charge" and women to "take care" of situations and people.[9] The consequences of such deeply embedded false mindsets are horrendous for women pursuing upward mobility, yet they are as likely to believe the stereotypes as men. A steady stream of contrary information must be presented to root out stereotypes if gender parity is to be a reality by 2019, as the optimistic Committee of 200, an elite group of powerful U.S. women, forecasts.[10] Otherwise, predictions of those who say gender equity will not occur for another 475 years may prove more accurate.[11]

Equity may not be achieved quickly if behavioral variations are primarily attributed to innate sex-based differences. Despite profuse apologies, former Harvard president Lawrence Summers, who resigned from that position on June 30, 2006, unleashed a controversy the previous spring by suggesting that the shortage of female science professors may be due to such distinctions. This rationale alarmed people who believe that nurture or socialization has far more to do with occupational choice than any internal differences, which they maintain are insignificant.

Baron-Cohen, who studies differences in empathizing and systematizing human brains that he believes are hard-wired but that appear in both women and men thinks the situation of those studying biological differences has improved since the 1960s and 1970s. In those days, serious researchers who recognized the role of socialization but wanted to study the impact of biology on sex differences in behaviors were "accused of oppression and of defending an essentialism that perpetuated inequalities between the sexes." Baron-Cohen argues that now the "pendulum has settled sensibly in the middle of the nature-nurture debate."[12]

His assessment is disputed by other researchers, notably Janet Hyde. Her meta-analysis revealed that gender-related behavioral differences long assumed to exist may not or may be highly exaggerated. She found few differences between the sexes and still fewer that were relevant to leadership or management in her studies of gender similarities.[13] False assumptions nonetheless persist and harm both sexes. Women who are not perceived as nice may be penalized in important selection and evaluation decisions; men may be perceived incorrectly and may see themselves as incapable of nurturing.[14]

Implications of many other factors based on which humans experience different workplace opportunity and treatment could have been explored; these volumes address only gender, race, and ethnicity for reasons of relative brevity. The socially constructed term *race* is used reluctantly, recognizing that it is not synonymous with skin color, differs from ethnicity, and may be unrelated to objective reality. The human race truly is the only one that exists.

Over the past two generations, much progress has been made. Things *have* changed, yet some issues in vogue today—such as "on-" and "off-ramps" for those who wish to step out of the fast track to provide care or get more education[15]—are essentially concerns from a quarter century ago that have been repackaged significantly.

A shortage of ideas for creating harmonious diverse workplaces in which all employees flourish is not the problem. We know what to do; now we must figure out how to do it. Ways to implement greater organizational equity must be considered carefully after they have been interiorized and are given high priority. Evaluation, accountability, and follow-up also are crucial to long-term success of equal opportunity efforts.

Consequences of failing in this endeavor could be dire. Some believe corporations are immune from the short-lived social disintegration and racial tension following Hurricane Katrina in 2005, but they may be deluded. Growing gaps between haves and have-nots in the United States, if not remedied, could result in chaos affecting all institutions, including businesses. Though many blacks have increased their incomes, their wealth trails that of the majority group.[16] Native Americans are virtually off the radar in terms of management of major firms, but the underlying leadership principles of some tribal nations are consistent with contemporary management theories, such as stewardship and servant leadership. Continuing to marginalize these and other racial and ethnic minorities is costly and must end.

This comprehensive set examines the status of women and racial/ethnic minorities and discusses challenges they face and the psychological, sociological, and legal contexts in which change must occur. It then suggests actions that organizations and individuals can take to deal with such challenges.

VOLUME 1

Volume 1 sets the stage for in-depth treatment of causes and consequences of workplace and leadership inequity. Perspectives of those who feel disconnected from or outside of the Eurocentric corporate mainstream in the United States, such as Asian Americans, Native American women, and black and white women are explored. Employment statistics pertaining to a spectrum of racial and ethnic minorities and to women are analyzed, as are those focused more narrowly on subgroups of Latinas.

Disaffection is expressed poignantly in the stories of those whose backgrounds would uniquely qualify them to make culturally rich, if thus far unrecognized and unrewarded, contributions to workplace management but for artificial barriers. This illustrates the amount of progress that must be made before those with different but equally valid and valuable perspectives become full partners in societal and business leadership.

Chapters in Volume 1 range from theoretical reflections on leadership to pragmatic analyses of employment statistics. The volume begins with conceptual discussions of leadership that draw on but go beyond experiences of diverse groups, including African American executives and entrepreneurs, skilled tradeswomen who perform managerial functions daily, Asian Americans, and Native American women. Advocated are flexible, holistic, situational leadership approaches that "give voice" to the marginalized, "give back" to the community, add value to society, and distance themselves from either/or dichotomies.

As a group, contributors largely reject hierarchical leadership but reach no consensus about what must replace it. Such agreement may be impossible if leadership depends on the circumstances. Leader effectiveness may demand both meticulous preparation through the study of related disciplines and a simultaneous willingness to "let go" and creatively combine a kaleidoscope of possibilities in new, different ways. The most fitting leadership analogy may be that of the artist whose painting-in-process evolves on an ever-changing canvas, suggested by Adler.

Though technically not managers, skilled craftswomen who eschew the title fulfill leadership roles and engage in traditional management functions of planning, organizing, directing, and controlling. The lack of attractiveness of management as an occupation is not an obstacle that the Glass Ceiling Commission of the 1990s envisioned but is nonetheless problematic. For most skilled tradeswomen, promotions to management would entail less flexible schedules, relative job insecurity associated with nonunionized supervisory positions, and short-term pay cuts due to necessary but unpaid overtime. Thus the short-run lack of incentives for tradeswomen to cross over to management may perpetuate occupational segregation at higher levels.

Such occupational segregation is the topic of later chapters in Volume 1. Contributors differ markedly in their views of this problem and related concepts. For example, Kim decries occupational segregation for its inefficiency in the use of human resources in a meritocracy where rewards are to be based on performance rather than on uncontrollable factors. Rosette, on the other hand, questions the existence of meritocracy due to unearned privilege, which gives advantages to some based on race, ethnicity, or gender.

VOLUME 2

Many legal, judicial, psychological, and sociological forces affect the treatment and advancement prospects of employees and executives based on their gender, race, and ethnicity. This volume discusses selected laws related to equal employment opportunity, affirmative action programs, and the relationship of the relatively neglected topics of racial and ethnic harassment to the more widely researched issue of sexual harassment and of the latter to workplace incivility (rudeness) and violence. The impact of stereotypes, socialization, and power-related concerns on the disenfranchised also are presented.

Twenty-five percent of human resource managers surveyed attribute sexual harassment lawsuits to failed romantic relationships in the workplace.[17] This worries some employers enough to ask the parties to sign so-called love contracts to release their firms from liability for harassment when or if the relationship ends. Unlike harassment, incivility, or violence, however, workplace romances may have a positive side, improving morale and satisfaction of the participants, possible charges of favoritism from co-workers notwithstanding. Romantic workplace relationships are addressed in Volume 2.

Though office romance may have unanticipated favorable effects on those directly involved, many laws and programs designed to rectify employment inequity have unintended harmful effects. For example, affirmative action has been wildly successful at opening previously closed doors for women and minorities—particularly white women—but also has led to consequences that some fear have hampered additional progress.

Furthermore, other equal employment opportunity–related programs focus on superficial problems and fail to discern (let alone address) their root causes. For example, Nydegger and coauthors point out in Volume 2 that workplace incivility and sexual harassment sometimes occur together. Rudeness at work, however, has been virtually ignored. Later, Callahan indicates that sexual harassment training implemented to deal with sexual assault by males in one branch of the military disregards the fact that its higher incidence and an increase in eating disorders among females in the same branch could be caused by perceived loss of personal control due to institutionalized resocialization practices.

In the first chapter of Volume 2, Heilman and Haynes argue that affirmative action may have unintended consequences that should be dealt with. The effects of the Pregnancy Discrimination Act of 1978 (PDA), intended or otherwise, could not be adequately assessed or addressed for many years due to different judicial interpretations. Not until enactment of the Family and Medical Leave Act in 1993 (FMLA) did the debate subside.

At issue was whether the PDA required employers to provide minimum job-protected leave when a woman was physically incapacitated during childbirth and recovery. In some jurisdictions, women could be fired for absenteeism associated with complications of pregnancy or time off for childbirth if their employers lacked temporary disability insurance. Those interpreting the PDA narrowly argued that pregnant women had to be treated only as well or as poorly as "non-pregnant persons" who were disabled for a time, assuming that their employers offered insurance or had other temporary disability policies. Even then, the controversy was resolved only for employees who met eligibility standards and worked for firms covered by the FMLA. Those employed by organizations not required to comply with the FMLA still may have to contend with such interpretations if their state laws provide no additional protection.

The FMLA allows all eligible employees, regardless of sex, unpaid, job-protected leave in an attempt to dispel gender stereotypes about responsibilities for caregiving. Some employees, however, fear their career commitment will be questioned if they take FMLA leave; others cannot afford to do so. Ironically, the FMLA, which was to protect employees' job rights when they needed time off work for caregiving, may deter employees—particularly women wishing to bear children—from job changes needed to advance in their careers because of its restrictive eligibility requirements.

Stereotypes about the career commitment of pregnant women harm all employed women. Such mindsets, though incorrect, readily extend to all in the same general category when they are grouped together based on one uncontrollable factor instead of viewed as individuals.

More than forty years after the *Harvard Business Review* published "Are Women Executives People?"[18] and over twenty-five years after "Women and Men as Managers: A Significant Case of No Significant Difference" appeared in *Organizational Dynamics*,[19] the perception (though not the reality) of a link between management and masculinity persists. Several contributors deal with these stereotypes and the difficulty in eradicating them despite evidence that any true gender differences in leadership are small and situational.[20] Such stereotypes may be all but intractable until women, who now represent half of all managers, professionals, and administrators, are no longer numerical tokens in the executive suite.

Tokenism is another subject examined in this volume. Though much empirical evidence describes the organizational consequences of tokenism for women, the few existing studies on the impact of racial and ethnic minorities are narrow. More should be conducted. Those researching women who are tokens believe the same concepts may apply to minorities and have seen positive results among token women in powerful positions when the organization employing them purposely legitimated their authority.

Any token group has far less power than the dominant class, but power can also be systematically taken from the numerical majority as is done in the military to resocialize recruits. Callahan's previously mentioned chapter illustrates how power and control of one's own life are systematically removed from both male and female air force cadets, resulting in dysfunctional consequences as both strive to regain it. An important distinction is that the women cadets seem to bear the brunt of the negative impact; not only do they experience eating disorders at a higher rate than other female college freshmen as they seek to control their bodies, but they also are targets of sexual assault by men cadets who react to being stripped of power by asserting control over women.

Whether they are military recruits or powerful corporate CEOs, women and men still seem to be evaluated differently. This occurs despite the notion that U.S. institutions including the judiciary are gender-neutral and fair. Those who do not conform to intensified gender-related prescriptions for behavior, which are especially strong stereotypical expectations based on gender, are punished harshly.[21] On the other hand, infractions of those violating relaxed gender-based proscriptions, or behaviors considered inappropriate for any U.S. adult but less so for males, may be dealt with less severely.[22] Though the final verdict is still out at this writing, these findings may be relevant in the respective cases of Martha Stewart and Ken Lay of Enron, discussed in the last chapter of Volume 2.

VOLUME 3

Organizational and individual strategies for dealing with challenges faced by people of color and women based on case studies, personal reflections, and research are presented in Volume 3. Face-to-face interpersonal communication is proposed as the new frontier in which the promised benefits of diversity management will be delivered as individuals begin to know and trust one another. Other chapters dealing with diversity focus on the path Shell Oil U.S. took to become a model firm in terms of not only cultivating a heterogeneous workforce but also using each employee's unique talents fully and best practices in diversity management, which include built-in accountability, top executive support, and aggressive promotion of diversity during recruitment.

Today's diverse workforce consists of about equal percentages of women and men. As the percent of sexual harassment cases filed by men increases, some might think harassment policies should be gender-neutral, but the authors of "Dirty Business," a chapter in Volume 3, disagree. They discuss why sexual objectification of women—even if it occurs off the job—has devastating effects on the workplace, what can be done to change the culture that perpetuates objectification, and who should be involved in effecting such widespread organizational change.

Another change in the workforce with implications for women and minorities involves career planning models. Vestiges from a bygone era that assume uninterrupted vertical movement within one company must be replaced by models with multiple career paths featuring flexible on- and off-ramps, lateral moves, and continuous learning.

Crucial to career advancement of women and racial/ethnic minorities is the cultivation of social capital through developmental opportunities. Those who have lower positions or have been historically underrepresented may need to temporarily gain legitimacy by reflecting that of more powerful organizational members. Role modeling, another avenue for development, deserves more study. Being perceived as and serving as role models also may affect women and minorities positively.

New forms of developmental relationships, such as a network of mentors, may be appropriate for a workplace in which demands for knowledge quickly outpace capabilities of any human, regardless of gender, race, or intellectual endowment. Other alternatives to the master-apprentice model are needed to ease the burden on executive women and minorities who are expected to help others advance but whose ability to sponsor protégés is limited due what has been dubbed a time famine.[23] Some options are virtual-, peer-, and co-mentoring, and mentors-for-hire.

If research supports the importance of developmental relationships for women and people of color, so does the life experience of contributors to this volume. Evans advocates greater use of peer mentoring and coaching and defines networking as "putting people together" for business reasons. Gee lists networking along with self-knowledge and reflection as strategies for dealing with gendered racism.

Though the business literature focuses on developmental relationships and activities occurring at work, one's personal life also can enhance leadership. Too often, personal life is assumed to detract from work, but that occurs only if resources are assumed to be limited. To the extent that multiple roles are energizing,[24] the net result of personal experiences that teach skills transferable to the workplace may be positive, especially for those who have lacked equal access to company-sponsored development programs historically.

Equal access and treatment are necessary but insufficient to create employment equity if certain groups face unequal limitations.[25] All organizations, including those in higher education, must seriously consider personal and professional needs and realities of the employees they seek to attract and retain when formulating work-life policies and programs to minimize disparities in constraints.

Perceived inequities may create stress. Thus, people of color and women are more likely than white male counterparts to encounter gender- and race-related stressors. Glass and concrete ceilings, manifestations of individual and institutional racism, and historical traumas deep enough to wound the soul represent unequal constraints.

The resilience some people of color and women exhibit in coping successfully with profound challenges or stressors is remarkable. It may lead to unparalleled gains in hardiness, self-efficacy, self-esteem, and empathy, qualities that can only help in future personal and professional endeavors. However, not all those in the workplace who have been harmed by "isms" related to gender, race, or ethnicity are gifted with such resilience. They must not be abandoned, nor must their possible future contributions as employees or executives be dismissed. Rather, organizations must fully commit not only to stress-reduction strategies but also to creation of an environment that optimizes the talents of all.

NOTES

1. E. Murphy, *Getting Even: Why Women Don't Get Paid Like Men—And What to Do about It* (New York: Touchstone, 2005).

2. S. A. Hewlett, "Executive Women and the Myth of Having it All," *Harvard Business Review* 80 (2002): 66–74.

3. J. S. Lublin, "Women Aspire to Be Chief as Much as Men Do," *Wall Street Journal* (2004, June 23): D2.

4. A. Bernstein, "Racism in the Workplace: In an Increasingly Multicultural U.S., Harassment of Minorities Is on the Rise," *Business Week* (2001, July 30): 37–43, 64–67.

5. L. Pitts, "Rosa Parks: She Taught Us the Power of One," *Wisconsin State Journal* (2005, Oct. 31): A6.

6. S. A. Hewlett and C. B. Luce, "Off-Ramps and On-Ramps: Keeping Talented Women on the Road to Success," *Harvard Business Review* (March 2005): 43–46, 48, 50–54.

7. T. Joyner, "Ethnicity, Gender Bias Remain Common at Work," *Wisconsin State Journal* (2005, April 15): C9.

8. S. Rynes and B. Rosen, "A Field Survey of Factors Affecting the Adoption and Perceived Success of Diversity Training," *Personnel Psychology* 48 (1995): 247–71.

9. Catalyst, *Women "Take Care," Men "Take Charge": Stereotyping of U.S. Business Leaders Exposed* (New York: Catalyst, 2005).

10. M. Llewellyn-Williams, *The C200 Business Leadership Index 2004: Annual Report on Women's Clout in Business* (Chicago: Committee of 200, 2001–2004).

11. D. L. Corsun and W. M. Costen, "Is the Glass Ceiling Unbreakable? Habitus, Fields, and the Stalling of Women and Minorities in Management," *Journal of Management Inquiry* 10 (March 2001): 16–25.

12. S. Baron-Cohen, "The Essential Difference: The Male and Female Brain," *Phi Kappa Phi Forum* 85(1) (2005): 23.

13. J. S. Hyde, "The Gender Similarities Hypothesis," *American Psychologist* 60 (2005): 581–92.

14. Ibid.

15. Hewlett and Luce, "Off-Ramps and On-Ramps: Keeping Talented Women on the Road to Success," 43–46, 48, 50–54.

16. D. Hajela, "The Color of Money Still Divides Blacks and Whites," *Wisconsin State Journal* (2005, January 18): D1, D9.

17. Society for Human Resource Management, "Workplace Romance Survey (item no. 62.17014)," Alexandria, VA: SHRM Public Affairs Department.

18. G. Bowman, N. Worthy, and S. Greyser, "Are Women Executives People?" *Harvard Business Review* (July–August 1965): 15–28, 164–78.

19. S. M. Donnell and J. Hall, "Men and Women as Managers: A Significant Case of No Significant Difference," *Organizational Dynamics* (Spring 1980): 71.

20. Hyde, "The Gender Similarities Hypothesis."

21. D. A. Prentice and E. Carranza, "What Women and Men Should Be, Shouldn't Be, Are Allowed to Be, and Don't Have to Be: The Contents of Prescriptive Gender Stereotypes," *Psychology of Women Quarterly* 26 (2002): 269–81.

22. Ibid.

23. L. A. Perlow, "The Time Famine: Toward a Sociology of Work Time," *Administrative Science Quarterly* 44 (1999): 57–81.

24. R. Barnett and G. Baruch, "Social Roles, Gender, and Psychological Distress," in R. Barnett, L. Biener, and G. Baruch, eds., *Gender and Stress* (New York: Free Press, 1987), pp. 122–41.

25. L. Bailyn, *Breaking the Mold: Women, Men, and Time in the New Corporate World.* (New York: Free Press, 1993).

Cross-Cultural Communication in the Diverse Workplace: A New Frontier for Managers

John F. Kikoski and Catherine Kano Kikoski

Don't be cynical about the American experiment because it has only now begun.
—Kurt Vonnegut Jr.

Could the new frontier of diversity management be the "ordinary," much overlooked area of face-to-face communication?

In the past, much effort in this important cause was focused on what may be called the macro of diversity—increasing awareness of the changing demographics of America and its workplaces, the pros and cons of affirmative action and initial efforts to extend existing laws affecting it, and more recently, efforts to retain equal employment opportunity laws and programs. Also included in the macro level of dealing with diversity, which is above the individual level, are the negative effects of discrimination and social injustice, which diminish organizational effectiveness, and new, more positive organizational restructuring and administrative innovations to "value differences" and "celebrate diversity" with an eye toward better "managing diversity."

Perhaps it is time to shift the focus of diversity management to the micro or to individuals and their relationships—to the hum-drum ordinary face-to-face communication and conversation conducted each day between individuals and among members of small groups or teams about matters both mundane and complex. Could it be that here, in one of the areas least studied by scholars of management yet most engaged in by managers, is the new frontier of the diverse workplace?

What does this mean to managers? The big question may not be "Are workplaces ready for diversity?" but "Is your workplace ready for diversity at the elementary level of work accomplishment—the face-to-face?"

This chapter proposes to address this question by examining the cultural paradigms—the values, nonverbal and verbal behaviors of the major demographic groups in the United States and its workplaces—white males, women, African Americans, Hispanics, and Asian Americans. Becoming aware of each group's cultural paradigm is essential to mutually effective communication among gender, ethnic, and racial groups. Doing so can also help reduce the misunderstandings and misinterpretations that limit the synchronized, unconscious behavior that is required for effective common action in groups.

This chapter also proposes an applied communication theory—reflexive communication—that can help access the uniqueness of each individual and create common ground. If there is an ethic to this chapter, it is that the only antidote to stereotyping and discrimination is to come to know each other as individuals.

DEMOGRAPHICS AND U.S. SOCIETY: INTO
THE TWENTY-FIRST CENTURY

In the late twentieth century, the overwhelmingly white America of Norman Rockwell's *Saturday Evening Post* with few minorities unexpectedly and rather rapidly disappeared. In the 1970s, approximately one American in eight was black, Hispanic, or Asian American; this ratio was one in four in the 1990s and will be one in three by 2010. By 2050, one American in two will be black, Hispanic, or Asian American.[1] The same discernible trend is evident in the workforce. From 1980 to 2000 to 2020, whites in the workforce are forecast to drop from 81.9 to 73.1 to 65 percent and by 2050, to 53.4 percent. Blacks in the labor force will increase from 10.2 to 11.8 to 13.3 percent, and by 2050 to 14.1 percent. Asian Americans will rise from 2.3 to 4.7 to 7.3 percent, and by 2050 to 10.9 percent. Hispanics will most dramatically increase from 5.73 to 10.9 to 16 percent and by 2050 to 23.7 percent.[2] Demographically, America and its workforce are changing at meteoric speeds.

During the late twentieth century, legal (and illegal) immigration also hit levels not reached since the 1900s: New York City, for example, had more foreign-born residents by 1989 than at any time since 1910.[3] Examining this rapid demographic shift, *The Economist* observed: "People of 30 and older will increasingly have the experience of growing up in one kind of country and growing old in another. In some parts of the U.S., Americans will thus share the experience of new immigrants simply by staying at home."[4] One demographer commenting on these developments forecast: "If current conditions continue the United States will become a nation with no racial or ethnic majority during the 21st century."[5] Kurt Vonnegut was presciently right.[6]

A NEW CHALLENGE FOR MANAGERS: FACE-TO FACE
COMMUNICATION IN THE MORE DIVERSE WORKPLACE

In some contexts—in offices, businesses, bureaucracies, educational establishments, etc.—knowing the order of talk required is a part of one's social competence as an adult.

—John Shotter

Face-to-face communication is the most frequent of a manager's activities, but perhaps the least analyzed by management scholars.[7] In a classic study, Henry Mintzberg found that managers engage in face-to-face communication for about 78 percent of their workday—far more than any other activity.[8] Even in the informational era, one high-technology company replete with IT hardware reported that "up to 80 percent of the information exchange within it takes place through personal dialogue."[9] However, often, such interpersonal communication was not clearly understood, as another study discovered: "Half the time what the manager thought what he was giving as instructions or decisions was being treated as information or advice."[10] Even in the relatively simple monocultural white male organizations of the twentieth century, interpersonal communication in the workplace was among the most common yet least effective activities in a manager's day.

Managers know that Shotter is right: "Knowing the order of talk" is important to organizational effectiveness. Linguists have concluded that communication tends to be more effective among those who share common traits, such as gender, race, ethnicity, or culture—elements of "fit"—than those who do not.[11] Other research finds that heterogeneous groups experience less effective face-to-face communication and more difficulty in performing tasks than homogenous groups.[12] Diversity researcher Taylor Cox Jr. arrived at a similar conclusion:

> There is reason to believe that the presence of cultural diversity does make certain aspects of group functioning more problematic. Misunderstandings may increase, conflict and anxiety may rise, and people may feel less comfortable with membership in the group. These effects may combine to make decision making more difficult and time-consuming. In certain respects, then, culturally diverse workgroups are more difficult to manage effectively than culturally homogenous workgroups.[13]

From his experience in the workplace, black American executive Edward W. Jones Jr. reported:

> One of the phenomena that develops in every corporation is a set of behavioral and personal norms that facilitates communication and aids cohesiveness. Moreover, because this "informal organization" is built on White norms it can reinforce ... black-white differences ... and thus reject and destroy all but the most persistent blacks. The informal organization operates at all levels in a corporation and the norms become more rigid the higher one goes in the hierarchy. While this phenomenon promotes efficiency and unity, it is also restrictive and very selective. It can preclude promotion or lead to failure on the basis of "fit" rather than competence.[14]

Problems with the "order of talk" or "fit" are not limited to black Americans. They also are experienced by women. Deborah Tannen, author of the best-selling book *You Just Don't Understand: Men and Women in Conversation*, concluded that:

> There are gender differences in ways of speaking, and we need to identify and understand them. Without such understanding we are doomed to blame others or ourselves—or the relationship for the otherwise mystifying and damaging effects of our contrasting conversational styles. . . . This book shows that many frictions arise because boys and girls grow up in what are essentially different cultures, so talk between women and men is *cross-cultural communication.*[15]

If frictions generated by gender differences can arise among boys and girls, brothers and sisters, husbands and wives, mothers and fathers who live their lives from birth to death in the same homes, what frictions may develop in the workplace? Here relative strangers from culturally diverse backgrounds encounter one another for the first time. It may be with good reason that proactive managers are realizing that they need to learn more about each other's communication styles, cultural values, and nonverbal as well as verbal behaviors— the stuff of effective and successful communication. How might managers begin to address the micro workplace issues that arise due to Shotter's "order of talk," Jones's lack of "fit," and Tannen's "frictions?" Cultural paradigms may offer one answer.

CULTURAL PARADIGMS

Cultural paradigms may be defined as a combination of the cultural values and communication styles of the major demographic categories or cultural groups in the American workforce—white males, females, African Americans, Hispanics, and Asian Americans.[16] The term *cultural paradigm* or *communication paradigm* henceforth may be used interchangeably to describe the unconsciously shared values and the verbal and nonverbal behaviors that guide individuals from differing demographic categories in their face-to-face communication interactions with others. All individuals unconsciously operate according to their own communication paradigms, which generally seem natural until they encounter another individual whose communication behavior unconsciously flows from a differing cultural paradigm. At such times we become aware of our own cultural paradigm, and our interactions with others become conscious, uncomfortable, and even strained. Each cultural paradigm encompasses an array of verbal and nonverbal behaviors that are subconsciously synchronized and may differ from one American subculture to another. *Culture* and *subculture* will be used interchangeably in this chapter to treat groups that live in and contribute to a rich, overarching, and common American culture and community.

The two channels for face-to face communication are nonverbal and verbal communication. Research indicates that most communication is nonverbal. Scholars have concluded that between 65 percent and 90 percent of inter-personal communication occurs nonverbally.[17] The channels for nonverbal communication include (1) gaze or eye contact behavior; (2) kinesics, or body movements; (3) proxemics or the spatial distance individuals unconsciously stand or sit from one another; (4) touch; and (5) the paralanguage, or vocal tones and rhythms by which one speaks.

One major purpose of this chapter is to help managers become aware of the cultural paradigms of the major demographic groups to more effectively communicate with their colleagues in the workplace. In the coming era, it may be imperative for managers to proactively understand the values as well as the nonverbal and verbal behaviors by which individuals from different demographic groups communicate if they are to manage effectively. Managers may not necessarily communicate or manage uniformly and similarly—as they have in the past. As one observer put it, "The labor force is going to look and be different. The challenge, then, is in learning how to manage this difference. And the manager who can successfully do so will be as indispensable to corporate management as working capital."[18]

Valuing Cultural Differences; Valuing the Individual

Using only the lens of culture can lead to stereotyping. Dealing with culture alone can logically lead to generalizations such as "whites are . . . ," "blacks are . . . ," "women are . . . ," which simply are not true. The briefest of contacts with individuals from any of these subcultures indicates how unique and different each of us is. However, culture does provide the vista, the broad context from which each one of us has come. Culture (or subculture) may provide the general context, but it does not account for each person's unique individuality. Each individual embodies the specific sum of his or her personal life experience, as well as other influences that include but are not limited to gender, ethnicity, race, education, social class, occupation, region, and religion. Mediating factors such as length of residence in the United States and level of acculturation also may need to be considered. This chapter in no way suggests that any of the cultural paradigms described below are dicta, but merely rough guides that are to be held lightly in view of the individual before us.

A personal experience may make our point. We will never forget a round table discussion at a scholarly conference we attended. The topic was race, and at the end of a long session the only African American who was present finally spoke for the first time to her white colleagues. She stated that she had listened attentively for ninety minutes to everything that had been said by her colleagues about black culture in general. She had only one point to make to her colleagues: "But I am more than that."

The Difficulty and the Necessity to Talk

Perhaps one other topic needs to be addressed—the frequent difficulty of entering into conversation about gender, race, ethnicity, and culture. There are times when such conversations may evoke pride or denial, assertion, or accusation. Such emotional reactions are understandable because these topics can be the source of personal identity, a larger group membership, as well as a temporal tradition that extends prior to as well as after one's own existence. One scholar observed: "Ethnicity can be equated along with sex and death as a subject that touches off deep unconscious feelings in most people."[19] Furthermore, there may be the risk of being labeled racist or sexist for the mere suggestion that different subcultures exist in the greater American community and that some groups of people may tend to behave differently because of them.

However, one wonders if such issues can create a double bind? On one hand, avoiding such conversations can create a situation for managers whereby they are passively managed by diversity. On the other hand, could it be that only by acquiring the knowledge and skills to communicate across differing subcultural paradigms and having those conversations that managers can actively manage diversity and surmount the problems of misinterpretation and miscommunication that it can bring.[20]

Could it now, in the twenty-first century, be time to begin to converse about gender, race, culture, and ethnicity literally, matter-of-factly, and rationally, especially in the workplace? Black journalist Ellis Cose suggests that such discussions tend to be difficult, for they generally happen as "shouts or as whispers"— shouters often are likely to be experiencing such pain "that spectators tune them out," whereas whisperers could be so intimated by the truth of the topic that "they avoid saying much of anything at all."[21] The Reverend Martin Luther King Jr. recognized the virtue of dialogue in his famous "Letter from Birmingham Jail." He wrote: "Too long has our beloved Southland been bogged down in a tragic effort to live in monologue rather than dialogue." He then called for negotiation with the Birmingham authorities to negotiate through dialogue and conversation—to achieve justice.[22]

This chapter proposes neither shouting nor whispering but addressing the issues that gender, race, ethnicity, and culture race in the workplace matter-of-factly and in calm, respectful voices. What might be some of these misperceptions or misinterpretations that culture can cause? Table 1.1 compares some of the most central values and behaviors of women, African Americans, Hispanics, and Asian Americans with one of the key white male values— hyperindividualism—as well as some differing nonverbal and verbal behaviors that can create cultural misunderstandings.

Knowledge and understanding of these differing paradigms and styles of communication may enable managers to transcend differences and bring about more effective understanding. In the twenty-first century, the U.S. workforce will be comprised of even more individuals with differing communication styles

TABLE 1.1. Values and Behaviors of Five American Cultural Paradigms

Paradigm	Values	Behaviors
White women	Connectedness	Maintain more eye contact in conversation; stand/sit closer together
White males	Hyperindividualism	Maintain less eye contact in conversation; stand/sit farther apart
Blacks	Community	Look at another when talking/ Look away when listening
White males	Hyperindividualism	Look away from another when talking/at another when listening
Hispanics	Personal relationships	Prefer to establish relationships before doing business
White males	Hyperindividualism	Prefer to "get right down to business"; relationship (if any) only after doing business
Asian Americans	Hierarchy	Ambiguous, subtle interpersonal communication; more meaning derived from body language than words; value indirectness
White males	Hyperindividualism	Words "mean what they say"; most meaning comes from words themselves; little from nonverbals; value directness

and cultural paradigms. As this century unfolds, the ability to deal with a more diverse workforce will become an asset of increasing importance to managers and their organizations.

THE WHITE MALE COMMUNICATION PARADIGM

We speak their language, read their novels, pledge allegiance to the political system they founded, and continue to be motivated by the ideals they inscribed in the Declaration of Independence. It is appropriate to begin by treating this demographic group, since it was the English or Anglo-Saxons who settled the continent of America, and thereby established the society, culture, and institutions that later attracted immigrants by the millions to become Americans.[23] The white Anglo-Saxon Protestants (WASPs), like every ethnic or racial group, are diverse. Initially inclusive only of those who were English or of English descent, the category now includes Americans who identify themselves as of German, Dutch, Scots-Irish, Scottish, Welsh, and/or Scandinavian descent.[24]

Because white males or (more precisely) WASP males established this society's institutions, it is natural that they dominated its leadership. This may be seen through the prism of the presidency: Every president from George Washington through George W. Bush has been a WASP male, with the partial exception of New England boarding school and Harvard-educated John Kennedy, who may be termed a (Catholic) or WASC male.[25] It was not until the 1960s and 1970s that WASP domination of America and its institutions began to fade and the term WASP male began to disappear from use and be replaced in the 1980s by a newer term—white male—as non-WASP males also began to realize the promise of America by ascending to its heights. The post–World War II expansion of the American economy was so great that the supply of WASP males was inadequate to meet demand. Simultaneously, the GI Bill opened the gates of higher education to many Catholic, Eastern and Southern European, and Jewish males for the first time. So, by the 1960s and 1970s these individuals, of whom Italian American Lee (originally Lido) Iacocca, the first non-WASP CEO of a major U.S. auto company, is a good example, had sufficient career experience to begin assuming high-ranking positions in corporate America. In so doing, these white males assimilated, largely conformed to, and enriched the WASP male communication paradigm that remains the core template for values and verbal and nonverbal behaviors in America's organizations. On this point, anthropologists Edward T. Hall and Mildred Reed Hall concluded:

> Despite its ethnic diversity, the U.S. has managed to absorb bits and pieces of many cultures and weave them into a unique culture that is strikingly consistent and distinct. . . . While the United States has absorbed millions of people from countries around the globe, the core culture of the United States has its roots in northern European or Anglo-Saxon culture . . . this dominant or mainstream business culture is the norm to which people with other cultural backgrounds are expected to conform, particularly in large corporations.[26]

Few may be aware of it, but approximately half of Americans are descendants of its early European settlers. As one statistical demographer concluded, "In 1990, 49 percent of the American population was attributable to the settler and Black populations of 1790 and 51 percent to immigration after that date."[27] So in terms of ideals, culture, and simple numbers, it may be appropriate that this treatment of subcultural diversity begins with the demographic group that today is called white male.

White Male Values

If any values are predominant in U.S. organizations today, they are WASP or white male values. They may seem common, for they are the mainstream values that are unconsciously taken for granted in American society.[28] They include hyperindividualism, self-control and limited expression of feeling, industry and work, achievement and success, self-reliance and self-sufficiency, practicality over theorizing, and doing over thinking and being.

As listed here (and as will be true with other demographic groups), these values are not necessarily prioritized in any order of significance. Only some can be addressed in this chapter.

Hyperindividualism

White males (as well as U.S. citizens generally) are not just individuals, they are hyperindividuals. Parents in the United States are almost unique in asking their young children what color candy, balloons, or food they want. Americans learn to be individuals at an early age.[29] All Americans also know that their country was founded to protect their right to life, liberty, and the pursuit of happiness—as individuals. While applauding team players, white males value those who can make tough decisions and amount to something—on their own.

Industry and Work

Americans work hard, as French visitor Alexis de Tocqueville observed.[30] Today, they still work more hours than any other workers in the world, especially managers, who are the "best-educated and best-paid."[31] They continue to value the story of an individual who has risen from "rags to riches" (or at least to middle-class status) through hard work. Americans do not respect people born to great wealth who remain idle rather than achieve. Rather, they respect those who, like the Rockefellers or Kennedys, work hard at other causes. Americans commonly speak of "working" on relationships and love, hobbies, and recreation with standards for achievement in each.

Achievement and Success

Careers are seen as individual trajectories toward achievement and success. Individuals should work hard to succeed, for life's justification lies in its accomplishments. Americans still believe in the secular version of sociologist Max Weber's "Protestant Ethic," according to which earthly attainment could be a sign that one is religiously "saved." Today, Americans believe that hard work and personal responsibility lead to earthly and secular success and the esteem of others.

Self-Control and Limited Expression of Emotions

White males are known for their self-control and limited expression of emotions. As did their English cultural forbearers, men should "maintain a stiff upper lip," bear pain, and "take it like a man." One also should repress the public expression of emotions. This value is reflected in the iconic image of the laconic frontiersman or silent cowboy who, after months on the frontier or trail, expresses little emotion and says little because he has little to say. Though this value has been breaking down, and it is more permissible for males to publicly express emotion (or even cry), the expectation remains that they should do so rarely, and certainly less often than women.

White Male Nonverbal Communication

Proxemics

Whether or not we are conscious of it, our subculture determines our proxemics—our customary use of space. In the mainstream white male business culture, managers typically stand about eighteen to thirty inches from one another—which is typically farther apart than many women or Hispanics. However, when white males approach one another, they tend to stop at greater distances than when they approach women. A white male manager who feels that a Hispanic colleague is aggressive because he has approached or is standing too close may not know and therefore misinterprets the impact of Hispanic proxemics.[32] Both managers may not only be advantaged, but may be better able to manage than be managed by cultural diversity.

Eye Contact and Gaze Patterns

Eye contact and gaze patterns may play an underappreciated role in conversation. As is true of every demographic group, white males have their own typical eye contact patterns. While listening, white males tend to look at the speaker much of the time. When speaking, they tend to look away from listeners much of the time, making eye contact with them to emphasize an important point or when beginning or ending a statement to signal turn-taking. At such times, white males tend to momentarily glance away from listeners and then reestablish eye contact to signify the start or completion of a statement.[33] Such eye contact also nonverbally cues listeners that it is their turn to talk. Some black Americans whose eye contact pattern may differ unknowingly could miss such a nonverbal cue and unintentionally hamper their chances for advancement.

Kinesics

Kinesic behavior refers to body posture, gesture, or movement. Kinesic behavior also sends powerful messages of which individuals may not always be aware. White males tend to have open and expansive body postures and movements that occupy more space than may be typical of women. Males also tend to swing their arms farther away from their bodies, lean backward more, and have open and relaxed body postures than is the tendency for women. Such male body postures and movements nonverbally convey messages of dominance and power. In addition, the white male norm is to gesture with restraint—more than Asian Americans or women, but less than Hispanics. Hands and the upper forearm are used for clipped, limited motions, whereas arms are rarely used to gesture. To gesture outside of these norms may be considered unfitting, and to gesture less may be considered uptight.[34]

Touch

The norm among white male managers is to touch rarely or not at all. White males touch more than Asians, but less than Hispanics. Generally, excessive touching among white males is viewed as aggressive and discomforting.[35]

Low Context

Another characteristic of the white male communication paradigm is a tendency to be low context. That is, white males tend to place more value on verbal than nonverbal communication. Words "mean what they say," and white males are likely to pay more attention to verbal (or low context) communication and less attention to nonverbal or (high context) communication than, for example, some Hispanics or Asian Americans.[36]

White Male Verbal Communication

Agonistic Verbal Communication

The white male style of verbal communication is rooted in the Western male model of discourse in the search for truth that Socrates practiced at his Academy in ancient Athens. There he asked questions of his students, listened to their responses, and then challenged and sometimes spiritedly debated with them. Later, in the early days of medieval universities, the highest academic status was awarded only after an agonistic (or combative) thesis-antithesis ritual. Students and teachers gathered in a church in the evening after worship hours. The candidate would climb the pulpit to proclaim his thesis ("I believe . . .") and then defend it against critics with their antitheses. Only after the candidate had strenuously defended his thesis against all opponents in the intellectual hand-to-hand combat of debate would a vote be taken of those assembled. Only the victorious candidates were invited to join their teachers as equals. Today's universities continue this agonistic practice of asking students to declare their thesis, which they must defend against those who pose antitheses before allowing only the most capable to assume the status of teacher.

The practices of Socrates and medieval universities embody male communication even today. Men tend to communicate more about general principles and abstractions in public and impersonal arenas and less about feelings and attending to others. Men's talk tends to reflect the public settings that males have dominated and that call for the direct expression of theoretical and conceptual content in the service of task achievement.[37] This could be why men interrupt to control the back-and-forth by challenging others and dominating and often rerouting the flow of conversation.[38]

For millennia, only white males spoke in public settings. As individuals, they discoursed on general principles that were detached, objective, and impersonal. Their speech tended to be agonistic—that is, forthright and above all combative. The agonistic style came to pervade male-dominated firms. Conventional managerial belief and practice have been that conflict is desirable because it causes employees to question their premises in the search for new solutions. To bring about change, some organizational scholars urged managers to engage in practices that deliberately create anxieties and "provoke unpleasant emotions in others."[39] Other scholars reflected this conventional belief when they wrote: "dialogue can . . . indeed, should, involve considerable conflict and disagreement. It is precisely such conflict that pushes employees to question existing premises and make sense of their experience in a new way."[40]

Males also encouraged one another to speak up and "say what's on your mind." WASP or white males should not be voluble. Speech serves a utilitarian purpose, and one should be brief and direct in organizational communication. "Let's lay our cards on the table" and "Let's stop beating around the bush and get to the point" are frequently heard expressions. Usually, little time is given to small talk. Generally, after brief pleasantries, the expectation is that the parties should get down to business. In their interactions, white males typically are more direct than some Hispanics or Asian Americans who often place a higher value on sensitivity and relationships in their communication—and hence sometimes are more circumspect and ambiguous. White male managers often have problems with silence. A silence that lasts longer than a minute or so is likely to generate a flurry of responses that range from introducing a new topic to a concession—a typical white male trait of which some Asians, and possibly Asian Americans, may already be aware.[41]

WOMEN'S COMMUNICATION PARADIGM

The status of women has changed more over the past 30 years than in the last 3000. Many reasons exist for this shift, but among the most important are the continuing expansion of the workforce; a move from the industrial to the information economy, which requires more positions of symbolic work than physical work; and the feminist movement, which is rooted in the American ideals of human dignity and individual equality. Women's values have changed, and more have sought higher education and entered the workplace. As a traditional German proverb points out, for thousands of years, women's' place was limited to the lifeworld of *"Kinder, Küche, Kirche"*—children, kitchen, church.[42] As the twentieth and twenty-first centuries unfolded, women's sphere of influence expanded, making this proverb less applicable. U.S. women are now employed at nearly the same rate as their male counterparts.[43] Given the unfolding of these new dynamics, women and minorities will first accommodate and then create a new "order of talk."

Women's Values

Education

This value is evidenced by the fact that the percentage of female students has increased substantially over recent decades.[44] Women in greater number seek education for reasons of emancipation.

Becoming Emancipated and Independent

Women today seek to become self-reliant and responsible for their own future. They pursue independence and responsibility to achieve their goals in life and to participate with significant others in sharing responsibilities and achievement of equality in their relationships. This also entails transcending the more limited roles that circumscribed the lives of their mothers and grandmothers.

Realization of One's Full Human Potential

Today's women seek to realize the goals they set for themselves not just by giving their all to succeed in their professional lives. Many women also seek to realize their full human potential in their personal lives as parents who participate with a significant other to raise a family, if this is the case.

Sharing Responsibility for Meeting the Needs of Family

Today's women do not see themselves as the sole source of nurturance and support for their children and families. Rather, the current ethic leans more toward sharing the responsibility for children and family. Not only is this a more egalitarian ideal; given the time and responsibility of a position in the paid workforce, it is pragmatic and necessary.

Self-Realization of Hopes and Dreams

Every goal-oriented person aims at the fulfillment of his or her dreams. A whole person gives her all to achieve the dreams that she has nurtured to attain her potential. As women's roles and expectations have grown, so have the number and variety of hopes and dreams they seek to realize.

Contributors to Society

Through their commitment to workplace success, women contribute their efforts to benefit not only their employers but also humanity, particularly the needy and helpless. In this way, women give witness to the commitment most seem to feel toward society.

Women's Nonverbal Communication

Eye Contact and Gaze

Generally, in the mainstream organizational culture, eye contact indicates attention and interest in what the speaker is saying. Research indicates that women engage in more eye contact than men in face-to-face interaction. Whether in mixed- or same-gender conversations, women are likely to maintain more eye contact than men when speaking or listening to others.[45] Women also are more likely than males to lower or break eye contact in uncomfortable or conflict-filled conversations.[46] Hence, in such situations, a female colleague who lowers or breaks eye contact may not be sending the message of compliance but merely responding according to the women's nonverbal paradigm.

Research suggests that the popular belief in women's intuition may have a nonverbal origin. Studies document that women gaze longer at others in conversation than men, and hence seem to be better able to read nonverbal cues, decode and encode nonverbal messages, and understand their meanings than males.[47] After reviewing more than sixty studies, one researcher concluded that women were more perceptive interpreters of nonverbal messages than males.[48]

Facial Expression

Women tend to express more emotion through their facial expressions than men, who are more likely to internalize and suppress their emotions. One laboratory study physiologically monitored male and female subjects and photographed their faces as they viewed emotional pictures. Though the male physiological responses were strong, their faces tended to remain expressionless. Although they also strongly responded physiologically, females were more open in expressing their emotions, particularly through their facial expressions.[49]

Many women also smile and return smiles more than men. Whereas 67 percent of male subjects returned smiles in one study, 93 percent of women did so.[50] Women also laugh more than men. They attentively combine more eye contact, smiles, and conversationally encouraging head nods than men.[51]

Vocal Qualities

The significance of voice as a channel of nonverbal communication is often underestimated. Women's voices are generally higher-pitched than men's. According to researchers, women's higher and more variably pitched voices may be heard as "unsure intonation patterns." They also found that such women with higher-pitched voices are less likely to be hired as broadcasters.[52] Other researchers reported that female and male subjects paid more attention to and recalled more information from male than female speakers.[53] Women with higher-pitched voices who report that they are not "heard" in the workplace often are correct. One strategy for women who confront this obstacle may be to speak more softly and lower the pitch of their voices.

Verbal Communication

Women's Connected Conversation

Women's conversation differs from men's. Generally, men's conversation has been more task- or goal-oriented, whereas conversation about relationships with family, friends, and colleagues has been more central for women.[54] Generally women have delighted in conversing, for it enables them to initiate and maintain relationships. In the past, women generally were more limited to the life world of home and family than the public forum of work. Because their traditional work and roles were circumscribed by child care and nurturance, women tended not to voice the public speech of facts and disputation but the private speech of caring and feeling.[55] For millennia, women were the muted gender.[56] This is no longer true. Today's women can make their points as forcefully and be as objective in the discussions as men. Since the rise of feminism in the 1970s, a shift in where and how women communicate has occurred. This is particularly true of members of the new generation of women, who are participating in the workforce at higher rates than before.

In the past, women's style has tended to be more polite and considerate. One researcher found that girls as young as four and five used more "would yous" and "could yous" than boys of the same age.[57] This research might be less descriptive of young girls' verbal communication today. Indeed, many women are urged to take assertiveness training to speak more assuredly. Interestingly, assertiveness tends to reduce the information flow from others, whereas women's considerate or tentative communication enhances it.[58] In today's high-velocity, complex environment, discovering which verbal communication style is more congruent with the needs of organizations for information could be vital for success (if not for survival).[59]

Women's conversation tends to be more participatory and interactive than men's, which tends to be more hierarchical and determined. Women who are conversing tend to freely share a two-way dialogue, which generates a flow of new ideas.[60] Perhaps women's more interactive and participatory conversational style also is more consistent with the needs of twenty-first-century organizations for which new thoughts and ideas are paramount.[61]

AFRICAN AMERICAN COMMUNICATION PARADIGM

For nine-tenths of the approximately 400 years that African Americans have lived in the United States, they either were subjected to slavery or the legal discrimination of Jim Crow laws that forbade them from drinking from white-only water fountains, let alone applying for jobs.[62] Not until the civil rights decade of the 1960s did black Americans gain the formal legal equality to vote. Having first arrived in America in 1619, blacks are among its oldest inhabitants but newest immigrants. Yet in examining their progress, Gregg Easterbrook concluded, "Black rates of social progress are little different from those previously displayed by white ethnic immigrant groups, which typically required two or three generations to take their places in the establishment. This suggests African Americans should be beginning to take their places in the establishment right now: exactly what is happening."[63]

Three cultural and historical forces have shaped the African American value system: a residual African heritage, almost four centuries of slavery and discrimination, and the internalization of mainstream American values. The residual African heritage embodies the values of community and kinship that were crucial to survival in Africa as well as to overcome the trials of slavery in America. Religion helped blacks overcome slavery experiences and later, discrimination. The strong commitment of black Americans to the core middle-class values of work, education, and achievement enable them to take full advantage of opportunities once unfairly denied them.

African American Values

Humanism and Relationships

Many African Americans place a high value on relationships and have fewer reservations about expressing care and concern for one another. Blacks may express their humanism through their open sharing and affiliative behaviors. In organizations, this often translates into informal and genuine concern for others and maintaining relationships. The value of expressive humanism could at times contrast with the white male self-control and restraint of emotion that is more characteristic of mainstream organizational culture.

Community and Kinship

Shared loyalty to group and bonds of kinship with family are values that most African Americans honor and uphold. It is not blood alone that makes one kin or family. African American families often are extended families, which include individuals who are called cousins or aunts or uncles by bonds of affection rather than ties of blood. The oft-quoted proverb "It takes a village to raise a child," embodies this value, as does the greater incidence with which African Americans appreciate and refer to community, even in the workplace. The community, and the high regard in which it was held, was an important resource for coping with slavery in the past and is a present resource for overcoming stressors that blacks encounter in a still discriminatory U.S. society. One African American scholar concluded that strong nuclear and extended family support are major factors in upward black mobility.[64] Another pointed out that this value has African roots: "Whatever happens to the individual happens to the whole group, and whatever happens to the whole group happens to the individual. The individual can only say: 'I am because we are, and since we are, therefore I am.'"[65] In addition to being a person unto him- or herself, in congruence with the individualistic premise "I think, therefore I am," many African Americans tend to prize relationships and see themselves as part of human networks. Recognizing and supporting this value in the workplace could yield dividends for all concerned.

Work, Education, and Achievement

Through history, blacks have passionately desired education.[66] After the Civil War and the abolition of slavery, the greatest desire of newly freed blacks was for land to farm self-reliantly and for schools to educate both children and adults.[67] High school graduation rates of blacks equaled those of whites in the United States for the first time in 1996. Though African Americans begin college with lower Scholastic Aptitude Test scores and grade point averages than whites, when they leave college and enter the real world, top black students more closely approximate career achievements of top white students.[68] Whereas black males typically earn 75 percent of the income of white males, the difference is cut in half for black male college graduates, and the earnings of black female college graduates are slightly higher than those of white female peers.[69]

Religion

For centuries, the black church was one of the few institutions that African Ameicans controlled and managed, where blacks could acquire experience needed to lead organizations. It is no accident that black men of the cloth like Martin Luther King Jr., Malcolm X, and Jessie Jackson were major leaders of the black community. Religion helped provide the strength and faith for African Americans to survive a discriminatory and painful society. The gospel and spirituals of the black church helped African Americans survive pain and find the solace to move forward. There is no end to the strength that church and faith have provided to black Americans.

African American Nonverbal Communication

Each human being is complex and multidimensional. Therefore, communication behavior is not only influenced by gender, race, ethnicity, or culture but also by education, region, income, and other factors. This section may provide an opportunity to use black communication patterns to illustrate the complexities that are true of every major demographic group.

As is true of all Americans, African Americans, like their community, are diverse. They live in the South and the North, in rural and urban settings. Some are poorly educated and unemployed, and others have earned Ivy League degrees and power elite positions. Some come from generations of grinding poverty, whereas others trace their ancestry to the 10 percent of blacks who were free at the time of the Civil War.

Today, black nonverbal communication ranges from patterns exhibited by those who are poor and educationally disadvantaged to those shown by former Chairman of the Joint Chiefs of Staff and Secretary of State Colin Powell, Secretary of State and former National Security Adviser Condoleezza Rice, Chairman of the Board and CEO of Merrill Lynch and Company Stan O'Neal, Chairman of the Board and CEO of Time Warner Richard Parsons, and CEO of American Express Kenneth I. Chenault. The nonverbal signals these individuals use tend to be typical of their socioeconomic peers.

Eye Contact and Gaze

Subject to the normal qualifiers of education, income, and occupation, research indicates that some black Americans may exhibit eye contact and gaze patterns that differ from other groups. The most striking difference may be between black and white patterns of eye contact behavior when speaking or listening.[70] These comparative eye contact patterns are as follows:

Speaking

Whites: Look away from the listener when speaking, except when initiating conversation, emphasizing points, or signaling that it is the listener's turn to speak.

Blacks: Look at the listener when speaking.

Listening

Whites: Look at the speaker when listening.

Blacks: Look away from the speaker when listening.

Some scholars believe that this eye contact pattern originated during the era of slavery when slaves were discouraged from looking their owners in the eye. Others attribute it to respect for elders and other authority figures. While disciplining children, whites told them, "You'd better look me in the eye" (a sign of respect), and blacks told their children, "You'd better not look me in the eye" (a sign of insolence). Still other studies indicate that these eye contact patterns may be more likely among rural or urban blacks, who may be somewhat lower in the educational or income rankings, and that eye contact patterns among other blacks of higher socioeconomic status (SES) can differ.[71]

Touch

Blacks in the United States tend to touch more than whites.[72] Research seems to indicate that some blacks may be members of a high-contact culture, whereas many whites belong to a low-contact culture. As members of a high-contact culture, many blacks touch more than whites, though not as much as Hispanic Americans. Such behavior is exhibited among blacks when they "give skin" or touch hands, especially with members of their in-group on meeting. However, caution is suggested, because such behaviors may be exhibited less by blacks of higher SES or educational status for whom understatement may typically apply.

Proxemics

Whether standing or seated, the distance between managers may make them feel more or less comfortable. Research seems to indicate that African Americans tend to greet or stand at a somewhat greater distance than other ethnic groups. Comparative studies indicate that blacks interact at the greatest distance, Hispanics (especially Mexican Americans) at the closest, and whites at an intermediate distance.[73] In reviewing research findings, one scholar stated that in three-fourths of the studies, "adolescent and adult Black males interacted at further distances than did adolescent and adult whites." However, the same review found that the small number of studies that controlled for social and economic status determined that "SES may well be influencing the spatial relations" of blacks and whites.[74]

African American Verbal Behavior

Research findings provide some general guidelines for managers about African American verbal communication. However, little research has been conducted in this area, and much of what has been done focuses on the least advantaged members of the black community. As is true of any demographic group, more studies need to be conducted among black Americans and other U.S. subcultures to provide the widest and most accurate knowledge base. More important, it is always vital to remember that research findings on the characteristics of various demographic groups should be held lightly. The best understanding is the one we arrive at because of our mutual experience with each other. Therefore, any generalizations should be tentative given the uniqueness of each individual before us.

This diversity is reflected in African American verbal and nonverbal behaviors. Some African Americans might speak in an identifiable Black English, while increasing numbers speak English in a manner unidentifiable from any other American of the same region, educational, or economic circumstance. Three overlapping groupings that black scholars have identified among African Americans are those who are:

1. proficient in both Black English and mainstream standard English,
2. fluent in Black English who may have difficulties with mainstream standard English, and
3. fluent in mainstream standard English who may experience problems speaking Black English.[75]

Such educational, regional, and income variations affect every demographic group treated in this chapter. Seeking to be true to our ethic of reducing discrimination by making unconscious communication behavior explicit, we ask readers to hold what is written lightly in view of the individual before them and create common ground. This section has described the values and nonverbal and verbal communication behaviors that can unknowingly create genuine but subtle barriers to the full participation of those who, more than any other racial or ethnic group, have earned the right to America's bounty.

HISPANIC COMMUNICATION PARADIGM

The term *Hispanic* is a racial-ethnic category that was created by a decision of a U.S. government agency. In 1978, the Office of Management and Budget decided to categorize as Hispanic those who lived in the United States and who were born in or could trace their ancestry to Puerto Rico, Mexico, Cuba, or any of seventeen other Spanish-speaking countries in Latin America (or Spain).[76] Though sharing a common language and cultural heritage, Hispanics, approximately 40 to 50 percent of whom were born outside the United States,[77] identify themselves, for example, as Mexican, Puerto Rican, Cuban (who make up nearly 80 percent of U.S. Hispanics), Argentinean, or Uruguayan,[78] based on their countries of origin or ethnic communities. Yet when asked how important it is for Hispanics to blend into U.S. society, 64 percent said it was very important and 24 percent indicated it was somewhat important.[79]

The Hispanic population of the U.S. is diverse. Beyond the standard categories of education, income, and occupation, Hispanics also differ by length of time in the United States, degree of acculturation, and English language fluency. They founded cities like San Francisco, Santa Fe, and El Paso in what is now the United States before the American Revolution. Other Hispanics are recent immigrants. Given their recent growth in numbers, Hispanics are only starting to reach the upper echelons of American society. Among those who have are Alberto Gonzalez, attorney general of the United States; Bill Richardson, governor of New Mexico; James Padilla, president of Ford Americas and executive vice president, Ford Motor Company; Carlos M. Gutierrez, an immigrant from Mexico who became chairman and CEO of cereal maker Kellogg Company and was appointed Secretary of Commerce by President George W. Bush; and Maria Elena Lagomasino, chair and CEO of J.P. Morgan. Having surpassed black Americans as the nation's largest minority group in 2005, the Hispanic wave is just beginning.

Hispanic Values

Hispanics' rich value system differs in certain ways from that of the mainstream U.S. organization. Non-Hispanic managers are well advised to become aware of Hispanic values, given their dramatic increase in numbers.[80]

Collectivism

One of the central values for Hispanic managers is collectivism—a sensitivity to and respect for the personal and interpersonal relationships that make up the group or collectivity. Studies of executives from forty counties, as well as Hispanic youths and adults from the United States and Latin America, agree on this point.[81] Other important values—such as "self-worth" (or *personalismo*), "dignity and respect" (or *dignidad*), "manliness" (or *machismo*), and "hierarchy"—are congruent and supportive of the overarching value of collectivism.

Family or Familism

The family (*familism*) is a critically important Hispanic value and manifestation of collectivism. The strong ties among members of nuclear and extended families tend to generate high levels of obligation, loyalty, and reciprocity. This value also provides support and strength to Hispanics. Visiting with family is important and frequent. Though they accept job changes requiring geographic moves at similar rates to whites or blacks, Hispanics may take longer to decide whether to do so, particularly if the new location has a low concentration of Hispanics.[82]

Self-Worth *or* Personalismo

Self-worth or *personalismo* recognizes the importance of each individual on the basis of his or her intrinsic self-worth. Each individual possesses inherent inner qualities that make that person worthy of respect regardless of worldly success or social status. *Personalismo* stands somewhat in contrast to the white male value of individual achievement.[83] It also may indicate why many Hispanics prefer face-to-face or personal contact rather than the more impersonal communication that is the norm in many mainstream American organizations.[84]

Dignity (Dignidad) *and* Respect (Respecto)

Dignity or *dignidad* and respect or *respecto* also are key values to Hispanics, given the wide gap in traditional Latin American societies between rich and poor, the powerful and powerless, for no one can grant or take away these inner qualities; they intrinsically belong to the person. In the mainstream white male paradigm, dignity and respect resonate with democratic equality as well as admiration for earned achievement. However, as one scholar put it, for Hispanics, "*Respecto* is acquired by virtue of being, not by virtue of doing."[85]

Dignidad and *respecto* also are accorded to those who exhibit courage and fearlessness in the face of death, sexual prowess, or intellectual accomplishment. Philosophers and writers are revered more in Latin America than in the United States. Respect also inheres in hierarchical position; superiors possess respect in organizations due to the position they occupy. Hispanic superiors may expect and demand more respect from subordinates than superiors who adhere to the white male paradigm. However, if the supervisor reciprocates by showing similar respect, the subordinate may become extremely loyal.

Manliness *or* Machismo, *Womanliness or* Marianismo

These two values are the gender-linked variants of the role models expected of adults. *Machismo*, the better-known value in the United States, refers to "manliness," or "being a man" via one's dignity, strength, and courage. One needs to respect each male's manliness, for not to do so via insensitivity or (worse yet) deliberate intent, would be to engage in a public humiliation or even insult of the highest order. One organizational implication of *machismo* could be a greater dominance, directiveness, and even authoritarianism in the superior–subordinate relationship.

According to the value of womanliness or *marianismo*, marriage, home, and children are the domains and chief concerns of Hispanic women, and work outside the home can be a source of conflict between women (who should be subordinate) and their husbands.[86] Self-sacrifice in these areas earns women respect from the community as well as self-respect. According to the value of *marianismo*, women should defer to men, especially in the area of decision making. However, research indicates that egalitarian (though covert) decision making between husband and wife are much more the norm than may be expected (to save the husband's "face" or dignity in the eyes of others).[87] Womanliness or *marianismo* may be among the earliest casualties to the acculturation by Hispanic women who appreciate the freedom and choice accorded them by the more egalitarian culture of the United States.

Hierarchy

Cross-cultural research of executives in forty countries indicates that Hispanic managers score high in what is termed "power distance" or hierarchy.[88] Hispanic managers tend to be outwardly respectful and deferential as well as conformist and obedient to their superiors who hold more power. Excessively agreeable behavior by subordinates and the autocratic exercise of power by superiors could be an organizational outcome. As is so often the case, care should be exercised here, because respect for hierarchy could be a weaker value among acculturated Hispanics who have lived and worked in the United States for a period of time.

Sensitivity

For all of the reasons just cited, Hispanics tend to be sensitive themselves, as well as toward others.[89] The value of sensitivity suggests that subtle, face-saving strategies be undertaken by managers, rather than the open (though they may be) constructive criticisms given in the spirit of impartial improvement that are common in mainstream U.S. firms. One Mexican psychologist speculates that two differing "realities" in U.S. and Mexican culture govern the "truth" of interpersonal relationships.[90] U.S. culture is characterized by an "objective reality," which encourages managers to "tell it like it is," painful though it may be. Mexican culture is characterized by an interpersonal reality according to which one should make another happy, not upset another, or jeopardize another's dignity. These differing realities might explain why some Hispanics may be more discreet or indirect in response to direct questions. They also may help Anglo managers understand why some Hispanic colleagues may be more likely to move away from the computer keyboard and listen to a person despite an impending deadline. One should always put people first because they have sensitivities.[91]

Hispanic Nonverbal Communication

High Context

The Hispanic culture is a high-context culture, meaning that it is characterized by the expectation that nonverbal behaviors will transmit as much if not more information than words alone.[92] However, in the low-context U.S. culture, the verbal channel of communication is considered paramount, for words—specific and concise—"mean what they say." In the high context Hispanic culture, nonverbal signals convey more of the message or meaning, which can be disconcertingly indirect and ambiguous to managers who may not be familiar with this increasingly important U.S. subculture.

Eye Contact and Gaze

Hispanics tend to avoid direct eye contact because it may be perceived as disrespectful or even confrontational, especially with male or higher status speakers.[93] However, as a high-context culture, many nonverbal cues are understood and much communication is received via peripheral or indirect gaze. Hence, although direct eye contact is avoided whenever possible, indirect gaze behavior is engaged in instead.

Proxemics

Body distances tend to be closer for Hispanics than the eighteen to thirty inches that is comfortably normal for whites in mainstream business culture.[94] A white manager may be backpedaling and thereby attempting to maintain his normal body distance (of about an arm's length or less), whereas a Hispanic manager may be advancing, attempting to do the same. In the first case, the other is interpreted as pushy, and in the second case the other is interpreted as cold. Neither understands the other as both walk away from the conversation with mutually negative feelings.[95] One study found that proxemic distances varied as much among Latin Americans as among North Americans.[96] Another study concluded that South Americans tended to stand farther from each other than Central Americans.[97] Once again, care should always be taken to avoid overgeneralizing about behaviors that tend to be more common about groups than individuals and about some groups than others.

Touch

Hispanics tend to engage in higher touch than whites. In the workplace, Hispanic males are more likely than whites to shake hands or touch or grasp a colleague's arm in a friendly gesture—behaviors that may make some white male manager uncomfortable or nervous.[98] Again, however, caution is in order. One scholar who researched Latin American nonverbal behavior concluded: "The results indicate that . . . the frequency of contact diminishes, and fewer touch and hold as one travels from Central to South America."[99] Though common cultural patterns exist, it is better to view the behavior of the person in front of you as an individual.

Verbal Communication

Establishing Relationships

Hispanics tend to have two styles in their verbal communication. With new acquaintances or business associates, they generally are formal, polite, and restrained. Being aware of the need to respect personal sensitivities, Hispanic managers may be more indirect and tactful than white male managers who generally may be more direct and specific in their statements.[100] What mainstream U.S. business culture may regard as the normal interplay of differing viewpoints may be interpreted by some Hispanic managers as evidence of conflict. Once trust and friendship have been established, the Hispanic style of verbal communication becomes more informal and even jovial, though always alert to sensitivities and dignity of others.

Culture also can influence establishing a business relationship, particularly if each party is unaware of his own or the other's cultural expectation. Mike and Miguel are midlevel executives from different corporations who are meeting for the first time to do business. Mike, a mainstream white businessman, expects to spend a few perfunctory minutes getting to know Miguel before getting down to business. In his cultural context, private and professional lives are separate. Generally, any personal relationship develops only after and as a result of their business relationship. Mike's attitude is: "Business is about money. Time is money. So let's get down to business."

When Miguel, an immigrant Mexican American who is now a U.S. citizen, meets someone the first time, he expects (according to his Hispanic culture) to spend some time getting to know the other person. For him, personal life and work are connected, and possess a higher priority than may be generally the case among "*gringos*." Hence, Miguel expects to learn a little about Mike, his background, and his character before, not after, any business relationship. Miguel's attitude is: "Business is about money. That is why I need to feel that I can trust Mike before I go further. However, business also is about life, and people are life. So let's get to know each other."

Hence, when these two individuals unconsciously are at odds about the process of initially establishing a business relationship, little hope exists that any business will be done. This scenario could unfold more frequently throughout the United States in the twenty-first century. Every counterpart of these two executives needs to be prepared.

Silence

Whether out of respect for age or due to politeness or hierarchal status or just out of a desire to ponder, Hispanic managers are more likely than their white counterparts to engage in silence in their dealings with others. Silence need not be interpreted as a negative or unfriendly message; Hispanics may often take more time to reflect and respond to queries than mainstream American managers do. Once again, however, one should exhibit care in such areas, for this generalization may apply more fully to some Hispanic subcultures in the United States than others. In the Hispanic community, Mexicans have a reputation for being stoic, whereas Cubans are typically considered to be more assertive.[101]

THE ASIAN AMERICAN COMMUNICATION PARADIGM

Few Americans are aware of the distance Asian Americans have traveled in their journey "from pariah to paragon."[102] Chinese Americans first immigrated to the United States during the 1849 California Gold Rush. In the nineteenth century, Chinese Americans were legally precluded from testifying against whites, denied the right to own land, and expelled from American cities. Such painful discrimination contributed to our language the once common but now tragically meaningful phrase, "Not a Chinaman's chance."

In the twentieth century, Executive Order 9066 placed Japanese Americans in often barren internment camps during World War II. Beginning for Chinese in 1882 and for Japanese in 1924, legal immigration to the United States ended for decades. Yet by 1959, a higher percentage of Chinese Americans than Caucasians were working in professional occupations,[103] and by 1940 the average Japanese American was more highly educated than the average white U.S. citizen.[104]

Asian Americans are a demographically diverse ethnic group. The category "Asian American" includes twenty-five groups from Asian Indian to Vietnamese. However, this chapter will focus only on Americans of Chinese, Japanese, and Vietnamese ancestry. Together, they make up the majority of Asian Americans and also share common Confucian and Buddhist roots and influences on their values and behaviors.

Asian American history in the United States can be divided into two waves: immigration before World War II and after the Immigration and Naturalization Act of 1965. In 1960, Asian Americans made up 0.5 percent of the U.S. population; by 2000, they grew eight times to 4.2 percent of the total population and are still growing. By 2050, Asian Americans are forecast to make up almost 10 percent of all Americans.[105]

The Asian American Value System: Confucianism

The teachings of Confucius (551–479 B.C.) left an enduring legacy for most Asian societies, particularly those of China, Japan, Korea, and Vietnam.[106]

Though these societies' cultures vary widely, Confucianism is a common unifying element that may help managers understand behavior patterns of their Asian American colleagues. Confucianism is part philosophical, religious, and political. It also is a body of precepts for daily living and social life and it helped organize Asian societies much as Christianity organized Europe. Though time and acculturation always weakens ties with ancestral homelands, Confucianism offers a useful prism through which to understand Asian American behaviors.

Four central principles of Confucianism offer prescriptions for the right conduct of individuals and ethical social behavior. They are: (1) benevolent humanism—putting oneself in another's position and seeing the world from that perspective; (2) reciprocity (and empathy) in dealing with others—the golden rule, which is common to all codes of ethical behavior; (3) devotion and allegiance to the long-term common good; and (4) discretion and deference in human behavior to achieve harmonious social relationships.

Confucian values stress a collectivist approach in that the harmonious equilibrium of the group tends to supersede individual needs, which are to be suppressed. Hierarchy in groups is important, and subordinates and superiors alike practice directness and deference in speech. Collectivist cultures tend to be normatively hierarchical—a younger person should respect an older person; a subordinate should not directly challenge or confront a superior.[107] The ideal of consensus is realized via attentive listening and patiently working to bring about harmonious unity.[108] Such collectivism sharply contrasts with the individualism that is at the core of American culture.[109] The group is primary and endures; the individual is secondary and serves the group. In one example of how collectivism was transplanted to America, scholars discovered that in Japanese American basketball leagues, individually oriented "hot doggers" who shot too much quickly found that their group-oriented teammates repressed their behavior by simply not passing them the basketball.[110]

In the organizational context, U.S. and Asian behaviors differ: Americans tend to expend much effort in communicating clearly and accurately. Logic is seen as linear, clear, and sequentially leading to a point. One should "stay on the point," "get to the point," and not "beat around the bush." Only communication which corresponds to such a subconscious structure of logic is deemed satisfying. In contrast, consciously communicating ambiguously or in a roundabout manner is common in Asian organizations. This could explain why the more indirect Asian American verbal behavior annoys some mainstream American managers who are frustrated by what they see as its length and ambiguity.[111] One scholar suggested that lines and points are metaphors for face-to-face communication in mainstream American culture, whereas for Asian and Asian Americans it is the circle and the curve.[112]

Managers should use care in applying these characteristics. Because so many Asian Americans have emigrated from their ancestral countries since 1965, their levels of acculturation may differ from those of other Asian Americans who have been in the United States since the mid-nineteenth century.

Differences also exist within demographic groups, as Korean Americans have the reputation within the Asian community for hard work and a direct communication style. Finally, every cultural generalization should be held lightly in view of the individual before us.

Asian American Nonverbal Communication

High Context

Asian societies are high-context cultures. One estimate holds that only 10 percent of the information in face-to-face communication in Japan is transmitted verbally; the remaining 90 percent is communicated nonverbally.[113] Such cultural influences can be relatively long lasting, especially in a social environment with a supportive critical mass. For example, among the two-thirds of Hawaiians who call themselves Asian American, researchers discovered that "Although assimilation is evident in dress, style of home, and religious affiliation, . . . in norms governing day-to-day interaction, the effects of the culture of origin remain influential."[114] The waves of emigration from Asian countries since 1965 may keep such influences alive, especially among relative newcomers.

Proxemics

Asian Americans tend to stand or sit at greater distances from others than major American demographic groups.[115] In one study in the United States, when speaking their own languages, Venezuelan students sat thirty-two inches apart while conversing, American students thirty-five inches apart, and Asian students forty inches apart. However, when speaking in English, both Japanese students sat closer and Venezuelan students farther away than their original distances, both approximating the distance of U.S. students.[116] One wonders about the impact of acculturation on newer generations of Asian Americans when simply speaking in English has such a profound effect on proxemic behavior. Furthermore, could this experiment that collapsed decades into minutes provide an illustration of how a new and common mainstream communication paradigm could come about?

Touch

Asian Americans trace their ancestry to low-contact cultures. One cross-cultural study concluded that the most touched Japanese students were touched less by friends as well as family than the least touched U.S. student. Some Asians reported extraordinarily low levels (and even the absence) of physical contact with parents after age fourteen. No U.S. students reported such low levels of touch.[117] Physical contact in the early stages of a relationship is likely to cause apprehension and discomfort among Asian Americans.[118] Because noncontact bowing is the norm in Asian cultures, some Asian American immigrants have had to be taught not only how to shake hands but how to do so firmly.[119]

Asian American Verbal Behaviors

Like their nonverbal communication, Asian American verbal communication tends to be indirect and constrained. Reflective of the Confucian values of individual respect for the harmony of the group, researchers found that Chinese and Japanese American parents talk less with their children than white parents. They also tend to be more restrained in their expressions of emotion while communicating verbally or nonverbally.[120] Among immigrant families from Asia, a chief complaint of children born in the more egalitarian and expressive U.S. society is that their Asian-born parents talk too little, and when they do, verbal communication tends to be too hierarchically top-down.[121] It seems that length of residence and level of acculturation can impact values and communication behaviors in one generation.

Silence

Few areas differentiate Asian American subculture from its mainstream counterpart more than the use of silence. In the mainstream culture of American managers, silence means awkwardness, discomfort, disinterest, and even rejection. Asian negotiators have learned that if they simply remain silent long enough, Americans often will make desired concessions with no further effort.[122] What can a mainstream American manager learn and apply in this situation? One professional working in Hawaii suggested that "greater acceptance of the positive aspects of silence is necessary when working with Japanese Americans. Within Japanese cultural traditions, a wise person uses silence as well as speech to communicate."[123]

Use of Questions

Their uses of questions reflect the central place of harmony and hierarchy in Asian American culture. Given the norm of polite, indirect, and considerate communication, Asian Americans do not tend to ask direct or closed questions that begin with "Do" or "Did," and which almost require a "yes" or "no" answer.[124] When they are asked direct questions, Asian Americans tend to respond indirectly for fear that a direct or honest answer might offend.[125]

Limited Expression of Emotions

True to their cultural norm of interpersonal harmony, Asian Americans are generally less likely to express their emotions than individuals from other subcultures.[126] When they do, Asian Americans tend to be less expressive and more subtle and understated than members of other racial or ethnic groups.[127]

Avoidance of Confrontation

In the Confucian view, if each person in a hierarchy acts in accord with the norm of harmony, social order is ensured. Asian Americans tend to avoid the directness and openness that can cause conflict. This stance is in marked contrast to the agonistic (or more combative) style of verbal communication that characterizes mainstream organizational culture in America. Even the very structure of Asian languages reflects this sensitivity to hierarchy and indirectness. In Japanese, the frequent utterance of *ne* (isn't it?) or *ka* (to avoid making too definitive a statement) softens statements and converts them from more direct, declarative sentences into less challenging questions.[128] The linguistic structure of English is subject-verb, thesis first, with supportive information later. In Chinese, speakers front-end load a sentence with large quantities of supportive data, and then put the main idea toward the end.[129] In both Chinese and Japanese, the goal is to lessen dissonance and create an affirming conversation, whereas the tacit Western approach tends to be to be more challenging and even confrontational. As one scholar put it, "Conversation proceeds not by negation or contradiction as in the West, but by affirmation where the speaker seeks continual affirmation and approval from the listener."[130]

REFLEXIVE COMMUNICATION: FINDING THE COMMON GROUND

How do managers transcend the differing values and nonverbal and verbal communication behaviors that are embodied in the communication paradigms we have examined? How do white males, women, African Americans, Hispanics, and Asian Americans find the common ground whereby they can create and maintain the rapid and effortless communication flows that characterize effective groups? One answer is reflexive communication.

What Is Reflexive Communication?

Reflexive communication assumes that various individuals have differing views of the same reality and therefore may derive differing meanings from the same experience. The mutual understanding that leads to common ground of any situation can only emerge from the mutual construction of a convergent view of that situation or experience. Such convergence is possible only via a specific process of conversation—reflexive communication.

The conventional model of face-to-face communication is of an input-output model with a single feedback loop that closes the circle. Reflexive communication reflects and folds back on itself—like a figure eight—which brings successively more information back to each conversant.[131] It is an active process that is especially useful in situations where more than one understanding or meaning may be derived from one situation or experience. Cultural diversity that differently conditions individuals and complicates interpersonal communication creates one such instance.

The theory and practice of reflexive communication rests on four premises and their attendant corollaries. Together, they provide the basis for finding the common ground in the vital area of diversity in America's organizations.

Premise 1: Reality always is viewed form a position or background; as one's position changes, so does one's view of reality.

Corollary to Premise 1: Reality always is viewed from a position that is the nexus into which flow the general cultural paradigm and the individual-specific experiences that make up that person at that point in time.

Premise 2: Mutual understandings of reality becomes progressively clearer with the exchange of different perspectives.

Corollary to Premise 2: We come to know human and organizational realities through conversations with each other.

Premise 3: Separate, uncommunicated realities divide us.

Corollary to Premise 3: The co-creation of realities that are shared provides a common understanding and reality so that common vision, action, and purpose can evolve.

Premise 4: Reflexive communication is a process-focused approach.

Corollary to Premise 4: This process of communication brings about the folding back of different views, meanings, and positions so that they eventually overlap and begin to converge.

Many managers are solution-focused in their approach to problems. Hence, Premise 4 especially may run counter to their mode of operation. Reflexive communication focuses much more on the process than the result of communication. However, a process focus tends to bring to the surface many more multiple views and understandings of situations. Triggering multiple new ideas for looking at a problem generates many new ideas for the construction of new solutions.

General Stances

Three general stances facilitate reflexive communication: the not-knowing, the curious, and the collaborative stance. Each provides the space for individuals to express and share their perspectives and meanings of situations that otherwise might keep them apart.

Not-Knowing Stance

By leveling the hierarchy, this stance encourages communication by taking the nonexpert position of not-knowing.[132] Such a stance with less hierarchy and more collaboration encourages the expression of viewpoints and meanings that otherwise might be suppressed. This stance sends the message that everyone may be equally qualified to suggest new ideas and perspectives on a situation or issue. It also encourages the listener to pay attention to not only the outer conversation about what others are actually saying but also the inner conversation of his or her thoughts and ideas that were triggered by the outer conversation. This criss-crossing continually triggers new meanings that unfold into additional new meanings about the situation.[133]

Curious Stance

In taking the curious stance, one simply expresses one's ideas in a curious or tentative manner.[134] To be dogmatic or assertive may be to hinder the creative process. To be curious or tentative may be to encourage others to take, leave, or develop ideas at will. In so doing, one helps multiply varying perspectives on a problem and encourages the evolved solutions that have been explored and found most fitting by those who will implement them. One takes the curious stance not by making statements but asking questions that might begin with the stems, "It's just an idea, but..." or "could it possibly be that...?"

Collaborative Stance

The collaborative stance is the result of the not-knowing and the curious stance. The joining of shared ideas and perspectives makes possible the co-creation of new and jointly owned outcomes. Others can be urged to add expressions of joining such as, "Well, I also find it uncomfortable when no one hears what I'm saying," or "Somehow, I feel this way, too. And I always thought it happened because I was a woman."[135]

CONCLUSION

The United States may be the only country that always has been diverse. Few may be aware that Paul (Revoire) Revere's father was a French Huguenot newcomer to America, that American Revolution heroine Molly Pitcher actually was a German American known as Maria Ludwig, that naval hero John Paul Jones was a Scot, and that the original surnames of frontier General George Custer, World War I General George Pershing, and President Herbert Hoover were Kuester, Pforshing, and Huever.[136]

Similarly, the history of newcomers to the American workplace is one of expanding—historically, waves of earlier immigrants and then-minorities (Jews and Catholics, for example) entered the workforce and, after initial discrimination, worked their way to the top as full participants of executive suites. We suggest that this process is underway again for women and today's minorities. The United States was originally settled by white Anglo-Saxon Protestant males who (more than the women of the era were permitted) created its culture and established its institutions. One of the most visible proofs is the continuing domination of the presidency, the most powerful executive position in the world, by WASP males—a domination that will most likely end in the twenty-first century. However, the post–World War II economic growth outstripped the pool of WASP males available for management. This economic growth, coupled with the deep-seated American ideals of the dignity and equality of the individual as well as greater educational access led to the entry and ascension of white males of the twentieth century who were Eastern and Southern European, Catholic and Jewish to every workplace level. Today, factors such as ethnicity and religion are of little or no significance in hiring or promotion. Now, in the twenty-first century, women, African Americans, Hispanics, and Asian Americans are following the same trajectory. And the same factors of economic growth that is outstripping the available pool of white males (coupled with the American ideals of equality and education) are operative for them. Progress is always trying, but might there be a responsible party who forecasts downward trends in any area of employment for women and (those who soon will cease being) "minorities"—from entry level to CEO?

In this environment, the micro becomes more important, as individuals from every demographic group in the United States come to work each day, all day, together. Their differing values and divergent nonverbal and verbal behaviors— precisely because they are unconscious—can complicate face-to-face communication, the most vital of managerial functions on which all others rest. The importance of face-to-face communication is escalating because of every organization's increasing need for the core resource of this era—information.

This chapter has attempted to sketch the general cultural paradigm of each major demographic group so that what is unconscious becomes conscious, and managers can actively influence cultural diversity rather than be passively managed by it. It also has sketched an applied theory of communication—reflexive communication—that can help managers access each other's individuality and create the common ground. All change, organizational or otherwise, begins with the individual. This fact may be especially true in the area of diversity. Perhaps it is time for managers and scholars to recognize the new frontier.

NOTES

Adapted from John F. Kikoski and Catherine Kano Kikoski, *Reflexive Communication in the Culturally Diverse Workplace* (Westport: Praeger, 1996/1999).

1. U.S. Bureau of the Census, No. 18, "Resident Population by Hispanic Origin Status, 1980 to 1992, and Projections, 1193 to 2050," in *Statistical Abstract of the United States* (Washington, DC: Government Printing Office, 1993); Melissa Therrien and Roberto R. Ramirez, "The Hispanic Population in the United States: Population Characteristics," in *Current Population Reports* (Washington, DC: Government Printing Office, 2001).

2. Mitra Toossi, "A Century of Change: The U.S. Labor Force, 1950–2050," *Monthly Labor Review* (May 2002): 15–28.

3. Edward B. Fiske, "Minorities a Majority in New York," *New York Times,* March 22, 1991, pp. 81–82.

4. "Poor Man at the Gate," *The Economist*, March 16, 1991, p. 9.

5. Martha Farnsworth Riche, "We're All Minorities Now," *American Demographics* (October 1991): 26–29.

6. "People in the News," *Hartford Courant*, May 28, 1990, p. A-2 reporting on Vonnegut's commencement speech at the University of Rhode Island.

7. Catherine Kano Kikoski and John F. Kikoski, *The Inquiring Organization: Tacit Knowledge, Conversation, and Knowledge Creation: Skills for 21st Century Organizations* (Westport: Praeger, 2004), pp. 7–8.

8. Henry Mintzberg, *The Nature of Managerial Work* (New York: Harper and Row, 1973), p. 38.

9. Ikujiro Nonaka, Georg Von Krogh, and Ichijo Kazuo, *Enabling Knowledge Creation: How to Unlock the Mystery of Tacit Knowledge and Realize the Power of Innovation* (New York: Oxford University Press, 2000), p. 131.

10. Tom Burns, "The Directions of Activity and Communication in a Departmental Executive Group," *Human Relations* 7(1) (1954): 73–97, especially 94.

11. Fred E. Fiedler, "The Effect of Leadership and Cultural Heterogeneity on Group Performance: A Test of the Contingency Model," *Journal of Experimental Social Psychology* 2 (1966): 237–64.

12. Ivan D. Steiner, *Group Process and Productivity* (New York: Academic Press, 1972).

13. Taylor Cox Jr., *Cultural Diversity in Organizations: Theory, Research and Practice* (San Francisco: Berrett-Koehler, 1993), p. 39.

14. Edward W. Jones Jr., "What It's Like to Be a Black Manager," *Harvard Business Review* (July–August, 1973): 108–16, especially 114.

15. Deborah Tannen, *You Just Don't Understand: Men and Women in Conversation* (New York: William Morrow, 1990), pp. 17–18; emphasis added.

16. The concept of a "speech community" that utilized "verbal signs" or "language use" was introduced by John Gumperz, "The Speech Community," in P. P. Gigliolli (ed.), *Language and Social Context* (Baltimore: Penguin, 1972), pp. 219–31, especially p. 219.

17. Ray Birdwhistell, *Kinesics and Context: Essays on Body Motion Communication* (Philadelphia: University of Pennsylvania Press, 1970), pp. 57–58. Birdwhistell estimated that approximately 30 to 35 percent of a face-to-face message is transmitted verbally and 65 to 70 percent is transmitted nonverbally. See also Edward T. Hall and Mildred Reed Hall, *Hidden Differences: Doing Business with the Japanese* (New York: Anchor Books/Doubleday, 1987), p. 3. The Halls estimated on the basis of their research that 80 to 90 percent of information conveyed among individuals occurs nonverbally.

18. Audrey Edwards, "The Enlightened Manager: How to Treat All Your Employees Fairly," *Working Woman* 16(1) (January 1991): 46.

19. Irving Levine, personal correspondence to Monica McGoldrick in Monica McGoldrick, John K. Pearce, and Joseph Giordano, eds., *Ethnicity and Family Therapy* (New York: Guilford Press,1982), p. 4.

20. Nancy J. Adler, *International Dimensions of Organizational Behavior* (Boston: Kent, 1986), pp. 77–78.

21. Ellis Cose, *The Rage of a Privileged Class: Why Are Middle-Class Blacks so Angry? Why Should America Care?* (New York: HarperCollins, 1993), p. 9.

22. See the Reverend Martin Luther King Jr.'s "Letter from Birmingham Jail," in Martin Luther King Jr., *Why We Can't Wait* (New York: New American Library, 1963/1964), pp. 76–95, especially p. 80.

23. Samuel Huntington, *Who Are We Now? The Challenges to America's National Identity* (New York: Simon and Shuster, 2004), pp. 36–46.

24. According to the *Ancestry 2000 Census 200 Brief* of the U.S. Census Bureau, nearly one-third of Americans self-identified themselves as Germans (15.2 percent or 42.8 million) of the U.S. population, English (8.7 percent or 24.5 million), Scottish (1.7 percent or 4.9 million), Dutch (1.6 or 4.5 million), Norwegian (1.6 percent or 4.5 million), Scots-Irish (1.5 percent or 4.3 million), and Swedish (1.4 percent or 4.0 million). Under a broad definition, WASPs total 31.7 percent or 89.5 million of the population of the United States. See Angela Brittingham and Patricia de la Cruz *Ancestry 2000: Census 2000 Brief* (Washington. DC: Government Printing Office, June 2004), pp. 1–12, especially p. 3.

25. Richard L. Zweigenhaft and G. William Domhoff, *Jews in the Protestant Establishment* (New York: Praeger, 1982), p. 110. See also Robert Christopher, *Crashing the Gates: The De-Wasping of America's Power Elite* (New York: Simon and Schuster, 1989) as well as Huntington, *Who Are We Now?*

26. Edward T. Hall and Mildred Reed Hall, *Understanding Cultural Differences* (Yarmouth, ME: Intercultural Press, 1990), pp. 139–40.

27. Huntington, *Who Are We Now?*, pp. 44–45 citing the work of Campbell Gibson, "The Contribution of Immigration to the Growth and Ethnic Diversity of the American Population," *Proceedings of the American Philosophical Society* 136 (June 1992): 157–75, especially 165 and 169. Campbell cites the 1790 census as enumerating 80.7 percent of the United States population as white and 19.3 percent as black.

28. For other sources on the WASP male or white male cultural paradigm, see Charles Anderson, *White Protestant Americans: From National Origins to Religious Groups* (Englewood Cliffs, NJ: Prentice Hall, 1970); Gary Althen, *American Ways: A Guide for Foreigners in the United States* (Yarmouth ME: Intercultural Press, 1988); Richard Brookhiser, *The Way of the WASP: How It Made America, and How It Can Save It, So to Speak* (New York: Free Press, 1991); David McGill and John K. Pearce, "British Families," in Monica McGoldrick, John K. Pierce, and Joseph Giordano, eds., *Ethnicity and Family Therapy* (New York: Guilford Press, 1982), pp. 457–79; Margaret Mead, *And Keep Your Powder Dry: An Anthropologist Looks at America* (New York: William Morrow, 1943); and Edward C. Stewart, *American Cultural Patterns: A Cross-Cultural Perspective* (Yarmouth, ME: Intercultural Press, 1972).

29. Althen, *American Ways*, pp. 4–5.

30. Alexis de Tocqueville, *Democracy in America*, ed. and abridged by Richard D. Heffner (New York: Mentor/New American Library, 1956), pp. 209–20.

31. Michael Mandel, "The Real Reasons You're Working So Hard...And What You Can Do about It," *Business Week* (October 3, 2005): 60–64, 66–70, 73.

32. Edward T. Hall, *The Hidden Dimension* (New York: Anchor Books/Doubleday, 1966/1969), pp. 114–25. The term *proxemics* was given currency by Edward T. Hall in "Proxemics," *Current Anthropology* 9(2–3) (April–June 1968): 83–107. See also Judith A. Hall, "Male and Female Nonverbal Behavior," in Aaron W. Siegman and Stanley Feldstein, eds., *Multicultural Integrations of Nonverbal Behavior* (Hillsdale, NJ: Lawrence Erlbaum Associates, 1985), pp. 195–225, especially pp. 213–17; and Anneke Vrugt and Ada Kerkstra, "Sex Differences in Nonverbal Communication," *Semiotica* 50(1–2) (1984): 1–41. See notes 94–97 below on Hispanic proxemics.

33. Ralph V. Exline, "Explorations in the Process of Person Perception: Visual Interaction in Relation to Competition, Sex, and Need for affiliation," *Journal of Personality* 31 (1963): 1–20; Michael Argyle, "New Developments in the Analysis of Social Skills," in Aaron Wolfgang, ed., *Nonverbal Behavior: Applications and Cultural Implications* (New York: Academic Press, 1993), p. 139; and Adam Kendon, "Some Functions of Gaze-Direction in Social Interaction," *Acta Psychologica* 26 (1967): 22–63.

34. Elizabeth Aries, "Verbal and Nonverbal Behavior in Single-Sex and Mixed-Sex Groups," *Psychological Reports* 51 (1982): 127–34, especially pp. 132–33; Hall, "Male and Female Nonverbal Behavior," p. 220.

35. Ibid., pp. 218–19.

36. Hall and Hall, *Understanding Cultural Differences*, pp. 6–10.

37. Fern Johnson, *Speaking Culturally: Language Diversity in the United States* (Thousands Oaks, CA: Sage, 2000), pp. 95–107.

38. Lea P. Stewart, Alan D. Stewart, Sheryl A. Friedley, and Pamela J. Cooper, *Communication between the Sexes: Sex Differences, and Sex Role Stereotypes*, 2nd ed. (Scottsdale, AZ: Gorsuch Scarisbrick, 1990), pp. 51–52.

39. Edgar Schein, "How Can Organizations Learn Faster? The Challenge of Entering the Green Room," *Sloan Management Review* 34(2) (Winter 1993): 85–92, especially 88–89.

40. Ikujiro Nonaka, "The Knowledge-Creating Company," *Harvard Business Review* 69(6) (November–December 1991): 96–104, especially 104.

41. Joel P. Bowman and Tsugihiro Okuda, "Japanese-American Communication: Mysteries, Enigmas and Possibilities," *Bulletin of the Association for Business Communication* 48(4) (December 1985): 18–21, especially 19.

42. For a description of the word *lifeworld* see Walter J. Ong, *Orality and Literacy: The Technologizing of the Word* (Ithaca, NY: Cornell University Press, 1982), p. 42.

43. Toossi, "A Century of Change," p. 16.

44. Ibid., p. 15.

45. John F. Dovidio and Steve L. Ellyson, "Patterns of Visual Dominance Behavior in Humans," in Steve L. Ellyson and John F. Dovidio, eds., *Power, Dominance and Nonverbal Behavior* (New York: Springer-Verlag, 1985), pp. 129–49, especially pp. 139–42; and Judee Burgoon, "Nonverbal Signals," in Mark L. Knapp and Gerald. R. Miller, eds., *Handbook of Interpersonal Communication*, 2nd ed. (Thousand Oaks, CA: Sage, 1994), pp. 229–85; especially p. 244.

46. Nancy M. Henley, *Body Politics: Power, Sex and Nonverbal Communication* (Englewood Cliffs, NJ: Prentice Hall, 1977), pp. 160–67, especially p. 165.

47. Alice H. Eagley, *Sex Differences in Social Behavior: A Social Role Interpretation* (Hillsdale, NJ: Lawrence ErlbaumAssociates, 1987), p. 103; and Burgoon, "Nonverbal Signals,", pp. 242–47.

48. Hall, "Male and Female Nonverbal Behavior," pp. 200–204.

49. Ross Buck, Robert E. Miller, and William F. Caul, "Sex, Personality and the Physiological Variables in the Communication of Affect via Facial Expression," *Journal of Personality and Social Psychology* 30 (1974): 587–96.

50. Henley, *Body Politics*, p. 165.

51. Eagley, *Sex Differences in Social Behavior*, p.103; Burgoon, "Nonverbal Signals," p. 247.

52. Nancy Henley and Barrie Thorne, "Womenspeak and Manspeak: Sex Differences and Sexism in Communication, Verbal and Nonverbal," in Alice G. Sargent, ed., *Beyond Sex Roles* (St. Paul, MN: West Publishing, 1977), pp. 201–18, especially p. 207.

53. Kenneth J. Gruber and Jacquelyne Gaebelein, "Sex Differences in Listening Comprehension," in *Sex Roles* 5(3) (1979): 299–310, especially 307–9.

54. Elizabeth J. Aries and Fern L. Johnson, "Close Friendships in Adulthood: Conversational Content Between Same-Sex Friends," *Sex Roles* 9(12) (1983): 1183–96; Pamela S. Kippers, "Gender and Topic," *Language and Society* 16(4) (1987): pp. 543–57; Fern Johnson, "Friendship Among Women: Closeness in Dialogue," in Julia T. Wood, ed., *Gendered Relationships: A Reader* (Mountain View, CA: Mayfield, 1996), pp. 79–94.

55. Ong, *Orality and Literacy*, p. 112.

56. Dorothy E. Smith, "A Peculiar Eclipsing: Women's Exclusion from Man's Culture," *Woman's Studies International Quarterly* 1(4) (1978): 281.

57. Robin Lakoff, "Language and Woman's Place," *Language in Society* 2 (1973): 45–79, especially 57.

58. Harlene Anderson and Harry Goulishian, "The Client Is the Expert: A Not-Knowing Approach to Therapy," in Sheila McNamee and Kenneth J. Gergen, eds., *Therapy as Social Construction* (London: Sage, 1992), pp. 25–39.

59. Kikoski and Kikoski, *The Inquiring Organization*, pp. 1–37.

60. Deanna L. Hall and Kristen M. Langellier, "Story Telling Strategies in Mother-Daughter Communication," in Barbara Bate and Anita Taylor, ed., *Women Communicating: Studies of Women's Talk* (Norwood, NJ: Ablex, 1988), pp. 107–26, especially pp. 117–18, 121–25.

61. Kikoski and Kikoski, *The Inquiring Organization*, pp. 1–37.

62. For other sources on the African American cultural paradigm, see John Hope Franklin, *From Slavery to Freedom: A History of Negro Americans*, 4th ed. (New York: Knopf, 1974); Thomas Sowell, *Ethnic America, a History* (New York: Basic Books, 1981), pp. 183–224; Paulette Moore Hines and Nancy Boyd Franklin, "Black Families," in Monica McGoldrick, John K. Pearce, and Joseph Giordano, eds., *Ethnicity and Family Therapy* (New York: Guilford Press, 1982); Elaine Pinderhughes, "Afro-American Families and the Victim System," in Monica McGoldrick, John K. Pearce, and Joseph Giordano, eds., *Ethnicity and Family Therapy* (New York: Guilford Press, 1982), pp. 84–107; Janet Brice, "West Indian Families," in Monica McGoldrick, John K. Pearce, and

Joseph Giordano, eds., *Ethnicity and Family Therapy* (New York: Guilford Press, 1982), pp. 123–33; Harriet Pipes McAdoo, "Factors Relating to Stability in Upwardly Mobile Black Families," *Journal of Marriage and the Family* 40(4) (November 1978): 761–76; Joseph White and Thomas Parham, *The Psychology of Blacks*, 2nd ed. (Englewood Cliffs, NJ: Prentice Hall, 1990); Nancy Boyd Franklin, *Black Families in Therapy* (New York: Guilford Press, 1989); Robert Hill, *The Strengths of Black Families* (New York: Emerson Hall, 1971).

63. Gregg Easterbrook, *The Progress Paradox: How Life Gets Better while People Feel Worse* (New York: Random House, 2003), p. 59.

64. McAdoo, "Factors Relating to Stability," pp. 761–76.

65. John S. Mbiti, *African Religions and Philosophy* (New York: Praeger, 1969), pp. 108–9.

66. Mary Frances Berry and John W. Blassingame, *Long Memory: The Black Experience in America* (New York: Oxford University Press, 1982), pp. 70–113; Hill, *The Strengths of Black Families*, p. 9.

67. Sowell, *Ethnic America, a History*, pp. 202–5.

68. Easterbrook, *The Progress Paradox*, p. 59, citing William Bowen and Derek Bok, *The Shape of the River* (Princeton, NJ: Princeton University Press, 1998), pp. 118–48.

69. Ibid., p. 59.

70. Marianne LaFrance and Clara Mayo, "Racial Differences in Gaze Behavior during Conversations: Two Systematic Observational Studies," *Journal of Personality and Social Psychology* 33(5) (1976), 547–52, especially 550–51. See also Amy G. Halberstadt, *Race, Socioeconomic Status, and Nonverbal Behavior*, ed. Aaron W. Seigman and Stanley Feldstein (Hillsdale, NJ: Lawrence Erlbaum Associates, 1985), pp. 227–66, especially p. 252.

71. Ibid., especially pp. 234–35, 250–53; Robert Shuter, "Gaze Behavior in Interracial and Intraracial Interactions," *International and Intercultural Communication Annual* (Falls Church, VA: Speech Communication Association, 1979): 48–55, especially pp. 53–54.

72. Halberstadt, *Race, Socioeconomic Status*, p. 247; Richard Majors, "Nonverbal Behaviors and Communication Styles among African Americans," in Reginald L. Jones, ed., *Black Psychology*, 3rd ed. (Berkeley, CA: Cobb and Henry, 1991), pp. 269–94, especially p. 283.

73. James C. Baxter, "Interpersonal Spacing in Natural Settings," *Sociometry* 33(4) (1970): 444–56; Daniel J. Thompson and James C. Baxter, "Interpersonal Spacing in Two-Person Cross-Cultural Interactions," *Man-Environment Systems* 3(2) (March 1973): 115–17.

74. Halberstadt, *Race, Socioeconomic Status*, pp. 240–42.

75. Harry N. Seymour and Charlena M. Seymour, "The Symbolism of Ebonics: I'd Rather Switch than Fight," *Journal of Black Studies* 9(4) (June 1979): 408–9.

76. Gerardo Marin and Barbara VanOss Marin, *Research with Hispanic Populations* (Newbury Park, CA: Sage, 1991), pp. 20–21.

77. Therrien and Ramirez, "The Hispanic Population in the United States," p. 3, estimated that 39.1 percent of Hispanics were foreign-born. Another survey of U.S. Hispanics conducted in 2005 estimated that 49 percent of Hispanics were born elsewhere than the mainland United States or Puerto Rico. *Time Magazine*, August 22, 2005, p. 56.

78. Therrien and Ramirez, "The Hispanic Population in the United States," p. 3. As of 2000, Mexicans made up 66.1 percent, Puerto Ricans 9 percent, and Cubans 4 percent—or 79.1 percent—of the U.S. population of 32.8 million Hispanics.

79. "Inside America's Largest Minority," *Time*, August 22, 2005, p. 56.

80. For other sources on the Hispanic cultural paradigm, see Leo Grebler, John W. Moore, and Ralph C. Guzman, *The Mexican-American People: The Nation's Second Largest Minority* (New York: Free Press, 1970); John W. Moore, *Mexican Americans* (Englewood Cliffs, NJ: Prentice Hall, 1970); Sowell, *Ethnic America, A History*, pp. 227–70; Earl Shorris, *The Latinos: A Biography of the People* (New York: Basic Books, 1992); Ronald Takaki, *From a Different Shore: A History of Multicultural America* (Boston: Little Brown, 1993).

81. Geert Hofstede, *Culture's Consequences: International; Differences in Work-Related Values* (Beverly Hills, CA: Sage, 1980), pp. 92–152; Gerardo Marin and Harry C. Triandis, "Allocentrism as an Important Characteristics of the Behavior of Latin Americans and Hispanics," in Rogelio Diaz-Guerrero, ed., *Cross-Cultural and National Studies in Social Psychology* (North Holland: Elsevier Science Publishers B.V., 1985), pp. 84–104.

82. Jack E. Edwards, Paul Rosenfeld, Patricia J. Thomas, and Marie D. Thomas, "Willingness to Relocate for Employment: A Survey of Hispanics, Non-Hispanic Whites, and Blacks," *Hispanic Journal of Behavioral Sciences* 15(1) (February 1993): 121–23.

83. Nydia Garcia-Preto, "Puerto Rican Families," in Monica McGoldrick, John K. Pearce, and Joseph Giordano, eds., *Ethnicity and Family Therapy* (New York: Guilford Press, 1982), pp. 164–86, especially p. 169.

84. Sally Innis Klitz, *Crosscultural Communication: The Hispanic Community of Connecticut* (Storrs: University of Connecticut, 1980), p. 15; Sidney W. Mintz, "Puerto Rico: An Essay in the Definition of a Natural Culture," in *The Puerto Rican Experience: A Sociological Source Book* (Totowa, NJ: Rowman and Littlefield, 1973), p. 68.

85. Orlando Isaza, personal communication, October 1995.

86. Maria Nieto Senour, "Psychology of the Chicana," in Joe L. Martinez Jr., ed., *Chicano Psychology* (New York: Academic Press, 1977), pp. 329–42, especially p. 333; Melba J. T. Vasquez, "Latinas," in Lillian Comas-Diaz and Beverly Greene, eds., *Women of Color: Integrating Ethnic and Gender Identities in Psychotherapy* (New York: Guilford Press, 1994), pp. 114–38.

87. Vicky L. Cromwell and Ronald E. Cromwell, "Perceived Dominance in Decision-Making and Conflict Resolution among Anglo, Black, and Chicano Couples," *Journal of Marriage and the Family* (November 1978): 745–58.

88. Hofstede, *Culture's Consequences*, pp. 92–152.

89. John C. Condon, *Good Neighbors: Communicating with the Mexicans* (Yarmouth, ME: Intercultural Press, 1985), pp. 41–46.

90. Rogelio Diaz-Guerrero, *Psychology of the Mexican: Culture and Personality* (Austin: University of Texas Press, 1967), pp. 44–45.

91. Eva S. Kras, *Management in Two Cultures: Bridging the Gap between U.S. and Mexican Managers* (Yarmouth, ME: Intercultural Press, 1989), pp. 44–45.

92. Hall and Hall, *Understanding Cultural Differences*, pp. 6–10.

93. Carmen Judith Nine Curt, *Non-Verbal Communication in Puerto Rico*, 2nd ed. (Cambridge, MA: Evaluation, Dissemination and Assessment Center, 1984), pp. 30–31.

94. Edward T. Hall, *The Silent Language* (Greenwich, CT: Fawcett, 1959), p. 164; Curt, *Non-Verbal Communication in Puerto Rico*, p. 21; Baxter, "Interpersonal Spacing in Natural Settings," pp. 444–56; Thompson and Baxter, "Interpersonal Spacing," pp. 115–17.

95. Curt, *Non-Verbal Communication in Puerto Rico*, p. 21.

96. Robert F. Forston and Charles Urban Larson, "The Dynamics of Space: An Experimental Study in Proxemic Behavior among Latin Americans and North Americans," *Journal of Communication* 18 (June 1968): 109–16.

97. Robert Shuter, "Proxemics and Tactility in Latin America," *Journal of Communication* 26(3) (1976): 46–52, especially 52.

98. Bernardo M. Ferdman and Angelica C. Cortes, "Culture and Identity among Hispanic Managers in an Anglo Business," in Stephen B. Knouse, Hall Rosenfeld, and Amy L. Culbertson, eds., *Hispanics in the Workplace* (Newbury Park CA: Sage, 1992), pp. 246–77, especially pp. 256–57; Baxter, "Interpersonal Spacing," pp. 444–56; Shuter, "Proxemics and Tactility," pp. 46–52.

99. Shuter, "Proxemics and Tactility," p. 52.

100. Celia Jaes Falicov, "Mexican Families, "in Monica McGoldrick, John K. Pearce, and Joseph Giordano, eds., *Ethnicity and Family Therapy* (New York: Guilford Press, 1982), pp. 134–63, especially p. 153; Condon, *Good Neighbors*, p. 45.

101. Calvin Sims, "The South American Art of Name-Calling," *New York Times*, July 30, 1995, sec. IV, p. 4.

102. For other sources on the Asian American cultural paradigm, see Peter L. Rose, "Asian Americans: From Pariahs to Paragons," in Nathan Glazer, ed., *Clamor at the Gates: The New American Immigration* (San Francisco: ICS Press, 1985), pp. 181–212, cited in Harry Kitano and Roger Daniels, *Asian Americans: Emerging Minorities* (Englewood Cliffs, NJ: Prentice Hall, 1998), p. 48. For the history of Asian Americans in America, see also Stanford Lyman, *Chinese Americans* (New York: Random House, 1974); William Petersen, *Japanese Americans* (New York: Random House, 1971); and Sowell, *Ethnic America, a History*, pp. 133–79. Perhaps the best single source of the World War II internment of Japanese Americans is Page Smith, *Democracy on Trial: The Japanese American Evacuation and Relocation in World War II* (New York: Simon and Shuster, 1995). For a briefer treatment, see also S. Frank Miyamoto, "The Forced Evacuation of the Japanese Minority during World War II," *Journal of Social Issues* 29(2) (1973): 11–32.

103. Sowell, *Ethnic America, A History*, pp. 138, 144–45.

104. Ibid., 175.

105. U.S. Bureau of the Census, No. 11, "Resident Population—Selected Characteristics, 1790 to 1992, and Projections, 1995 to 2050," in *Statistical Abstract of the United States* (Washington, DC: Government Printing Office, 1994); Jessica S. Barnes and Claudette E. Bennett, "The Asian Population: 2000, Census 2000 Brief," Washington, DC: Government Printing Office, 2002), pp. 1–10, especially p. 1.

106. June Ock Yum, "The Impact of Confucianism on Interpersonal Relationships and Communication Patterns in East Asia," in Larry A Samovar and Richard E. Porter, eds., *Intercultural Communication: A Reader*, 6th ed. (Belmont, CA: Wadsworth, 1991), pp. 66–78.

107. Frank Johnson, Anthony Marsella, and Colleen Johnson, "Social and Psychological Aspects of Verbal Behavior in Japanese-Americans," *American Journal of Psychiatry* 131 (1974): 580–83.

108. John C. Condon, *With Respect to the Japanese: A Guide for Americans* (Yarmouth, ME: Intercultural Press, 1984), p. 9; Hall and Hall, *Hidden Differences*, pp. 78–79.

109. Tocqueville, *Democracy in America*; Robert N. Bellah, Richard Madsen, William M. Sullivan, Ann Swidler, and Steven M. Tipton, *Habits of the Heart: Individualism and Commitment in American Life* (Berkeley: University of California Press, 1985).

110. Kitano & Daniels, *Asian Americans*, p. 72.

111. Richard Tanner Pascale, "Zen and the Art of Management," *Harvard Business Review* 56 (1978): 153–62.

112. Condon, *With Respect to the Japanese*, pp. 42–44.

113. Colleen Leahy Johnson and Frank Arvid Johnson, "Interaction Rules and Ethnicity: The Japanese and Caucasians in Honolulu," *Social Forces* 54(2) (December 1975): 452–56, especially 453.

114. Johnson et al., "Social and Psychological Aspects," p. 453.

115. Nan M. Sussman and Howard M. Rosenfeld, "Influence of Culture, Language, and Sex on Conversational Distance," *Journal of Personality and Social Psychology* 42(1) (1982): 66–74.

116. Ibid., pp. 71–73.

117. Dean Barnlund, "Communicative Styles in Two Cultures: Japan and the United States," in Adam Kendon, Richard M. Harris, and Mary Ritchie Key, eds., *Organization of Behavior in Face-to-Face Interaction* (The Hague: Mouton, 1975), pp. 444–57.

118. Anthony J. Marsella, "Counseling and Psychotherapy with Japanese Americans," *American Journal of Orthopsychiatry* 63 (April 1993): 200–208, especially 203.

119. James Morishima, "Special Employment Issues for Asian Americans," *Public Personnel Management Journal* 10 (1981): 384–92, especially 389.

120. Jing Hsu, Weng-Shing Tseng, Geoffrey Ashton, John F. McDermott Jr., and Walter Char, "Family Interaction Patterns among Japanese-American and Caucasian Families in Hawaii," *American Journal of Psychiatry* 142(5) (1985): 577–81.

121. Colin Watanabe, "Self-Expression and the Asian-American Experience," *Personnel and Guidance Journal* 51(6) (February 1973): 393–94; Kitano and Daniels, *Asian Americans*, p. 72.

122. Bowman and Okuda, "Japanese-American Communication," p. 19.

123. Marsella, "Counseling and Psychotherapy," p. 204.

124. Barnlund, "Communicative Styles in Two Cultures," pp. 429–36.

125. Bowman and Okuda, "Japanese-American Communication," p. 19.

126. Frederick T. L. Leong, "Counseling and Psychotherapy with Asian-Americans: Review of the Literature," *Journal of Counseling and Psychology* 31(2) (1986): 196–206, especially 197; Karen Huang, "Chinese Americans," in Noreen Mokuau, ed., *Handbook of Social Services for Asian and Pacific Islanders* (New York: Greenwood Press, 1991), pp. 79–96, especially p. 91.

127. Marsella, "Counseling and Psychotherapy," p. 205.

128. Barnlund, "Communicative Styles in Two Cultures," pp. 450–51.

129. Linda Wai Ling Young, "Inscrutability Revisited," in John Gumperz, ed., *Language and Social Identity* (Cambridge: Cambridge University Press, 1982), pp. 72–84, especially p. 79.

130. Barnlund, "Communicative Styles in Two Cultures," pp. 450–51.

131. Vernon E. Cronen, Kenneth M. Johnson, and John W. Lannamann, "Paradoxes, Double Binds, and Reflexive Loops: An Alternative Theoretical Perspective," in

Family Process 20 (March 1982): 91–112; Frederick Steier, "Introduction: Research as Self-Reflexivity," in Frederick Steier, ed., *Research and Reflexivity* (London: Sage, 1991), pp. 1–11; Frederick Steier, "Reflexivity and Methodology: An Ecological Construction-ism," in Frederick Steier, ed., *Research and Reflexivity* (London: Sage, 1991), pp. 163–85; Lynn Hoffman, "A Reflexive Stance for Family Therapy," *Journal of Strategic and Systemic Therapies* 10(3,4) (Fall/Winter 1991): 4–17.

132. Anderson and Goolishian, "The Client Is the Expert," pp. 25–39.

133. Harlene Anderson, "Then and Now: From Knowing to Not-Knowing," *Contemporary Family Therapy Journal* 12 (1990): 193–98.

134. Harlene Anderson and Susan Swim, "Learning as Collaborative Conversation: Combining the Student's and Teacher's Expertise," *Human Systems: The Journal of Systemic Consultation and Management* (1993): 145–60.

135. Kenneth J. Gergen, "The Social Constructionist Movement in Modern Psychology," *American Psychologist* 40(3) (March 1985): 266–75.

136. Esther Forbes, *Paul Revere and the World He Lived In* (Boston: Houghton Mifflin, 1942), pp. 1–17; Frederick Harling and Martin Kaufman, *The Ethnic Contribution to the American Revolution* (Westfield MA: Westfield Bicentennial Committee and Historical Journal of Western Massachusetts, 1976), p. 30; and Christopher, *Crashing the Gates.*

2

Dirty Business: Women Managing Sexual Objectification in the Workplace

Britain A. Scott and Sidney W. Scott

Twenty-two years after the Civil Rights Act of 1964 placed a prohibition on sex discrimination in workplace and organizational settings, the Supreme Court officially recognized sexual harassment as a form of such discrimination.[1] The 1986 *Meritor Savings Bank v. Vinson* ruling distinguished between two types of harassment: the less frequent quid pro quo harassment, which typically involves a superior asking for sexual favors in exchange for employment or consideration for promotion, and the more pervasive hostile workplace harassment, which may involve a variety of behaviors such as the use of sexist language (e.g., referring to women administrative assistants as "the girls"), telling sexist or sexually graphic jokes, displaying sexually graphic pictures, engaging in sexual innuendo, groping or fondling, exhibitionism, and so on.

In this chapter, we will not attempt to comprehensively address the broad topic of sexual harassment. Instead, we will focus on two distinct developments in the commercial sex industry that contribute to a hostile workplace climate for women, and may encourage all forms of sexual harassment, because of their psychological impact on both women and men. Specifically, we address the problem of Internet pornography in the workplace and the growing popularity of "gentlemen's clubs" that market themselves to a business clientele. We will describe social psychological theory and research on how the sexual objectification of women—which is pervasive in both of these forms of entertainment—affects the thoughts and behaviors of men, and the women with whom they interact, in ways that are distinctly negative for the workplace.

If current occupational trends continue, more of the leaders and managers who will be called on to deal with sexual harassment in the next decades will be women. According to a 2003 Catalyst report, women make up almost half of the paid workforce and hold just over half of managerial and professional specialty jobs in the United States.[2] The report cites a prediction that by 2010, the number of women in the U.S. workforce will have increased at a rate almost one-third higher than that of men.[3] For women in leadership and management positions, the challenges of addressing sexual harassment are complicated by the fact that they *are* women. After we discuss the problem of women's objectification in the workplace, we will recommend ways in which employers in general, and women specifically, can address it.

OBJECTIFICATION IN THE OFFICE

When we say a woman is being *objectified*, we mean that she is being perceived not as a whole person but in a way that dehumanizes her, sexualizes her, and reduces her to her body—or just parts of her body. When a woman is referred to as a "blonde" or a "babe," she is being objectified. When an image features a close-up shot of just a woman's cleavage, butt, or glossy lips, objectification is occurring. Women's objectification pervades our popular culture. Women are commonly turned into sex objects in advertising and entertainment venues. In the sections that follow, we discuss two specific ways that women's objectification is increasingly seeping into our workplace and organizational settings.

Web Women in the Workplace

Live women are not the only ones present in today's workplace settings. Girlie calenders on the walls may be mostly a thing of the past, but swimsuit model screensavers and pin-up planners are taking their place. Less visible but more insidious in the office are other sexually charged images and descriptions of women that are distributed via spam email, accessed online, or downloaded and tucked away in electronic file folders. During the past several years, many businesses and other organizations have made headlines for disciplining or dismissing employees for accessing sexually related Internet content at work.

The Pervasiveness of Internet Porn

Estimates of the number of pornography pages currently on the Internet range upward of 260 million. A 2001 Kaiser Family Foundation study surveyed fifteen- to seventeen-year-olds and found that 95 percent of those who had ever gone online had "accidentally" encountered pornography.[4] According to Sex-Tracker, a service that monitors the use of sexually related Web sites, as much as 70 percent of Internet traffic on porn sites occurs during the workday.[5]

In 1999, Xerox fired forty employees for accessing inappropriate Web sites, many of which were sexually related,[6] and the *New York Times* fired twenty-three employees for distributing sexually explicit images via email.[7] In 2000, Dow Chemical Company fired fifty employees for circulating images ranging from "material comparable to a swimsuit catalog all the way to hard-core violence and depictions of sadomasochistic sex" via the company's internal network.[8] A 2000 survey of 224 human resource directors at U.S. companies revealed that although more than 80 percent of the companies had Internet access policies, over 60 percent of them had disciplined employees for inappropriate use of the Internet.[9] The most common reason for disciplinary action—and dismissal—was accessing sexually oriented sites.

This phenomenon is not limited to the United States. In 2004, the British government fired 19 civil servants and disciplined 200 more for viewing sexually explicit Web sites at work.[10] The researchers who conducted the 2000 U.S. survey of human resource directors collected similar data in 2002 from 544 HR personnel in the United Kingdom and found that the majority of dismissals for inappropriate Internet use (69 percent) were related to sexual sites.[11] A third to a half of workplace computers in New Zealand have been found to contain downloaded images of a sexual nature ranging from swimsuit models to bestiality.[12] A 2004 study conducted by researchers from Queens University in Belfast found that 28 percent of workers at 350 companies in the United States, the United Kingdom, and Australia admitted downloading sexually explicit content while at work.[13]

The Content of Internet Porn

When most people hear the word *pornography*, they think of photographs or films of people who are nude or engaged in sex. Although much of the sexually related Internet content that workers are perusing probably fits this description, it would be naive to assume that the content is limited to graphic depictions of sex. Women especially may be unaware of the misogynist, violent, and racist content on many Internet sites.

Women in pornography are mostly presented as sex objects, dehumanized bodies on display for the pleasure of the viewer. What many women may not realize is that women in pornography are categorized and marketed according to factors such as their race, ethnicity, age, body types, and occupational status. No matter what the viewer's personal predilection, he can undoubtedly find Internet sites tailored to his preferences. The Web hosts "naughty housewives" and "barely legal teens," as well as sites featuring "sexy secretaries" and other women in workplace settings. There are sites devoted to women with lots of hair and women with no hair, women with very large breasts and women with very small breasts. Racist stereotypes include black women as sexual slaves or animal-like savages and Asian women suffering bondage and torture.[14]

Women in pornography are frequently portrayed as deriving pleasure from their own pain or humiliation. Such depictions reinforce the myth that women are masochistic and enjoy sexual harassment and abuse.[15] When women are portrayed as suffering without enjoyment, the tone is typically hostile and often boastful. For example, in 2003, an amateur videographer filmed nude women being hunted in the desert by camouflage-clad men wielding paintball guns. The video, called "Hunting for Bambi," was available on his Web site (and from mainstream outlets including Best Buy and Amazon.com). At the time of this writing, the Web site it still active and welcomes viewers with the copy,

> Guys would rather see naked women running around the woods with their beautiful, voluptuous "racks" jiggling all over, versus a hairy, four-legged deer anyways, right? Let's face it. For those of you that have a wife, girlfriend, significant other, even an ex-wife, or ex-girlfriend (you get the point) or some other Bambi Bitch that has done you wrong in the past, nagged you to death over the stupidest things, complained and whined that you didn't spend enough time with her, didn't take out the garbage, yada, yada, yada. . . . Here's a question. Wouldn't you just like to "Busta Bambi" sometime? I mean, if you had a paintball gun, and she was running for her hide through the woods, and you busted her in the ass with a paintball, you would feel just a little bit of gratification, wouldn't you? Okay, maybe some of you *really wouldn't want to see* your wife or girlfriend running naked through the woods with their fat rolls wiggling all over. But, you get the point.[16]

This site is a relatively tame example of the woman-hating and violent content that can be easily accessed on the Internet. Other sites feature images and descriptions of gang rape and "sexy torture."

In addition to virtual sexualized women that inhabit the workplace electronically, live sexy women serve as the backdrop for business that occurs outside the office. Although these women are not physically present at the workplace site, they are present in the memories of men when they return to the office.

BUSINESS AT THE BOYS' CLUB

In the mid-1990s, while the first author was a doctoral student at the University of Minnesota, women who worked in downtown Minneapolis and were members of the newly formed Skyway Business and Professional Women (SBPW) organization became concerned about the growing proliferation of so-called gentlemen's clubs in the heart of the city's business district. The women were particularly outraged by the free lunch buffets that their male colleagues were frequenting. These women suspected that the combination of lunch and lap dances might have a negative effect on gender relations during the second half of the workday.[17] During this same period, also in the Twin Cities, a local citizens' group formed in response to the announcement that the planners of the Mall of America intended to include a Hooters restaurant. Although the "Give Hooters the Boot" campaign was ultimately unsuccessful at keeping the restaurant out of the mall, it temporarily raised public awareness about the company's use of scantily clad, buxom "Hooters girls" to attract customers. Since the early 1990s, strip clubs and Hooters restaurants have become more numerous, more mainstream, and more common as locations for conducting business.

Growth of the Adult Hospitality Industry

Since the opening of the first restaurant in 1983, Hooters has expanded its scope to include over 375 restaurants in 46 states and 15 countries, novelty items such as calendars and DVDs, a magazine, swimsuit contests, sports sponsorship, and an airline. The company describes itself on its Web site as follows:

> The element of female sex appeal is prevalent in the restaurants, and the company believes the Hooters Girl is as socially acceptable as a Dallas Cowboy cheerleader, Sports Illustrated swimsuit model, or Radio City Rockette. . . . Claims that Hooters exploits attractive women are as ridiculous as saying the NFL exploits men who are big and fast. . . . To Hooters, the women's rights movement is important because it guarantees women have the right to choose their own careers, be it a Supreme Court Justice or Hooters Girl. . . . The chain acknowledges that many consider "Hooters" a slang term for a portion of the female anatomy. Hooters does have an owl inside its logo and uses an owl theme sufficiently to allow debate to occur over the meaning's intent. The chain enjoys and benefits from this debate. . . . Sixty-eight percent of customers are male, most between the ages of 25–54. . . . Hooters believes critics of the concept are a vocal minority of politically correct minded individuals.[18]

The company itself reports that many of its customers are businesspeople and 45 percent of its food sales occur during lunch.[19]

More extreme than Hooters are the growing number of strip clubs that have gone from being considered seedy to sophisticated. Clubs in many major U.S. cities, including New York, Dallas, and Miami Beach, have recently hired gourmet chefs and now offer fine dining comparable to upscale restaurants.[20] Tourist publications in hotel rooms now typically include advertisements for gentlemen's clubs, often targeting business travelers in particular. In 1995, Houston-based Rick's Cabaret became the first ever publicly traded adult nightclub stock. According to a 2000 episode of the Arts & Entertainment network's *Investigative Reports*, the number of gentlemen's clubs in North America doubled over the decade of the 1990s.[21]

Babes as a Backdrop for Business

In 2004, Wal-Mart stores faced a class-action sexual harassment lawsuit in which one store manager claimed that monthly sales meetings were held at a Hooters restaurant and that she had been pressured to visit a strip club during a business trip.[22] That same year, Wall Street giant Morgan Stanley paid a $54 million settlement in a sex discrimination suit that included complaints about women being routinely excluded from deal-making meetings at strip clubs.[23] When the huge Houston-based energy trading company Enron collapsed in bankruptcy in 2001, ugly truths about the spending habits of its top executives made national news. Reports came in that Enron executives had frequented

Houston strip clubs, in one instance attempting to charge to a business account more than \$750 for a single lunch for three or four men.[24] In 1995, *Sales and Marketing Management* magazine surveyed 228 U.S. salespeople and found that 49 percent of the men had entertained clients at topless bars.[25] In 1998, the growing trend toward conducting business at strip clubs caught the attention of ABC news and served as the theme of a *20/20* segment.[26]

Like the increasingly popularity of Internet pornography in the workplace, the mainstreaming of strip clubs as business venues is an international phenomenon. For example, strip clubs in Canada lure business clients with perks such as complimentary hotel pick-up service, VIP meeting rooms, and preferential "front of the line" admission passes.[27] A strip club in Oslo, Norway, specializes in major corporate events and several other Norwegian strip clubs rent their dancers for events at company offices.[28]

In 1997, two women employees sued Magna International, one of North America's largest auto parts companies, for sexual harassment by their male co-workers that they claimed was fueled by the men spending their lunch hours entertaining clients at strip clubs.[29] The women claimed that female employees were regularly fondled and called harassing names (such as "cupcake") by the men who frequented the clubs during work hours.[30] Like the women working on the Minneapolis skyway, these women made a connection between lunches spent ogling nude dancers and the treatment they received in the afternoon. In the next section we discuss psychological theory and research that supports such a connection.

HOW OBJECTIFICATION CREATES A HOSTILE WORKPLACE

As described earlier, when a woman is objectified, she is stripped of her individual personhood and reduced to a collection of body parts. Clearly, the Web women, waitresses, and strippers discussed previously are objectified. So how does their objectification affect the experience of women in the workplace? When considering the potential negative psychological and behavioral impacts of these women's objectification on women in the workplace, we must separately address the effects on men and the effects on their female co-workers.

From Sexual Objectification to Sexual Harassment: Effects on Men

Social psychological research studies clearly demonstrate that sexual objectification of women affects men's attitudes and behavior toward women and their perceptions of women. Effects vary depending on whether the sexual objectification involves hostility and violence. The effects of violent sexual objectification are most disturbing, but the effects of nonviolent objectification—which is more common in the workplace—also can contribute to a hostile climate.

It is important to recognize that to some extent this issue is circular: men who are already inclined toward sexist attitudes and harassment of women may be more inclined to download porn or take a business client to Hooters. We do not presume to suggest that the objectification of women as described is the sole or primary cause of sexual harassment; we will explain, however, that the practices mentioned can contribute to or exacerbate a hostile climate because of their psychological effects on men.

Nonviolent Objectification

In 1995, social psychologists Laurie Rudman and Eugene Borgida published an award-winning study in the *Journal of Experimental Social Psychology* that was inspired by a sexual harassment suit against Stroh's Brewery.[31] Although the lawsuit eventually settled out of court, it made headlines for a while because of the plantiffs' attorney's plan to use Stroh's own advertising as evidence that the company supported a hostile workplace.[32] Specifically targeted was the brewery's use of the "Swedish bikini team" in its television and print promotions. The bikini team consisted of five clone-like busty blonde bimbos who would conveniently show up with Old Milwaukee beer to entertain a bored and lonely guy. The attorney intended to argue that the portrayal of women in these ads contributed to a climate of sexual harassment at the company. At the time, there was a dearth of empirical research evidence to support the attorney's claim, so Rudman and Borgida stepped up to the plate.

In their experiment, male college students were recruited to individually participate in a consumer research study. The men were told that they would view twenty television commercials and rate them for their consumer appeal. Half of the men saw commercials that portrayed women as sex objects; the other half saw commercials for similar products with no women in them. All were actual commercials taped from television. After watching and rating one of the sets of commercials, each man was asked if he would do a favor for the experimenter and meet with a prospective research assistant who was due to arrive momentarily. The researcher explained that a participant's evaluation of the candidate would be helpful to her in deciding whether to hire the person for the position. All of the men agreed to help.

In each case, the researcher gave the man a set of questions from which he was instructed to select a few to ask the job candidate. The man was left alone in a room with the "candidate," who was portrayed by the same actress every time—dressed the same, acting the same, and unaware of which set of commercials the man had viewed. Unbeknownst to the man, the interaction was surreptitiously videotaped so the researcher could later assess his behaviors. After the interview, the man was asked his opinion about the candidate and tested on his memory for her personal characteristics.

The findings were startling. Men who had viewed the commercials that portrayed women as sex objects (certainly a more tame stimulus than a restaurant full of Hooters girls or nude table dancers), sat closer to the woman, acted in a more dominating manner toward her, chose more sex-stereotypical questions to ask her (e.g., "do you have a good phone voice" versus "are you good at statistics"), and recalled more about her physical appearance—and less about her as a person—than did men who had viewed the commercials without sexualized women in them.

The reason the study was award-winning was because Rudman and Borgida also collected data that explained *why* the men who had viewed the sex-object commercials treated the woman in a more sexist manner. The motivation for their behavior came from the mindset that the commercials put them in; specifically, the men had been unconsciously *primed* to think of women as sex objects. The well-learned cultural stereotype woman-as-sex-object had been triggered in their brains and had then acted as a filter for their perceptions of the woman and as a guide for their behavior toward her. How did Rudman and Borgida determine that the stereotype was triggered in these men's minds? After each man interviewed the candidate, he did a computer task in which strings of letters flashed on the screen and he indicated by pressing a key as quickly as possible whether the string was a real word or a nonsense word. Embedded among these letter strings were words that are commonly associated in people's minds with the woman as sex object stereotype: *bimbo, blonde, babe, Playboy, breasts,* and *panties.* Men who had viewed the commercials portraying women as sex objects recognized these words as words significantly more quickly than did the other men. Because the sex object stereotype had been activated, all ideas associated with that stereotype were in the forefront of these men's brains, making the recognition of them easier.

The activation of the sex object stereotype motivates and directs men's thoughts and behaviors in a sexual direction as demonstrated in this study and several others.[34] Activation of this stereotype also limits men's thinking in the following way: the perception of women as sex objects is inconsistent with the perception of them as professionals. Researchers have found that women are generally stereotyped as belonging to one of three categories: sexy woman, housewife, or career woman—categories that differ in terms of the women's power, competence, and moral virtue.[34] When people are asked to list the characteristics of the "sexy woman" and of the "career woman," the lists are distinctly different and nonoverlapping.[35] Sexy women are not perceived as powerful, competent, or virtuous, whereas career women are perceived as all three of these. Men who are primed to think of their female co-workers through the filter of the sex object stereotype are not likely to be tuned in to the women's intelligence, skills, or authority.

The activation of the sex object stereotype in the minds of male co-workers has implications for how all women in the workplace are perceived; however, the phenomenon is particularly problematic for women of lesser status. In general, higher power persons stereotype lower power persons more commonly than the other way around because powerful people can afford to generalize and ignore the individual characteristics of insignificant others.[36] Experimental research suggests that for men who are already prone to sexual aggression, just being in a position of power relative to a woman is an automatic trigger for stereotyping the woman sexually instead of professionally.[37] Women of "lesser status" include not only women in subordinate jobs (where most employed women find themselves) but also women who are younger or less experienced than the men or have minority racial or ethnic status relative to the men. Women whose lesser status is defined by more than one of these attributes may be especially vulnerable targets of sexual objectification and harassment.

Psychologist Kay Deaux has studied gender stereotypes extensively. She sums up the relationship between the sex object stereotype and the hostile workplace as follows:

> A hostile work environment might be defined as one in which a particular subtype of woman—one emphasizing sexual characteristics rather than professional ones—is primed, encouraged, and supported. To the extent, for example, that pornographic pictures, photos of women in bathing suits, and sexually explicit jokes and language are part of the work environment, then sexual stereotypes of women are going to be far more accessible than they would otherwise, and sexual harassment is more likely to occur.[38]

We know that nonviolent objectification of women, such as what occurs at Hooters, in strip clubs, and on many Internet sites, causes men to perceive women as sex objects. What happens when the objectification also involves hostility or violence?

Violent Objectification

When the sexual objectification involves hostility or violence toward the objectified women (as in the "Hunting for Bambi" example), the psychological and behavioral effects are more extreme. Experimental research suggests that exposure to material that combines the sexual objectification of women with violence lowers men's support of sexual equality, desensitizes men to violence against women, increases men's acceptance of rape myths, such as "all women secretly want to be raped," and increases men's physical aggression toward women in the laboratory.[39]

For example, in one study researchers Daniel Linz, Edward Donnerstein, and Steven Penrod exposed male college students to ten hours of R-rated or X-rated movies (two hours a day for five days).[40] Some men saw films that were sexually explicit and included sexual assault; some saw films that were sexually explicit but portrayed consensual sex; and the rest saw films that were less sexually explicit but portrayed violence against women within a sexual context. At the end of the five days, the three groups of men, along with a control group who had not seen any films, were asked to watch a reenactment of a rape trial and make several judgments about the case. Compared to the control group and the group that had seen the X-rated nonviolent films, the two groups who had seen sexually violent films judged the rape victim's injury to be less severe and rated her significantly more worthless as a person.

Importantly, it is the *combination* of sex and violence—rather than the sexual explicitness of the material—that leads to the more extreme effects. This means that Internet content such as the "Hunting for Bambi" site should not be dismissed as a harmless joke. Even nonexplicit sites that objectify women in a hostile or violent way may lower men's inhibitions regarding sexual harassment. For practical and ethical reasons, experimental research cannot address the possible links between sexually violent material and men's behaviors toward women in the real world; however, numerous interview studies with abused women support the connection.

When researchers have interviewed battered women about their partners' use of pornography, they have typically found that about 40 to 60 percent of the women report that their batterers use of violent pornography was intimately tied to their abuse in that they had been asked or forced to act out violent sexual encounters the men had seen in the porn.[41] In their study on the sexual abuse of prostitutes, Mimi Silbert and Ayala Pines had not planned to study pornography, but were confronted with the subject when 24 percent of their study participants implicated violent pornography in their open-ended accounts of rape. One rape survivor recalled her attacker saying, "I know all about you bitches, you're no different; you're like all of them. I seen it in all the movies. You love being beaten."[42] We cannot conclude from accounts like these that violent sexual objectification of women directly causes otherwise harmless and respectful men to harass or abuse women, but it is clear that such pornography can provide sexually arousing behavioral scripts for men with aggressive impulses.

From Sexual Objectification to Performance Problems: Effects on Women

The negative effects of objectification on women manifest as performance deficits—a serious concern for workplace productivity. We will describe two ways that women's workplace performance may be hindered when their male colleagues have been primed to perceive them as sex objects. We first review experimental research that suggests women's performance may suffer when male superiors stereotype them. Then we describe theory that predicts that a woman's awareness (or suspicion) that she is being objectified may interfere with her performance.

Responses to Being Stereotyped

As described, the stereotypes "sex object" and "career woman" have been found to be incompatible and nonoverlapping in U.S. culture. When a woman is perceived as one, she is not likely to be simultaneously perceived as the other. When the sex object lens is in place, a woman's competence, intelligence, leadership skills, and so on will be out of focus. As the Rudman and Borgida study demonstrated, the sex object stereotype will then guide the behavior of the perceiver and direct him to treat the woman in a more sexist—and possibly harassing—manner. The effects do not stop there. When a person is the target of a stereotype, her behavior is affected in turn.

When an individual is stereotyped, he or she is likely to unintentionally behave in ways consistent with the stereotype. This phenomenon, labeled *behavioral confirmation*, has been demonstrated in numerous experiments since the late 1970s. In the first laboratory investigation, pairs of opposite-sex strangers were seated in separate rooms and asked to have a "getting acquainted" conversation over an intercom.[43] The man in each pair was given a photograph, ostensibly of his interaction partner. In reality, the photo was one of only two: either a photo of an attractive woman or a photo of an unattractive woman. Before the conversation, the man was asked about his expectations of his partner. Consistent with our culture's "what is beautiful is good" stereotype, if he was looking at the attractive photo, he expected her to be more intelligent, more socially skilled, and so on. Importantly, the woman participant was unaware that he had a photo he believed to be of her.

After the man and woman had their conversation, the man was asked what his partner had actually been like. Men who had looked at the attractive picture reported that their partners possessed significantly more positive qualities than did the men who had looked at the unattractive picture. This finding is not surprising given the effect of stereotypes on our perceptions: we see (and hear) what we expect to. The surprising finding surfaced later when other people judged the women's behaviors in the conversations.

Each conversation had been audiotaped with the man and woman on separate channels. The researchers asked a few people to listen to just the women's sides of the conversations and rate each woman on the same qualities the men had (intelligence, social skills, etc.). Like the women participants, the listeners were unaware of the photos. Still, what the listeners heard led them to rate the women whose partners had been looking at an attractive picture more positively than the women whose partners had been looking at an unattractive picture. In other words, because the pictures led the men to treat the women differently, the women ended up *actually behaving differently*—specifically, the women unintentionally behaved in ways consistent with the men's expectations of them. The stereotype had become a self-fulfilling prophecy.

Consider the implications when a woman is being stereotyped as a sex object by her male colleague. Not only is he likely to interpret her behavior as consistent with his expectations about her, she may very well end up behaving in stereotype-consistent ways because of the way he treats her. If he expects her to be incompetent and unintelligent because she is merely a sex object in his eyes, he may not give her the opportunity to disconfirm his preconceived notions. For example, if the stereotype leads him to not ask for her opinion about an important decision, her silence may reinforce his belief that she is not bright. She may underperform because she is expected to underperform.

Since the late 1970s, behavioral confirmation has been studied in a variety of contexts. Researchers have found that the effects are strongest when the perceiver is more powerful than the target of the stereotype because powerful people have more influence over the way an interaction happens.[44] In the case of mixed-sex interaction, not only do men in our culture have higher social status in general, most workplaces are characterized by sex stratification in which men occupy the majority of higher power positions while women are concentrated in lower power roles.[45]

Recent work by social psychologist Theresa Vescio and colleagues suggests that powerful men do not always automatically stereotype subordinate women, even in masculine domains (such as the majority of both blue-collar and white-collar workplaces in the United States).[46] When the context leads to gender stereotyping, however, powerful men tend to behave toward subordinate women in patronizing ways, offering praise and compliments but withholding tangible resources such as money and power. What women receive is a condescending mixed message: "wow, what surprisingly good work [for a woman or a sex object]; still, it's not worthy of real rewards." As a result, the women tend to feel anger and a lack of confidence, and their performance suffers.

The effects of stereotyping that we have described can occur without men being primed to view women specifically as sex objects; merely stereotyping women as women (i.e., emotional, dependent, nurturing) can cause women to behaviorally confirm the stereotype or experience feelings of anger and frustration. When the stereotype is the woman as sex object, these effects will likely happen along with the woman's own internal response to being objectified.

Self-Objectification

According to Barbara Frederickson and Tomi-Ann Roberts, girls and women in our culture are taught to routinely objectify themselves.[47] When girls grow up surrounded by sexually objectified representations of women, they learn to perceive themselves as objects and adopt an observer's perspective on their own bodies. This *self-objectification* involves habitual self-surveillance and body monitoring that places demands on attention. Frederickson and Roberts do not suggest that women are naturally vain or self-absorbed, but instead explain that women learn to be vigilant about their appearance because it is a practical strategy in a culture in which a woman's appearance may significantly affect her life outcomes.

When women engage in appearance monitoring, their attention is directed away from the tasks at hand and toward feelings of anxiety (that their appearance will be scrutinized by others), shame (that their appearance doesn't measure up to some ideal), and fear (that if their appearance is too appealing they may become targets of unwanted sexual attention). When women self-objectify, they enter a self-conscious preoccupation in which they find themselves not subjectively experiencing a situation but thinking about how they appear to others in the situation. For example, in one study of young adult women, approximately a third admitted being preoccupied with concerns about their appearance during sexual intimacy, instead of being tuned in to their own desires and physical sensations.[48]

Not only does self-objectification direct attention away from subjective experience, it divides attention between self-surveillance and other tasks. We know from cognitive psychology research (and personal experience trying to multitask) that our mental resources are limited; we can only think about so many things at once. Frederickson and Roberts suggest that when women devote mental resources to self-objectification, fewer resources are available for other tasks. Support for this proposition comes from experiments that put women in situations that temporarily heighten their self-objectification.

For example, in one study researchers had individual women and men try on either a sweater or a swimsuit.[49] The researchers predicted that the women would be in a more self-objectifying state of mind after trying on the swimsuit than after trying on the sweater and that the men would be unaffected by the clothing manipulation. They were correct. Why this study is remarkable, however, has to do with what happened next. After trying on either the sweater or the swimsuit, each participant's available mental resources were assessed by the administration of a set of fairly challenging math problems. The researchers found that the math performance of women who had tried on the swimsuit was significantly worse than the performance of women who had tried on the sweater. Men's math performance was unaffected.

Granted, it is not very often that women find themselves in situations in which they are wearing a swimsuit and doing math problems; however, even subtle situational cues can trigger women's self-objectification. For example, in one study feelings of self-objectification were significantly heightened after women participants had simply unscrambled sentences that contained appearance-related words such as *weight, slender, beauty*, and *shapely*.[50] Consider the implications of both the swimsuit study and the scrambled sentence study for the situation of a woman in the workplace who is aware that her male colleague has just been in his office surfing porn sites or has just returned from lunch at the local topless bar.

In the only published study to date that looked at how interacting with a man might heighten a woman's self-objectification, researcher Rachel Calogero led women participants to believe that they would be engaging in small talk with either a male or female stranger for five minutes.[51] Before the interaction (which never actually happened), the women's self-objectification was measured. Women who anticipated interacting with a male stranger reported significantly greater body shame and anxiety than did women who anticipated interacting with another woman. These participants merely had to anticipate interacting with a man for their self-objectification to be heightened. When a woman has to interact with a male co-worker she suspects is objectifying her, due to her awareness of his Web surfing, for example—or one whom she *knows* is objectifying her, due to his verbal or physical behavior—heightened self-objectification will almost certainly occur. How might a woman's heightened appearance monitoring, feelings of shame and anxiety, and mental pre-occupation affect her ability to concentrate on her work?

MANAGING OBJECTIFICATION

In the preceding sections we presented the issue of women's objectification in the workplace and have described psychological research that supports our thesis that it is a problem warranting attention. The remainder of the chapter will address the challenges of dealing with this problem, some of which pertain to employers in general and others that are specific to women managers.

Objectification and Sexual Harassment Policy

Sexual harassment has always been difficult to delineate, even with the often cited guidelines presented by the Equal Employment Opportunity Commission (EEOC) in the 1980s and approved by the U.S. Supreme Court in 1986.[52] According to the EEOC,

> Unwelcome sexual advances, requests for sexual favors, and other verbal or physical conduct of a sexual nature constitutes sexual harassment when submission to or rejection of this conduct explicitly or implicitly affects an individual's employment [quid pro quo], unreasonably interferes with an individual's work performance or creates an intimidating, hostile or offensive work environment.[53]

Quid pro quo harassment is a clear violation of Section 703 of Title VII of the Civil Rights Act of 1964, and there is no defense on the part of the company when this happens. Less clear-cut yet far more common is the situation of the hostile workplace environment.

A recent trend has been toward organizations adopting general harassment policies to encompass not only sexual harassment but also any form of harassment that contributes to a hostile workplace in general. The Massachusetts Commission Against Discrimination has urged employers to supplement sexual harassment policies with broader harassment policies to identify that all forms of discriminatory practices can have a negative effect on workplace relationships, morale, and productivity.[54] Although the obvious intent of a general harassment policy is to protect and prevent all types of unwelcome behavior, the unintended result may be that managers and employees will think of harassment in a gender-neutral manner.

This may be a problem given that the vast majority of sexual harassment remains male-to-female. Situations of female-to-male harassment, such as the one portrayed in the 1994 film *Disclosure*, in which supervisor Demi Moore created a quid pro quo situation with subordinate manager Michael Douglas, are relatively rare. The latest EEOC data for FY 2004 indicate sexual harassment claims by men, though rising since 1993, still only constitute 15.1 percent of the claims, and women are filing nearly 85 percent of them.[55] Gender-neutral approaches to harassment policy may be detrimental because they obscure the fact that objectification and stereotyping of women in the workplace is not balanced by similar stereotyping and objectification of men. There are no *Sports Illustrated* swimsuit hunk desk planners or "Cocks" restaurants for business lunches.

In 1993, the American Psychological Association filed an amicus brief with the Supreme Court in the case of *Harris v. Forklift Systems* that reviewed research on gender differences in perceptions of sexual harassment. The plaintiff in the case claimed that the company president created a hostile workplace with his jokes about her attracting customers with sexual favors and his requests to female employees to pull coins out of his front pants pocket. The amicus brief explained that women and men tend to have different ideas about what constitutes harassment.[56] A recent meta-analytic review of sixty-two individual studies on women's and men's perceptions of sexual harassment concluded that women tend to perceive a broader range of behaviors as harassing than men do and that some of the largest differences are in perceptions of what qualifies as a hostile workplace and whether derogatory attitudes toward women are present.[57] With support from these psychological research studies and a legal precedent from the 1991 case *Ellison v. Brady*, many have argued that the courts should employ a "reasonable woman" standard in place of a "reasonable person" or "reasonable man" standard in sexual harassment cases.[58] This standard allows that a woman need not prove psychological harm to claim sexual harassment and that a hostile workplace may exist when a reasonable woman would find the environment offensive (even if a reasonable man would not).

The EEOC description of the hostile workplace is intentionally vague so as to encompass a variety of scenarios, and the reasonable woman standard seems to treat women's subjective experience as sufficient evidence that a workplace climate is hostile; however, both the EEOC guidelines and the reasonable woman standard were created with only overt behavior in mind. Neither was crafted to address those subtle behaviors (e.g., men privately accessing Internet sites that sexually objectify women and conducting business at establishments that do the same) that may lead to women experiencing a hostile workplace merely because of the way these activities affect men psychologically and the way women's awareness of these activities may undermine women's performance.

A recent case in the United Kingdom tested the idea that a woman's awareness of sexually objectifying behavior could, in and of itself, constitute sexual harassment. A female data entry clerk worked in close proximity to male colleagues who allegedly downloaded pornographic images from the Internet on three occasions when she was in the room. A tribunal originally rejected her sexual harassment claim on the basis that the images had not been shown to her. The Employment Appeal Tribunal (EAT) overturned the decision, recognizing that downloading porn in the presence of a female co-worker was potentially degrading and an affront to her dignity.[59] It is unclear whether the EAT would have ruled the same had she not been present when the behavior was happening.

Human resources professionals in enlightened organizations adopt strict policies against sexual harassing behaviors and regularly train employees to recognize, prevent, and stop these behaviors from occurring. This training is primarily conducted to keep the employer out of court with an important secondary objective of making the workplace safer and less threatening. Most training, though necessary and helpful, does not adequately address the problem of women's objectification. Employees are informed about which behaviors are legally prohibited but are not normally educated about how a hostile workplace can be created by invisible influences, such as the clandestine use of a bikini babe screen saver or lunch at the strip club. Nor are employees typically asked to think critically about how the hostile workplace may be related to underlying male attitudes toward women in general that are reinforced by societal norms, mass media, and our institutional structures.

Compounding the problem, courts have held that companies can comply with their obligation to prevent further sexual harassment *after* an incident by simply removing offending items and reminding employees of the rules. For example, in a Tenth Circuit court decision in 2003, Exxon Mobile Oil was deemed to have responded adequately to a sexual harassment charge by removing "demeaning graffiti" from a female worker's area, increasing security, and calling all employees into meetings to reinforce the sexual harassment policy even though these actions likely did little to change situational factors, beliefs, and attitudes that prompted the sexually harassing behavior in the first place.[60]

Companies can address overt behavior, but the activities in question are difficult to monitor. In the next section we will describe how many companies are proactively attempting to address Internet usage (including the accessing of sexual content), while at the same time some companies may actually be resistant to tackling the issue of meetings at sexually objectifying venues because of the belief that it would be bad for business.

E-Harassment

When the definition of sexual harassment became a part of the language of human resources policies, many forms of communication commonly used today did not exist. For example, use of the Internet has grown astronomically since 1994, the year Netscape launched Netscape Navigator, the first widely used browser. Although an estimated 3 million persons worldwide, mostly located in the United States, were using the Internet in 1994, by 2004, estimates of global usage ranged to 945 million, with 140 million U.S. citizens going online every month.[61]

With the ease of access to the Internet in the workplace, employers have had to contend with the potential loss of productivity associated with employees spending time browsing for non–work-related information and shopping for personal items. Some non–work-related Internet activity, though publicly discouraged in policies, is tolerated by employers who try to balance productivity wants with employees' needs for periodic breaks from the work at hand. Actually, taking a break at one's work area is probably less disruptive than going for a break in a remote, designated area of the building. This may explain why in a Vault.com study of over 1,400 employers, 82 percent indicated it was appropriate for employees to view non–work-related Web sites, and 58 percent felt it was permissible to spend fifteen to thirty minutes each day in these activities.[62]

The problem arises from the tendency of the Internet to become habitual and even addictive.[63] While employees' use includes personal email, chat rooms, games, sports, music downloads, shopping, gambling, and online stock trading, the most commonly reported form of Internet misuse is the accessing and downloading of pornography. A 2002 study found that pornography was the issue in 51 percent of the complaints and 69 percent of Internet misuse dismissals.[64] Pornography has addictive properties that have been described by some experts as comparable to those found in heroin or crack cocaine. In a recent testimony before a Senate subcommittee, Mary Anne Layden, codirector of the University of Pennsylvania's Sexual Trauma and Psychopathology Program, described pornography as, "the most concerning thing to psychological health . . . existing today," and described how the Internet is "a perfect drug delivery system because you are anonymous, aroused, and have role models for . . . behaviors."[65] When we understand that an estimated 260 new porn sites are added each day, and that nearly three-quarters of all pornographic traffic on the Internet is occurring during the workday, then we begin to realize the depth and breadth of the problem facing employers.[66]

In addition to the misuse of company resources and wasted time, a concern for employers is how to prevent the Internet itself from becoming another vehicle for sexual harassment. The illusion of anonymity and impersonality created by electronic communication may give encouragement to harassers to take even more risks to transmit discriminatory statements, lewd images, and abusive messages than live interaction that forces the offender to face his victim. In response to Internet misuse and the potential for electronic forms of sexual harassment, many companies have not only written strict rules and policies forbidding harassing behavior and outlining severe consequences, up to and including dismissal, but have also added provisions for monitoring and limiting access to email and the Internet. Employers walk a fine line, however, as their rules, policies, and procedures must also protect employee rights to privacy afforded by federal and state laws.[67]

Objectification Is Business as Usual

At the same time that employers are cracking down on Internet porn in the workplace, the mixing of business and objectified women appears to be increasing outside the workplace. As described, sexual harassment cases at large companies, including Wal-Mart and Morgan Stanley, have involved accusations that business was conducted at strip clubs. In the high-profile 1996 Mitsubishi case, women workers described how their male colleagues took photos of each other with strippers and prostitutes at off-site parties (including some that managers attended in Japan) and then displayed the photos in the employee break room.[68] This specific behavior was only one of a plethora that occurred in what the EEOC ultimately deemed a "hyper-sexual environment." Women were routinely groped, subjected to lewd and threatening comments, and made to witness to exhibitionism and simulated masturbation.

Women's objectification is an integral part of the business culture in many more organizations than Mitsubishi. For example, in her book *Tales from the Boom Boom Room*, Susan Antilla describes the sexism and sexual harassment that pervade Wall Street and reports that strip clubs are a favorite hangout for brokers.[69] After the CEO of the newly formed Rent-A-Center essentially dismantled the human resources department, problem behaviors flourished—including hiring go-go dancers to entertain at a company meeting in Las Vegas.[70] Not only are objectified women considered acceptable in many business circles, they also are seen as lucrative. When women sued in the aforementioned Magna International case, auto industry salesmen explained that the habit of conducting business at strip clubs was a profitable practice. Men, they said, are happy when they are surrounded by beautiful nude women—and happy men are more agreeable clients and collaborators.[71]

When strip clubs are lauded as bonding environments that facilitate positive relationships between men, a company is most likely going to look the other way when they are used as settings for business. Objectification of women in forms such as the Hooters lunch may also be a part of the routine script because it serves as a means for men to express and reinforce their masculinity and dominance to each other.[72] Given that most workplaces are still male-dominated, what will it take to break the tradition of women's objectification in the workplace? We think it will take women.

Women Managers Challenging Objectification

We do not want to be misunderstood as unfairly putting the burden on women to remedy a problem that originates with men's behavior; instead, we intend to promote an optimistic and pragmatic perspective that women in positions of authority are the ones best poised to tackle the problem of objectification in the workplace. History tells us that social change comes about when those who are wronged fight against the status quo (e.g., the civil rights movement, the women's movement). Allies can be found among the dominant group, but the momentum for change comes from the bottom up. Women managers may be more influential than other women employees in eliciting change because they at least have some authority; however, we predict that action on the part of women managers will not be risk-free.

Women Managers in a Double-Bind

When a woman occupies a role that requires her to behave in "unfeminine" ways, she may find herself in a double bind; in other words, she is damned if she does and damned if she doesn't. If she acts appropriately for the occupational role (e.g., a woman manager disciplining an employee for tardiness) she may be seen as harsh and unlikable; if she acts in more feminine ways (e.g., gently reminding the employee about the time), she may be considered ineffective and unsuited for her job. For example, in a highly publicized 1988 case against accounting firm Price Waterhouse, senior manager Ann Hopkins described how she was denied a partnership—in spite of her outstanding record—because several colleagues thought she had been acting too masculine and needed to walk, talk, and dress more femininely.[73] Presumably, she would not have been so successful in her job had she not displayed so-called masculine qualities, such as agency and assertiveness.

Just by being in positions of authority, women managers are in a chronic double bind. When it comes to challenging women's objectification, women managers will likely find themselves in a situation-specific double bind. If they do not address the problem, the negative effects we have already described will potentially produce a hostile working environment for themselves and their female colleagues. In addition, the glass ceiling may be reinforced as they are left out of important networking that takes place in settings where women are thought of only as objects. If they *do* address the issue, however, they minimally run the risk of being labeled oversensitive, not a team player, or bitchy. More seriously, they may jeopardize their careers.

Several studies conducted in the 1980s and 1990s found that when women challenge sexual harassment, they may face retaliation, poor performance evaluations, denial of promotions, or even dismissal.[74] These studies were conducted before the Internet was popular and before business at Hooters and strip clubs was trendy, so the harassment the women were reporting was probably more blatant than the hostile objectifying climate we have discussed. If a woman faces retaliation for complaining about blatant harassment, what can she expect when she tries to argue the subtleties of the problem of objectification?

Though the situation sounds bleak, we are confident that women who are in influential positions within their organizations can serve both as catalysts for change as well as activists in bringing about necessary progress. We think the crucial goal is systemic change. Isolated lawsuits may yield positive benefits for individual women or groups of women at a particular workplace, but they do not necessarily challenge the pervasive problem of women's objectified status.

Women Changing the System

Lasting change will require nothing less than a shift in cultural norms. Large system change has been the purview of organization development (OD) professionals since the 1960s. The standard OD approach is based on the work of Kurt Lewin, a social psychologist who proposed that systemic change requires three steps: organizations and individuals need to "unfreeze" present behavior, take action (called movement) that will change the original social system, and then "refreeze" the new standard of behavior so that it is resistant to change.[75]

We anticipate that the unfreezing of the objectifying behavior that creates a chilly climate for women will be the most challenging step in the process given that the trends we have described are toward more objectification of women in the workplace. As long as workplaces remain male-dominated—or at least employ primarily men in influential positions—a sexually objectifying ideology is likely to prevail. Still, the unfreezing is already in progress to some extent. The fact that the issues of Internet porn in the workplace and strip clubs catering to business clients have both received widespread media attention is a hopeful sign. The media have not delved into the social science research on why these things are a problem, but at least they have been considered worthy of discussion and debate.

As the thaw proceeds, action will need to come from women who will create the new norms for appropriate conduct. One way to shape the norms is to occupy positions of greater influence. Of course, we recognize that this is easier said than done. It is no easy task for women to just step into higher-level positions (for the reasons we have discussed and more). Currently only ten women rank among the Fortune 500 CEOs. Although some women are opting out of high-power (high-demand) positions because of the difficulty of balancing work and family, women's absence in the upper ranks of corporate America cannot be attributed entirely to them prioritizing family. According to a recent article in *Chief Executive*, 50 percent of today's private businesses are run or owned by women.[76] Women are still in the workforce, but they are leaving corporate structures that they perceive to be inflexible or not accommodating of diversity. We respect this decision, yet we encourage women who are able to stay within the system where they can change it. Women in visible positions of responsibility can act as role models for respectful behavior.

As workplaces become more women-friendly and women-managed, we think the refreezing will happen naturally when companies come to recognize the benefits of the changed climate. We are already seeing data that suggest potential benefits include not only improved employee morale but also significantly higher profits. In 2004, the Calvert Group, the largest family of socially responsible mutual funds, unveiled its *Calvert Women's Principles*, a set of corporate guidelines intended to economically empower women worldwide.[77] The first two companies that adopted the Calvert principles were Dell computers and Starbucks coffee. Dell is the 28th largest company in the United States, and Starbucks is in 372nd place on the 2005 list of the 500 largest corporations.[78] Not coincidentally, Starbucks is ranked eleventh on the 2005 Fortune "100 Best Companies to Work For" list, and 63 percent of its workforce is female.[79] Calvert asserts that changing corporate conduct and structures will not only help eliminate entrenched gender bias and sex discrimination but will be economically advantageous. As president and CEO of Calvert Barbara Krumsiek put it, "As a result of gender inequities, women remain . . . an untapped economic resource and an underutilized economic asset."[80]

Support for the claim that woman-friendly environments are good for profits comes from a 2004 Catalyst study of 353 of the Fortune 500, which found a significant connection between representation of women on top management teams and two common measures of financial performance—return on equity and total return to shareholders. In the largest public companies with the highest representation of women on their top management teams, return on equity was 35.1 percent higher and total return to shareholders was 34.0 percent higher than the companies with the lowest representation of women in top management teams.[81] As women move up, profits go up—what better argument is there for workplaces changing their objectifying ways?

CONCLUSION

The December 2003 issue of *Playboy* magazine included a cartoon of a secretary seated outside the open office door of a lecherous-looking boss, warning a woman who was about to enter the office, "Watch yourself—he had lunch at Hooters."[82] It may seem paradoxical to consider *Playboy* a definitive source on the negative effects of women's objectification in the workplace. Still, we see the presence of this cartoon in the magazine as a hint that men are not completely oblivious to the connection between exposure to objectified women during work hours and subsequent sexual harassment of female colleagues; otherwise, why would it be funny?

Men know what's going on, and women are beginning to catch on as well. Social psychologists clearly know what's going on is problematic. It is time that we all stopped dismissing women's objectification in the workplace with the excuse "boys will be boys," because these days more of the "boys" in the business world are actually girls. And these "girls" are entitled to respect, dignity, and fully human status.

NOTES

1. *Meritor Savings Bank v. Vinson*, 474 U.S. 57 (1986).

2. Catalyst, "2003 Catalyst Census of Women Board Directors: A Call to Action in a New Era of Corporate Governance," available online at www.catalystwomen.org; accessed June 11, 2005.

3. Howard N. Fullerton Jr. and Mitsa Toosi, "Labor Force Projections to 2010: Steady Growth and Changing Composition," *Monthly Labor Review* November (2001): 35.

4. Kaiser Family Foundation, *Generation Rx.com: How Young People Use the Internet for Health Information*. Publication #3202 available from the Kaiser Family Foundation, 2001.

5. Michelle Conlin, "Workers, Surf at your Own Risk," *Business Week* (June 2000).

6. Lisa Guernsey, "Surfing the Web: New Ticket to a Pink Slip," *New York Times*, December 16, 1999.

7. Thomas York, "Invasion of Privacy: E-Mail Monitoring is on the Rise," *Information Week*, February 21, 2000.

8. Vito Pilieci, "Dow Fires 50 over Porn Email: Company Only Latest to Take Action," *Chicago Sun Times*, July 30, 2000, p. 3.

9. David N. Greenfield and Richard A. Davis, "Lost in Cyberspace: The Web @ Work," *CyberPsychology and Behavior* 5 (2002): 347–53.

10. Reuters, "Britain Fires Porn Surfers," *Toronto Sun*, August 27, 2004, p. 54.

11. Paul Kelso, "Most Internet Sackings Linked to Visiting Porn Sites," *Guardian*, July 10, 2002, p. 11.

12. "Police Culture: Workplace Porn," *New Zealand Herald*, April 23, 2005.

13. Bob Sullivan, "Porn at Work Problem Persists: Study Says 50 Percent Receive Unwanted Sex Messages," *MSNBC*, September 6, 2004; available online at msnbc .msn.com/id/5899345; accessed May 27, 2005.

14. Patricia Hill Collins, "Pornography and Black Women's Bodies," in L. L. O'Toole and J. R. Schiffmann, eds., *Gender Violence: Interdisciplinary Perspectives* (New York: New York University Press, 1997), pp. 395–99.

15. Diana Russell, *Against Pornography: The Evidence of Harm* (Berkley, CA: Russell Publications, 1993).

16. Bambi Bob, "Men Hunting Naked Women. It's About F**k'in Time!" Hunting for Bambi 2; available online at huntingforbambi.com; accessed May 25, 2005.

17. Jill Hodges, "Doing in Doing Lunch: Women Articulate Growing Concerns about Noon-Hour Adult Entertainment," *Star Tribune*, January 26, 1995, sec. D, p. 1.

18. Hooters, "About Hooters," available online at www.hooters.com/company/about_ hooters; accessed June 2, 2005.

19. Andrew Gomes, "Hooters Okay for Business Lunch? Depends on Definition of 'Business,'" *Pacific Business News*, February 5, 1999.

20. Milford Prewitt, "Top 10 Restaurant Trends," *Nation's Restaurant News*, December 20, 2004.

21. Arts & Entertainment Network, *Investigative Reports: Gentlemen's Clubs*, aired January 4, 2000.

22. Stephanie Armour, "Rife with Discrimination," *USA Today*, June 24, 2004, sec. B, p. 3.

23. Jenny Anderson, "Wall St. Women Win: Morgan OKs $54M Payout in Bias Suit," *New York Post*, July 13, 2004, p. 5.

24. Robert Bryce, *Pipe Dreams: Greed, Ego, and the Death of Enron* (New York: Public Affairs, 2002).

25. Robyn Meredith, "Strip Clubs under Siege as Salesmen's Haven," *New York Times*, September 20, 1997, sec. A, p. 1.

26. ABC News, "A Day at the Office: Entertaining Business Clients at Strip Clubs," aired August 3, 1998.

27. Betsy Powell, "Strip Clubs Lure Business Clients," *Toronto Star*, February 23, 2003, p. 7; Charlie Fidelman, "The Naked Lunch: Is Doing Business in a Strip Club Just Like Taking a Client to Play Golf? Or Is it Discriminatory?" *Gazette*, August 3, 1998, sec. C, p. 5.

28. Jonathan Tisdall, "Bosses Prefer Strip Clubs," *Aftenposten: News from Norway*, February 20, 2003.

29. Kathleen Parker, "Worked up over Lap Dancing at Lunch," *Des Moines Register*, September 24, 1997, p. 2.

30. Fidelman, "The Naked Lunch."

31. Laurie A. Rudman and Eugene Borgida, "The Afterglow of Construct Accessibility: The Behavioral Consequences of Priming Men to View Women as Sexual Objects," *Journal of Experimental Social Psychology* 31 (1995): 493–517.

32. Tony Kennedy, "Stroh Must Surrender Ad Material, Judge Says; Women's Attorney Says She Will Show that Sexism Is Prevalent at Company," *Star Tribune*, May 5, 1992, sec. D, p. 3.

33. For example, Doug McKenzie-Mohr and Mark Zanna, "Treating Women as Sexual Objects: Look to the (Gender Schematic) Male Who has Viewed Pornography," *Personality and Social Psychology Bulletin* 16 (1990): 296–308.

34. T. William Altermatt, Nathan DeWall, and Emily Leskinen, "Agency and Virtue: Dimensions Underlying Subgroups of Women," *Sex Roles: A Journal of Research* 49 (2003): 631–42.

35. Kay Deaux, "How Basic Can You Be? The Evolution of Research on Gender Stereotypes," *Journal of Social Issues* 51 (1995): 11–20.

36. Susan T. Fiske, "Controlling Other People: The Impact of Power on Stereotyping," *American Psychologist* 48 (1993): 621–28.

37. John Bargh and Paula Raymond, "The Naïve Misuse of Power: Nonconscious Sources of Sexual Harassment," *Journal of Social Issues* 51 (1995): 85–96.

38. Deaux, "How Basic Can You Be?" p. 16.

39. Daniel Linz, Edward Donnerstein, and Steven Penrod, "Sexual Violence in the Mass Media: Social Psychological Implications," in P. Shaver and C. Hendrick, eds., *Review of Personality and Social Psychology: Vol. 7. Sex and Gender* (Newbury Park, CA: Sage, 1987), pp. 95–123.

40. Daniel Linz, Edward Donnerstein, and Steven Penrod, "The Effects of Long-Term Exposure to Filmed Violence against Women," *Journal of Communication* 34 (1984): 130–47.

41. Evelyn K. Sommers and James V. Check, "An Empirical Investigation of the Role of Pornography in the Verbal and Physical Abuse of Women," *Violence and Victims* 2 (1987): 189–209; Elizabeth Cramer, Judith McFarlane, Barbara Parker, Karen Soeken, Concepcion Silva, and Sally Reel, "Violent Pornography and Abuse of Women: Theory to Practice," *Violence and Victims* 13 (1998): 319–32.

42. Mimi H. Silbert and Ayala M. Pines, "Pornography and Sexual Abuse of Women," *Sex Roles* 21 (1984): 857–68, quote from p. 864.

43. Mark Snyder, Elizabeth D. Tanke, and Ellen Berscheid, "Social Perception and Interpersonal Behavior: On the Self-Fulfilling Nature of Social Stereotypes," *Journal of Personality and Social Psychology* 35 (1977): 656–66.

44. John T. Copeland, "Prophecies of Power: Motivational Implications of Social Power for Behavioral Confirmation," *Journal of Personality and Social Psychology* 67(1994): 264–77.

45. Barbara Reskin, "Sex-Segregation in the Workplace," *Annual Review of Sociology* 19 (1993): 241–70.

46. Theresa K. Vescio, Sarah J. Gervais, Mark Snyder, and Ann Hoover, "The Stereotype-Based Behaviors of the Powerful and their Effects on Female Performance in Masculine Domains," *Journal of Personality and Social Psychology* 88 (2005): 658–72.

47. Barbara L. Frederickson and Tomi-Ann Roberts, "Objectification Theory: Toward Understanding Women's Lived Experiences and Mental Health Risks," *Psychology of Women Quarterly* 21 (1997): 173–206.

48. Michael W. Wiederman, "Women's Body Image Self-Consciousness during Physical Intimacy with a Partner," *Journal of Sex Research* 37 (2002): 60–68.

49. Barbara L. Frederickson, Tomi-Ann Roberts, Stephanie M. Noll, Diane M. Quinn, and Jean M. Twenge, "That Swimsuit Becomes You: Sex Differences in Self-Objectification, Restrained Eating, and Math Performance," *Journal of Personality and Social Psychology* 75(1998): 269–84.

50. Tomi-Ann Roberts and Jennifer Y. Gettman, "Mere Exposure: Gender Differences in the Negative Effects of Priming a State of Self-objectification," *Sex Roles: A Journal of Research* 51 (2004): 17–28.

51. Rachel M. Calogero, "A Test of Objectification Theory: The Effect of the Male Gaze on Appearance Concerns in College Women," *Psychology of Women Quarterly* 28 (2004): 16–21.

52. Amy Oppenheimer and Craig Pratt, *Investigating Workplace Harassment: How to be Fair, Thorough, and Legal* (Alexandria, VA: Society for Human Resource Management, 2003).

53. EEOC, "Facts about Sexual Harassment" available online at www.eeoc.gov/facts/fs-sex.html; accessed June 13, 2005.

54. "Model Sexual Harassment Policy," MCAD Policy 96-2 Adopted by the Commission on October 25, 1996, Massachusetts Commission Against Discrimination.

55. Equal Employment Opportunity Commission, Office of Research, Information and Planning national database, 2005.

56. American Psychological Association, *In the Supreme Court of the United States: Teresa Harris v. Forklift Systems, Inc.: Brief for amicus curiae American Psychological Association in Support of Neither Party* (Washington, DC: American Psychological Association, 1993).

57. Maria Rotundo, Dung-Hanh Nguyen, and Paul R. Sackett, "A Meta-Analytic Review of Gender Differences in Perceptions of Sexual Harassment," *Journal of Applied Psychology* 86 (2001): 914–22.

58. Frances J. Ranney, "What's a Reasonable Woman to Do? The Judicial Rhetoric of Sexual Harassment," *NWSA Journal* 9 (1997): 1–27.

59. Christina Tolvas-Vincent, Nikki Duncan, Alison Bell, and Ken Allison, "X-rated Behavior . . . Not What You'd Expect to Find in the Office!" *Bond Pearce Employment Briefing* (November 5, 2004), available online at www.bondpearce.co.uk/publications/bppubs112004_01.pdf; accessed June 17, 2005.

60. *Scarberry v. ExxonMobil Oil Corp.*, 328 F. 3d 1255 (10th Cir.2003).

61. The World Almanac and Book of Facts, "About the Internet," (World Almanac Books, 2005, p. 390).

62. Charles J. Muhl, "Workplace E-Mail and Internet Use: Employees and Employers Beware," *Monthly Labor Review* (February 2003).

63. Mark Griffiths, "Internet Abuse in the Workplace: Issues and Concerns for Employers and Employment Counselors," *Journal of Employment Counseling* 40 (2003): 87–96.

64. Personnel Today and Websense International, "Internet Misuse Survey 2002," July 2002, available online at www.websense.com/company/news/research/Internet_Misuse_Survey_2002.pdf; accessed June 1, 2005.

65. Ryan Singel, "Internet Porn: Worse than Crack?" *Wired News* (November 19, 2004), available online at www.wired.com/news/technology/0,1282,65772,00.html; accessed June 17, 2005.

66. Douglas M. Towns and Mark S. Johnson, "Sexual Harassment in the 21st Century—E-Harassment in the Workplace," *Employee Relations Law Journal* 29 (2003): 7–24.

67. Ibid., pp. 17–18.

68. Kathy McKinney, "Detailing a Pattern of Harassment, EEOC Calls Mitsubishi 'A Hyper-Sexual Environment,'" *Pantagraph* (September 20, 1997): A1.

69. Susan Antilla, *Tales from the Boom Boom Room: Women vs. Wall Street* (Princeton, NJ: Bloomberg Press, 2002).

70. Robert J. Grossman, "Paying the Price," *HR Magazine* (August 2002): 33.

71. Meredith, "Strip Clubs under Siege."

72. Beth A. Quinn, "Sexual Harassment and Masculinity: The Power and Meaning of Girl Watching," *Gender and Society* 16 (2002): 386–402.

73. Ann B. Hopkins, *So Ordered: Making Partner the Hard Way* (AmherstA: University of Massachusetts Press 1996).

74. Louise Fitzgerald, Susan Swan, and Karla Fischer, "Why Didn't She Just Report Him? The Psychological and Legal Implications of Women's Responses to Sexual Harassment," *Journal of Social Issues* 51 (1995): 117–38.

75. W. Warner Burke, *Organization Development: A Normative View* (Reading, MA: Addison Wesley, 1987), pp. 53–57.

76. C. J. Prince, "Where Are the Women?" *Chief Executive* 209 (1995): 28–29.

77. William Baue, "Calvert Group Launches Code for Corporations to Profit by Promoting Gender Equality," *SocialFunds.com* (June 29, 2004), available online at www.socialfunds.com/news/article.cgi/article1454.html; accessed June 11, 2005.

78. Fortune, "The Fortune 500: America's Largest Corporations," *Fortune* (April 18, 2005).

79. Robert Levering and Milton Moskowitz, "The 100 Best Companies to Work for in America 2005," Great Place to Work Institute, available online at www.greatplace towork.com/best/list-bestusa.htm; accessed June 12, 2005.

80. Baue, "Calvert Group Launches Code," p. 2.

81. Catalyst, "The Bottom Line: Connecting Corporate Performance and Gender Diversity," 2004, available online at www.catalystwomen.org/knowledge/titles/files/full/financialperformancereport.pdf; accessed June 12, 2005.

82. *Playboy* (December 2003): 186.

3

Best Practices in Diversity Management

Kecia M. Thomas and Jimmy L. Davis

For some organizations, 2002 brought more expenses and negative press than revenue. In February 2002, a federal jury awarded $1.1 million to a white former executive of the Metropolitan Atlanta Transit Authority in a discrimination case that centered on racial politics, alleging that white executives were fired to appease African American critics. In the same month a Chicago federal jury awarded $2.2 million to ten white firefighters who were passed over for promotion due to the use of race norming to benefit minority firefighters. Later that year, MetLife announced it would take a $250 million pretax charge against earnings to cover costs arising out of class-action lawsuits and an investigation of allegations that it charged black customers higher rates than white customers.

For other companies, the problems with diversity and management continue. In February 2003, a federal judge approved a settlement of $2.5 million between the Sacramento, California, Regional Transit District and 200 women claiming sex discrimination in pay, promotion, and training. A separate attorney's fee award was made in the amount of $900,000. In 2004, a judge approved a potential base of 1.5 million plaintiffs for class-action status in their suit against Wal-Mart for discriminating against women.[1] The plaintiffs contend that Wal-Mart discriminates in both the recruitment and promotion of female workers. Although this case is pending at this writing, the ramifications from a negative outcome will prove to be damaging to the company listed as second on the 2005 Fortune 500 list.

Almost twenty years after the release of *Workforce 2000*,[2] workplace diversity remains one of the most compelling issues facing organizations today. Increasing demographic diversity within the labor force, a less than stable economy, growing global competition, and an evolving consumer market have made diversity management a core platform of top leadership teams regardless of organization, industry, geographic location, or size.

Clearly diversity management is not going away, and expenses paid by organizations to put in place diversity initiatives and training programs have been extensive and perhaps unnecessary given the unending tide of employment litigation. In 1996, Texaco settled a class-action lawsuit alleging race discrimination for $176 million, and in 2000, Coca-Cola settled a race discrimination case for $192.5 million.[3] In 2002, fifteen minority workers filed a $7.4 billion race discrimination lawsuit against General Motors Corporation (GM), the world's largest automaker.[4] The complaint alleged that GM failed to stop employees from discriminating against minority workers at its truck assembly plant and truck engineering and development center.

Despite the availability of diversity consultants, training, and packaged initiatives and programs, many organizations still lack guidance regarding the best practices for diversity management. The persistent costs of defending organizations against allegations of discrimination and harassment, settlement costs, and at times, fines, demonstrate that organizations still struggle with issues of diversity and inclusion. Therefore, this chapter will integrate and summarize the management literature related to the best diversity management practices in four core areas of human resource management: leadership, recruitment, training, and executive development. The identification of best practices related to each of these core HR areas will culminate in a discussion of common themes that extend across them and that can themselves promote better diversity management.

The first section of this chapter discusses a topic that diversity scholars consistently identify as a critical focal area and management practice—leadership. Beginning with leaders is crucial, given their impact on diversity outcomes across every area of organizational life. Second, the chapter will turn to strategic recruitment of a diverse workforce. Our focus will be on how to best attract a diverse workforce while not deterring traditional workers (i.e., white males) from applying to or entering the organization. After creating a diverse workplace, how does an organization ensure that individuals are able to work together? One way is through training. Therefore the role of diversity training and suggestions for its design and delivery will be presented third. Finally, we will turn to the issue of executive development specifically as it relates to breaking the glass ceiling. The essay will conclude with an integration of the strategies reviewed as an opportunity for identifying human resource strategies for creative, inclusive organizations. To make the case for these best practices, we begin our discussion by highlighting the complex relationship between diversity and organizational performance.

DIVERSITY AND ORGANIZATIONAL PERFORMANCE: A COMPLEX RELATIONSHIP

There are many ways to define performance within organizations. We could consider individual productivity or prosocial behavior. Another distinction could be made between team processes in organizations and team productivity. Those responsible for leading organizations, however, are likely most concerned with the relationship between diversity and a firm's productivity and ultimately its financial performance. Yet like other performance indicators, financial performance can be defined in myriad ways, and each has a potential relationship to firm diversity.

Financial performance could be defined as return on investment, return on equity, cost savings, and other financial outcomes. In thinking about the best practices related to diversity in organizations, we will take a broad lens to highlight the many ways in which diversity can impact the organization's bottom line. One way to think about the diversity-organizational performance relationship would be to consider the direct and indirect effects of diversity on financial performance.

Direct Financial Outcomes

The most obvious way to consider the diversity–organizational performance relationship is simply to assess profit. A study across multiple branches of a Canadian bank revealed that those with racial-ethnic diversity attained higher levels of financial profitability than culturally homogenous branches.[5] For example, the culturally diverse branches reported a growth rate in profit per full-time employee of 52 percent over a two-year period, as compared to 42 percent and 10 percent for the primarily Caucasian and Asian branches, respectively. These results were found despite lower scores on employees' job satisfaction, organizational commitment, and workplace coherence and higher rates of turnover in the more diverse branches. On all these factors, an expectation that employees' responses and workplace reactions could lead to decreased levels of financial performance would be reasonable. The relationship between employees' responses and workplace reactions was, however, moderated by many demographic variables, such as age, job tenure, organizational position, children's age, location of education and previous employment, birthplace, and education level.

Another study in the banking industry, this time in three U.S. states, demonstrated that racial diversity was positively associated with both intermediate and bottom-line firm performance.[6] However, this relationship was only found in firms that pursued a growth strategy. Furthermore, the relationship between diversity and firm performance was negative within companies pursuing a downsizing strategy. Thus the relationship of racial diversity to firm performance may depend on the organizational context and business strategy. This research is important in that it demonstrates that failure to consider strategic context can lead researchers to incorrectly conclude that diversity is always negatively associated with firm performance and profit.

Direct financial benefits may also accrue from an organization's image or reputation related to diversity. Research conducted by the Business and Higher

Education Forum cites evidence that when organizations are commended for their diversity efforts, stock prices rise.[7] For example, the 50 best companies for minorities have beaten the S&P 500 over the past three and five years.

The need for best practices related to diversity management can be substantiated by also looking at the indirect financial outcomes of sound diversity practices, especially as diversity relates to costs associated with human resources.

Indirect Financial Outcomes

One method of examining the diversity–financial performance relationship is to consider costs incurred rather than profit or income. The lack of effective diversity management practices can lead to substantial turnover costs. For example, the total cost of replacing a salaried worker (including recruitment, training, lost productivity, placement fees, relocation, human resource processing, etc.) is estimated to be as much as 1.2 to 2.0 times the worker's salary. For hourly workers, the estimate is somewhat less and may be approximately 0.75 times their salary.[8] Imagine that an organization has 1000 employees, each with an annual salary of $30,000. If that organization loses 10 percent of its workforce annually due to poor diversity management practices, and the cost of the loss of each worker is 100 percent of salary, the cost to the company is $3 million per year and potentially $150 million over five years.

Although not every unhappy worker will leave the organization, those who stay may be less engaged in their work. These workers' lack of productivity, absenteeism, and job search behaviors while in their current positions will cost the organization financially.

Certainly, a major indirect cost associated with the mismanagement of a diverse workforce involves defending the organization against allegations of harassment and discrimination. For example, the Rand Institute estimates that the cost of defending a wrongful termination lawsuit is at least $100,000.[9] Nationally, this cost is significant given the steady growth in charges of employment discrimination. According to the EEOC, 79,432 individual charges of discrimination were filed in its offices in 2004. Of these, 34.9 percent were related to race, 30.5 percent related to sex, 10.5 percent to national origin, and 3.1 percent to religion.[10]

In cases where the organization is found guilty of discriminatory practices, the costs associated with the mismanagement of a diverse workforce become even more significant. For example, in September 1999, the Bureau of Justice Statistics,[11] an agency of the U.S. Department of Justice, reported survey results from 15,613 state court civil trials in the nation's largest 75 counties during 1996. The median judgment in all such cases where the plaintiff won was $33,000. For employment discrimination cases, the median judgment where plaintiffs won was $200,000. Plaintiffs in the employment discrimination suits were awarded a total of $56 million. Settlements also are expensive and typically involve back pay to the plaintiff, attorney costs, expert witness costs, as well as court costs.

Even successfully defending a discrimination lawsuit can be costly. Legal fees can average between $100,000 and $500,000. In addition, companies bear significant intangible costs, such as lost productivity of employees who must spend time with lawyers or gather information they require.[12]

The relationship between diversity and organizational performance is indeed complex. It appears that when organizations and their leaders work toward creating an inclusive climate for diversity, the costs are minimal compared to potential rewards. However, when organizations discriminate subtly or overtly, potential costs associated with firm liability can be significant.

BEST PRACTICES RELATED TO INDIVIDUAL WORKERS AND THEIR EMPLOYERS

There is also a potential cost to the individual worker in regard to opportunities for new jobs, development, and promotion. Therefore this section will focus on the best diversity practices as they affect workers and, subsequently, the organization. In each case, we will define existing organizational problems and barriers as they affect workers and then recommend ways for organizations to resolve or avoid them.

Leadership

Almost every best practice for diversity management relates to thoughts and/or actions of organizational leaders. Probably the most consistent recommendation regarding managing diversity is that leaders must value and commit to a diverse and inclusive workplace. However, major challenges exist regarding what that means in terms of leadership behavior, organizational policies and practices, and broader organizational behavior. David Thomas, professor at the Harvard School of Business, suggests that despite the sentiment that "leadership matters," leaders are frequently ineffectual in achieving an organization's diversity goals and mission. In fact, leaders may behave in ways that are inconsistent with their diversity-related beliefs.[13]

Committed leaders can adopt several behaviors to improve their odds of being effective diversity change agents. These relate to goal setting, framing, accountability, and establishing diversity readiness.

Goal Setting

Leaders and their organizations may be ineffective in accomplishing their diversity-related goals and mission because such goals are crafted too broadly to be accomplished or measured. Sometimes leaders even confuse diversity goals with illegal quotas. Measurable diversity goals would be to establish relationships with minority communities in and outside of the organization, increase the number of mentoring relationships available to female and minority employees, or raise retention rates of high-potential and minority managers.

One strategy for establishing diversity-related goals may be to conduct an organizational diversity climate assessment that also can serve as a needs assessment. Tracking such climate data over time can help leaders develop needs-based diversity initiatives that those responsible for their implementation are more likely to accept. Periodic assessment of the climate for diversity also can enable leaders to learn about successes as well as areas for improvement. These data also give the organization an opportunity to benchmark best practices within departments or functions that could have utility organization-wide.

Framing

In addition to developing needs-based goals and initiatives, leaders must communicate about diversity in ways that positively frame[14] it as a strategic learning opportunity for the organization that will also enhance its effectiveness.[15] Rather than telling top managers that diversity is a barrier to effectiveness to be overcome, leaders should instead communicate that diversity is an opportunity to learn about new practices and markets that can improve and expand the business. Another part of effective framing involves tying diversity goals to business goals. In other words, leaders consistently communicate the role of diversity in helping the organization accomplish diversity at every opportunity.[16]

Accountability

Establishing accountability is another way that leaders can promote effective diversity management. One way to do this is to make sure that human resource practices and decisions, such as those related to selection, promotion, and compensation, consider diversity goals and values. For example, one criterion based on which managers are promoted to senior levels may be the extent to which they have identified and developed effective workers regardless of race, gender, sexuality, or physical ability. Those who are effective in developing diverse talent also could be rewarded with special assignments or bonuses.

Readiness

Diversity readiness refers to leaders' understanding of the complexities of diversity in the organization and society.[17] In addition, readiness for diversity leadership means that leaders have explored diversity's complexities for their own lives. Specifically, they have engaged in self-exploration and, as a result, understand how privilege and ethnocentrism operate within their organizations and lives. Leaders are growing in knowledge of their own racial, gender, or sexual identity.

Leaders establish diversity readiness by reflecting on their own identity and the ways it has afforded the leaders advantages (privilege) and disadvantages. They may ask themselves, "Are there ways in which this organization privileges sameness or the status quo? In what ways does the organization resist differences in its many forms? How does this resistance keep us from recruiting the best talent, using better ideas, and being more effective?"

These questions not only provide the opportunity for leader self-reflection but also create an opportunity to establish intraorganizational dialogue about the pulls toward and pushes against diversity. These provide new areas in which organizational members can hold each other accountable for achieving the organization's diversity goals and mission.

Recruitment

According to the Bureau of Labor Statistics,[18] most future labor force growth will occur in nonwhite segments, especially among blacks, Latinos, and Asians. This labor force shift will accelerate in the period through 2020 because of the retirement of white Baby Boomers and their replacement by a younger, more diverse generation. By 2028, the number of jobs will exceed the number of workers trained to fill them by 19 million.[19] Approximately 40 percent of those available to take these jobs will be members of minority groups. Therefore, major questions for organizations are, "How do we attract and retain the best of this new workforce?" and "Are the strategies by which we have engaged in recruitment going to be effective with this more diverse workforce?"

Based on extensive scholarship about recruitment of a diverse workforce, two best practices have emerged. They relate to who is depicted in recruitment advertisements and the messages that these ads convey.

A best practice that has emerged in this area of research pertains to the demographic composition of individuals portrayed in company recruitment advertisements.[20] Studies have demonstrated that minority and female job seekers value diversity in recruitment advertisements somewhat differently than their nonminority and male counterparts. Female and minority job seekers are more attracted to demographic diversity among those in recruitment advertisements than to a portrayal of a homogenous, white workforce. Unexpectedly, this research also has shown that diversity depicted in recruitment advertisements has little impact on white male job seekers. Their attraction remains stable regardless of the level of diversity represented in such ads.

A second best recruitment practice relates to messages conveyed in recruitment advertisements. As was the case when analyzing job seekers' responses to people portrayed in these ads, jobs seekers also respond differently based on their gender and racial identities. Again, female and minority job seekers' attraction to organizations relates to the strength of the diversity statements embedded in recruitment advertisements. White male job seekers' attraction to organizations again remains stable regardless of the diversity statement. The message from both lines of research suggests that organizations can aggressively promote diversity in recruitment campaigns, including advertisements, to attract minority and female job seekers without losing white male job seekers.

Another practice related to an organization's recruitment strategy is to broaden its recruitment net. That is, if vehicles that were successful in the past no longer yield a diverse applicant pool, then the organization should consider new alternatives. Additional options are minority-serving institutions, such as historically black colleges and universities and tribal colleges, and minority professional associations, such as the Black MBA Association, the American Indian Science and Engineering Society, and the Association for Women in Science and Engineering. Networking within regional offices of social justice organizations, such as the Urban League, National Organization of Women, and the National Council of La Raza, is another possibility. Electronic and online resources such as Monster.com, online mailing lists, and one-on-one referrals can create opportunities to communicate with the new workforce. Having a friendly image and reputation should not be underestimated; this may be another best practice that helps recruit diverse workers.

Diversity Training and Multicultural Competence

Diversity training is perhaps the oldest intervention associated with diversity management. Organizations often attempt to provide some form of diversity training even when leaders have not yet worked out their own beliefs regarding diversity's role in their workplace or determined whether it adds value to their organization. In fact, most organizations provide some form of diversity training, yet may still become defendants in discrimination-related litigation. Texaco,[21] which spent millions of dollars on an organization-wide diversity training campaign but was still sued,[22] is a notable example. Various reasons exist for conducting diversity training, and its objectives may differ. Legal and social pressure, business necessity, and a belief that providing diversity training is morally imperative can drive leaders to offer it in their workplaces. Training objectives may be to provide knowledge, enhance self-awareness, change behavior, develop skills, or use the training as a tool for larger organizational change. Within the organization, it can be positioned as a personal growth or skills-based training opportunity or used as a strategic intervention or an impetus for change in the organizational culture.

Diversity training's success rests often on leadership. In a study of over 700 human resource professionals, such training's perceived success was largely related to perceived support of the top leadership team.[23] Leadership support came about through several best practices, including mandatory attendance of all managers in the training, long-term evaluation of its results, rewards for managers who increased diversity, and the adoption and framing of diversity as an inclusive rather than an exclusive goal within the organization.

Other best practices concern diversity training's delivery. A study of the perceived effectiveness of such training offered to graduate teaching assistants found that trainee group composition mattered regarding the material to be delivered.[24] Graduate assistants without prior diversity training did not seem to care about the racial diversity of the group, but those who had experienced diversity training previously preferred racially homogenous groups. This research may suggest another best practice related to diversity training. During a training campaign's early stages or when dealing with organizational newcomers, diversity training can be offered to large, diverse groups. Advanced training, relying on the analysis of more personal and sensitive issues, however, should occur within smaller, racially homogenous groups.

EXECUTIVE DEVELOPMENT AND BREAKING THE GLASS CEILING

Best practices related to leadership behavior are important and certainly affect subsequent organizational practices related to recruitment and to diversity training. Access to leadership and leadership development, however, also are core areas of diversity management. The following sections addresses the issue of the glass ceiling as a common barrier for women, people of color, and members of other marginalized groups who seek development via upward career mobility.

The glass ceiling refers to artificial barriers to the advancement of women and minorities. It is the invisible, impermeable barrier that keeps minorities and women from rising to the upper rungs of the corporate ladder, regardless of their qualifications or achievements.[25] A study of career paths of women and people of color found, consistent with the glass ceiling theory, that women and minorities wait longer for promotions than do white men.[26] In fact, this study suggested that within industries of increasing racial and gender diversity, white men receive career benefits; this phenomenon is known as the glass escalator. Due to the glass escalator effect, white men's long history as leaders may create favorable conditions for their upward mobility, especially in situations where they are becoming a minority.

Many organizations have been scrutinized for issues associated with the glass ceiling. Major Fortune 500 companies, such as Wal-Mart, Home Depot, Coca-Cola, and FedEx, are defendants in class-action lawsuits regarding selection and advancement of women and minorities each year. Governmental regulations have curbed many overt systems of employment discrimination, but most companies do not respond until they are sued. For example, plaintiffs in *Satchell, et al. v. Federal Express*, filed in the U.S. District Court in San Francisco in 2003, allege that FedEx violated federal and California law by discriminating against minority employees based on race in promotion, compensation, and discipline practices. The motion for class certification is still pending at this writing. Plaintiffs, African American and Latino hourly employees and African American operations managers at FedEx, charge that FedEx treats minority group members worse than similarly situated white employees.

Lawsuits such as these are far too common in today's environment, and the ramifications of one successful lawsuit can either cripple an organization or become a point where diversity within the organization can be recognized and embraced. Most companies that lose a class-action lawsuit must make major changes in policies and practices to improve their environment. In August 2004, Home Depot settled a $5.5 million class-action lawsuit alleging that it discriminated against a group of employees in its Colorado stores. Home Depot paid the $5.5 million to current and former employees and had to provide significant injunctive relief. In addition to the settlement, Home Depot signed a consent decree, a voluntary agreement with the EEOC, which provides for $3 million to resolve charges of discrimination filed by thirty-eight individuals, and paid an additional $2.5 million into a class settlement fund to provide relief for others who were harmed by the alleged unlawful conduct. Besides the monetary relief, the consent decree requires Home Depot to provide training on anti-discrimination law requirements with appropriate levels of information presented to nonsupervisory employees, managers, and human resource employees. Home Depot also agreed to submit quarterly reports to the EEOC and remain under the agency's continued monitoring.

These actions will affect women and minorities in similar firms in the future. With a governmental body monitoring their employment practice numbers, companies must make sure that they are not discriminating against women and minorities and that their practices are favorable to all groups. This helps break the glass ceiling to a certain extent in many organizations.

The glass ceiling cannot be broken until leaders are convinced of its existence, and then they must understand the realities of being a member of a minority group in the workplace. For this to occur, some CEOs' perceptions must change. A study of male CEOs and executive women suggests that the two groups see the glass ceiling differently.[27] Male CEOs believed that women's lack of interest, family responsibilities, and lack of representation in the leadership pipeline prevent them from reaching top corporate positions. In contrast, executive women mentioned as barriers women's lack of access to frequently male-dominated networks, their shortage of mentoring opportunities, and their lack of access to developmental opportunitities that would place them in the leadership pipeline.

Companies wishing to embrace diversity and build capacity for diverse leadership should pay close attention to these findings. A significant lesson from this research on the gap between the way CEOs and executive women see the glass ceiling is that both groups acknowledge that women are not in the pipeline but differ as to why.

Human Resource Development Practices

One best practice may be to develop communication structures allowing top leadership to hear underrepresented workers' voices. Human resource development strategies such as coaching, networking, and mentoring can facilitate this by placing senior executives and more junior minority group members in developmental and productive relationships. Xerox has accomplished this through its Mentor Up program,[28] which pairs senior executives with junior female engineers. These women get the traditional benefits of mentoring, such as career advice, expanded networks, and advocacy. Senior executives also gain from learning about the experiences of female engineeers in their organizations and the conflicts they confront that can stifle their careers. The organization benefits through the learning that occurs for both the protégée and the mentor. Besides attending to the development of all employees, organizations must critically review human resource practices that may inadvertently leave minority workers underdeveloped and out of the leadership pipeline.

Human Resource Management Practices

Another best practice may be to monitor all selection materials and procedures. Many companies have flawed selection methods, which have adverse impact on women and minority applicants. An examination of the selection procedures may reveal that some groups are disproportionably advantaged or disadvantaged because of the tools being used. Organizations can increase the diversity of their applicant pool by using different, nondiscriminatory selection methods.

A related recommendation is to monitor diversity resulting from an organization's promotion policies. Many firms use slating and other promotion methods to monitor top talent in key positions.[29] Making sure that the slates are diverse and representative of the organization in terms of gender and race will increase the likelihood that more diverse candidates are promoted. Leaders' willingness to collect data on diversity regularly and monitor and evaluate human resource systems and diversity initiatives generates more work, but ongoing measurement and evaluation can reinforce the organization's commitment to diversity and help hold it accountable to related goals.

IBM has instituted management accountability for developing and promoting diverse talent informally through what its managers refer to as the five-minute drill.

> The five minute drill takes place during the discussion of management talent at the corporate and business unit levels. During meetings of the senior team, executives are expected at any moment to be able to discuss any high-potential manager . . . an explicit effort is made to ensure that minorities and females are discussed along with white males. The result has been to make the executives more accountable for spotting and grooming high-potential minority managers both in their own areas and across the business.[30]

Positive Examples of Workplace Diversity

Given many negative examples of ways in which diversity's absence can cause problems for organizations, we want to note that not all discriminate against minorities and some have embraced diversity. Firms such as IBM and Xerox have been diversity champions. Their programs demonstrate a culture that integrates diversity at all levels. We applaud these organizations for their efforts but also want to highlight other companies, such as Procter & Gamble (P&G).[31]

P&G is a $51 billion company with 110,000 employees. The awards it has received and its initiatives reflect the firm's commitment to diversity. P&G is ranked at number forty-five on the 2005 Fortune Best Company for Minorities list. Other examples of its many accolades include being ranked among several of Diversity Inc.'s Top Companies for Diversity (number thirty), which includes being a top company for Executive Women and Latinas. In addition, P&G was ranked first in its industry on Fortune's World's Most Admired Companies, and *Black Enterprise* included it as one of the 2005's 30 Best Companies for Diversity.

The company sponsors one of the oldest supplier diversity programs in the United States, spending more than $1.1 billion across nearly 700 minority- and women-owned suppliers. Additionally, P&G provides continuing leadership in the advertising industry by partnering with agencies to refer applicants to each other and help minorities enter commercial production companies.

Not only is P&G devoting funds to diversity efforts, it is also making diversity a key performance determinant for management. Diversity results are tied to stock option awards for the top thirty company officers. Clearly, P&G is another premier company in terms of its diversity efforts.

CONCLUSION

This chapter has provided insight into issues dealing with workplace diversity. Common best practices emerged across the issues of leadership, recruitment, training, and executive development. One theme related to these best practices is needs assessment. To be effective, diversity initiatives generally should be developed with an expressed need in mind; otherwise, they lack a purpose.

Another best practice theme involves communication. A needs assessment can certainly help open communication avenues throughout the organization. Diversity-related task groups, affinity groups, and mentoring programs, however, can also provide new opportunities for underrepresented or marginalized groups to speak to the organization regarding their concerns and realities.

A final theme relates to data collection, monitoring, and evaluation. Diversity initiatives and practices are rarely assessed for several reasons. At times the goal is only to put an initiative in place, so no need for evaluation exists. In other circumstances, fear arises that evaluation data will increase the potential for organizational liability, open new opportunities for litigation, or create unrealistic employee expectations. Diversity-related data must be collected to understand the diversity climate and evaluate outcomes of expensive initiatives. Without data collection, reduced accountability for the success of diversity campaigns and goals occurs. Organizations should think broadly and creatively about the data they can obtain, such as applicant pool data, information about the amount and types of outreach to target communities, and organizational tenure and promotion rates.

We have set the foundation for workplace diversity, given examples of the detriments organizations face if it is mismanaged, and provided best practices for the incorporation of positive diversity initiatives within an organization. As the popularity of diversity management grows, we hope that more researchers study and benchmark best practices across all areas of organizational life as they affect all segments of an increasingly diverse workforce.

NOTES

1. Anthony J. Sebok, "The Huge Class Action Sex Discrimination Suit against Wal-Mart: Should It Proceed as a Class Action, or Be Decertified?" online document available at writ.news.findlaw.com/sebok/20040809.htm (accessed July 29, 2005).

2. William Johnston and Arnold Packer, *Workforce 2000: Work and Workers for the Twenty-First Century* (Indianapolis, IN: Hudson Institute, 1987).

3. Ben White, "Black Coca-Cola Workers Still Angry Despite 2002 Legal Settlement, Protesters Say Little Has Changed," *Washington Post*, April 18, 2002, p. E3; available online at www.washingtonpost.com/ac2/wp-dyn?pagename=article&contentId=A4802-2002Apr17&notFound=true.

4. "$7.4 Billion Race Discrimination Suit Filed Against General Motors," online document available at www.injuryboard.com/view.cfm/Article=1358.

5. Eddy Ng and Rosalie L. Tung, "Ethno-Cultural Diversity and Organizational Effectiveness: A Field Study," *International Journal of Human Resource Management* 9 (1998): 980–95.

6. Orlando C. Richard, "Racial Diversity, Business Strategy, and Firm Performance: A Resource-Based View," *Academy of Management Journal* 43 (2000): 164–77.

7. The Business and Higher Education Forum is a nonprofit organization comprised of leaders from American businesses, nonprofit organizations, and institutions of higher education. Its goal is to examine and create dialogue around issues of national importance. Originally sponsored by the American Council on Education, it became an independent entity in 2004. See www.bhef.com.

8. Charles R. McConnell, "Staff Turnover: Occasional Friend, Frequent Foe, and Continuing Frustration," *Health Care Manager* 18(1) (1999): 1–13; J. D. Phillips, "The Price Tag on Turnover," *Personnel Journal* 69(12) (1990): 58–61.

9. Rita Risser, *Stay Out of Court: The Manager's Guide to Preventing Employees' Lawsuits* (Englewood Cliffs, NJ: Prentice Hall, 1993).

10. See the EEOC's 1992–2004 charge statistics at www.eeoc.gov/stats/charges .html.

11. Bureau of Justice Statistics, *Civil Trial Cases and Vertices in Large Counties 1996*. Bureau of Justice Statistics Bulletin, NCJ 173426 (1999). Report can be found online at: www.ojp.usdoj.gov/bjs/pub/pdf/ctcvlc96.pdf.

12. "What Is This Going to Cost Me?" *Delaware Employment Law Letter* 7(6) (2002).

13. David A. Thomas, "Diversity as Strategy," *Harvard Business Review* (2004): 98–108.

14. Michele E. Jayne and Robert L. Dipboye, "Leveraging Diversity to Improve Business Performance: Research Findings and Recommendations for Organizations," *Human Resource Management* 43(4) (2004): 409–24.

15. David A. Thomas and Robin Ely, "Making Differences Matter: A New Paradigm for Managing Diversity," *Harvard Business Review* 74(5) (1996): 79–90.

16. Thomas, "Diversity as Strategy," p. 107.

17. Kecia M. Thomas, "Psychological Readiness for Multicultural Leadership," *Management Development Forum* 1(2) (1998): 99–112.

18. Projections of the civil labor force through 2012 by sex, race, age, and Hispanic origin can be found online at www.bls.gov/emp/emplab2002-01.htm.

19. Business and Higher Education Forum.

20. Kecia M. Thomas and P. Gail Wise, "Organizational Attractiveness and Individual Differences: Are Diverse Applicants Attracted by Different Factors?" *Journal of Business and Psychology* 13(3) (1999): 375–90; Lesley Perkins, Kecia M. Thomas, and Gail A. Taylor, "Advertising and Recruitment: Marketing to Minorities," *Psychology and Marketing* [Special Issue on Emerging Topics in Marketing] 17(3) (2000): 1–21.

21. Shari Caudron, "Don't Make Texaco's $175 Million Mistake," *Workforce* 75(3) (1997): 58–65.

22. Jenny C. McCune, "Diversity Training: A Competitive Weapon," *Management Review* 85(6) (1996): 25–28.

23. Sara Rhynes and Benson Rosen, "A Field Survey of Factors Affecting the Adoption and Perceived Success of Diversity Training," *Personnel Psychology* 48 (1995): 247–70.

24. Loriann Roberson, Carol T. Kulik, and Molly B. Pepper, "Designing Effective Diversity Training: Influence of Group Composition and Trainee Experience," *Journal of Organizational Behavior* 22(2001): 871–85.

25. Federal Glass Ceiling Commission, Department of Labor, *Good for Business: Making Full Use of the Nation's Capital* (Washington, D.C.: Government Printing Office, 1995).

26. David Maume, "Glass Ceilings and Glass Escalators," *Work and Occupations* 26(4) (1999): 483–510.

27. Belle R. Ragins, Bickley B. Townsend, and Mary M. Mattis, "Gender Gap in the Executive Suite: CEOs and Female Executives Report on Breaking the Glass Ceiling," *Academy of Management Executive* 12 (1998): 28–42.

28. Margaret B. White, "Organization 2005: New Strategies at P & G," *Diversity Factor* 18 (1999): 16–20.

29. *Slating* is the concept whereby a company will create a list of possible candidates for promotion to a new or vacant position. It requires the company to pull together

information on each possible candidate and then rank candidates for their current position and other future positions in the company. Slates are the pipeline of future talent for each key position.

30. Thomas, "Diversity as Strategy," p. 107.

31. "Linking Opportunity with Responsibility: Sustainability Report" (2004). Available online at www.pg.com/content/pdf/01_about_pg/corporate_citizenship/sustainability/reports/sustainability_report_2004.pdf.

_____ 4 _____

The Diversity Journey at Shell

Catherine A. Lamboley

Looking back on the Shell Oil Company diversity journey in the United States, one event stands out as a turning point: a two-day diversity awareness seminar for Shell management in 1996. The CEO and other top U.S. executive leaders—all white males—participated in the event along with senior-level women and people of color. As a manager in Shell's legal department at the time, I was one of those women. At one point, we were invited to talk about what our lives were like at Shell. We were brutally candid. Anger and pain came pouring out. The executives were stunned. We were stunned, too, at the powerful feelings that had been unleashed.

The seminar was a watershed for Shell U.S. At the end of the two days, the CEO stated that things would change going forward. Most important, he made a commitment to set goals for diversity. "Without accountability," he said, "we will continue to select people who are just like us, and we won't change fast enough."

One year later, at a conference for the top 200 leaders of Shell U.S., the change was clearly evident. In fact, women applauded because for the first time there was a line for the restroom.

A decade later, the values of diversity and inclusiveness are woven into the fabric of Shell. Our leadership firmly believes that diversity is both the right thing to do and critical to our success. Our major businesses are held accountable annually through a diversity scorecard, and our leaders know that their compensation is partly tied to their individual diversity performance.

It has been an incredible journey.

WHITE, MALE, AND MARRIED

The 1996 diversity workshop was actually the outgrowth of an initiative that began a year earlier, when the CEO of Shell Oil Company, the U.S. business of the global Shell Group,[1] convened a strategic planning team to discuss the direction the company would take on diversity in the future. The Strategic Team on Diversity—one woman, one Hispanic male, two African American males, and four white males—set out as its mission "to understand the human and business possibilities of a culture in which all types of differences are valued—a culture in which diversity is appreciated as a means to high performance rather than an obstacle."

The mid-1990s may strike some as rather late for a major corporation to have embraced the concept of diversity. In fact, Shell U.S. at the time was like most of its peers in the oil industry. Antidiscrimination policies were in place, and the company met all the requirements for equal opportunity compliance, but little was done beyond the minimum. The work environment was dominated by white males and characterized by conservatism and formality. In employee focus groups conducted at the time, when men and women were asked what qualities were required to be a senior leader at Shell, the consensus was "white, male, and married."

But forces for change were emerging both externally and internally. Outside Shell, other major corporations in the oil industry and elsewhere were facing highly publicized lawsuits on diversity issues. This external pressure reinforced a growing recognition among some senior leaders that the company's compliance-based approach to diversity issues was not enough—something needed to change. Employee feedback indicated dissatisfaction with access to development opportunities for women and employees of color. The demographics of the labor market were shifting, and it was becoming clear that if Shell continued down the path it was on, the company would not be able to attract, retain, and develop the people it needed to continue to succeed.

Another force was influencing change as well. About this time, the global Shell Group had begun a broader business initiative to transform the organization from its old, cumbersome structures and processes to a more nimble organization able to respond to change quickly. The concept of a more responsive organization, more reflective of the outside environment, was linked with the need for a workforce that was more representative of the society as a whole.

A STRATEGIC IMPERATIVE

Cumulatively, these forces led Shell U.S. to the realization that diversity was a strategic imperative for success, both in the marketplace and in the attraction and recruitment of the most talented employees. As we have embarked on this journey, the business rationale has only become stronger over time. We articulated the business case for diversity and inclusiveness a few years ago in words that have continued to drive our efforts:

- As the workforce becomes increasingly diverse, the company can gain a distinct competitive advantage by attracting, retaining, and developing talented people with diverse backgrounds and perspectives.
- Effective diversity and inclusiveness management helps remove barriers to productivity and provides an environment in which these employees can contribute fully toward achieving Shell's business goals.
- Employees who feel respected, valued, and connected develop stronger relationships and become more involved in their work, which leads to enhanced teamwork, increased innovation and productivity, lower staff turnover, lower absenteeism, and reduced costs.
- Shell's customer base is becoming more diverse. By having a workforce that reflects the demographics of the consuming public, we can more effectively understand, anticipate, and respond to customers' needs.
- Encouraging diversity and inclusiveness enables the company to build relationships and demonstrate respect and fairness in its dealings with suppliers, partners, the government, and other stakeholders.
- Promoting diversity and inclusiveness enhances our reputation and increases loyalty, which, in turn, earns us the right of access and the license to operate and grow.
- Promoting supplier diversity and supporting the growth and development of women- and minority-owned businesses within our community helps improve the climate in which our partners and we conduct business.
- By promoting diversity not only within our own ranks but also in the communities in which it operates, Shell is helping make these communities better places for its employees to live and work.
- Finally, an effective diversity process helps ensure that federally mandated affirmative action goals are addressed and achieved.

LEADERSHIP ENDORSEMENT

In January 1996, the Strategic Team on Diversity reviewed its findings and recommendations with the senior leadership team of Shell U.S. The team endorsed the report, paving the way for the formal establishment of a diversity process.

The first step was to create a structure to manage the process. A function now known as the Shell Diversity Practice was established to provide thought leadership and consulting services to the Shell U.S. companies. An executive director of diversity was hired to spearhead its activities and begin the efforts to train all managers and employees on the concept and practice of inclusiveness in the workplace.

Over the next year, Shell U.S. began engaging senior leadership in the diversity process. By mid-1997, each business unit and firm within the company had established diversity councils and had begun creating diversity action teams charged with continuing to educate and inform their fellow employees regarding diversity and inclusiveness. This multilevel approach, a change management technique that has been used in other initiatives within Shell, has been one of the keys to our success in permeating an organization of more than 20,000 Shell employees in multiple U.S. locations.

- The Strategic Team on Diversity, a small, senior-level team, provided direction and vision for the change process.
- The director of diversity position created one focal point for communication, implementation, and accountability. The Diversity Practice influences the integration of diversity into business and human resource strategies and develops and provides processes, tools, training, and consultative services.
- Diversity councils, which reflected a cross-section of employees from different grade levels, years of service, functions, races, genders, sexual orientations, and ages, brought ownership of the issue into each business unit. These councils began by collecting data, doing needs assessments, and creating specific plans for each unit. They now support the leaders of their respective organizations with ongoing assessments, feedback, goal-setting, and action plans that link diversity efforts to the goals of the respective businesses.
- Diversity action teams, larger groups also representative of the workforce demographics, created a critical mass of employees committed to the change who could keep the messages flowing through both formal and informal communication channels. These groups implement diversity activities that can cross business unit or departmental boundaries. They are charged with integrating diversity into all aspects of the business and with promoting linkage and resource sharing across and within the businesses to realize the greatest possible efficiency, value, and quality.

A VISIBLE COMMITMENT

Two actions that Shell U.S. took early in the process provided highly visible symbols of the company's commitment to diversity. The first was the appointment of the first woman—a Hispanic woman—to the 1997 Shell U.S. Board of Directors. The second was a restructured employee benefits package introduced in 1997. Reflecting the needs of a diverse employee population, the package included benefits for domestic partners, open resourcing (an internal electronic job posting system accessible to all employees), work-schedule flexibility, and a more flexible pension plan. Later that year, Shell U.S. also initiated a program, called RESOLVE, that provides employees with additional support, tools, and processes for resolving diversity-related and other conflicts in the workplace.

Although informal employee networking had been in place for many years, the Strategic Team on Diversity report recommended supporting the creation of formal employee network groups. Such groups created another highly visible internal reminder of Shell's commitment. In 1997, guidelines were issued for these networks, which would serve two roles: as resources to leadership teams, councils, and diversity action teams for business and people/strategy issues and as a support system and forum for development, information sharing, and education among their members. Although sanctioned and funded by the company, the networks are managed entirely by employee volunteers. The first five employee networks represented Asian Pacific, African American, female, Hispanic and GLBT (gay, lesbian, bisexual, and transgendered) employee populations.

ACCOUNTABILITY FROM THE OUTSET

True to the CEO's commitment, accountability was built into the program early on. By fall 1997, Shell U.S. had adopted balanced workforce goals. These goals accelerated targets that the Strategic Team on Diversity had originally recommended for achievement by 2005. We also started tracking supplier diversity spend data. These two elements provided the much-needed backbone for Shell's diversity efforts and raised them to a higher level for making change happen and ensuring continuous progress.

Progress continued toward laying the foundation for diversity within Shell U.S. as Diversity Practice staff began establishing processes for incorporating diversity into the company's business model and leadership succession planning. At the same time, they began developing company-wide diversity recruitment strategies as well as procedures for incorporating the company's specific diversity goals into future joint ventures and alliance agreements.

MAKING PROGRESS

In 1999, Shell U.S. built a formal goal of becoming a model for diversity in corporate America into a broad business initiative we called the Blueprint for Success—a plan for ensuring that the company maintains its leadership role in the United States. We also held our first diversity conference, which brought representatives from leading companies and thought leaders in the diversity field to Houston, Shell's main office in the United States, to share their views and experiences with more than 300 conference attendees. This conference has since become an annual event.

By 2000, the Shell U.S. commitment to diversity was beginning to bring results. The company had women on all of its executive committees, and representation at management levels had improved by 136 percent for women and 61 percent for people of color.

The number of employee networks had grown to nine with the addition of a network for employees with disabilities, regional networks in Louisiana (where 20 percent of Shell's U.S. employees are located) for African Americans and women, and a network for Generation Xers. In addition, Shell expanded the role of the networks, increasing their influence in the business and in the community, and using them as the basis for a mentoring program to support the development of diverse leaders. Shell U.S. also launched a new cross-functional Diversity Change Agent Network, aimed at supporting management's efforts to achieve diversity results. The network organized Shell's first women's conference and began piloting a tool for assessing the progress of employee network groups.

By 2001, five years into the initiative, Shell U.S. shifted leadership responsibility for diversity to its individual businesses, with the corporate group taking on the support role. This brought accountability home to the level where most of the workforce decisions—hiring, promotion, and development—were made.

CHALLENGES AND SETBACKS

Although progress was made, the first five years were not easy. Shell U.S. learned from the experiences of other firms, but none seemed to provide a complete model of diversity and inclusiveness, and in some areas the company had to forge its own path. Changing an organization as large and as set in its ways as Shell historically had been is a long-term effort. Considerable education and culture change was required at all levels of the organization, top to bottom. Compounding the challenge was the outside economic environment. Though the economy as a whole was growing, energy prices were relatively low and declining further from 1997 to early 1999, which meant that few new employees were hired while this initiative was getting under way. In fact, the organization had been focused on operating with a lean staff for several years. That approach, which still underlies Shell's business strategy, coupled with a low employee turnover, meant that changing the demographic makeup of the organization would not happen as quickly as it might have in a high-growth or highly mobile organization.

In addition, some diversity efforts have moved forward more consistently than others. Since 1997, women's presence in leadership roles at Shell U.S. has increased significantly and continuously. However, to date we have not been as successful in advancing people of color, whether women or men. This remains a challenge, and we continue to work to identify and remove barriers and ensure there are continuous opportunities for advancement.

TAKING IT TO THE NEXT LEVEL

In 2002, recognizing the need to accelerate diversity efforts and ensure alignment of business and diversity goals, the Shell U.S. leadership team commissioned a cross-business diversity enhancement project team of human resource and diversity leaders to develop a plan to take the company's diversity efforts to the next level.

After brainstorming about barriers to achieving diversity progress and gathering information from employees, members of employee networks, and leaders on their perspectives about diversity, the team drafted and gained approval for a common diversity vision for all Shell operations throughout the United States: "Shell U.S. will value and leverage diversity to become a model of an inclusive working environment."

The team made a series of recommendations to management for achieving this goal:

- Make diversity data more transparent to all employees and leaders to identify gaps and demonstrate progress toward closing them.
- Develop workforce representation goals that are tied to Shell's affirmative action plans.
- Develop a scorecard for measuring progress within each business toward achieving diversity goals.
- Link progress toward diversity goal achievement to compensation.
- Involve Shell employee networks in recruiting and retaining talented employees, helping acclimate new hires to Shell's culture of diversity and inclusiveness, and promoting the Shell brand and image in the community.
- Give high-potential people of color and female employees expanded, cross-organizational experience to prepare them for management positions, which will help close gaps in representation of people of color and females in management.
- Consider diversity when recruiting external consultants and suppliers.
- Review supplier diversity certification systems and procedures, mentoring programs, and measurement and tracking systems with a goal of creating a more robust minority/women business enterprise program across the businesses.

These recommendations became the driving force for the next level of progress in the Shell U.S. diversity journey.

At the same time, the Shell Group enhanced its accountability system to ensure progress on diversity goals, requiring each country's business leader to submit an annual in-depth report to the group's managing directors outlining progress. The goals are based on a Global Diversity and Inclusiveness Standard that includes six components:

- Leadership, commitment, and accountability for change;
- Standards development and governance;
- Strategic plans and objectives;

- Supporting systems and resources;
- Human resources systems integration; and
- Monitoring performance, communication, and continuous learning.

Based on the enhancement team's recommendations, in 2003 Shell U.S. began evaluating managers as well as selected employees in diversity-related functions against performance on a diversity scorecard. The scorecard includes such elements as supplier diversity/economic development, workforce representation goals, and workplace climate. That performance is considered in making individual pay decisions.

Feedback from women and people of color has been valuable in helping us stay on track. At a roundtable luncheon in 2003, for example, thirty women representing a cross-section of Shell shared insights, experiences, and concerns with the top global leadership of the Shell Group and its businesses. Issues discussed ranged from gender style differences to Shell's culture and retention strategy for women. The Shell U.S. Asian Pacific employee network group organized a similar session with leaders of several of Shell's U.S. businesses in 2004.

Shell U.S. also began including questions aimed at assessing the company's diversity and inclusiveness climate in its employee survey. Employees are asked to indicate if they believe leadership supports diversity and inclusiveness, if people are treated fairly, and if different lifestyles, cultural backgrounds, views, and values are respected.

ENHANCING CAREER DEVELOPMENT

Shell U.S. leaders learned that creating workforce representation goals and standards would be ineffective if no women and people of color were available and prepared to take on increased responsibility. In response to this issue, Shell U.S. began looking for ways to build the talent pipeline through recruitment of new and experienced personnel, assess and develop potential leaders, and help equip the business units for succession planning. This issue has taken on increased urgency as a large percentage of the current workforce—the Baby Boom generation—nears retirement. At the same time, the number of students pursuing geosciences and other technical careers critical to Shell's business has declined over the past two decades.

Internally, Shell U.S. created a career development program to help high-potential women increase their understanding of issues affecting them in business, review their approach to professional and personal development, clarify career and life goals and develop strategies for implementation, learn tactics and develop confidence and skills for upward mobility, gain an understanding of their leadership style and perception by others, obtain mentors and seek mentoring opportunities, develop work-life balance strategies, and create networking opportunities.

Externally, Shell U.S. has refocused its social and community investment funds to align with the business need to strengthen its talent pipeline. The company's workforce development initiative was launched in 2004 to increase the flow of candidates, with special emphasis on women and people of color, to meet future workforce needs in engineering, geosciences, and operator, crafts, and technician areas. The program includes scholarships, science teacher training and support, and a stronger presence on key campuses to position Shell as an employer of choice.

Reaching further down to primary education, Shell U.S. has provided volunteer and financial support to programs such as the Education Rainbow Challenge, which promotes interest in math to all inner-city children, and other programs that support math and science learning.

MAINTAINING THE MOMENTUM

With strong support from Shell U.S. leadership, much of the daily implementation of Shell's diversity strategy at the business and department levels is driven by diversity and human resources staffs, the company's diversity councils, diversity action teams, and employee network groups. These teams have organized a wide range of activities aimed at improving the work environment and promoting development opportunities for women and people of color. A few examples:

- The employee network group for women sponsored a workshop in which four senior women from Shell U.S. shared their personal learnings and best practices around three key ingredients for increasing career opportunity: defining success, becoming known, and finding and/or being a mentor.
- The diversity council in Shell U.S.'s information technology business put diversity into terms that resonated within the organization, creating a talent pipeline flow model that helped leadership understand the demographic composition of people joining, moving through, and leaving the organization at various levels with an eye on identifying systemic changes that are needed to eliminate bottlenecks in the pipeline and achieve desired results.
- Members of Shell's Asian Pacific employee network group worked with the diversity office of Shell U.S.'s information technology business to identify opportunities to improve retention of Asian Pacific information technology employees. A network team assisted in determining background factors and developing suggestions for improvement, such as training mid-level managers about Asian Pacific value systems and culture.
- A Women of Color conference focused on issues faced by African American women working for Shell U.S. Over 150 people attended; about

one-half were African American women from the organization, about one-quarter were supervisors and managers, and the rest were supportive male and female colleagues.

- Shell's Hispanic employee network group has organized a series of *juntas*, based on the Spanish conversational term for "meetings." These limited-size sessions bring employees together with experienced leaders in a format that allows everyone to participate.
- At a Shell U.S. manufacturing facility, the local diversity council created a six-month structured curriculum to help employees learn about diversity and inclusiveness philosophies and about their own perceptions. Employees can meet once a month to discuss specific topics.
- To involve field operations employees in isolated locations, the diversity action team for Shell's exploration and production business in the U.S. held a contest among employees and contractors to submit quotes relating to diversity along with three or more discussion questions related to the quote. The winning submissions were used to create four professionally designed posters distributed to field locations on a quarterly basis.
- The Generation X, Hispanic, and women's networks collaborated to present a seminar on career paths, including presentations from a female supervisor who began as an hourly operations employee, a manager who discussed how to cross over to a different functional or skill area, the chief financial officer of Shell U.S., and a human resources professional.

BEYOND THE WALLS

Early in Shell's diversity journey, it became clear that to create a diverse workplace, achieve sustainable change, and enhance the reputation of Shell U.S. as an employer of choice and a socially conscious and progressive organization, the company's diversity and inclusiveness activities would have to extend beyond the walls of Shell. The two components of this effort—encouraging supplier diversity and promoting diversity in the communities where Shell operates—were articulated in the business rationale almost from the outset and were reemphasized in the enhancement team's recommendations in 2002.

One of the clearest success stories for our supplier diversity efforts has been in our legal area. Nationwide as of 2004, only 4 percent of partners in law firms were of color and 16 percent of partners were women. In 2000, we launched an initiative with our key law firms to require that they enumerate for us on invoices the hours all women and men of color worked and fees they generated. We began reporting these figures back to the firms along with a blind comparison of how their totals compare to other firms with which we do business. Where we do not see at least a gradual improvement in diversity, we ask the firm to submit an action plan on the issue.

In 2003, we decided to reduce the number of law firms with which we work by selecting a core group of firms to handle most of our legal work. By doing so, we believed we could build stronger relationships with firms that had a deeper understanding of our business. In choosing the firms with which to build this strategic partnership, we included a commitment to diversity as one of our selection criteria. Though many factors went into our decision process, at least one firm did not make the list primarily because it lacked diversity. Of the twenty-seven firms we selected, seven have partnerships where women and men of color outnumber white males.

Why exert this market pressure? We value diversity among our suppliers for the same reasons we value it internally—because it is good business as well as the right thing to do. As we explain to our suppliers, we value having people of diverse backgrounds—employees and suppliers alike—who can provide different ways of looking at things that can lead to better solutions. If law firms wish to retain and advance talented women and men of color, their attorneys must have the chance to do challenging work and have meaningful interaction with clients, such as Shell, so that relationships can grow. Tracking, reporting, and follow-up help ensure the opportunities are provided and cause the firms to be very focused on training, mentoring, work assignments, and leadership development so that the women and men of color are prepared to take on those opportunities.

We don't stop at tracking and reporting. We also provide support for our vendors' diversity programs. In the legal arena, we hold an annual symposium, which brings us together with our law firms to hear from leading experts on diversity in the legal profession and share best practices. The symposium addresses advancement, retention, and similar issues law firms face and has included such topics as how to create additional opportunities/exposure for women and men of color and factors that may inhibit their abilities to succeed in law firms.

We also have reached out to other companies and national organizations to join us in supporting diversity. Alone, Shell has pressure it can bring to bear. But with many more corporations, together we have significant buying power and can achieve real change.

Shell U.S. serves as a visible, proactive proponent of diversity in the community. When we announced our new benefits package in 1997, we were among the first major corporations to announce benefits for domestic partners. We have continued to take the lead on this and other diversity issues. The CEO of Shell U.S. endorsed efforts by the mayor of Houston to include sexual orientation in the city's nondiscrimination policy and also testified before the Senate endorsing the Employment Non-Discrimination Act.

TODAY: MODELING DIVERSITY AND INCLUSIVENESS

The vision of Shell U.S. as a "model of diversity and inclusiveness" that was articulated in 2002 continues to move into reality. The company has been widely recognized, especially for its success in advancing women. Shell received an award in 2004 that Catalyst, the leading U.S. nonprofit organization focused on the advancement of women, gives annually to showcase firms using innovative approaches with proven results to address the recruitment, development, and advancement of all professional women, including women of color.

More important than the recognition, however, are the results we have achieved. We have made significant progress, but we still have work to do, both globally and in the United States. Globally, the first woman was appointed to the Shell Group's committee of managing directors in 2003. As of this writing, three members of the Shell Oil Leadership Team (U.S.) are women; previously, the percentage of positions held by women on this team has been slightly higher.

In the United States, as of this writing, women represent 26.5 percent of the total employee population, compared with 22 percent at year end 1997. Women comprise about 32.6 percent of senior executives and 19 percent of the management-level workforce; about 2.2 percent of senior executives and 2.7 percent of managers are women of color.

Although Shell's workforce representation of people of color showed an initial increase after the diversity initiative began, it has not made the dramatic strides that our women's initiative has made. To close this gap, in 2004 Shell enhanced its focus on increasing the pool of qualified people of color who are candidates for employment, promotion, or development. Our goal is to close existing gaps between our workforce representation and the market demographics by 2010.

We continue to actively pursue supplier diversity as a way to achieve a competitive advantage, enhance our brand image and reputation, and support sustainable development of minority firms. Shell U.S.'s active involvement with business and community organizations also fosters a vigorous and sustained business environment. Having a team of supplier diversity advocates in each Shell U.S. business unit, we have developed an infrastructure to identify strategies and provide access for minority and women business owners.

Our proactive supplier diversity program has succeeded in increasing the number of women- and minority-owned business enterprises that conduct business with Shell U.S. During 2004, Shell businesses in the United States recorded expenditures of $439 million (approximately 8.6 percent of total spend) with women- and minority-owned businesses—up from approximately $40 million (approximately 2 percent of total spend) in 1994.

For the past two years, Shell has been listed as one of America's Top Corporations for Women's Business Enterprises by the Women's Business Enterprise National Council. The Shell U.S. manager of Corporate Supplier Diversity was recognized by *Women's Enterprise Magazine* with a 2003 Women of Excellence Award for her personal and professional accomplishments and continuous efforts on behalf of women in business. In 2003 Shell U.S. was named one of the Top 5 Companies for Supplier Diversity in DiversityInc.com's rankings. The Houston Area Women's Business Enterprise Alliance, the Houston Minority Business Council, and the Louisiana Minority Business Council also recognized Shell U.S. as Corporation of the Year in 2004. These awards recognize Shell's commitment and success in creating contract opportunities for minority and women business owners.

Shell's diversity efforts are also paying off in new business opportunities. In 2004, two members of Shell U.S.'s Asia Pacific network group participated in organizing a global symposium on petroleum and petrochemical opportunities in China. As a result of the company's involvement in the symposium, a partnership was forged between Shell's exploration and production arm in China and the Chinese national petroleum company to develop a major natural gas field.

We continue to track and refine our efforts on all diversity fronts. In addition to annual tracking at the individual, business unit, and national level, a quarterly progress enhancement team meeting provides an additional opportunity for key diversity leaders to review progress, share best practices, and identify gaps across businesses.

Decisions about managers' compensation are based in part on progress made by women and people of color who report to them. Diversity demographic data also is shared with employees on a regular basis.

USING THE SHELL MODEL

Along Shell's diversity journey, the company learned many lessons that can be of value to others following in our footsteps. Three key learnings stand out.

- To be successful, diversity and inclusiveness require a commitment of time and energy by many people at all levels of the organization.
- Over time, diversity must be integrated into the business processes and systems of the company to ensure consistent, effective implementation.
- Finally, diversity processes must include measurable, achievable goals and clear accountability.

These three lessons are closely linked. Underlying them all is the understanding that diversity is not just another corporate program—it is a business imperative. Diversity and inclusiveness enable a company to attract, retain, and develop the people it needs to execute its business plan. Managed strategically, diversity and inclusiveness create a competitive advantage as the company becomes an employer of choice, a partner of choice, and a supplier of choice. At Shell, we have taken that lesson to heart, and it has guided and will continue to guide our diversity journey.

NOTE

1. Previously the Royal Dutch/Shell Group. "The Shell Group" is a collective term referring to the global enterprise as a whole, of which Shell Oil Company is an affiliate. "Shell U.S." refers to the collective businesses and operations of the Shell Group in the United States.

5

Career Planning: Toward an Inclusive Model

Claretha H. Banks

Many organizations today discuss career planning for women and diverse individuals from the perspective of workforce diversity, which Robbins defines as the "concept that organizations are becoming more heterogeneous in terms of gender, race, ethnicity, sexual orientation and inclusion of other diverse groups."[1] The word *individual* is used as opposed to *populations* because career planning is an individual endeavor, although the individual may be assisted by others. Many individuals, situations, and events may influence an individual's career planning; yet ultimately, the individual must live with and execute the plan.

CAREER PLANNING

A career is a pattern of work-related experiences that encompass the course of a person's life.[2] According to Robbins, career planning has made a transition from a traditional to a boundaryless approach. In the traditional approach, organizations took responsibility for managing their employees' careers. In the boundaryless method, which crosses boundaries, functions, and levels, individuals take responsibility for their futures.[3] Therefore, employees must become astute at managing their own careers.[4]

Beverly Kaye identifies career planning as the "specific strategy and methods of the career development effort. It involves setting objectives, designing an evaluation scheme, assigning responsibilities for the entire effort, and determining methodologies, resources and support."[5] According to Lee Isaacson and Duane Brown, however, career counselors have not begun to answer the classic question, "What types of intervention are most useful with which types of clients?"[6]

CAREER PLANNING MODELS

Many career planning models have been identified, but very few specifically address career issues of concern to women and diverse individuals who wish to succeed in U.S. corporations. Writers have proposed that many of the theories are oriented primarily toward white males and are inappropriate for women and diverse individuals; others have argued that there is no need for a specific model for diverse individuals.[7]

Super's Models

Super's Life-Career Rainbow, six life roles in schematic life space model, initially was developed in 1953.[8] The major concepts of his models included vocational stages; vocational tasks to achieve if one is to successfully pass through the stage; implementation of the self-concept in developing a career identity; the development of vocational maturity; and career patterns.[9] It associates age with five stages of career development. They are: growth (4–13), exploration (14–24), establishment (25–44), maintenance (45–65), and decline (65 and over).[10] Super's theory suggests that everyone does not progress through the stages at fixed ages or in the same manner. Individuals develop and mature at different stages. Their life experiences also play a role within career progression.

In the 1990 segmental model of career development, Super based his life span development theory on fourteen propositions. His propositions suggest that biographical and geographical influences affect individuals as they progress through the career cycle. This model was designed to address the differences in people and explain how their personality and social policy play a role in their career success. Super also proposed a ladder model of life career stages, developmental tasks, and behaviors to express his theory regarding to the life stages and the ages at which they occur.[11]

Super's theory is very familiar to individuals in occupations dealing with career development. Most seem to prefer Super's model and use it within organizations. This preference produces many questions not only with respect to women and diverse individuals but also with respect to white males. Questions of interest include the following:

1. If Super's model is being used within organizations, what aspect of it is relevant and/or applicable to anyone other than white males?
2. How well do the individuals using Super's model understand it?
3. In what way(s) is Super's model being effectively communicated to women and diverse individuals?
4. Are women and diverse individuals aware that Super's model is the model of choice in today's workplace? Do they consider this information as they plan their careers?

Career planning for women and diverse individuals is often written about and researched from a group perspective. Characteristics among like groups of people are indeed similar; yet unless they have the same jobs and display similar personal characteristics including attitude and behavior, their career planning should be based on individual assessment and evaluation. The assessments and evaluations should be strongly based on individual self-perception.

Self-perception theory supports the notion that individuals come to know their own attitudes, emotions, and other internal states partially by inferring them from observations of their own overt behavior or the circumstances in which this behavior occurs. To the extent internal cues are weak, ambiguous, or uninterpretable, the individual is functionally in the same position as an outside observer, who must necessarily rely on those same external cues to infer the individuals' inner states.[12] Individuals use self-perception to explain their behavior by noting the conditions under which it occurs.[13]

Super's is not the only career planning model; however, it is one of the most accepted. Other models of interest include Holland's Theory of Vocational Choice, the National Career Development Guidelines (NCDG) Model, Beverly Kaye's Six Stages of Career Development, the Hayes Career Transition Model, and Karsten and Igou's Career Planning Model for a Diverse Workforce. Specific details of each model are described here.

Holland's Theory of Vocational Choice

Holland's theory suggests that a person expresses personality through the choice of a vocation and that interest inventories are really personality inventories. He also suggests that individuals hold stereotypical views regarding vocations. His perception is that individuals in like vocations have similar personalities and will respond to situations and problems in comparable ways. Holland's view is that the success of a person on a job depends on the extent to which the individual's personality and work environment are compatible.[14]

Holland's theory is considered to be the most influential of the extant theories and is used frequently to assess personality types. It identifies six personality types: realistic, investigative, artistic, social, enterprising, and conventional. Holland's Self-Directed Search instrument is used to match the person with the model work environment. He has also developed a Model for Interpreting Interclass and Intraclass Relationships for assessing the different inventories.[15]

Because Holland's theory and model are designed to assess personality traits and match them with potential vocations, women and diverse individuals may want to explore them further. This theory may provide information that helps them understand how their personalities can have an impact on job success. They must realize that this is a method of selecting options and depends on an objective self-assessment.

National Career Development Guidelines (NCDG) Model

The NCDG Model is a competency based model that is designed for elementary, middle, and high school students.[16] It is a framework for thinking about the knowledge and skills young people and adults need to manage their careers effectively, from their first job to their last.[17] At the high school level, students are to be introduced to an individual career plan process. Individuals can use the goals and indicators obtained from the model as an informal checklist to determine areas of competency and gaps that need attention. Questions that arise regarding this model include:

1. Are all high school students introduced to this model?
2. In what way(s) does this model address the unique needs of female and minority students?

Isaacson and Brown devote sections of their book to the special needs of gifted and physically, emotionally, and learning disabled students regarding career planning;[18] however, there is no specific reference to gender, race and ethnicity.

Kaye's Six Stages of Career Development

Kaye's model is designed from the organizational perspective and is focused toward the organization developing and sustaining a career development plan that will be beneficial for itself and its employees. Kaye's perspective arises from the notion that:

> Career development is ideally a joint effort...[among] the individual, the manager or leader, and the organization. While the individual has the primary responsibility for his or her own career, the leader is a supportive coach, and the organization provides the necessary systems and information. Career development involves looking realistically at the present conditions and at the career environment of today and tomorrow in order to regain the control necessary to ensure future productivity and job satisfaction.[19]

Kaye suggests that six stages of the career development cycle exist; they are as follows:

1. Preparing (Analyzing, Planning). During this phase, organizations are to determine the scope and nature of the career development effort through analyzing the needs, problems, and activities that led to the career development effort and that will eventually determine its objectives.[20]
2. Profiling (Identifying, Reality Testing). In the profiling stage, the employee is responsible for identifying skills and interests; the leader must support the effort by providing opportunities for discussion; and the practitioner makes a variety of assessment tools available.[21]

3. Targeting (Exploring, Specifying). During the targeting phase the employee is to explore possibilities and specify goals. The organization is to provide guidance that points employees' exploration efforts in a direction consistent with the organization. Leaders and practitioners are challenged to make exploration and opening of possibilities and goal setting a realistic and profitable exercise.[22]

4. Strategizing (Understanding, Synthesizing). The strategizing stage involves formulating a comprehensive strategy to accomplish the goals identified in stage 3.[23] Change is of the essence within this stage of development.

5. Implementing (Acquiring, Demonstrating). During the implementing stage employees seek information, opportunities, people, or groups to provide support and resources to attain goals. The organization, through practitioners, provides financial resources and developmental activities, monitors progress, establishes motivation and reward systems, and documents activities and results. Managers provide information, encourage employees, provide necessary time for employee development activities, and establish internal means for using new employee capacities. The three groups share responsibility for two-way, effective communication, ongoing feedback, change in support of career development, and improved utilization of the workforce.[24]

6. Sustaining (Maintaining, Evaluating).[25] Kaye suggests several actions to sustain career development programs. They must be adapted to changing conditions, which can be done by designing various sustaining systems that keep the program alive during the preparation stage.[26] Some questions to consider throughout this phase include:

   a. How do identified career development needs match our overall business direction?

   b. How can we create interventions that are flexible and adaptable enough to meet changing needs and audiences?

   c. How can our career development efforts be made to outlive individual stakeholders and particular actions so they become part of the fiber of the organization?[27]

Kaye suggests that individual movement among stages may proceed sequentially or oscillate; yet all six must be experienced at least once for one complete cycle ending at the sustaining phase.[28] She considers career planning to be essential in stage 1 of her career development model. Little information in this model is specifically devoted to diverse populations and their individual career planning efforts. Kaye's model is developed from the organizational and practitioner perspective, which, in most cases, differs markedly from the individual perspectives of diverse employees. Women and diverse individuals can use this model as a guide to take individual responsibility for their own career planning. Kaye's model is not specifically designed for individual career planning purposes, however. It is intended primarily for practitioners inside organizations to advance the goals of the organization. It focuses on the needs of the organization, not necessarily those of the employee. Some stages of Kaye's model, specifically stages 2, 3, 4, and 5, give the employees an opportunity to assess their positions and goals and take personal responsibility for their career development both from an individual and organizational perspective. Stages 1 and 6 of her model indicate that it is a model with organizational, not individual, goals in mind unless those goals are the same, which may not be the case.

Kaye suggests that a diverse workforce poses both challenges and opportunities to an organization. Its main challenge is to develop the knowledge and flexibility of its diverse workforce to its highest potential. She suggests that organizational leaders ask the following questions to evaluate diversity development:

1. Are we satisfied with the state of the art of this organization's development opportunities for special needs groups?
2. How will each career development stage make our organization more responsive to diversity needs?
3. Are we using the skill identification information developed at the Profiling Stage, to give us a better picture of needs of any underrepresented groups?
4. Are the goals for developing diversity, set at the Targeting Stage, realistic?
5. Is the organization doing all it can to support these goals?[29]

These questions continue to support the fact that much work is needed within organizations to make them level playing fields for women and diverse individuals. Communication channels must be constantly open to women and diverse individuals so that they can express their concerns and develop their careers within organizations that may not be receptive to their presence.

Hayes Career Transition Model

Hayes identifies six steps for managing career transitions. She suggests that adults will go through this model several times during their career. The steps are as follows:

1. Self-assessment: Employees get to know themselves very well by looking at their skills, values, interests, and personality preferences.
2. Career exploration: Individuals open up to career possibilities and let go of stereotypes.
3. Decision making: People synthesize information and seek similarities among jobs and the marketplace and their own values, interests, personalities, and skills.

4. Goal setting: Individuals establish goals to move forward toward their career choices.
5. Acquiring job search skills: People build networks of professional contacts and develop skills to market themselves to employers of choice.
6. Acquiring career success skills: Individuals learn ongoing career management skills and those that will help them fit into a new organization.[30]

Hayes presents an objective model for individuals who want to change careers. No specific reference is made to the use of the model by women and/or diverse individuals. It is an objective model that can be used to help people assess their ideas regarding career transitions to enhance their opportunities within the workforce.

Career Planning Model for a Diverse Workforce

Karsten and Igou suggest a need for a career planning model that addresses the unique needs of a diverse workforce.[31] They have proposed a model that combines the efforts of Bowden[32] and Ibarra[33] along with their original ideas. Their model primarily focuses on environmental and personal factors. The phases that they describe are career preparation, entry and progress, reassessment, and career change.

Karsten and Igou disagree with Super's theory from the perspective that

> until recently, white women tended to leave and re-enter the workforce to deal with non-work responsibilities more than their male peers. Thus, their age may have placed them in the maintenance stage of Super's model, but, based on their development, they may have fit better in the establishment phase. Because of prior discrimination, experiences of racial and ethnic minorities also may differ from those assumed in Super's model.[34]

They also argue that due to the impact of personal and environmental factors associated with women and diverse individuals, inventories and other questionnaires designed to increase self-knowledge are not effective because women and diverse individuals have a greater tendency to select jobs based on community needs as opposed to personal preference.[35]

During career preparation they suggest using self-knowledge inventories but only to the extent that personal and environment factors specific to women and diverse individuals are considered. They also include developing an understanding of occupational information resources and how they explain career choices within this stage.

During the entry and progress phase, they use Bowden's Career States System model with regard to launching, building, sustaining, subsisting, and searching within a career.[36] During the reassessment and career change stage, Karsten and Igou emphasize Ibarra's model of career change, in which she stresses doing over planning. Her suggestions are to try out change, make new connections, and make sense of change.[37] They emphasize that career models should allow for career breaks and that employees should be able to determine their own career success measures within their own timeframes.[38]

Karsten and Igou have developed a complex model that tries to address the needs of women and diverse individuals from a group and individual perspective. This in itself is a very difficult to accomplish. All of the variables that they mention should be explored with regard to women and minorities; however, it may make the model too cumbersome for individuals to navigate effectively.

ORGANIZATIONAL PERSPECTIVE

Within organizations one typically finds the individual, the group, the organization system, and organizational dynamics. Each aspect of the organization must be clearly understood by women and diverse individuals to help them attain success within the organization. The characteristics of each of these elements of the organization vary among organizations. As women and diverse individuals enter the workplace, they must recognize these elements and prepare to develop their careers within the opportunities presented and despite the constraints that they may encounter on entry.

Robbins suggests that in the boundaryless career, the organization's responsibility is to build employees' self-reliance and help them maintain marketability through continuous learning.[39] Specific ways in which this can be accomplished are to clearly communicate the organization's goals and future strategies, create growth opportunities, offer financial assistance, and provide time for employees to learn.[40] Women and diverse candidates must be aware of this shift in career planning and adapt accordingly. They have a tendency to enter and reenter the workplace;[41] however, women and diverse individuals must remain aware of trends and changes in the world's workplaces by keeping informed and participating in community and professional organizations.

CAREER PATHS

Citing Leibowitz, Farren, and Kaye,[42] Isaacson and Brown refer to career paths as a representation of the sequential lines of career progression in an organization.[43] Career paths can be used to develop career plans for individuals. Consistency is crucial when developing, explaining, and administering procedures related to career paths within an organization. Individuals progressing along a specified path should encounter no discriminatory experiences concerning gender, race, or ethnicity.

Usually, career paths for each job are developed based on employees' experiences that reflect organizational promotion practices.[44] However, few organizations provide career counseling or planning assistance to help employees, particularly diverse employees, progress along the paths.

BANKS'S SELF-ASSESSMENT AND SUFFICIENCY MODEL

The Self-Assessment and Sufficiency Model is developed with consideration for all of the previously identified models. Perspectives from each model may be relevant to women and diverse individuals; however, the author believes that they must be most diligent at organizational entry. Many models help prepare women and diverse individuals obtain a job; however, little emphasis is placed on the unique characteristics they must understand to succeed after job entry. After joining the workplace, women and diverse individuals must emphasize extensive planning and execution of strategy in three distinct career phases—entry, sustainability, and advancement. Internal factors, which are within individuals, and external factors, inherent in the organizations employing them, affect these stages. Processes within the three phases are as follows:

1. Entry Phase
   a. Relationships within Organizations
   b. Job Choice
2. Sustainability Phase
   a. Training and Professional Development
   b. Personal Development
3. Advancement Phase
   a. Criteria for Selection
   b. Skills
   c. Continuous Learning

Goals and Expectations

The central theme of Banks's model is goals and expectations. Women and diverse individuals often enter the workplace for survival reasons, without having identified their goals and expectations. Personal responsibilities are such that they often accept the first available position without considering career plans, goals, or personal expectations. Research also shows that culture, gender, and socioeconomic status influence career choice and development.[45]

The arrows from goals and expectations are double pointed to represent continuous feedback in both directions (see Figure 5.1). A two-way arrow from the goals and expectations to the organizations represents the fact that individuals will receive feedback from the organization; however, it may or may not affect their progress through the career planning model. Arrows around the model go in one direction only.

Goals are crucial in motivational theories. Pfeffer, referring to George Gallup, notes that "People tend to judge a man by his goals, by what he's trying to do, and not necessarily by what he accomplishes or by how well he succeeds."[46] Having goals can only be an asset for women and diverse individuals.

According to Ormond, the general effects of motivation are to:

1. increase an individual's energy and activity level;
2. direct an individual toward certain goals;
3. promote initiation of certain activities and persistence in those activities; and
4. affect the learning strategies and cognitive processes an individual employs.[47]

Victor Vroom first proposed expectancy theory to explain work behavior. He developed three models dealing with job satisfaction, work motivation, and job performance to address people's choices among work roles, the extent of their satisfaction with their chosen work roles, and their level of effectiveness in such roles.[48] Vroom's model has been used primarily to predict job satisfaction

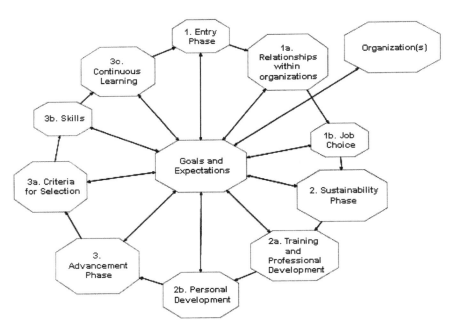

FIGURE 5.1. Self-Assessment and Sufficiency Model for career planning.

and occupational preference.[49] Adaptations including the Porter-Lawler Expectancy Model and Porter-Steers Met Expectations Hypothesis have been used to measure effort and job satisfaction.

The Porter-Lawler model has been used mainly to measure supervisor, peer, and self-effort. It focused on the value of the reward, the perceived and actual effort required to attain the expected reward, the actual effort, abilities and traits, role perceptions, performance (accomplishment), rewards (fulfillment), perceived equity of rewards, and satisfaction.[50] Porter and Lawler's value of reward variable referred to the attractiveness of possible outcomes to individuals. At a given point, individuals attach different values to a variety of potential rewards.[51] The value of the rewards to a person can be measured in several ways, including asking that individual to (1) make an actual choice among two or more alternatives in a situation in which she anticipates that her behavior will affect these outcomes; (2) rank or rate, on an attitude scaling device, the value of different rewards to himself; or (3) complete a projective device, such as the Thematic Apperception Test or a sentence completion test, from which some other person (i.e., the tester) infers the values of different rewards to the individual under consideration.[52]

The Porter-Steers Met Expectations Hypothesis describes "three common denominators that characterize motivation: (1) what energizes human behavior; (2) what directs or channels such behavior; and (3) how this behavior is maintained or sustained."[53] Motivational theories also have models that help explain their characteristics. According to Porter and Steers, "the basic building blocks of a generalized model of motivation are: (1) needs or expectations; (2) behavior; (3) goals; and (4) some form of feedback."[54] Banks's model incorporates all of these elements from the perspective that women and diverse individuals must address their personal goals and expectations, which will affect job choice and on-the-job behavior. Their feedback will be internal, within themselves, and external, from others in their organization.

Porter and Steers were concerned with the potential role of "met expectations" on a person's withdrawal behavior,[55] which is their tendency to be absent, avoid participation in optional organizational activities, or, in the extreme, quit. They define met expectations as the "discrepancy between what a person encounters on this job in the way of positive and negative experiences and what he expected to encounter."[56] Women and diverse individuals must be able to establish expectations when they start a job and progress through the career model, allowing them to adjust to positive and negative experiences based on an understanding of the way such experiences relate to their expectations. Using met expectations hypothesis, Porter and Steers predict that when an individual's expectations are unmet, that person's propensity to withdraw will increase.[57]

Irving and Meyer felt that the met expectations hypothesis could be tested by using difference scores reflecting the discrepancy between postentry experiences and preentry expectations and found problems. The difference scores yielded artificial relationships with outcome variables. The use of direct measures generally requires respondents to indicate the extent to which they perceive that their preentry expectations concerning their jobs have been confirmed.[58]

Thus, when direct measures of met expectations are used, respondents are implicitly assumed to compare their expectations and experiences mentally. Scores on the measure are assumed to reflect the match between these variables. If this is true, it should be possible to show that direct measures of met expectations reflect independently obtained measures of expectation and experiences approximately equally.[59]

Requiring individuals to recall their prior expectations after having been on the job for some time is a weakness of direct measures of met expectations. Recollections of preentry expectations are filtered by more recent experiences and behaviors.[60]

By establishing goals and expectations upfront and throughout the career planning process, women and diverse individuals can establish baselines to determine how well their expectations are being met through their own and organizational efforts, as applicable. This is an area where more research is needed. A study that measures the gap, if any, between expectations and experiences of women and diverse individuals from their point of entry into the workplace and a predetermined time frame that they remain within the organization could be beneficial to career planning professionals. A study that determines whether successful women and diverse individuals had personal goals and expectations and the extent to which they believe those goals and expectations influenced their success could also be beneficial to career planning professionals.

Entry Phase

Relationships within Organizations

During the entry phase, women and diverse individuals should try to establish relationships within the organization. The most important relationship will be with their immediate supervisor or manager. They must understand the culture and power dynamics that play a major role in decisions to remain in or leave the organization. Historically, women and diverse individuals have been the last to be hired and the first to be dismissed when workforce reductions are necessary. Labor laws and affirmative action practices have enabled women and diverse individuals to enter workplaces to which they previously were denied access. "Employers are now seeking to create workplaces where employees from all backgrounds fully utilize their skills and feel personally comfortable."[61] This is not intended to infer that they are unqualified and/or being hired to meet a quota, though some organizational members may think so. Some prejudge women and diverse individuals and do not view them as valuable team members who bring essential knowledge, skills, and abilities into the workplace. Because of these issues, women and diverse individuals must understand how their hierarchical positions within their respective organizations can be used to help them gain power and influence. The connotation of the word *power* is often negative; however, individuals and organizations must use power to remain effective. Each day, people use it to ensure success of organizational initiatives; women and diverse individuals may as well use power, too.

According to Pfeffer, "organizations have career systems in place that tend to reward and encourage activities and skills more generously than others.... Therefore, those who rise to positions of influence and who benefit from this career system have a particular set of skills and have engaged in a particular set of activities—those favored by the system."[62] Therefore, on entry into any organizational system, women and diverse individuals must build relationships and develop an understanding of the culture and career system they have entered.

Pfeffer notes that "the essence of organizations is interdependence."[63] Individuals must obtain power and the capacity to influence others to be successful within organizations. "It is critical that one be able to diagnose the relative power of various participants and comprehend the patterns of interdependence. One needs to know and understand not only the game, but also the players.[64]

Job Choice

Women and diverse individuals must become very selective about jobs they choose after organizational entry. In most instances, they consider particular jobs without thinking about the comprehensive career paths they want to follow. They must become aware of career paths to avoid becoming entrenched in positions with no advancement opportunities. They must navigate the organizational landscape and not end up in controversial positions that can become dead-ends for their careers.

Kaye provides a comprehensive analysis that women and diverse individuals can use to acquire an understanding of why job choice is essential. Once understanding is achieved, they can begin to develop and move from the concept of job choice to the idea of career planning.

Throughout this phase, establishing goals and expectations is critical to the success of women and diverse individuals. Without such goals, they can be steered into jobs and career paths that they may not desire or understand.

Sustainability Phase

The sustainability phase is the model's most important stage. This is the point at which women and diverse individuals must be most astute. They must realize that others within the organizations may expect them to fail or may develop schemes to sabotage their success. Having clear goals and expectations with an active execution strategy is essential to their sustainability. This is the point at which they should have solid relationships with others within their organization and an understanding of their ability to use power and influence to accomplish assigned tasks.

They must execute details of their jobs effectively and be open to learning new skills. The methods by which they acquire these new skills can vary; however, they must use opportunities to network with others in their chosen career field and remain current in essential skills that are necessary for success.

Training and Professional Development

Women and diverse individuals should take advantage of all training and professional development opportunities available within their organizations. Training usually includes skills taught on a need-to-know basis. Therefore, if the organization is offering training in a skill, employees most likely will need it to accomplish their jobs effectively. Professional development often consists of opportunities to attend training workshops and seminars or gain additional education by using tuition aid programs.[65] Cascio identifies training and development activities as "planned programs of organizational improvement undertaken to bring about a relatively permanent change in employee knowledge, skills, attitudes, or social behavior."[66] Human resource development focuses on the individual's ability to perform what she has learned in training and development activities after returning to the job.[67] Performance, as defined by Cascio, is the "observable, measurable behavior from which we infer learning."[68] Women and diverse individuals must understand how training and professional development provide organizational support to help them acquire knowledge, skills, and abilities.

Personal Development

Women and diverse individuals should be active participants in their own personal development. They can do this by reading trade journals, joining professional organizations, and networking with peers. Desire cannot be taught, however; people must *want* to succeed. According to Pfeffer, "developing and exercising power requires having both will and skill. It is the will that often seems to be missing."[69] Women and diverse individuals must use their acquired skills. Pfeffer also notes that "there is a greater sin than making mistakes or influencing others—the sin of doing nothing, of being passive in the face of great challenges and opportunities, and even great problems."[70]

Goals and Expectations

Throughout this phase, goals and expectations of individuals may be adjusted to fit their change in skill level and personal development. Understanding change as related to personal growth and development will assist them as they make career adjustments. Organizations will change; so must those they employ. According to Moran and Brightman, to manage change, leaders must understand the three most powerful drivers of work behavior: purpose, identity, and mastery. Change leaders must inspire individuals to align their purpose, or what they desire and value, identity, which is their sense of who they are, and mastery, their ability to manage themselves and the environment, with the necessary organizational change effort.[71]

Advancement Phase

To reach the advancement phase, with few exceptions, women and minorities must have mastered the previous stages. They must be prepared to showcase their knowledge, skills, and abilities to move forward. Though not all organizations reward them based on performance, women and diverse individuals should avoid using that as an excuse for failure to perform.

Criteria for Selection

If they have succeeded in previous phases, by the time they reach the advancement stage, women and diverse individuals must clearly understand promotion criteria. They should be able to match their accomplishments to the criteria to assess their career progress and advancement potential. This is a point where mentoring could be essential. A mentor who has successfully advanced through this phase could be able to assist women and diverse individuals understand the criteria and may even be at the table when the selection for promotion is made.

Skills

During the advancement stage, women and diverse individuals will be asked to display their skills constantly. Having knowledge is not enough. Most often women and diverse individuals are watched more closely than others and are expected to prove that they have what it takes to succeed in the job before being promoted into it. White males, on the other hand, have traditionally been promoted based on potential to succeed. Though this double standard is unfair, it exists and must be recognized. Women and diverse individuals do not have to accept the double standard, but they still must perform.

Continuous Learning

Continuous learning is essential during the advancement phase. Throughout the career cycle, there will be many opportunities to obtain new information both inside and outside of the organization. Gathering new information is also essential when changing units or moving to a different organization. Continuous learning can include obtaining higher education if a terminal degree has not been earned, attending training and professional development seminars, or engaging in individualized study. Learning from peers and co-workers is another possibility.

During this phase, maintaining a record of goals and expectations is crucial. Individuals can assess where they started and to what extent they have progressed in achieving their goals and meeting expectations. Many resources on setting goals and expectations are available; however, individuals must determine which goals and expectations are necessary and feasible for their own success.

CONCLUSION

In today's global economy, all members of the workforce must perform at their best. Women and diverse individuals want to succeed but may be unsure of their acceptance within organizations. Historically, they have struggled to participate actively even in workplaces that recruited them aggressively and welcomed them warmly at first. After entry, however, some have been surprised that other organizational members were far less congenial than the recruiters. If they continue to feel as if they are outsiders, they may not achieve their full potential in the workplace.

Women and diverse individuals can use all models of career planning and development described in this chapter in some way. It is up to them to assess themselves to determine if they have sufficient knowledge, skills, and abilities to succeed. This does not suggest that others are unavailable or unwilling to assist them. Rather, it points out that their personal motivation, desire, and will are more important to their success than the influence of others.

NOTES

1. Stephen P. Robbins, *Organizational Behavior*, 11th ed. (New Jersey: Pearson Prentice Hall, 2005), p. 17.

2. Ibid., p. 593.

3. Ibid.

4. Ibid., p. 594.

5. Beverly Kaye, *Up Is Not the Only Way* (New Jersey: Davies-Black, 1997), p. 59.

6. Lee E. Isaacson and Duane Brown, *Career Information, Career Counseling, and Career Development*, 6th ed. (Boston: Allyn and Bacon, 1997), p. 499.

7. Ibid.

8. R. L. Gibson and M. H. Mitchell, *Introduction to Career Counseling for the 21st Century* (New Jersey: Pearson Prentice Hall, 2006), p. 72.

9. Ibid., p. 71.

10. D. Super, "A Life-Span, Life-Space Approach to Career Development," in D. Brown and L. Brooks, eds., *Career Choice and Development*, 2nd ed. (San Francisco: Jossey-Bass, 2002), pp. 197–261.

11. Gibson and Mitchell, *Introduction to Career Counseling*, p. 75.

12. D. J. Bem, "Self-Perception Theory," in L. Berkowitz, ed., *Advances in Experimental and Social Psychology*, vol. 6 (New York: Academic Press, 1972), pp. 1–62.

13. P. G. Irving and J. P. Meyer, "On Using Direct Measures of Met Expectations: A Methological Note," *Journal of Management* 21 (1995): 1159–76.

14. Isaacson and Brown, *Career Information*, p. 21.

15. Ibid., p. 25.

16. Ibid.

17. Linda Kobylarz, Cal Crow, and Judith Ettinger, *America's Career Resource Network* (Virginia: National Training Support Center, 2005), online at www.acrnetwork.org/ncdg/ncdg_what.htm.

18. Ibid.

19. Kaye, *Up Is Not the Only Way*, p. 2.

20. Ibid., p. 21.

21. Ibid., p. 75.

22. Ibid., p. 107.

23. Ibid., p. 155.

24. Ibid., p. 198.

25. Ibid., p. 9.

26. Ibid., p. 227.

27. Ibid., pp. 227–28.

28. Ibid., p. 14–15.

29. Ibid., p. 39.

30. Katherine Harrington Hayes, *Managing Career Transitions*, 2nd ed. (New Jersey: Prentice Hall, 2000), pp. 14–16.

31. M. F. Karsten and F. Igou, "Career Planning: A Model for a Diverse Workforce," *Proceedings of the North American Management Society track at the 2005 Midwest Business Administration Association Conference* (Illinois: MBAA, 2005), p. 97.

32. V. Bowden, "The 'Career States System Model': A New Approach to Analyzing Careers," *British Journal of Guidance and Counseling* 25 (1997): 473–90.

33. H. Ibarra, "How to Stay Stuck in the Wrong Career," *Harvard Business Review* 80 (2002): 40–47.

34. Ibid.

35. Ibid., pp. 98–99.

36. Bowden, "The 'Career States System Model,'" pp. 473–90.

37. Ibarra, "How to Stay Stuck in the Wrong Career," pp. 40–47.

38. Karsten and Igou, "Career Planning," p. 104.

39. Robbins, *Organizational Behavior*, p. 594.

40. Ibid.

41. Karsten and Igou, "Career Planning."

42. Z. B. Leibowitz, C. Farren, and B. L. Kaye, *Designing Career Development Systems* (San Francisco: Jossey-Bass, 1986), p. 4.

43. Isaacson and Brown, *Career Information*, p. 457.

44. Ibid.

45. Ibid., p. 21.

46. Jeffrey Pfeffer, *Managing with Power* (Cambridge, MA: Harvard Business School Press, 1992), p. 288.

47. J. E. Ormond, *Human Learning*, 3rd ed. (New Jersey: Prentice Hall, 1999).

48. Victor Vroom, *Work and Motivation* (San Francisco: Jossey-Bass, 1995).

49. Claretha Hughes Banks, "A Descriptive Analysis of the Perceived Effectiveness of Virginia Tech's Faculty Development Institute." PhD diss., Virginia Tech, 2002.

50. L. W. Porter and E. E. Lawler, *Managerial Attitudes and Performance* (Illinois: Richard D. Irwin, 1968).

51. Banks, "A Descriptive Analysis."

52. Porter Lawler, *Managerial Attitudes and Performance.*

53. L. W. Porter and R. M. Steers, "Organizational, Work, and Personal Factors in Employee Turnover and Absenteeism," *Journal of Management* 80 (1973): 151–76.

54. Ibid.

55. Banks, "A Descriptive Analysis."

56. Ibid.

57. Ibid.

58. P. G. Irving and J. P. Meyer, "On Using Direct Measures of Met Expectations: A Methological Note," *Journal of Management* 21 (1995): 1159–76.

59. Ibid.

60. Ibid.

61. S. Jackson and A. Joshi, *Research on Domestic and International Diversity in Organizations: A Merger that Works*, Handbook of Industrial, Work and Organizational Psychology (California: Sage, 2001) vol. 2, pp. 206–31.

62. Pfeffer, *Managing with Power*, p. 318.

63. Ibid., p. 38.

64. Ibid., p. 49.

65. Banks, "A Descriptive Analysis."

66. W. F. Cascio, *Applied Psychology in Human Resource Management*, 5th ed. (New Jersey: Prentice Hall, 1998).

67. Banks, "A Descriptive Analysis."

68. Cascio, *Applied Psychology in Human Resource Management.*

69. Pfeffer, *Managing with Power*, p. 338.

70. Ibid., p. 300.

71. J. W. Moran and B. K. Brightman, "Leading Organizational Change," *Journal of Workplace Learning: Employee Counseling Today* 12 (2000): 66–74.

6

Gender, Race, and Role Model Status: Exploring the Impact of Informal Developmental Relationships on Management Careers

Audrey J. Murrell and Thomas J. Zagenczyk

Changes in the employer–employee relationship, organizational structure, and diversity of the workforce have had a major impact on today's work environment. The dynamic nature of today's organizations often means that individuals must be more actively involved in managing their careers than was necessary years ago.[1] Recognizing the importance of these changing career dynamics, much research has focused on the increasing need for employees to form their own networks of informal developmental relationships rather than relying solely on formal relationships (e.g., supervisors) provided by the organization to support and advance their careers.[2]

A variety of informal developmental relationships can significantly influence the outcomes of management careers. For example, peer networks play an important role in shaping career interests, career choice, job seeking, socialization, and career mobility as well as work-related attitudes.[3] Formal organization-sponsored networks, often called employee affinity groups, are powerful tools for employee recruitment, socialization, and retention.[4] Most recently, research has revealed that peer networks are a vital resource for career mobility and enhancement for women and people of color within organizations.[5]

The range of different developmental relationships that can be beneficial to one's career is extensive. Influential work by Kathy Kram outlines a number of mentoring or developmental functions that apply to both formal and informal relationships.[6] The work of Kram and her colleagues explains that developmental relationships shaping one's career are diverse in both form and function. Thus it is vital that we not treat all types of informal (as well as formal) developmental relationships in the same manner; instead, we should focus on the unique set of features associated with a particular type and function. Based on this fundamental assumption, we explore the impact of one aspect of informal mentoring relationships on the outcomes of management careers: role models.

In addition to the changing relationship between employees and the firm, the overall composition of the workforce continues to change substantially. Although women and people of color have made some advancement in organizations, both groups are still underrepresented in senior management positions and executive levels within most companies, regardless of size, industry, structure, or geographic location.[7] When examining the impact of role models as informal developmental relationships, considering the specific context in which these relationships form and develop is necessary. Work on concepts such as distinctiveness, tokenism, and power dynamics in organizations reveals that factors such as gender and race provide the context surrounding interactions between individuals within the workplace that produce either favorable or unfavorable outcomes. Though a wide variety of research examines the impact of role models, this work often omits any discussion of their importance within an organizational context for people who traditionally have been left out of the formal structure and process. Thus we examine the importance of role models for career outcomes and also look at the similarities and differences based on race and gender in the identification and impact of informal role models within organizations.

MENTORING AND THE FUNCTION OF ROLE MODELS

Mentoring is a process that assists employees in their career development and advancement that has gained considerable attention from organizations and management research over the past three decades.[8] Although much of this previous work concentrated on the impact of formal mentoring relationships between a senior mentor and a junior protégé, much recent work has examined the importance of peers as well as informal developmental relationships in shaping management careers. This is consistent with the original idea developed by Kram of "relationship constellations" reflecting the range of people who are important to support an individual's career development and success.[9]

Within this classic perspective, primary mentoring relationships have been the focus. Kram's original distinction between career and psychosocial functions also has been central to this traditional approach.[10] This work helped us unpack the complexity of a single mentor–protégé relationship to better understand the different types of mentoring functions, such as sponsorship, protection, exposure/visibility, coaching, counseling, acceptance, and role modeling. From a developmental perspective, mentoring also takes into account the various forms of these relationships, such as the number of mentors an individual has and the level or status of the mentor in relation to the protégé. These factors can affect the dynamic nature of the developmental relationship across the various phases of the mentoring (i.e., initiation, cultivation, separation, redefinition).

Regardless of whether one considers mentoring relationships that are primary or secondary, single or multiple, hierarchical or peer, the importance of the function served by the relationship must be defined and examined. As Higgins and Kram argue, "the provision of developmental assistance defines the boundaries of the developmental network construct."[11] Thus diverse mentoring networks provide an important vantage point from which to view the range of career and psychosocial assistance necessary to guide individuals throughout their professional and personal development.

RACE, GENDER, AND MENTORING RELATIONSHIPS

Mentoring relationships have been noted as particularly important for women and people of color in organizations. For example, research by the Catalyst organization finds that women who have broken through to high-level positions usually credit mentors with their success, whereas those still struggling to advance cite lack of access to mentors as a key barrier.[12] Thomas tracked the careers of African American managers who were successful in reaching the executive levels of their organizations. His work clearly highlights the importance of mentoring and sponsorship early in one's career. However, his data also showed that although sponsorship from senior-level managers is important, a network of developmental relationships that served both career and psychosocial functions is essential for long-term success.

Studies have consistently shown that those who have mentors have higher salaries, achieve higher level positions in organizations, are more satisfied at work, and have lower turnover rates than those without mentors.[13] Not only does the presence of a mentor matter, but the race and gender of the mentor is also important. Mentoring research shows that women and minorities who have white male sponsors generally are promoted more quickly and earn higher salaries than those with minority and female mentors.[14] A study of graduates from top MBA programs also found that mentoring helped explain the differences in career outcomes between those with and without access to these developmental relationships. In addition, the presence of mentoring helped account for the persistent gap in pay based on race and gender found among managers across various types of firms.[15] Recent work in this area examines the interaction of gender and race in mentoring relationships.[16]

Ragins's work on "diversified mentoring relationships" explains why issues of race and gender are important to the outcomes of development relationships.[17] Mentors and protégés in diverse mentoring relationships have different group memberships (e.g., gender or race) that are related to power differences in organizations. Mentoring relationships do not occur independently of context, but are influenced by macro-dynamics of power relationships between groups embedded within organizations. The influence of each party in the mentor–protégé dyad is affected by the individual's group membership and the group's access to key organizational resources.

Consistent with the logic of Ragins's work, social networks research also explains why groups have differential access to resources and power within organizations. A social network is defined as a specific set of relations among a defined set of people. Social networks analysis is based on the premise that the pattern of interpersonal relationships explains attitudinal and behavioral outcomes better than individual characteristics alone. For example, Brass investigated the interaction patterns of women and men to explain why women have not acquired status and influence similar to men in organizations. He found that how central a person is within the organization's informal network was significantly related to the influence that he or she had in the organization, and that women were generally less central than men.[18] Although women were aware of the importance of social networks and developed networks of their own, they still were not well integrated into the informal networks (particularly those of leaders and managers) and thus did not receive promotions at the same rate as men. Social networks research has revealed that an individual's race has similar effects on his or her position in a social network.[19]

The concept of distinctiveness offers another way to understand why gender and race will affect the pattern and nature of informal social networks. People identify with others who share similar characteristics that are relatively rare in the specific environment. Based on this concept, women are more likely to identify with other women, African Americans with other African Americans, and white males with other white males. Mehra and colleagues found that the drive for distinctiveness resulted in white males being highly central in organizational networks because of their greater numbers. Minorities and women, on the other hand, tended to be marginalized.[20] Ibarra found a similar pattern in her comparison of minority and white managers' networks. "High-potential" minority managers had more cross-race ties than did average-potential minority managers and thus were more central within the informal network inside the organization.[21]

Burt's work on social networks is also quite relevant to our discussion.[22] He argued that women are unable to duplicate men's networks because they lack legitimacy in the organization. To be successful, women need to effectively borrow the social network of a male sponsor who is influential in the organization. This borrowing of social power makes other organizational members believe that the individual with whom they are dealing is legitimate because that person is being treated as a source of organizational power by proxy. Burt's research found that women who borrowed male managers' social networks were promoted more quickly than women who attempted to develop their own networks. Borrowing the social capital of an influential white male sponsor was also an effective strategy for African Americans who broke through to senior levels within organizations, according to Thomas.[23]

Thus, research on mentoring, social networks, and distinctiveness suggests that developmental relationships may be sources of power and legitimacy (or a signal for a lack thereof) for those typically less central in informal organizational networks. Without this support, these individuals may be marginalized within the organization, experience fewer (or slower) promotions, and be seen as lacking leadership potential. Because people tend to use stereotypes in judgments about knowledge, expertise, and competence, the member of a work group who knows or is expected to know more about a particular domain is typically assigned responsibility for it.[24] Clearly, issues of power, expertise, and legitimacy are both defined and understood by the social context in which they are formed.

It is reasonable to expect that fundamental beliefs and biases surrounding race and gender also influence these definitions. Thus if people wish to advance within organizations or be perceived as having power, status, or legitimacy, they should seek role models who not only share some similar attributes but also can be a signal to others of the employees' own level of competence, knowledge, or status (i.e., borrowing social capital). In other words, for women and people of color in organizations, developmental networks may be important not only to provide models of and information about career and organizational success but also to share power, legitimacy, and social capital necessary to make that success a reality.

THE IMPORTANCE OF ROLE MODELS

Among key developmental relationships is the connection between an individual and any person he or she designates as a role model. Gibson defines a role model as "person(s) an individual perceives to be similar . . . [to himself or herself] to some extent, and because of that similarity the individual desires to emulate (or specifically avoid) aspects of that person's attributes or behaviors."[25] This definition implies that role models can serve three main functions to individuals: motivation, self-definition, and learning.

Gibson draws on role identification and social learning theories to explain the function of role models.[26] The motivation and self-definition component of role models draws on role identification theories. They propose that people are attracted to others who they believe are similar to themselves in terms of attitudes, behavior, goals, or status position, and are motivated to make themselves similar to those others through observation and learning.[27] The idea of learning draws on social learning theories, which suggest that people pay attention to models because they may be useful in learning new tasks, skills, or norms.[28] In their research, psychologists and organizational scholars contend that having role models is important to an individual's growth and development because of the various functions provided by these figures.

Role models expand our traditional understanding of developmental relationships in several respects. First, role models are informally selected by organizational members themselves rather than formally assigned by the organization. Second, a role model–employee relationship does not necessarily require direct interaction, although it may occur. Because individuals can observe role models without actually interacting with them, relationships with role models may be low-cost compared to those with formal mentors, as no reciprocity is expected or required. Individuals also can benefit by observing different role models who have different skills and styles while expending less time and effort.[29] Finally, traditional definitions specify that a mentor is older and hierarchically superior to the protégé.[30] A role model, however, may be anyone in an organization regardless of hierarchical position. Because role models afford flexibility, efficiency, and access to a wider array of individuals with diverse skill sets, maintenance of role model relationships may give employees an important source of informal developmental relationships within a dynamic career environment. Indeed, flexibility and choices are valuable given that an employee's career success may depend on the availability of diverse role models.[31]

Despite this range of benefits, few organizational studies have examined the impact of diversity on those individuals selected to be role models. This question is important because the very definition of role models involves a status that is socially constructed or based on subjective judgments of knowledge, expertise, and competence. For example, in one study of Canadian managers, researchers showed that managers' perceived effectiveness was positively associated with being considered a role model by subordinates.[32] Investigating consulting and law firm employees, Gibson and Cordova found that employees selected role models based on technical expertise, leadership ability, organizational and financial success, ability to balance personal and professional life, interpersonal skills, and personal traits and values.[33] Similarly, Zagenczyk and colleagues found that leadership positions, advice-giving, performance rewards, and tenure were positively associated with being perceived as a role model by others.[34]

Previous work has shown that role models are frequently selected as representations of an individual's ideal self.[35] Individuals perceived as highly effective and successful are often selected as role models. Thus to help shape their own career and organizational goals, employees who aspire to organizational success will look to those who hold leadership positions, are perceived to have expertise, or who have been honored with performance-related awards or some other formal recognition. In addition, individuals with desirable organizational positions or resources are frequently chosen as role models.

Role models differ in terms of whether they are positive or negative; whether they are above, below, or equal to the observer within the organizational structure; and whether they are close or distant to the observer in terms of strength of relationship.[36] Positive role models have attributes or achievements that others wish to emulate. On the other hand, negative role models have undesirable attributes and are used by employees as an example of what not to do. Upward role models have higher-level positions in the organizational hierarchy, whereas downward role models have lower-level positions. Finally, close role models are those with whom an employee interacts frequently or maintains close ties, whereas no interaction or direct relationship occurs between a distant role model and an observer. Distant role models are monitored vicariously by those who observe them. Thus, role models can be distinguished based on valence (positive, negative), status (upward, downward) or closeness (close, distant) to the individual.

Besides Gibson's initial investigation from which he derived these dimensions[37] and experimental work by Lockwood and colleagues[38] on positive and negative role models, little research has investigated the various dimensions of role models. In addition, few studies consider race and gender along with the status of the role model in the organizational context. In fact, most research on the effects of role models examines merely the presence versus absence of role models on career choice or on how hypothetical role models affect an individual's motivation within an experimental context.[39] This limited view of role models may underestimate their importance for shaping management careers, particularly for women and people of color within organizations.

Employees form a connection or identify with the firm when they define themselves at least partly in terms of what it values or represents.[40] Role models are a useful way of transferring information about an organization's values and norms to its employees.[41] In addition, organizational leaders recognize that their observable behavior is a strong signal of what the organization stands for in terms of its embedded culture.[42] Thus, because they provide information to an employee concerning the values and culture of the organization and help employees define themselves, having a diverse array of role models should be critical for the success of individuals attempting to better understand and navigate the organization and build informal developmental relationships. Clearly role models serve as important social referents for other employees, and in the case of close relationships, they may dispense advice that can be particularly valuable to employees. Last, as a social referent, they may drive not only aspirations but also the performance of individuals who use role models as a personal benchmark for their own career progress and outcomes.

ROLE MODELS: EXPLORING THE IMPACT OF GENDER AND RACE

A small number of studies has focused on attributes of role models in organizations, but even fewer empirical studies have focused on how either gender or race influences whether an individual is perceived to be a role model and the attributes that drive this identification. One exception is provided by Javidan and colleagues,[43] who included gender in their study of managers, but found that it did not predict (explaining only 1 percent of the variance) whether an employee considered his or her manager to be a role model. The study only examined the impact of gender in the context of the supervisor–subordinate relationship; it did not include any dimension of race or ethnicity. In addition, because the women in this study had already achieved formal recognition within the organization (i.e., supervisor) as part of being included as a role model, this study does not really speak to the issue of how role models are identified within informal relationships among peers within the same organization.

More recent research examines co-worker relationships.[44] Interestingly, the selection and perception of role models was very consistent with gender-based stereotypes. Female role models were more likely to be described as balancing work and personal life, being hard workers, and having a positive attitude and less likely to be described as organizationally effective, or as leaders, teachers, managers, or coaches than men were. In addition women selected the same number of female role models regardless of the proportion of females within the organization. Thus, even when more female role models were available, women did not seem to identify them as role models. Perhaps female employees may not be viewed as influential because the specific context does not identify women as having power, status, or expertise within the organization. This leaves open the important question of whether the gendered nature of organizations may serve to either prevent women from being identified as role models or place on them a different (and perhaps higher) set of criteria to be perceived as a role model by both men and women. The same logic could be applied to the effect of race and role model status. However, so far, research has failed to examine either of these critical issues.

The effect of gender and race on role model status within informal developmental relationships is clearly affected by the representation of women and people of color within organizations. Within the existing literature on diversity in organizations, notions of leadership, expertise, success, and status are viewed as social constructs influenced by the skewed nature (in terms of gender and race) of the portion of individuals occupying formal and informal leadership roles. Because of their relatively scant representation in managerial ranks, women and people of color are often underrepresented within leadership or other positions of influence. Kanter's classic discussion of organizational tokens as individuals belonging to a numerical minority describes the workplace in which people of color and women reside and must navigate.[45]

Several conditions accompany being a token: high visibility, high risk, low tolerance for mistakes, and hyperrepresentation. Tokens' distinctiveness makes them stand out in ways that can be detrimental to building interpersonal relationships and being selected as role models. Interacting with highly visible tokens is risky; if a mistake is made, everyone will see that error because everyone is already looking. This is particularly true in the case of close (versus distant) role models. Because any mistake made is so public, tokens also face far more severe penalties if they make an error. Finally, the success or failure of tokens is not attributed just to their own merit; in success and, more important, failure, they are seen as representing their whole demographic group (e.g., women, African Americans).

Thus, although token status increases the visibility of women and people of color in organizations, it may discourage others from choosing them as role models. For close, informal peer relationships, each condition just described can hamper the creation of effective developmental relationships. Although the dynamics of tokenism have been studied in a variety of situations, their application to the identification and selection of role models across gender and race is a wide open area for future research exploration.

In addition to the effects of numerical representation on role model status, the overall subjective nature of how success, expertise, and leadership competence are defined within an organization's culture should significantly affect the attributes and criteria used for identifying women or people of color as role models. This conclusion points to a need to better understand how expert status is conveyed within an organization's culture and how perceptions of expertise are affected by gender and race. This is a critical issue because to the extent that employees wish to be successful in their organization, they will look to those who are perceived as being successful and who have achieved either formal or informal recognition as experts. A more complete understanding of the relationship between judgments of expertise within organizations would contribute significantly to clarification of the effects of race and gender on informal role models within organizations.

Some work on transactive memory finds early support for this line of reasoning. Transactive memory systems occur when individuals' memory becomes involved in larger, organized social systems that have knowledge that is not traceable to individuals.[46] For example, research by Hollingshead shows a strong gender bias in the assignment of knowledge expertise among peers. She notes, "people who are interdependent often develop an implicit plan for learning new information based on their shared conception of another's expertise."[47] Transactive memory, along with judgments of expertise, develops naturally in relationships, particularly informal ones. It is no surprise that existing stereotypes should affect how people make judgments about relative knowledge and how they assign labels (e.g., expert or role model) to particular individuals. We need to understand more about how race and gender impact social judgments of expertise within organizations. This will help increase our understanding of when and how women and people of color are identified and nurtured as experts within informal role model relationships.

Some might argue that perceptions of expertise are really about organizational legitimacy and the pattern of relationships that helps establish and support it. Social networks and mentoring research show that women and people of color often have difficulty gaining legitimacy in organizations. Recent research on gender and role model status by Murrell and colleagues found that females who were identified as a source of advice by peers were considered to be role models, whereas females who received advice from their co-workers were not. Perhaps females must share their expertise to validate themselves as role models, but to avoid being affected by negative cues that can detract from their legitimacy, they must request advice from others infrequently. Females seeking job-related information or advice may not be considered role models because such requests detract from their organizational legitimacy (i.e., those who ask clearly lack the necessary knowledge).

On the other hand, Murrell's research revealed that frequently requesting advice did not affect employees' beliefs that a male was a role model. Thus it seems that behaviors such as advice-seeking may reduce legitimacy for women (and perhaps also people of color) in their peers' eyes. This suggests the need to identify a set of distinctive behavioral cues that determine organizational legitimacy and thus make it more or less likely that an individual will be afforded role model status in a manner that is affected by gender and race. Perhaps the cues for legitimacy differ based on race and gender. Identifying how legitimating behaviors are viewed differently based on gender and race would help provide concrete strategies for reducing the bias in the subjective nature of organizational legitimacy and role model status.

Last, although issues such as expertise and legitimacy may play an important part in informal role model relationships, the strength of these relationships is critical in helping explain the impact on management careers. Though the reasons for conferring role model status matter, the strength of the relationship is also an important determining factor. Relationships that can be described as strong ties are often reciprocal and characterized by frequent contact and strong levels of identification.[48] Previous work has clearly shown that strength of ties affect a range of attitudinal and behavioral outcomes.[49] Murrell and Zagenczyk found that the number and strength of advice and friendship ties a female employee maintained was significantly and positively associated with her being perceived as a role model. However, only the number of advice and friendship ties maintained, not the strength of these ties, was significantly related to a male being considered a role model.[50] Thomas reported similar findings in his work on African Americans and career mobility.[51] These results suggest that to be considered a role model, strength of ties matters more for women and people of color, particularly in terms of their relationships with their coworkers.

Though speculative at this point, exploring the effect of tie strength on role model relationships that differ based on race and gender is an important area for future research. Perhaps strong ties help reduce some of the biased or stereotyped judgments that might affect how women and people of color are evaluated within these informal relationships. In addition, establishing legitimacy and expert status may be a function of both the strength of one's relationships and the type of network involved (e.g., friendship, advice). Although it might be difficult for women and people of color to be included within interpersonal networks (e.g., friendship networks), they may gain access to information networks because their knowledge can be useful to those within the network. These are important questions that require further exploration.

SOME CONCLUDING THOUGHTS

Though much research has explored the power of developmental relationships within organizations, many questions remain. For women or people of color to be identified as role models, what attributes are key? What are the benefits versus the costs of asking for as opposed to providing advice within the organization in terms of being seen as a role model? How important are formal organizational cues such as titles and leadership positions for women and people of color in being perceived as role models? Is it enough for women and people of color to be connected with high-status or powerful individuals as role models, or does the strength of these informal relationships matter for career success?

Understanding the identification, cultivation, and impact of informal role models provides a number of important and interesting questions, only some of which are explored here. The argument is made that for women and people of color, role models may provide an invaluable source of support, knowledge, and legitimacy that has been overlooked by the previous work on mentoring and diversity in organizations. Being seen as a role model is also an important signal of organizational values and culture and is affected by the lack of representation of women and minorities in leadership roles and the persistent stereotypes of what it means to be a knowledge expert in today's organization. This review argues that having access to and being seen as a role model are both important for the management careers of women and people of color and that these issues warrant further research attention.

We see work on mentoring, social networks, organizational learning, and transactive memory as key areas to help shape the answers to many of these crucial questions. In addition, such answers may have major implications for individual careers and organizational effectiveness. This is important because role models are expected to be primary sources of learning for the individual and the organization. As the nature of organizations and management careers continues to change and become more complex, the need to expand and cultivate formal and informal systems of knowledge and continuous learning also increases. One important source of knowledge that has gained recent attention involves learning about the context of work called relational job learning.[52] This type of knowledge relies on understanding that extends beyond the technical aspects of work to the interdependence of one's job to systems and to other people. Clearly, developmental relationships can be invaluable tools that facilitate relational job learning. We see role models that can cut across traditional boundaries of race and gender as an untapped resource for innovative relational job learning. Although the effective use of role models is not a panacea, it deserves more attention due to its potential to unlock important aspects of organizational learning and shape the unrealized potential of management careers for women and people of color.

NOTES

1. Michael B. Arthur and Denise M. Rousseau, *The Boundaryless Career* (New York: Oxford University press, 1996).

2. Monica C. Higgins and Kathy E. Kram, "Reconceptualizing Mentoring at Work: A Developmental Network Perspective," *Academy of Management Review* 26 (2001): 264–98.

3. Scott E. Seibert, Maria L. Kraimer, and Robert C. Liden, "A Social Capital Theory of Career Success," *Academy of Management Journal* 44 (2001): 219–37.

4. Ray Friedman, Melinda Kane, and Daniel B. Cornfield, "Social Support and Career Optimism: Examining the Effectiveness of Network Groups among Black Managers," *Human Relations* 51 (1998): 1155–77.

5. Herminia Ibarra, "Personal Networks of Women and Minorities in Management: A Conceptual Framework," *Academy of Management Review* 18 (1993): 56–87.

6. Kathy Kram and Douglas T. Hall, "Mentoring in a Context of Diversity and Turbulence," in Ellen Kossek and Sharon Lobel, eds., *Managing Diversity: Human Resource Strategies for Transforming the Workplace* (Cambridge, MA: Blackwell, 1996).

7. Lotte Bailyn, *Breaking the Mold: Women, Men and Time in the New Corporate World* (New York: Free Press, 1993); Sharon M. Collins, "The Marginalization of Black Executives," *Social Problems* 36 (1989): 317–31.

8. Higgins and Kram, "Reconceptualizing Mentoring at Work," pp. 264–98.

9. David A. Thomas, "Racial Dynamics in Cross-Race Developmental Relationships," *Administrative Science Quarterly* 38 (1993): 169–94.

10. Kathy E. Kram, "Phases of the Mentoring Relationship." *Academy of Management Journal* 26 (1983): 608–25.

11. Higgins and Kram, "Reconceptualizing Mentoring at Work."

12. Catalyst, *Women of Color Executives: Their Voices, Their Journeys* (New York: Catalyst, 2001).

13. Ellen A. Fagenson, "The Mentor Advantage: Perceived Career/Job Experiences of Protégés versus Non-Protégés," *Journal of Organizational Behavior* 10 (1989): 309–20.

14. George F. Dreher and J. A. Chargois, "Gender, Mentoring Experiences and Salary Attainment among Graduates of an Historically Black University," *Journal of Vocational Behavior* 53 (1998): 501–16; George F. Dreher and Taylor H. Cox, "Race, Gender, and Opportunity: A Study of Compensation Attainment and the Establishment of Mentoring Relationships," *Journal of Applied Psychology* 81 (1996): 297–308; Katherine Giscombe, Stacy Blake-Beard, Audrey J. Murrell, and Faye J. Crosby, "Race, Gender and Mentoring: A Study of African-American Women in the Corporate Sector," unpublished manuscript.

15. Dreher and Cox, "Race, Gender, and Opportunity."

16. Giscombe et al., "Race, Gender and Mentoring."

17. Belle R. Ragins, "Diversified Mentoring Relationships in Organizations: A Power Perspective," *Academy of Management Journal* 22 (1997): 482–521.

18. Daniel J. Brass, "Men's and Women's Networks: A Study of Interaction Patterns and Influence in an Organization," *Academy of Management Journal* 28 (1994): 327–43.

19. Reed E. Nelson, "The Strength of Strong Ties: Social Networks and Intergroup Conflict in Organizations," *Academy of Management Journal* 32 (1989): 377–401.

20. Ajay Mehra, Martin Kilduff, and Daniel J. Brass, "At the Margins: A Distinctiveness Approach to the Social Identity and Social Networks of Underrepresented Groups," *Academy of Management Journal* 41 (1998): 441–52.

21. Herminia Ibarra, "Race, Opportunity, and Diversity of Social Circles in Managerial Networks," *Academy of Management Journal* 38 (1995): 673–703.

22. Ronald Burt, "The Gender of Social Capital," *Rationality and Society* 10 (1998): 5–46.

23. David A. Thomas and John J. Gabarro, *Breaking Through: The Making of Minority Executives in Corporate America* (Boston: Harvard Business School Press, 1999).

24. David M. Wegner, "Transactive Memory: A Contemporary Analysis of the Group Mind," in Brian Mullen and George R. Goethals, eds., *Theories of Group Behavior* (New York: Springer-Verlag, 1987), pp. 185–208.

25. Donald E. Gibson, "Developing the Professional Self-Concept: Role Model Construals in Early, Middle, and Late Career Stages," *Organization Science* 14 (2003): 591–610; quote on p. 592.

26. Donald E. Gibson, "Role Models in Career Development: New Directions for Theory and Research," *Journal of Vocational Behavior* 65 (2004): 134–56.

27. Lawrence Kohlberg, "Moral Development and Identification," in Harold W. Stevenson, ed., *Child Psychology: The Sixty-Second Yearbook of the National Society for the Study of Education* (Chicago: University of Chicago Press, 1963), pp. 277–332.

28. Albert Bandura, *Social Foundations of Thought and Action* (Englewood Cliffs, NJ: Prentice Hall, 1986).

29. Herminia Ibarra, "Provisional Selves: Experimenting with Image and Identity in Professional Adaptation," *Administrative Science Quarterly* 44 (1999): 764–91.

30. Ragins, "Diversified Mentoring Relationships in Organizations."

31. Gibson, "Role Models in Career Development."

32. Monsour Javidan, Brian Bemmels, Kay Stratton-Devine, and Ali Dastmalchian, "Superior and Subordinate Gender and the Acceptance of Superiors as Role Models," *Human Relations* 48 (1995): 1271–84.

33. Donald E. Gibson and Diane I. Cordova, "Women's and Men's Role Models: The Importance of Exemplars," in Audrey J. Murrell, Faye J. Crosby, and Robin J. Ely, eds., *Mentoring Dilemmas: Developmental Relationships within Multicultural Organizations* (Mahwah, NJ: Lawrence Erlbaum Associates, 1999), pp. 121–42.

34. Thomas J. Zagenczyk, Audrey J. Murrell, Tanvi Guatam, and Mike Ptaszenski, "Following the Muse: Role Models, Their Social Networks and Impact on Employees' Work-Related Attitudes," *Midwest Academy of Management Conference Proceedings* (2005).

35. Ibarra, "Provisional Selves."

36. Penelope Lockwood, Christian H. Jordan, and Ziva Kunda, "Motivation by Positive or Negative Role Models: Regulatory Focus Determines Who Will Inspire Us," *Journal of Personality and Social Psychology* 83 (2002): 854–64.

37. Gibson, "Developing the Professional Self-Concept."

38. Lockwood et al., "Motivation by Positive or Negative Role Models"; Penelope Lockwood and Ziva Kunda, "Superstars and Me: Predicting the Impact of Role Models on the Self," *Journal of Personality and Social Psychology* 73 (1997): 91–103; Penelope Lockwood and Ziva Kunda, "Increasing the Salience of One's Best Selves Can

Undermine Inspiration by Outstanding Role Models," *Journal of Personality and Social Psychology* 76 (1999): 214–28.

39. Lockwood and Kunda, "Increasing the Salience of One's Best Selves."

40. Glen E. Kreiner and Blake E. Ashforth, "Evidence towards an Expanded Model of Organizational Identification," *Journal of Organizational Behavior* 25 (2004): 1–27.

41. Cheri Ostroff and Steve W. J. Kozlowski, "Organizational Socialization as a Learning Process: The Role of Information Acquisition," *Personnel Psychology* 45 (1992): 849–74.

42. Edgar H. Schein, *Career Dynamics: Matching Individual and Organizational Needs* (Reading, MA: Addison-Wesley, 1978).

43. Javidan et al., "Superior and Subordinate Gender."

44. Gibson and Cordova, "Women's and Men's Role Models."

45. Rosabeth M. Kanter, "Some Effects of Proportion on Group Life: Skewed Sex Ratios and Responses to Token Women," *American Journal of Sociology* 82 (1977): 965–90.

46. Wegner, "Transactive Memory."

47. Andrea B. Hollingshead and Samuel N. Fraidin, "Gender Stereotypes and Assumptions about Expertise in Transactive Memory," *Journal of Experimental Social Psychology* 39 (2003): 355–63.

48. Mark Granovetter, "The Strength of Weak Ties," *American Journal of Sociology* 78 (1973): 1360–80.

49. Mark Granovetter, "The Strength of Weak Ties: A Network Theory Revisited," in Peter V. Marsden and Nan Lin, eds., *Social Structure and Network Analysis* (Beverly Hills, CA: Sage, 1982), pp. 105–30; Nelson, "The Strength of Strong Ties."

50. Audrey J. Murrell and Thomas J. Zagenczyk, "The Gendered Nature of Role Model Status: An Empirical Study," unpublished manuscript, University of Pittsburgh.

51. Thomas and Gabarro, *Breaking Through*.

52. Melenie J. Lankau and Terri A. Scandura, "An Investigation of Personal Learning in Mentoring Relationships: Content, Antecedents and Consequences," *Academy of Management Journal* 45 (2002): 779–90.

7

Alternative Approaches to Mentoring in the New Millennium

Suzanne C. de Janasz

Few would argue the value of mentoring in the development of one's career. Experts agree that individuals with mentors earn higher salaries, have higher job satisfaction, get more promotions, and have greater organizational commitment.[1] In addition, protégés gain confidence and self-awareness through these developmental relationships (and friendships), learn increasingly valuable interpersonal skills by observing a more experienced individual in practice, and expand associations in related networks.[2] All individuals, especially women and minorities, miss an important career developmental experience if they do not have a mentor.[3] Implementing formalized mentoring programs benefits organizations as well by facilitating the socialization process and hastening the acculturation of junior members of the organization.[4] In fact, 60 percent of the Fortune 100 Best U.S. Companies to Work For have formal mentor programs.[5]

Traditionally, mentoring has been described as a long-term, intense developmental relationship where a mentor—generally a higher-ranking employee with advanced organizational (or industry) experience and knowledge—shapes a protégé's career by providing advice, coaching, and career opportunities to him or her.[6] More specifically, mentors provide protégés with two types of support. Career development support is provided when a mentor attempts to enhance a protégé's career advancement through sponsorship, exposure and visibility, coaching, protection, challenging assignments, and career strategizing. Psychosocial support enhances the protégé's sense of competency, identity, and effectiveness in a professional role; this is done when a mentor provides role modeling, acceptance and confirmation, counseling, friendship and support, and personal feedback.[7] The amount and mix of support varies according to the protégé's needs and mentor's abilities.

Mirroring recent changes in the contemporary environment, mentoring has transformed into diverse relationships that often extend beyond traditional organizational, geographical, and functional boundaries.[8] This chapter discusses several trends necessitating new forms of mentoring and explains how these alternate forms facilitate career development for protégés and mentors alike.

TRENDS NECESSITATING ALTERNATE FORMS
OF MENTORING BOUNDARYLESS CAREERS

The career, once synonymous with a well-defined ladder and advancement in one or two paternalistic organizations, has become boundaryless, with individuals changing jobs an average of every four and a half years.[9] One explanation for this shift is changes in the organization's psychological contract with employees.[10] Whereas decades ago most employees could expect to remain with a firm from the start of their professional career through retirement, competitive and global pressures have undermined this implied loyalty. As the business landscape evolves, organizations wishing to remain viable businesses also must change. Accompanying the trend toward free agency among employees and organizations has been a shift of employees' allegiance—from their organizations to their industry or profession—and career approach. The new protean careerists,[11] like the Greek god Proteus they were named after, reshape themselves, repackaging and remarketing their abilities and skills, to find new jobs, challenges, and learning experiences across organizational and occupational boundaries.[12] Others following protean strategies do so for more utilitarian reasons: to maintain their standard of living. In either case, each time employees relocate they must learn new organizational rules, procedures, and politics while simultaneously mastering the technical aspects of the job.[13] To effectively assimilate new skills and environments and navigate the boundaryless career landscape,[14] individuals must consider relying not only on one mentor but on multiple, diverse individuals.[15] A variety of mentors—also known as a developmental network[16]— can provide different perspectives, knowledge, and skills while serving different mentoring functions, such as providing emotional support or protection from political enemies, in a way perhaps no one individual can.

In the same way firms are using organizational networks to facilitate increased knowledge for a competitive advantage,[17] individuals can—and should—use mentor networks to facilitate access to the knowledge and experiences of others for a competitive career advantage. Although relationships within this developmental network may not be as intense as the traditional one-on-one master–apprentice model,[18] a developmental or mentor network can become an important conduit by which individuals increase their social capital, work performance, and career success. More than ever, mentors are needed to help protégés navigate the less secure waters of today's careers, learn specific skills, and establish connections with influential decision makers.

In tandem with the shift toward the boundaryless career is the transfer in accountability for one's career from the organization to oneself.[19] When both parties anticipated a long-term association, actively guiding employees' careers was an expected, practical role for managers, who sent direct reports on important developmental assignments or recommended participation in professional conferences or training programs. Without this paternalistic approach, employees are on their own to determine and pursue developmental opportunities through relationships and connections with superiors, peers, and those external to the organization.

People as a Source of Knowledge and Social Capital

Another trend responsible for the increasing reliance on alternative forms of mentoring is the fact that more organizations are viewing their people—as opposed to their products, services, or assets—as the chief source of sustainable competitive advantage.[20] In today's knowledge economy,[21] the people within whom knowledge resides become the firm's primary assets. Rapid environmental and technological changes render previously valuable skills sets obsolete and require that knowledge continuously change and evolve. As such, it becomes difficult, if not impossible, for individuals—or individual mentors—to possess all the requisite knowledge.[22] Individuals need to continually tap many knowledge sources to remain valuable to their organizations.[23] Even organizations made up of primarily senior-level, highly educated employees (think tenured faculty!) realize that regardless of education, experience, or career stage, individuals' need for continuous learning goes on, particularly in turbulent times.[24] The most valuable employees are those who use their skills and resources to remain on the cutting edge of what is known and who adapt and are flexible learners.[25]

Because of the value of sharing knowledge, involvement in productive mentoring relationships clearly would benefit participants and the organization.[26] As the competition for highly skilled and dedicated professionals heats up, firms focus more attention on developing their current employees. Companies implementing mentoring programs—in traditional and nontraditional formats, such as group mentoring and e-mentoring—have a leg up in recruiting candidates, particularly in tight labor markets.[27] Candidates view such firms as people-oriented places where they can develop valuable job- and career-related knowledge and skills. This is critical as personal competencies reflect different forms of knowledge that can be applied and adapted to the shifting career opportunities in today's turbulent workplace.[28] Helping a protégé build this diverse set of career competencies amid environmental change and uncertainty requires the services of not one but a diverse set of mentors[29] who will expand the protégé's competencies as well as beliefs about career possibilities.[30]

Need to Manage a Diverse Workforce

The applicability of traditional and nontraditional mentoring programs to corporate diversity initiatives is another trend driving its increased implementation.

Many companies now offer mentoring programs, which bolster a person's chance for advancement. All employees are eligible, but many organizations pay special attention to underrepresented groups, such as women and minorities, to help them overcome additional barriers (i.e., individual, interpersonal, and organizational) they face.[31] Moreover, these programs assist women and minorities in finding senior managers with whom to enter into developmental relationships.[32] This is important because senior-level mentors (primarily men) are more likely to choose a protégé who is "a younger version of himself."[33] Without this assistance, female and minority employees may ignore their desire for a mentor or look outside the organization or industry for one. Companies are finding that offering mentoring programs is an excellent way to boost the performance and advancement rates of minorities and women, as well as build confidence and boost morale.

In tandem with changes in organizational and job structures are major changes in the demographic makeup of the global workplace. William Johnston, author of *Global Workforce 2000*, notes that there are "massive relocations of people including immigrants, temporary workers, retirees and visitors. The greatest relocations will involve young, well-educated workers flocking to the cities of the developed world."[34] These immigrants are expected to flock to Japan, Germany, and the United States; in addition, millions of women in industrializing nations are entering the paid workforce.[35] In this new, diverse global context, managers must bridge the variety of employee expectations, values, and work habits while simultaneously taking advantage of the diversity this new workforce offers. Changing labor force demographics have altered the work of and created additional challenges for managers, necessitating the development of not just one but a cadre of mentor relationships. In addition, as the number of dual-career and single parents continues to grow, organizations increasingly adopt family-friendly policies and other supportive practices and expect their managers to implement them.[36] The changing composition of employees and shifts in the work they do create two reasons to seek mentor guidance: to learn how to deal with employees' diverse employment expectations and how to balance one's work and family roles and responsibilities. As these reasons for seeking mentors are fairly recent, at least among certain populations, human resource or other formalized functions may provide only minimal guidance. Current and future organizational leaders would benefit greatly from developing mentor relationships with those who have successfully addressed these challenges to provide valuable knowledge and support.

The anticipated mass global worker migration suggests increasingly diverse work populations who face challenges emanating from minority status. However, the limited supply of minorities in high-level positions necessitates protégés to search for mentors beyond organizational and geographic boundaries. As an added bonus, each new mentor in the protégé's network—whether cultivated face to face or electronically—provides potential access to an exponentially greater number of individuals with similar or compatible values and characteristics.

Along with the global mass migration of workers into the North American workforce, we are seeing an employee migration out of companies' physical locations. Organizations implementing teleworking arrangements—also known as boundaryless work practices[37]—realize significant gains through reduced real estate expenses, enhanced productivity, increased access to global markets, reduced pollution, and greater ability to attract and retain high-quality workers.[38] Ceridian Group reported that 90 percent of firms use boundaryless work arrangements, including telecommuting (i.e., completing all or most of one's work from a home office), flexible scheduling, and project work.[39] Furthermore, the International Telework Association and Council reports that in 1999, nearly 20 million workers telecommuted; that number exceeded 44 million in 2004.[40] Given societal concerns about traffic, pollution, and disaster preparedness and the passage of a law that requires federal agencies to enact plans to maximize the number of telecommuters, this trend will continue.[41] However, this technology-facilitated working arrangement presents a unique set of challenges to executives and managers whose experience is limited to traditional office environments. Today's managers are challenged to establish organizational and individual goals, provide performance feedback, and lead culturally and geographically diverse teams and meetings, while simultaneously maintaining a positive work climate and tracking productivity, quality, costs, and adherence to regulations with minimal if any face-to-face interaction.[42] These skills were likely not part of managers' formal education; thus, they would benefit from associating with mentors who have the technological and managerial expertise to succeed in this venue.

ALTERNATIVE FORMS OF MENTORING

Multiple Mentors

Perhaps the most significant change in mentoring theory and practice is protégés' cultivation of simultaneous multiple mentors in their developmental network.[43] Effectively responding to the many trends such as those discussed requires an individual to seek advice of not one but multiple mentors.[44] These shifting demands make it impossible for one person—or mentor—to possess the requisite skills, knowledge, and experience to excel in the ever-changing workplace. Bill Radiger, president of Karma Media, reflects this view when he says: "One mentor is not enough. You have to rely on a number of mentors to allow you to see values in action, to develop business acumen and product knowledge. If you do choose to rely on one mentor, that mentor had better know everything, otherwise you will end up with their bad habits along with the good."[45]

A diverse set of mentors—also known as a constellation of developmental relationships[46]—can provide different perspectives, knowledge, and skills while serving different mentoring functions, such as providing emotional support or protection from political enemies, in a way perhaps no one individual can. By cultivating and maintaining a cadre of developers—peers, managers, sponsors, or friends—individuals are using their mentor networks to facilitate access to others' knowledge and experiences to increase their social capital, work performance, and career success.[47]

Realistically, the individual mentor relationships within one's developmental network will vary in strength or intensity (degree of closeness, reciprocity), amount and type of assistance provided (career, psychosocial, role modeling), and duration (project or longer term).[48] Some may be as intense as the traditional one-on-one master–apprentice model, and others may take the form of an occasional phone call or lunch. Furthermore, all mentor relationships change over time, and at some point end. As an added benefit, unlike in traditional mentoring relationships, protégés with multiple mentors can rely on others for career assistance should one relationship in the network become dysfunctional or a mentor becomes unavailable.

Peer Mentoring

Peer mentoring is a relationship between group members at the same level, wherein both parties acknowledge that they can and do learn from and assist one another with professional development.[49] Whereas traditional mentors provide both career and psychosocial support as a means to advance in an organization, peer support has not always been thought of as—or been the focus of much research on[50]—mentoring. Early research by Kram and Isabella demonstrated that although the nature and amount of support that superiors and peers provide differs, peer assistance encompassed career and psychosocial functions.[51] Recent conceptualizing by Kram and others recognizes the need for broader notions of what constitutes (and plays out as) mentoring,[52] given the changes in the environment, organizations, and individuals' careers. Interestingly, many refer to a peer or friend as a mentor only in hindsight, as illustrated by Ed Hartman, director of Technical Services with Avaya Corporation,[53] "Working with Jim, Scott, and Ann on the management team was the best time I had at work. We had fun; we made things happen. Jim retired, Scott took a new job, and Ann moved. With them gone, suddenly I realized that I counted on these people for more than support and fun. . . . I had lost a trusted group of advisors."

Many peer relationships develop spontaneously without a specific plan. They occur when a mentor and protégé find each other, such as when an employee seeks counsel or offers advice based on having learned the ropes in an organization. In their study on the effectiveness of formal mentoring programs, Ragins, Cotton, and Miller note that "mentors choose protégés whom they view as younger versions of themselves, and protégés select mentors whom they view as role models."[54] Because they share commonalities—similar position, professional experience, values, or aspirations—those involved in a peer relationship develop trust and disclose more deeply and more quickly than in a traditional mentoring relationship. For example, a protégé with a more senior mentor may be so concerned with ensuring a positive impression with the higher-ups that she glosses over weaknesses or mistakes that if shared, could form the basis of a valuable learning experience. With trust, which is developed more quickly in peer relationships, protégés are more likely to assume the risk inherent in sharing "what happened as opposed to the story we all made up about what happened," and thus reap the benefit of their mentor's advice and support.[55]

Whereas traditional senior/junior mentoring relationships signify a strategy to aid protégés' career advancement, today's flatter, more participative environments have given rise to peer relationships focused on developing job-related skills.[56] With fewer managers available or able to mentor nonmanagers, employees are likely to feel a sense of vulnerability or isolation,[57] making the need for support—and fear in admitting that need to one's manager—even greater. Moreover, because employees' loyalty to the profession increasingly exceeds their loyalty to the firm,[58] managers' motivation to fulfill company succession objectives by mentoring employees "on deck" is reduced.

Given the current work environment, we would expect to see a rise in the popularity and efficacy of the various types of peer mentoring relationships—those involving co-worker, teammates, and co-mentors. As organizations become flatter and employees increasingly must do more with fewer resources—particularly following organizational restructuring or downsizing—they naturally seek assistance from co-workers. Even in the absence of formal work teams, co-workers are required to interact with one another to complete tasks, provide services, and improve processes. Through these interactions, employees share technical and organizational information; they also share—and support one another on—personal issues.[59] Thus, this type of mentoring is consistent with the peer developmental relationships described by Kram and colleagues.[60]

Eby discusses the increasing preponderance of interdependent work teams and notes how the transfer of traditional management responsibilities (e.g., planning, organizing, coaching, training) to team members creates opportunities for job and career support and development.[61] In addition, because teams possess accumulated organizational knowledge and history, they can transmit this knowledge to—and help socialize—members of a team.[62] Like other peer developmental relationships, intragroup or team mentoring relationships represent a mutually reinforcing ideal wherein mentor and protégé help each another.

Co-mentors are a pair of close, collegial friends who are committed to facilitating each other's development and take turns mentoring each other at particular stages of their careers/lives.[63] This idea of friends as developers is not new; however, the recognition that friendship can serve as a mentoring relationship is novel. In their study of high-ranking executive women in the male-dominated entertainment industry, Ensher and her colleagues found that many shared information and strove to maintain good relationships with those above, below, and at the same status level as themselves.[64] Their social lives were built around and integrated with work contacts and friendships. Hiking outings or monthly women-only industry parties provided social satisfaction as well as a means to connect and share resources with many different types of developers. These findings echo another study wherein the participants did not recognize the significant contribution of the friendships to their professional and personal lives until they narrated their experiences for the researcher.[65] This notion of co-mentoring clearly demonstrates mentoring as a reciprocal relationship—a concept that has become more common in both the popular and academic press. Wayne Baker, author of *Achieving Success through Social Capital*, reminds professionals that "the goal of building networks is to contribute to others."[66] Similarly, de Janasz et al. advise protégés to seek out opportunities to provide their mentors with technical information, new knowledge, or emotional support.[67] By helping another, individuals increase the likelihood of receiving assistance in the future as well as increasing the trust and credibility of the developmental relationship.[68]

Virtual or Electronic Mentoring

Recently, electronic or e-mentoring programs have burgeoned,[69] reflecting changes in our conceptualization of mentoring and reliance on technology for communication. Also known as tele-, online, cyber- or virtual mentoring, e-mentoring—the merger of mentoring with electronic communications— exists within major corporations, connects members of an industry or profession, and supports students and professionals at various levels. Like its traditional counterpart, the goal of e-mentoring is the creation of a mutually beneficial relationship between a mentor and a protégé. Unlike traditional mentoring, however, the personal and professional learning and support come primarily through e-mail and other electronic means.[70] Given the billion—and growing— worldwide Internet users,[71] and the business climate characterized by layoffs, worker mobility, and increased work demands, the use of electronic means to find and cultivate a mentor makes e-mentoring more tenable and important than ever.[72]

Responding to the need to foster multiple mentor relationships in the current environment requires individuals to augment traditional, face-to-face mechanisms with electronic means. Preliminary evidence from program evaluations and scholarly work suggests that e-mentoring is extremely beneficial both to mentors and protégés.[73] Aside from freeing up geographic, time, and space constraints, participants in e-mentoring relationships benefit in other important ways. Past research in traditional mentoring has found that particularly early in the relationship, demographic similarity between mentors and protégés is directly related to mentoring effectiveness.[74] More recently, a study examining the importance of gender and racial similarity among mentor–protégé pairs demonstrated that protégés (students) were more likely to initiate relationships with mentors who were similar in gender and race, even though such similarity was unrelated to the type of or amount of mentoring received.[75] One advantage of electronic communication is that it lacks the visual cues that can lead to bias and stereotypes based on demographics or reminders of status differences.[76] This is particularly important as women and minorities— suggested by some to have the greatest need for and difficulty finding mentors[77]— may develop their relationship without the distortion of demographic cues.[78]

Another benefit arising from the fact that e-mentoring relationships are carried out through electronic means is the evidence that mentors and protégés develop trust and disclose more quickly and readily in electronic than in traditional mentoring relationships, possibly due to minimal (if any) role played by visual, demographic differences.[79] Without trust, protégés are less likely to disclose their weaknesses or learning needs and receive the needed support and guidance from their mentors.[80]

E-mentoring is not without its limitations, however. Much has been written about the inability of electronic conversations to convey tone, body language, and other nonverbal cues. E-mentors and e-protégés may be at greater risk for experiencing misunderstandings as compared to their traditional counterparts. Furthermore, in addition to receiving career and psychosocial support from their mentors, protégés often benefit from role modeling—learning through informal observation, job shadowing, feedback on career assignments, discussion of professional challenges, and reviewing samples of their mentors' work.[81] Although protégés might receive some role modeling online, this aspect will likely play a limited role in a virtual mentoring relationship.

Mentors for Hire

Another alternative approach to mentoring involves the paid mentor. Along with rapid rise in the number of small and start-up businesses—particularly among women and minorities—is the popularity of mentors for hire. Starting or running an organization is complex. Knowledge of marketing, laws, operations, human resources, finance, accounting, as well as an ability to interact with and persuade others to realize favorable pricing and treatment from larger, well-established firms is critical. Assuming initial capital can be raised—which is a major feat in itself, few individuals possess the requisite knowledge and experience, a fact borne out by the alarming failure rate of start-ups. With a need for just-in-time knowledge, few developers who can "show you the ropes," and little time to cultivate a trusting and reciprocal relationship, entrepreneurs and small business owners are turning to mentors for hire. These mentors may be part of a formal program or agency that pairs mentors and protégés for a fee or might even be a competitor who agrees to provide training and assistance within agreed-on constraints.[82]

Although not feasible or desirable for all employees, mentors for hire may be a viable alternative to traditional mentoring. One benefit is the protégé's ability to shop around for and "buy" specific guidance without investing time to develop a close, trusting relationship. Reciprocity—in the traditional sense—is not expected. Guidance is offered in exchange for money or a percentage of future profits, depending on the nature of the agreement between the parties. The protégé need not worry about appearances or filtering their mistakes or needs, as the mentor does not control future raises or promotions. Finally, because it is formal, time- and cost-bound, a protégé can more easily (and contractually) discontinue a mentor-for-hire relationship that is ineffective or dysfunctional, something that traditional protégés cannot do.

Some disadvantages—beyond the financial cost—are inherent in this alternative mentoring arrangement. Because protégés have paid for a mentor's advice and support, they may believe that the mentor can and should help them overcome all challenges. For the reasons discussed earlier in this chapter, the likelihood that one mentor, albeit a paid one, can address all of the protégé's needs approaches zero. By deciding to invest in one formal mentor, the protégé may develop a false sense of security in the short run, and a one-sided view of the environment and how best to operate within it in the long run. Either situation may spell disaster for the protégé.

In summary, the current environment requires individuals to seek advice and support of not one but many, diverse mentors. Some relationships may be of the traditional, long-term, master/apprentice variety; others may involve peer, virtual, or paid mentors. Each mentor relationship can and should vary according to protégé's current and future needs and abilities.

IMPLICATIONS AND FUTURE RESEARCH

Since the publication of Kram's seminal book, *Mentoring at Work*, mentoring practice and research has grown and shifted dramatically, reflecting concurrent changes in the business environment. We know much about the nature, function, and outcomes of traditional mentoring. We know less about alternative forms of mentoring that have emerged in response to environmental trends and changes, prompting important implications for scholars and practitioners alike.

1. *Career satisfaction and success are no longer possible without the assistance of multiple mentor relationships that vary in intensity, duration, and function over the course of one's career.* Organizational downsizing, mergers and acquisitions, global competition, and the growth of small entrepreneurial startups have altered the "company man" ideal of stability and upward mobility. Today, people have careers characterized by flexibility, project work across multiple firms, and an emphasis on learning rather than promotions and salary increases.[83] As protégés attempt to navigate within boundaryless or protean

career paths,[84] they must seek a diverse set of mentors who can provide needed visibility, access to opportunities, and help in developing specific skills or competencies from within and outside their functional area, peer group, and organizations.

The notion and purported benefits of using not one but multiple mentors has received a fair amount of attention in the past decade; however, efforts to conceptualize and empirically test the simultaneous impact of multiple mentors on protégé outcomes is lacking.[85] With the exception of one study,[86] mentoring research has focused on one primary relationship or the accumulated mentoring a protégé has received over time.[87] What configuration of how large a mentor network is optimal and during which stage of one's career? What is the best way to measure the collective impact of a mentor network?

Moreover, although multiple mentors may be better than one, individuals may lack the time and emotional energy needed to maintain effective relationships with mentors whose styles, practices, and preferences might differ dramatically. Furthermore, the law of numbers suggests that the more mentor relationships the greater the probability that one or more would be ineffective or dysfunctional.[88] For example, some mentors, feeling threatened by the protégé's success and seeing the protégé as a rival who could threaten their professional or personal image, might subtly (or not so subtly) attempt to sabotage their protégé's career. Other mentors, in demand because of their wisdom and reputation for developing others, may have insufficient time to devote to each protégé. Mentoring scholars Eby and Allen found that 55 percent of the 242 protégés studied reported that their mentors had occasionally neglected them.[89] Still other relationships, though not rising to the level of dysfunctional, may simply be ineffective or fail to live up to the expectations of one or both parties. Individuals' goals may change, or the organization may withdraw its formal support for—or be revealed to be paying lip service to—mentoring activities; situations like these can undermine mentoring's effectiveness.[90] Additional unanswered questions include: How many effective mentors in a network are needed to overcome an ineffective or dysfunctional one? How can the combined effects of mentors (good and bad) at one time be measured and compared to the combined effects of mentors at another time?

2. *Protégés who cultivate mentoring relationships only with those who are formally assigned, in their organization, senior to them, or of the same gender and ethnicity will benefit less than those cultivating a diverse mentor network.* The current business environment—characterized by rapid changes in markets, technology, workforce demographics, and demands—renders traditional mentoring models and processes woefully inadequate. Long-term master–apprentice relationships are incompatible with organizational and career realities and are ill-advised for protégés who seek to continuously learn and update marketable skills. Today's managers are asked to assume more and different roles than a decade ago. Managing virtual employees and teams, demonstrating ethical leadership, building knowledge capital within and outside organizational

boundaries, and helping employees (and themselves) balance often competing work and nonwork demands are some challenges for which few managers are prepared. Relying on one's superior for career advice and development—a traditional mentoring approach—will limit the breadth and depth of information available to the protégé. It may also present potential problems emanating from the power differences and a protégé's need to "look good" to the person in charge of distributing rewards, thereby missing out on learning or developmental experiences. Future research is needed to perhaps identify a contingency model to match protégé needs with mentor types. Scholars might consider applying past research on person–organization fit to inform this area.[91]

While increasing numbers of organizations are implementing formal mentoring programs, protégés should avail themselves of an assigned mentor and also should seek support from informal mentors who might be peers, colleagues, or others who share similar values. Research on formal and informal mentors demonstrates that each type has benefits and drawbacks, and mentors have different motivations for entering into relationships. Additional questions to be explored include: What is the relationship between mentor network diversity and protégé success? Is there an optimal mix of formal/informal, internal/external, or traditional/alternative mentors? Finally, drawing on the growing use of paid mentors, researchers should examine how the processes and outcomes associated with "free" mentor relationships might differ with those of paid mentor relationships.

3. *Electronic or virtual mentoring is a viable means for cultivating one or more mentors in a network; it is especially helpful for women and minorities.* Despite the proliferation and availability of online mentoring Web sites and opportunities, empirical research on this topic has been extremely limited with a few exceptions.[92] As much of the relationship is carried out using electronic, as opposed to face-to-face means, mentors and protégés likely realize benefits and pitfalls unique to this exponentially growing phenomenon. Representing an entirely new context, e-mentoring creates opportunities for scholars and practitioners alike to clarify which traditional mentoring constructs and measures are applicable and which are not. For example, is role modeling a relevant mentoring function to measure in an e-mentoring relationship? Should we consider participants' preferences for face-to-face versus electronic communication? Might preferences for visual versus other (e.g., auditory, kinesthetic) forms of communication or learning be important? Does mentor dysfunctionality look the same in electronic versus traditional relationships? Again, more research is needed.

Without a doubt, mentors remain critical for individual career development and satisfaction. Career changes, precipitated by business environment changes, have necessitated the evolution of alternate forms of mentoring. Researchers and practitioners must continue their efforts to understand the intricacies, predictors, and outcomes of traditional and alternative mentoring relationships that occur separately and simultaneously, as in the case of multiple mentor networks.

NOTES

1. A number of recent articles have demonstrated the benefits of mentoring. See Tammy Allen, Joyce Russell, and Sabine Maetzke, "Formal Peer Mentoring: Factors Related to Protégés Satisfaction and Willingness to Mentor Others," *Group and Organization Management* 22 (1997): 488–507; George Dreher and R. A. Ash, "A Comparative Study of Mentoring among Men and Women in Managerial, Professional, and Technological Positions," *Journal of Applied Psychology* 75 (1990): 539–46; Ellen Fagenson, "The Mentor Advantage: Perceived Career/Job Experiences of Protégés v. Nonprotégés," *Journal of Organizational Behavior* 10 (1989): 309–20; and Terri Scandura and Ralph Viator, "Mentoring in Public Accounting Firms: An Analysis of Mentoring-Protégé Relationships, Mentorship Functions, and Protégé Turnover Intentions," *Accounting, Organizations and Society* 19 (1994): 717–34.

2. R. Alsop, "Playing Well with Others," *Wall Street Journal*, September 9, 2002, p. R11; Albert Bandura, *A Social Learning Theory* (Englewood Cliffs, NJ: Prentice Hall, 1977); and Patricia M. Buhler, "A New Role for Managers: The Move from Directing to Coaching," *Supervision* (October 1, 1998): 16.

3. D. J. Levinson, C. N. Darrow, E. B. Klein, M. A. Levinson and B. McKee, *The Seasons of a Man's Life* (New York: Knopf, 1978).

4. D. M. Hunt and C. Michael, "Mentorship: A Career Training and Development Tool," *Academy of Management Review* 8 (1983): 475–85; Kathy Kram, *Mentoring at Work: Developmental Relationships in Organizational Life* (Glenview, IL: Scott, Foresman, 1985); and J. A. Wilson and N. S. Elman, "Organizational Benefits of Mentoring," *Academy of Management Executive* 4(4) (1990): 88–94.

5. S. Branch, "The 100 Best Companies to Work for in America," *Fortune* 139(1) (1999): 118–30.

6. Kram, *Mentoring at Work*; and Vicki Whiting and Suzanne de Janasz, "Mentoring in the 21st Century: Using the Internet to Build and Network," *Journal of Management Education* 28(3) (2004): 275–93.

7. Kram, *Mentoring at Work*.

8. Suzanne de Janasz, Sherry Sullivan, and Vicki Whiting, "Mentor Networks and Career Success: Lessons for Turbulent Times," *Academy of Management Executive* 17(4) (2003): 78–91.

9. Michael Arthur and Denise Rousseau, "The Boundaryless Career as a New Employment Principle," in M. B. Arthur and D. M. Rousseau, eds., *The Boundaryless Career* (New York: Oxford University Press, 1996), pp. 3–20; and R. Osterman, *Broken Ladders* (New York: Oxford University Press, 1996).

10. Denise Rousseau, *Psychological Contracts in Organizations: Understanding Written and Unwritten Agreements* (Newbury Park, CA: Sage, 1995).

11. Sherry Sullivan, "The Changing Nature of Careers: A Review and Research Agenda," *Journal of Management* 25 (1999): 457–84.

12. Tim Hall, *The Career Is Dead—Long Live the Career* (San Francisco: Jossey-Bass, 1996).

13. Suzanne de Janasz and Sherry Sullivan, "Multiple Mentoring in Academe: Developing the Professorial Network," *Journal of Vocational Behavior* 64(2) (2004): 263–83.

14. See Kenneth Brousseau, Michael Driver, K. Eneroth, and Rickard Larsson, "Career Pandemonium: Realigning Organizations and Individuals," *Academy of Management Executive* 10 (1996): 52–66; and Kathy Kram and Tim Hall, "Mentoring in a Context of Diversity and Turbulence," in E. E. Kossek and S. A. Lobel, eds., *Managing Diversity: Human Resource Strategies for Transforming the Workplace* (Cambridge, MA: Blackwell Business, 1996), pp. 108–36.

15. See, for example, Gayle Baugh and Terri Scandura, "The Effect of Multiple Mentors on Protégé Attitudes toward the Work Setting," *Journal of Social Behavior and Personality* 14 (1999): 503–22; Monica Higgins, "The More, the Merrier? Multiple Developmental Relationships and Work Satisfaction," *Journal of Management Development* 19(4) (2000): 277–96; Higgins and Kram, "Reconceptualizing Mentoring"; Kram, *Mentoring at Work*; and David Thomas and Monica Higgins, "Mentoring and the Boundaryless Career: Lessons from the Minority Experience," in M. B. Arthur and D. M. Rousseau, eds., *The Boundaryless Career: A New Employment Principle for a New Organizational Era* (New York: Oxford University Press, 1996), pp. 268–81.

16. Higgins and Kram, "Reconceptualizing Mentoring."

17. Rosalie Tung, "Building Effective Networks," *Journal of Management Inquiry* 11 (2002): 94–101.

18. Higgins and Kram, "Reconceptualizing Mentoring."

19. S. K. Johnson, G. D. Geroy, and O. V. Griego, "The Mentoring Model Theory: Dimensions in Mentoring Protocols," *Career Development International* 4(7) (1999): 384–91.

20. Peter F. Drucker, *The Practice of Management* (New York: HarperCollins, 1993); Jeffrey Pfeffer, "Competitive Advantage Through People: Unleashing the Power of the Work Force," *Administrative Science Quarterly* 40(3) (1995): 524–27.

21. James Clawson, "Mentoring in the Information Age," *Leadership and Organization Development Journal* 17(3) (1996): 6–15; and G. Pinchot and E. Pinchot, *The End of Bureaucracy and the Rise of the Intelligent Organization* (San Francisco: Berrett-Koehler, 1994).

22. V. Anand, W. Glick, and C. Manz, "Thriving on the Knowledge of Outsiders: Tapping Organizational Social Capital," *Academy of Management Executive* 16 (2002): 87–101.

23. Tim Hall, "Protean Careers of the 21st Century," *Academy of Management Executive* 10(4) (1996): 8–16; Higgins and Kram, "Reconceptualizing Mentoring," p. 267.

24. Melenie Lankau and Terri Scandura, "An Investigation of Personal Learning in Mentoring Relationships: Content, Antecedents, and Consequences," *Academy of Management Journal* 45 (2002): 779–90.

25. Higgins and Kram, "Reconceptualizing Mentoring," p. 267; Kram and Hall, "Mentoring in a Context of Diversity."

26. Troy Nielson, "The Developmental Journey of Mentoring Research and Practice," Presented at the Academy of Management Annual Meeting in Chicago (1999).

27. See, for example, K. Tyler, "Mentoring Programs Link Employees and Experienced Execs," *HR Magazine* 43(5) (1998): 98–103.

28. Robert DeFillippi and Michael Arthur, "The Boundaryless Career: A Competency-Based Perspective," *Journal of Organizational Behavior* 15 (1994): 307–24.

29. de Janasz et al., "Mentor Networks."

30. Baugh and Scandura, "Effect of Multiple Mentors."

31. Belle Rose Ragins, John Cotton, and Janice Miller, "Marginal Mentoring: The Effects and Type of Mentor, Quality of Relationships, and Program Design on Work and Career Attitudes," *Academy of Management Journal* 43(6) (2000): 1177–94; R. J. Burke and C. A. McKeen, "Developing Formal Mentoring Programs in Organizations," *Business Quarterly* 53 (1989): 76–99; Rosabeth Moss Kanter, *Men and Women of the Corporation* (New York: Basic Books, 1977).

32. Belle Rose Ragins, "Barriers to Mentoring: The Female Manager's Dilemma," *Human Relations* 42 (1989): 1–22.

33. Margaret Linehan and James Walsh, "Mentoring Relationships and the Female Managerial Career," *Career Development International* 4(7) (1999): 348–52; p. 350.

34. William Johnston, "Global Workforce 2000: The New World Labor Market," *Harvard Business Review* (1991): 115–26.

35. Ibid.

36. S. D. Friedman and Jeff Greenhaus, *Work and Family—Allies or Enemies?* (New York: Oxford University Press, 2000).

37. de Janasz et al., "Mentor Networks."

38. Wayne Cascio, "Managing a Virtual Workplace," *Academy of Management Executive* 14(3) (2000): 81–90. See also A. M. Townsend, S.M. DeMarie, and A. R. Hendrickson, "Virtual Teams: Technology and the Workplace of the Future," *Academy of Management Executive* 12(3) (1998): 17–29.

39. "Boundaryless Workforce Vary by Workers' Age, Position, Company Size," Ceridian Employer Services, January 27, 1999, Canadian Telework Association Web site.

40. "Telework Facts," International Telework Association and Council, www.telcoa.org/id33.htm (retrieved June 21, 2003).

41. Grant Goss, "Group Encourages Government Workers to Telecommute," Networkworld.com, April 5, 2005; www.networkworld.com/net.worker/news/2005/0405groupencou.html (retrieved September 10, 2005).

42. C. Sandlund, "Remote Control: As the Virtual Workforce Grows, So Does the Challenge for Managers. Here's How to Keep it Together," *Business Week* 27 (March 2000): F14.

43. Higgins and Kram, "Reconceptualizing Mentoring."

44. See, for example, Baugh and Scandura, "Effect of Multiple Mentors"; Higgins, "The More, the Merrier"; Higgins and Kram, "Reconceptualizing Mentoring"; Kram, *Mentoring at Work*; and Thomas and Higgins, "Mentoring and the Boundaryless Career."

45. Quoted in de Janasz et al., "Mentor Networks."

46. Kram, *Mentoring at Work*.

47. Tung, "Building Effective Networks."

48. Higgins and Kram, "Reconceptualizing Mentoring."

49. Linda Holbeche, "Peer Mentoring: The Challenges and Ppportunities," *Career Development International* 1(7) (1996): 24–27.

50. Kathy Kram and Lynn Isabella, "Mentoring Alternatives: The Role of Peer Relationships in Career Development," *Academy of Management Journal* 28 (1985): 110–32.

51. Ibid.

52. See for example Kram and Higgins, "Reconceptualizing Mentoring"; Lillian T. Eby, "Alternative Forms of Mentoring in Changing Organizational Environments: A Conceptual Extension of the Mentoring Literature," *Journal of Vocational Behavior* 51 (1997): 125–44; and Kram and Hall, "Mentoring in a Context of Diversity."

53. de Janasz et al., "Mentor Networks," p. 85.

54. Ragins et al., "Marginal Mentoring," p. 1179.

55. Todd Smart, quoted in J. H. Maxwell and M. Hopkins, "Who Do You Call When No One Has the Answers? Where the Smartest CEOs Turn for Guidance and Perspective When Company Building Gets Personal," *Inc.* (September 2002): 38–45.

56. Eby, "Alternative Forms of Mentoring."

57. de Janasz et al., "Mentor Networks"; Holbeche, "Peer Mentoring."

58. Sullivan, "Changing Nature of Careers."

59. Eby, "Alternative Forms of Mentoring"; Kram, *Mentoring at Work.*

60. Kram, *Mentoring at Work.*; Kram and Isabella, "Mentoring Alternatives."

61. Eby, "Alternative Forms of Mentoring."

62. Ibid.; and Richard Hackman, "Group Effectiveness in Organizations," in M. D. Dunnette and L. M. Hough, eds., *Handbook of Industrial and Organizational Psychology* (Palo Alto, CA: Consulting Academic Press, 1992), vol. 3, 199–267.

63. J. Rymer, "Only Connect: Transforming Ourselves and Our Discipline through Co-Mentoring," *Journal of Business Communication* 39(3) (2002): 342–63.

64. Ellen Ensher, Susan Murphy, and Sherry Sullivan, "Reel Women: Lessons from Female TV Executives on Managing Work and Real Life," *Academy of Management Executive* 16(2) (2002): 106–21.

65. T. J. Carter, "The Importance of Talk to Midcareer Women's Development: A Collaborative Inquiry," *Journal of Business Communication* 39(1) (2002): 55–91.

66. Wayne Baker, *Achieving Success through Social Capital: Tapping Hidden Resources in Your Personal and Business Networks* (San Francisco: Jossey-Bass, 2000).

67. de Janasz et al., "Mentor Networks."

68. For a review, see Monica Forret and Sherry Sullivan, "A Balanced Scorecard Approach to Networking and Career Development," *Organizational Dynamics* 31(3) (2002): 1–15.

69. P. B. Single and Carol Muller, "When E-Mail and Mentoring Unite: The Implementation of Nationwide Electronic Mentoring Program," in L. Stromei, ed., *Implementing Successful Coaching and Mentoring Programs* (Cambridge, MA: American Society for Training and Development, 2001), pp. 107–22; and Ellen Ensher, Christian Heun, and Anita Blanchard, "Online Mentoring and Computer-Mediated Communication: New Directions in Research," *Journal of Vocational Behavior* 63(2) (2003): 264–88.

70. Ensher et al., "Online Mentoring."

71. R. Hof, "The Power of Us," *BusinessWeek* (June 20, 2005): 75.

72. Ellen Ensher, Suzanne de Janasz, and Christian Heun, "E-Mentoring: Virtual Relationships and Real Benefits," manuscript under review.

73. Whiting and de Janasz, "Mentoring in the 21st Century"; C. W. Lewis, *International Telementoring Report* (2002), www.telementor.org (retrieved March 5, 2004); and MentorNet's 2002-03 *MentorNet Evaluation Report* (2003), www.mentornet.net/documents/files/Eval.0203.Report.pdf (retrieved March 5, 2004).

74. David Thomas, "The Impact of Race on Manager's Experiences of Developmental Relationships (Mentorship and Sponsorship): An Intra-Organizational Study," *Journal of Organizational Behavior* 11 (1990): 479–92.

75. D. B. Turban, Thomas Dougherty, and F. K. Lee, "Gender, Race, and Perceived Similarity Effects in Developmental Relationships: The Moderating Role of Relationship Duration," *Journal of Vocational Behavior* 61 (2002): 240–62.

76. L. Sproull and S. Kiesler, "Computers, Networks, and Work," *Scientific American* 265(3) (1999): 116–23.

77. Ragins, "Barriers to Mentoring"; and Thomas, "The Impact of Race."

78. Ensher et al., "Online Mentoring"; and Betti Hamilton and Terri Scandura, "E-Mentoring: Implications for Organizational Learning and Development in a Wired World," *Organizational Dynamics* 31(4) (2003): 388–402.

79. S. Turkle, *Life on the Screen* (New York: Simon & Schuster, 1995); and Ensher et al., "Virtual Relationships and Real Benefits."

80. de Janasz et al., "Mentor Networks."

81. C. R. Bell, *Managers as Mentors* (San Francisco: Berrett-Koehler, 1996).

82. For a review of one such program, see Leonard Bisk, "Formal Entrepreneurial Mentoring: The Efficacy of Third Party Managed Programs," *Career Development International* 7(2) (2002): 262–70; also see Shane McLaughlin, "New Business Owners Hire Experienced Mentors in Their Fields to Show Them the Ropes," *Inc.* December (2002).

83. Arthur and Rousseau, *Boundaryless Career.*

84. Ibid.; Hall, *The Career Is Dead.*

85. de Janasz and Sullivan, "Multiple Mentoring in Academe," p. 278.

86. Baugh and Scandura, "Effect of Multiple Mentors."

87. Higgins and Kram, "Reconceptualizing Mentoring."

88. Scandura, "Dysfunctional Mentoring."

89. Lillian Eby and Tammy Allen, "Further Investigation of Protégés' Negative Mentoring Experiences: Patterns and Outcomes," *Group & Organization Management* 27(4) (2002): 456–79.

90. de Janasz et al., "Mentor Networks."

91. See, for example, Jennifer Chatman, "Matching People and Organizations: Selection and Socialization in Public Accounting Firms," *Administrative Science Quarterly* 36 (1991): 459–84.

92. Single and Muller, "When E-Mail and Mentoring Unite"; Ensher et al., "Virtual Relationships and Real Benefits."

8

Impact of Social Networks on the Advancement of Women and Racial/Ethnic Minority Groups

Monica L. Forret

There have been glimmers of progress in U.S. corporations for women and members of racial and ethnic minority groups. In 2002, *Fortune* published its first list of the 50 Most Powerful Black Executives in America.[1] The Executive Leadership Council, a professional network for senior African American executives in Fortune 500 firms, has grown from 19 members in 1986 to over 340 members today, with women making up one-third of the membership. Although the signs of upward movement are becoming more visible, the pace is slow. For instance, although women account for about half of all managerial and professional positions, they hold only 8 percent of executive vice president positions and higher at Fortune 500 companies, and only 5 percent are among the top five highest paid for each company.[2]

A number of explanations exist for the lack of upward advancement for women and minorities. A Catalyst study found that both Fortune 1000 CEOs and women executives agreed that lack of line experience was a major factor preventing women's upward movement. Other major barriers cited include exclusion from informal networks, negative stereotypes about women, lack of accountability of top leaders for advancing women, lack of role models, lack of mentoring, and lack of awareness of organizational politics.[3] Constraints posed by social networks can help explain the obstacles women and minorities face that result in their restricted upward movement in organizations. The constraints come in a variety of forms, such as increased difficulty in forming social networks and lower levels of influence held by the members of their social networks. Consistent with Ragins's definition, the term *minority* will be used here to refer to those groups traditionally lacking power in organizations—including women and members of racial and ethnic groups.[4]

In this chapter, I will first discuss the need for more attention to the social capital of minorities and important factors to consider in building social networks. Second, I explore three major barriers minorities face in developing their social networks. Third, the success of three strategies—mentoring, networking, and network groups—minorities use for altering their social networks to improve their opportunities in organizations will be examined. Finally, suggestions for individuals and organizations to help women and minorities improve their social networks to increase their advancement prospects will be proposed.

HUMAN CAPITAL IS NOT ENOUGH:
THE NEED FOR SOCIAL CAPITAL

Human capital represents the investments we make in ourselves to help us become and stay marketable. Our education, prior work experiences, training, knowledge, skills, and abilities all represent critical sources of human capital that increase our value in the workplace.[5] Although human capital theory assumes that similar investments will pay off equally, minorities do not reap the same rewards from their investments as white males.[6]

Examples of the disparity abound. Stroh, Brett, and Reilly found that women lagged behind men with respect to salary progression and frequency of job transfers in a sample of 1,029 male and female managers even though women had done "all the right stuff," such as obtaining similar education as men and not moving in and out of the workforce.[7] A follow-up survey conducted on this sample by Brett and Stroh showed that only male managers benefited in terms of salary progression by pursuing an external labor market strategy.[8] Extending this finding to include race as well as gender, Dreher and Cox showed that an external labor market strategy increased compensation for white males only.[9] Controlling for many human capital variables, Landau found females to be rated lower than males and African Americans and Asians to be rated lower than whites in promotion potential in a sample of 1,268 managers and professionals from a Fortune 500 company.[10] Furthermore, training seems more beneficial for the advancement of males than females; and women, but not men, who experience a mid-career gap suffer drawbacks in attaining higher management levels.[11]

Whereas career development efforts have tended to focus on improving human capital, managers and professionals need to evaluate their social capital as well. In his book *Achieving Success through Social Capital*, Wayne Baker describes social capital as the resources available to an individual as a result of one's personal network of contacts. Social capital can provide new ideas, timely information, job opportunities, business leads, influence, and social support.[12] Social capital is a valuable resource that gives individuals a formidable career advantage.[13] For instance, Seibert, Kraimer, and Liden found that the structure of an individual's network provided access to information, resources, and career sponsorship, which in turn were related to longer term career success outcomes (i.e., current salary, promotions, and career satisfaction).[14]

Moreover, social capital is more difficult to imitate than human capital. Similar education, training, and work experiences are easier to obtain and replicate than relationships with others.[15] The individuals we know, the quality of our relationships, and the resources available through our relationships are a unique, valuable, nonreplicable asset. One explanation for the slow rate of advancement for minorities is that within organizations members of the majority group — typically white males — tend to possess larger inventories of valuable social capital.

BUILDING SOCIAL NETWORKS

Four important factors to consider in building social networks to gain access to social capital are the size of the network, strength of the tie, pattern of ties, and resources of the tie. *Size* refers to the number of members in a network. To illustrate the importance of size, Morrison's study of the socialization of auditors showed that having a larger friendship network was positively related to social integration, and having a larger information network was associated with increased organizational knowledge and task mastery.[16] In their study of managers and professionals in a high-technology company, Podolny and Baron found that the size of one's strategic information network was positively related to number of promotions.[17] In general, having a larger network translates into more individuals to turn to for friendship, information, resources, and advice.

Strength of the tie refers to the degree of closeness that characterizes a relationship. For instance, strong ties are denoted by frequent contact, a degree of intimacy, and emotional investment in the relationship.[18] According to Granovetter, because our strong ties (i.e., close friends) tend to know one another and share information, our weak ties (i.e., acquaintances) are more likely to be a richer source of unique information benefits (such as job openings). His research concluded that job seekers with weak ties were more successful in finding jobs than those with strong ties.[19] However, recent research has questioned the level of assistance provided by strong versus weak ties. In a study of new product development teams, Hansen showed that weak interunit ties were helpful for gaining quick access to routine information, but strong ties were necessary for obtaining complex knowledge.[20] Strong ties may be more important for the transfer of sensitive or complex information than weak ties due to the higher risk and effort involved.[21]

Burt's structural hole theory focuses on the pattern of ties in a network, that is, whether the members of an individual's social network are connected to one another. A structural hole exists when there is no connection between two members of a social network. Having structural holes in one's network is beneficial in two important ways. First, members of a network who do not know one another are more likely to provide access to diverse information. Second, the absence of a relationship between network members offers an opportunity to control the flow of information between them, which may be used to one's advantage.[22] In addition to Burt, Podolny and Baron found that structural holes were associated with upward mobility, and Rodan and Galunic showed that they were related to greater managerial performance.[23]

Finally, the resources of a tie refer to the benefits that may be derived from a relationship. These benefits may take a wide variety of forms, including information, friendship, materials/services, and influence.[24] In particular, relationships with high-status individuals have the potential to provide valued outcomes. To illustrate, in their study of job seekers, Lin, Ensel, and Vaughn found that the status of the contact had a strong positive effect on the prestige of the attained job, indicating the ability of powerful contacts to exert influence on one's behalf.[25]

To summarize, network size, tie strength, pattern of ties, and resources of ties are critical factors to consider in building one's social network. However, minorities experience unique barriers in their attempts to develop their social networks, which will now be considered.

BARRIERS MINORITIES FACE IN BUILDING THEIR SOCIAL NETWORKS

Three explanations for the difficulties minorities experience in building their social networks are centered on: (1) the similarity-attraction paradigm, (2) tokenism theory, and (3) existing organizational structures.

Similarity-Attraction Paradigm

Using Byrne's similarity-attraction paradigm, those who are considered similar on ascriptive characteristics (e.g., gender, race, ethnicity) are likely to perceive greater interpersonal similarities, which in turn leads to increased attraction and more frequent communication.[26] Gender, racial, and ethnic similarities facilitate interactions with others like oneself. Similarity on these factors increases the likelihood of shared values, beliefs, and attitudes, which helps reduce uncertainty and create trusting relationships. For example, Tsui and O'Reilly found that subordinates in same-gender superior–subordinate dyads were rated higher in perceived effectiveness and liking by their superiors and experienced lower role conflict and ambiguity than subordinates in mixed-gender dyads.[27]

According to March and Simon, similarity on ascribed characteristics influences the "language compatibility" between two people and makes communication easier.[28] Roberts and O'Reilly found that participants in a communication network tend to have higher job satisfaction, more organizational commitment, and higher job performance than isolates.[29] Furthermore, by communicating frequently, individuals develop similar attitudes and beliefs, which facilitate their integration into the organization.[30]

However, the similarity-attraction paradigm poses a problem for minorities in organizations in that the demographic makeup offers fewer opportunities for interactions with others like themselves based on gender, race, or ethnicity.[31] For example, based on a sample of managers from four Fortune 500 companies, Ibarra found that minorities had fewer same-race ties and fewer strong ties than white managers.[32] This lack of similarity affects the availability of social support for minority employees. Furthermore, given that minorities have less power in organizations, ties to other minorities are less instrumental in their ability to provide access to valued resources. Therefore, minorities have to seek out dissimilar others to obtain what they need. This necessity was illustrated in Ibarra's study of an advertising firm, in which men developed both instrumental and expressive (i.e., friendship) contacts with other males, whereas females developed instrumental contacts with men and expressive contacts with women.[33]

Tokenism Theory

According to Kanter, the presence of a small, easily identifiable minority group of individuals (referred to as tokens) results in increased performance pressures and boundary heightening. Given that minorities are highly visible in organizations, they face added pressures to perform. If a minority employee performs poorly, it is more likely to be known throughout the organization. This may encourage majority employees to distance themselves from minorities to avoid negative perceptions that association might convey. Furthermore, the behavior of a minority employee is likely to be construed as being symbolic for the group. For example, if a woman fails at her position, majority members are likely to view this as evidence that women as a group are unable to handle those types of jobs.[34]

Boundary heightening occurs due to polarization that magnifies distinctions between minority and majority groups. Boundary heightening results in an increase in stereotyping and isolation of minorities from areas where informal socializing and politicking take place.[35] To illustrate, Ely found that sex-role stereotypes were exaggerated in law firms dominated by men, in contrast to firms with a more balanced gender representation.[36] Furthermore, Lyness and Thompson found that female executives were more likely than male executives to report lack of culture fit and being excluded from informal networks as barriers to their career advancement.[37] These results support the research on organizational interaction networks in that minorities, due to their token status, have less access to members of the dominant power structures.[38]

According to Baron and Pfeffer, white males are motivated to preserve the ingroup/outgroup distinctions to protect their status and privilege in organizations.[39] Applying tokenism theory to the building of social networks, one can surmise that there will be a tendency for white males to avoid developing relationships with minority employees, resulting in smaller social networks comprised of less instrumental contacts.

Existing Organizational Structures

An individual's position in the organizational structure influences that person's social network.[40] The hierarchy of authority indicated by an organization chart determines the superior and subordinates one interacts with to facilitate vertical coordination. Furthermore, the design and flow of the work necessitates coordination with other individuals, and changes in the technology used have been found to affect communication patterns.[41] To the extent that the job held calls for coordination with individuals from a variety of work units, there is more opportunity to develop personal relationships, which may influence network size, the strength of ties, the pattern of ties, and the resources available.

Brass and colleagues also argue that the location of a person in the physical and temporal space of an organization influences interaction patterns.[42] We tend to communicate with individuals who are in close proximity to us and who work the same hours we do. One drawback of telecommuting and other types of flexible work arrangements (which are frequently marketed to women) is the negative impact on informal learning and relationship development due to the lower rates of interaction with members of the organization.[43] Similarly, Meyerson and Fletcher emphasize the importance of time boundaries in organizations. If strategic decisions are frequently made outside of normal working hours (e.g., while socializing after work), women are less likely to have input into them due to the need to attend to child care and other responsibilities at home.[44]

Also, as individuals move into different positions in an organization, their social networks change. New relationships must be developed to meet the demands required by the new position, and former relationships may erode through nonuse.[45] Starting a new position poses an extra challenge for minorities in that they are more likely to have to develop relationships with others who are dissimilar on the basis of gender, race, or ethnic status. Therefore, organizational decision makers may believe that promoting a minority will result in a slower transition and reduced levels of effectiveness.

Furthermore, Pfeffer states that examining the job structure to ensure that minorities are located in jobs that lead to higher positions in the organization is crucial.[46] Because lack of line experience is a major factor preventing upward movement, it is important for minorities to obtain jobs that have career ladders.[47] Although minorities may hold staff positions that call for extensive interaction with others, those holding line positions with profit and loss responsibility have access to the most powerful decision makers and opportunities to prove their value to the organization. Competition for such line positions is intense and political. Having a powerful sponsor in the upper levels of an organization advocating on one's behalf provides a strong advantage to obtaining these jobs. Minorities are much less likely to have such sponsors.

In sum, research shows that multiple forces help maintain existing power structures. What is being done to address this situation? Next, I discuss the success of three strategies women and minorities are using to alter their social networks and improve their opportunities in organizations, namely, mentoring, networking, and network groups.

MENTORING

Mentoring has been defined as a relationship whereby a more senior, experienced individual is committed to providing developmental assistance and guidance to a less experienced protégé.[48] Obtaining a powerful mentor represents the addition of a strong tie to an individual's social network that provides access to valued resources.[49] Mentors provide protégés with career development and psychosocial support.[50] They nominate protégés for challenging and visible assignments and provide coaching to help ensure that their protégés succeed. By introducing protégés to influential individuals, mentors confer a sense of legitimacy on their protégés.[51] Mentors serve as role models for protégés and affirm their worthiness and identity by offering counseling and friendship. The benefits of mentoring for protégés as a result of such assistance have been well established. Protégés have greater opportunities and higher compensation and receive more promotions than those who have not received mentoring.[52] Protégés also are more satisfied with their jobs and careers and have greater intentions to remain in their organizations.[53]

Many researchers have discussed barriers that women and minorities face in finding potential mentors.[54] Given that the upper echelons of organizations are dominated by white males, there is a lack of role models available to serve as mentors. The few women and minorities in the upper ranks may feel overwhelmed by the number of individuals who might desire a mentoring relationship, and cross-race and cross-gender relationships are more difficult to develop. Cross-gender and cross-race mentoring relationships are highly visible, which might invoke feelings of envy and accusations of favoritism by peers, especially if the protégé is perceived as less competent.[55] In addition, the high visibility of the relationship makes it more likely that a failure by the protégé will be known in the organization and may reflect poorly on the mentor. Furthermore, men and women may avoid participating in a cross-gender mentoring relationship due to concerns that a sexual relationship might develop or to avoid damaging gossip and rumors that a sexual relationship exists.[56]

However, even though these barriers are present, several studies show no differences between men and women in the number of mentoring relationships or the amount of mentoring received.[57] According to Thomas, due to the scarcity of demographically similar relationships in an organization, minorities are more likely to search outside their organization to find individuals willing to provide developmental assistance.[58] Although benefits such as career advice and acceptance can be gained from these relationships, a mentor outside one's organization is unlikely to wield the type of power and influence needed to help the protégé land prestigious assignments and move up the career ladder in his or her organization.[59]

Some evidence suggests that cross-gender or cross-race relationships yield fewer benefits than those accruing to white male protégés with white male mentors. Although Dreher and Cox identified no gender or racial differences in forming mentoring relationships, they found preferences for similarity. African American, Hispanic, and female MBAs were less likely to establish mentoring relationships with white male mentors, despite a compensation advantage for those with white male mentors.[60] In his examination of cross-race mentoring relationships, Thomas found that protégés receive more psychosocial support from mentors of the same race.[61] Furthermore, some research suggests that role modeling is more likely to occur in same-gender mentoring relationships.[62] The increased psychosocial functions protégés receive in same-gender, same-race relationships are not surprising given the greater social identification based on sex and race.[63]

Given the widespread benefits of mentoring and the additional barriers women and minorities face in developing a mentoring relationship, organizations have implemented formal mentoring programs to ensure that mentoring relationships are accessible to employees.[64] However, several studies show that formal mentoring programs tend to be ineffective for advancing a protégé's career.[65] Noe argues that one should not expect the same benefits from both formal and informal mentoring relationships because the latter develop naturally based on mutual attraction and interest.[66] In contrast, formal mentoring programs tend to be for a limited time period (such as a year) in which mentors and protégés are paired through a matching process that may not be based on mutual identification given the shortage of mentors in organizations.[67] For strong sponsorship to occur, the mentoring relationship needs to be characterized by identification and trust between the mentor and protégé, confidence in the mentor of the protégé's abilities and potential, and a commitment to helping the protégé succeed. Although formal mentoring programs may provide some benefits to minorities, it is unlikely that they will receive the powerful backing an informal mentor can provide.

NETWORKING

In light of the difficulties in finding a high-ranking senior manager to take a strong interest in one's development, and given the current boundaryless work environment characterized by frequent movement within and across organizations, a new focus has emerged on forming multiple developmental relationships to support one's career.[68] Multiple developmental relationships build on Kram's concept of the relationship constellation, which proposes that career and psychosocial support can come from a multitude of people both within and outside the organization.[69] Research has shown that having multiple developmental relationships is associated with greater work satisfaction, career progress, and retention in the organization.[70]

Individuals engage in networking to help build developmental relationships that in turn improve their social networks by influencing the size of their networks, their pattern of ties, and the resources available through their ties. Networking behaviors are proactive attempts by individuals to develop and maintain relationships with others for the purpose of mutual benefit in their work or career.[71] Networking expands an individual's relationship constellation by forming relationships with those internal to the organization (e.g., peers) and those external to it (e.g., members of professional associations).[72] The relationships formed through networking tend to be characterized by less interaction and intimacy than informal mentoring relationships, and hence are considered to be weaker ties.[73]

Forret and Sullivan advocate taking a strategic approach to networking, in that individuals should determine their career goals; assess their current social capital; align their networking efforts accordingly to reach individuals in their organization, profession, or community; and invest the time, energy, and effort to develop mutually beneficial relationships.[74] Developing interpersonal relationships through networking is considered to be a specific competency vital for managing one's career.[75]

Networking is related to career outcomes of managers, such as promotions and salary progression.[76] Forret and Dougherty identified five types of networking behaviors: maintaining external contacts, socializing, engaging in professional activities, participating in community, and increasing internal visibility.[77] In a study examining the relationship between types of networking behaviors and career outcomes for men and women, Forret and Dougherty found increasing internal visibility to be significantly related to number of promotions and total compensation for men, but not for women. Also, a marginal relationship between engaging in professional activities and total compensation was found. However, the relationship was positive for men and negative for women.[78] Although women make attempts to increase their internal visibility, the work assignments and taskforces in which they participate may be less prestigious than those of men, given their lack of access to members of the organization's power structure.[79] With regard to engaging in professional activities, organizations may assign a higher value to the professional involvement of men than of women.[80]

The few studies examining gender differences in networking behaviors show little difference between men and women. In the Gould and Penley study, men reported engaging in networking (measured via the extent to which respondents reported building a network of contacts and friendships in the organization) more than women, but the result was marginally significant.[81] Similarly, Forret and Dougherty found few differences. Men were more likely to engage in socializing behaviors than women; however, a subsequent analysis comparing men with single women found no difference in socializing behaviors.[82] Because married women tend to carry a disproportionate share of family and household responsibilities, it is not surprising that little time is left for socializing with colleagues outside of work.[83]

Although writings on protean careers stress the importance of networking, especially because the burden of responsibility for one's career has shifted from the organization to the individual, research on the benefits of networking for the careers of women and minorities is lacking.[84] The little existing evidence shows women benefit less than men from networking efforts. One explanation may be that because women's contacts are more likely to be at lower levels in organizations, they have less ability to provide influence and access to resources. Studies examining the success of networking behaviors of minorities need to be conducted.

NETWORK GROUPS

Network groups are defined as intraorganizational groups composed of members who share a common social identity (e.g., gender, race, ethnicity) who have formally organized themselves to provide support for their members.[85] African American employees at Xerox organized one of the first network groups. After an African American colleague left the company in 1971, a group of African American employees started meeting to practice their presentation skills, share sales techniques, and provide tips for navigating the corporate culture to help each other succeed.[86]

According to Catalyst, 33 percent of Fortune 100 companies have women's networks, including IBM, Procter & Gamble, Ford, Merck, Kraft, and 3M. Organizations with women's networks are much more likely to have other network groups (e.g., based on race or sexual orientation) than companies without women's networks.[87] Network groups provide networking opportunities, social support, and career development for their members. They also advise senior management and human resource managers on issues that concern their members and attempt to create positive organizational change.[88] In a survey of 20 HR managers, 70 Executive Leadership Council members, and 397 National Black MBA Association members, similar findings regarding the effectiveness of network groups were found. Networks groups were consistently rated as most effective at providing social support, informal advice, support for younger employees, and voicing concerns to management.[89]

Network groups meet regularly, often on company premises, where they hold a variety of events (e.g., speakers, seminars, workshops, career development sessions) for their members. Network groups are a means by which minorities can find and meet other minorities in their organization, thereby affecting the number, strength, pattern, and resources of their network ties. This reduces feelings of isolation, and allows them to act as "majority" members for a period of time.[90] In a sample of members of the National Black MBA Association, respondents with network groups in their organization reported more support and ties with other African Americans, were more likely to receive support from a mentor, and felt they were better able to interact with white mentors.[91] The presence of a network group was positively related to optimism about career progress in the organization, although this relationship was mediated by the presence of a mentor. Network groups also may influence job performance. According to Catalyst, sales for women brokers who started a network group at Dain Rauscher increased 19.2 percent compared with 5 percent for the rest of the firm.[92]

There is some concern that forming a network group will promote backlash by the majority members in an organization. As Friedman discussed, a voluntarily formed group of minorities signals that social identity makes a difference. Majority group members may see a network group as a threat to the existing power structure, and its existence may result in heightened tension and avoidance behaviors. Those who might benefit from participation in a network group may choose to decline membership over fears that it will highlight their social identity and negatively influence their career progress.[93] In a Catalyst survey of management representatives and leaders of the women's network at 132 companies, close to 75 percent of both groups indicated the presence of some minor negative reactions to the network group, such as males feeling threatened, concerns over elitism, women's fears about how participation might affect their careers, conflicts between the group's and HR management's role, and lack of management support for the network group. However, 20 percent expressed no negative responses, and only a very few experienced significant backlash.[94] In *Creating Women's Networks*, Catalyst outlines steps for creating or revamping women's networks and advocates finding the right goals for the network, responding to member needs, and making positive contributions to the organization.[95]

Overall, although network groups can provide a variety of benefits to their members, their ability to advance minorities to upper organizational levels may be limited due to the lack of interaction with members of the majority group. Research is needed to examine the linkages between network groups and advancement of minorities.

SUGGESTIONS FOR IMPROVING SOCIAL NETWORKS

The results of proactive attempts such as mentoring, networking, and network groups that minorities use to alter their networks have been somewhat successful in providing work-related and psychosocial benefits. However, the analysis of these strategies shows they may not attain the desired results in terms of advancing minorities into the upper ranks of organizations. To get past the barriers presented by the similarity-attraction paradigm, tokenism theory, and existing organizational structures, organizations need to ensure opportunities for substantive interaction take place between the organization's minority and majority members.

As Laurence Prusak and Don Cohen discuss in their book, *In Good Company: How Social Capital Makes Organizations Work*, social capital is created when employees have the opportunity to participate in "real work" with one another that accomplishes organizational objectives.[96] Sponsoring the occasional social gathering to provide opportunities for majority and minority employees to interact is not sufficient for developing the types of trusting relationships that are crucial for successful organizational functioning. In the context of performing real work, employees can discover similar values, attitudes, and beliefs held by individuals who initially appear dissimilar. Hence, employees are able to look beyond initial differences and communicate more effectively with each other.

Collaborative relationships need to be developed between majority and minority employees. Collaborative relationships are characterized by knowledge of each person's expertise, a willingness to engage in active and timely problem solving, and trust.[97] Building social networks composed of individuals diverse in gender, race, and ethnic background increases the likelihood of receiving novel ideas and a greater variety of feedback, which should enhance knowledge sharing and creation.[98]

Furthermore, Meyerson and Fletcher advocate experimenting with incremental structural changes to eradicate sources of inequity. By questioning organizational procedures and assumptions, practices that undermine equity for women and minorities can be modified or removed.[99] For example, requirements for a line position that are unnecessary for performance but eliminate minorities from the applicant pool can be dropped. By providing women with advancement opportunities, battling gender stereotypes, and rewarding managers based on achieving diversity goals, Georgia-Pacific increased its percentage of top women executives from 9 percent in 2001 to 29 percent in 2004.[100]

Breaking down the barriers to advancement for women and minorities must become a corporate imperative, not just because it is the ethical step to take but also because it is good for business. A recent study by Catalyst of 353 Fortune 500 companies found that those with the highest representation of senior women had a 35 percent higher return on equity and a 34 percent higher return to shareholders than those companies with the lowest number of high-ranking women.[101] Perhaps organizations with higher proportions of minorities in upper management ranks are taking better advantage of both their employees' human and social capital, a worthy goal for every company.

NOTES

1. Cora Daniels, "The Most Powerful Black Executives in America," *Fortune* (July 22, 2002): 60–80.

2. Betsy Morris, Kate Bonamici, Susan M. Kaufman, and Patricia Neering, "How Corporate America Is Betraying Women," *Fortune* (January 10, 2005): 65–74.

3. Sheila Wellington, Marcia Brumit Kropf, and Paulette R. Gerkovich, "What's Holding Women Back?," *Harvard Business Review* (June 2003): 18–19.

4. Belle Rose Ragins, "Diversified Mentoring Relationships in Organizations: A Power Perspective," *Academy of Management Review* 22 (1997): 482–521.

5. Gary S. Becker, *Human Capital* (Chicago: University of Chicago Press, 1975); Francine D. Blau and Marianne A. Ferber, *The Economics of Women, Men and Work* (Englewood Cliffs, NJ: Prentice Hall, 1987).

6. Ann M. Morrison and Mary Ann Von Glinow, "Women and Minorities in Management," *American Psychologist* 45 (1990): 200–208.

7. Linda K. Stroh, Jeanne M. Brett, and Anne H. Reilly, "All the Right Stuff: A Comparison of Female and Male Managers' Career Progression," *Journal of Applied Psychology* 77 (1992): 251–60.

8. Jeanne M. Brett and Linda K. Stroh, "Jumping Ship: Who Benefits from an External Labor Market Career Strategy?," *Journal of Applied Psychology* 82 (1997): 331–41.

9. George F. Dreher and Taylor H. Cox Jr., "Labor Market Mobility and Cash Compensation: The Moderating Effects of Race and Gender," *Academy of Management Journal* 43 (2000): 890–900.

10. Jacqueline Landau, "The Relationship of Race and Gender to Managers' Ratings of Promotion Potential," *Journal of Organizational Behavior* 16 (1995): 391–400.

11. Phyllis Tharenou, Shane Latimer, and Denise Conroy, "How Do You Make It to the Top? An Examination of Influences on Women's and Men's Managerial Advancement," *Academy of Management Journal* 37 (1994): 899–931; Joy A. Schneer and Frieda Reitman, "The Interrupted Managerial Career Path: A Longitudinal Study of MBAs," *Journal of Vocational Behavior* 51 (1997): 411–34.

12. Wayne Baker, *Achieving Success through Social Capital: Tapping the Hidden Resources in Your Personal and Business Networks* (San Francisco: Jossey-Bass, 2000).

13. Paul S. Adler and Seok-Woo Kwon, "Social Capital: Prospects for a New Concept," *Academy of Management Review* 27 (2002): 17–40.

14. Scott E. Seibert, Maria L. Kraimer, and Robert C. Liden, "A Social Capital Theory of Career Success," *Academy of Management Journal* 44 (2001): 219–37.

15. Monica L. Forret and Sherry E. Sullivan, "A Balanced Scorecard Approach to Networking: A Guide to Successfully Navigating Career Changes," *Organizational Dynamics* 31 (2002): 245–58.

16. Elizabeth Wolfe Morrison, "Newcomers' Relationships: The Role of Social Network Ties During Socialization," *Academy of Management Journal* 45 (2002): 1149–60.

17. Joel M. Podolny and James N. Baron, "Resources and Relationships: Social Networks and Mobility in the Workplace," *American Sociological Review* 62 (1997): 673–93.

18. Mark S. Granovetter, "The Strength of Weak Ties," *American Journal of Sociology* 78 (1973): 1360–80.

19. Mark S. Granovetter, *Getting a Job: A Study of Contacts and Careers* (Cambridge, MA: Harvard University Press, 1974).

20. Morten T. Hansen, "The Search-Transfer Problem: The Role of Weak Ties in Sharing Knowledge across Organizational Subunits," *Administrative Science Quarterly* 44 (1999): 82–111.

21. Marc-David L. Seidel, Jeffrey T. Polzer, and Katherine J. Stewart, "Friends in High Places: The Effects of Social Networks on Discrimination in Salary Negotiations," *Administrative Science Quarterly* 45 (2000): 1–24.

22. Ronald S. Burt, *Structural Holes: The Social Structure of Competition* (Cambridge, MA: Harvard University Press, 1992).

23. Ibid.; Podolny and Baron, "Resources and Relationships"; Simon Rodan and Charles Galunic, "More than Network Structure: How Knowledge Heterogeneity Influences Managerial Performance and Innovativeness," *Strategic Management Journal* 25 (2004): 541–62.

24. Noel M. Tichy, Michael L. Tushman, and Charles Fombrun, "Social Network Analysis for Organizations," *Academy of Management Review* 4 (1979): 507–19.

25. Nan Lin, Walter M. Ensel, and John C. Vaughn, "Social Resources and Strength of Ties: Structural Factors in Occupational Status Attainment," *American Sociological Review* 46 (1981): 393–405.

26. Donn E. Byrne, *The Attraction Paradigm* (New York: Academic Press, 1971); Karlene H. Roberts and Charles A. O'Reilly III, "Some Correlations of Communication Roles in Organizations," *Academy of Management Journal* 22 (1979): 42–57.

27. Anne S. Tsui and Charles A. O'Reilly III, "Beyond Simple Demographic Effects: The Importance of Relational Demography in Superior-Subordinate Dyads," *Academy of Management Journal* 32 (1989): 402–23.

28. James G. March and Herbert A. Simon, *Organizations* (New York: Wiley, 1958).

29. See Roberts and O'Reilly, "Some Correlations."

30. W. Gary Wagner, Jeffrey Pfeffer, and Charles A. O'Reilly III, "Organizational Demography and Turnover in Top-Management Groups," *Administrative Science Quarterly* 29 (1984): 74–92.

31. Herminia Ibarra, "Personal Networks of Women and Minorities in Management: A Conceptual Framework," *Academy of Management Review* 18 (1993): 56–87.

32. Herminia Ibarra, "Race, Opportunity, and Diversity of Social Circles in Managerial Networks," *Academy of Management Journal* 38 (1995): 673–703.

33. Herminia Ibarra, "Homophily and Differential Returns: Sex Differences in Network Structure and Access in an Advertising Firm," *Administrative Science Quarterly* 37 (1992): 422–47.

34. Rosabeth Moss Kanter, "Some Effects of Proportions on Group Life: Skewed Sex Ratios and Responses to Token Women," *American Journal of Sociology* 82 (1977): 965–90.

35. Ibid.

36. Robin J. Ely, "The Power in Demography: Women's Social Constructions of Gender Identity at Work," *Academy of Management Journal* 38 (1995): 589–634.

37. Karen S. Lyness and Donna E. Thompson, "Above the Glass Ceiling? A Comparison of Matched Samples of Female and Male Executives," *Journal of Applied Psychology* 82 (1997): 359–75.

38. Daniel J. Brass, "Men's and Women's Networks: A Study of Interaction Patterns and Influence in an Organization," *Academy of Management Journal* 28 (1985): 327–43; Ibarra, "Personal Networks of Women and Minorities"; Ibarra, "Homophily and Differential Returns."

39. James N. Baron and Jeffrey Pfeffer, "The Social Psychology of Organizations and Inequality," *Social Psychology Quarterly* 57 (1994): 190–209.

40. Daniel J. Brass, "A Social Network Perspective on Human Resources Management," in Gerald R. Ferris, ed., *Research in Personnel and Human Resources Management* (Greenwich, CT: JAI Press, 2004), pp. 13:39–79; Daniel J. Brass, Joseph Galaskiewicz, Henrich R. Greve, and Wenpin Tsai, "Taking Stock of Networks and Organizations: A Multilevel Perspective," *Academy of Management Journal* 47 (2004): 795–817; Podolny and Baron, "Resources and Relationships."

41. Marlene E. Burkhardt and Daniel J. Brass, "Changing Patterns or Patterns of Change: The Effect of a Change in Technology on Social Network Structure and Power," *Administrative Science Quarterly* 35 (1990): 104–27.

42. See Brass, "A Social Network"; see Brass et al., "Taking Stock."

43. Cecily D. Cooper and Nancy B. Kurland, "Telecommuting, Professional Isolation, and Employee Development in Public and Private Organizations," *Journal of Organizational Behavior* 23 (2002): 511–32.

44. Debra E. Meyerson and Joyce K. Fletcher, "A Modest Manifesto for Shattering the Glass Ceiling," *Harvard Business Review* (January/February 2000): 126–36.

45. Podolny and Baron, "Resources and Relationships."

46. Jeffrey Pfeffer, "A Political Perspective on Careers: Interests, Networks, and Environments," in Michael B. Arthur, Douglas T. Hall, and Barbara S. Lawrence, eds., *Handbook of Career Theory* (Cambridge: Cambridge University Press, 1989), pp. 380–96.

47. Wellington et al., "What's Holding Women Back?"

48. Kathy E. Kram, *Mentoring at Work: Developmental Relationships in Organizational Life* (Glenview, IL: Scott Foresman, 1985).

49. Reba Keele, "Mentoring or Networking? Strong and Weak Ties in Career Development," in Lynda L. Moore, ed., *Not as Far as You Think: The Realities of Working Women* (Lexington, MA: Lexington Books, 1986), pp. 53–68.

50. Kram, *Mentoring at Work*.

51. Belle Rose Ragins, "Barriers to Mentoring: The Female Manager's Dilemma," *Human Relations* 42 (1989): 1–22.

52. Ellen A. Fagenson, "The Mentor Advantage: Perceived Career/Job Experiences of Protégés versus Non-Protégés," *Journal of Organizational Behavior* 10 (1989): 309–20; Terri A. Scandura, "Mentorship and Career Mobility: An Empirical Investigation," *Journal of Organizational Behavior* 13 (1992): 169–74; William Whitely, Thomas W. Dougherty, and George F. Dreher, "Relationship of Career Mentoring and Socioeconomic Origin to Managers' and Professionals' Early Career Progress," *Academy of Management Journal* 34 (1991): 331–51.

53. Monica C. Higgins and David A. Thomas, "Constellations and Careers: Toward Understanding the Effects of Multiple Developmental Relationships," *Journal of Organizational Behavior* 22 (2001): 223–47; Ralph E. Viator, "An Analysis of Formal Mentoring Programs and Perceived Barriers to Obtaining a Mentor at Large Public Accounting Firms," *Accounting Horizons* 13 (1999): 37–53; Ralph E. Viator and Terri A. Scandura, "A Study of Mentor-Protégé Relationships in Large Public Accounting Firms," *Accounting Horizons* 5 (1991): 20–30.

54. Kram, *Mentoring at Work*; Ragins, "Barriers to Mentoring"; Belle Rose Ragins and John L. Cotton, "Easier Said than Done: Gender Differences in Perceived Barriers

to Gaining a Mentor," *Academy of Management Journal* 34 (1991): 939–51; Raymond A. Noe, "Women and Mentoring: A Review and Research Agenda," *Academy of Management Review* 13 (1988): 65–78.

55. See Ragins, "Diversified Mentoring Relationships"; Kram, *Mentoring at Work*.

56. Kram, *Mentoring at Work*; Ragins, "Barriers to Mentoring."

57. George F. Dreher and Ronald A. Ash, "A Comparative Study of Mentoring among Men and Women in Managerial, Professional, and Technical Positions," *Journal of Applied Psychology* 75 (1990): 539–46; Belle Rose Ragins and Terri A. Scandura, "The Way We Were: Gender and the Termination of Mentoring Relationships," *Journal of Applied Psychology* 82 (1997): 945–53; Whitely et al., "Relationship of Career."

58. David A. Thomas, "The Impact of Race on Managers' Experiences of Developmental Relationships (Mentoring and Sponsorship): An Inter-Organizational Study," *Journal of Organizational Behavior* 11 (1990): 479–92.

59. Ragins, "Diversified Mentoring Relationships."

60. George F. Dreher and Taylor H. Cox Jr., "Race, Gender, and Opportunity: A Study of Compensation Attainment and the Establishment of Mentoring Relationships," *Journal of Applied Psychology* 81 (1996): 297–308.

61. Thomas, "The Impact of Race on Managers' Experiences."

62. Belle Rose Ragins and Dean B. McFarlin, "Perceptions of Mentor Roles in Cross-Gender Mentoring Relationships," *Journal of Vocational Behavior* 37 (1990): 321–39; Terri A. Scandura and Ethlyn A. Williams, "An Investigation of the Moderating Effects of Gender on the Relationships between Mentorship Initiation and Protégé Perceptions of Mentoring Functions," *Journal of Vocational Behavior* 59 (2001): 342–63.

63. Ragins, "Diversified Mentoring Relationships."

64. Monica L. Forret, Daniel B. Turban, and Thomas W. Dougherty, "Issues Facing Organizations When Implementing Formal Mentoring Programmes," *Leadership and Organization Development Journal* 17 (1996): 27–30; Kathryn Tyler, "Mentoring Programs Link Employees and Experienced Execs," *HR Magazine* 43 (1998): 98–103.

65. Georgia T. Chao, Pat M. Walz, and Philip D. Gardner, "Formal and Informal Mentorships: A Comparison on Mentoring Functions and Contrast with Nonmentored Counterparts," *Personnel Psychology* 45 (1992): 619–36; Belle Rose Ragins and John L. Cotton, "Mentor Functions and Outcomes: A Comparison of Men and Women in Formal and Informal Mentoring Relationships," *Journal of Applied Psychology* 84 (1999): 529–50; Belle Rose Ragins, John L. Cotton, and Janice S. Miller, "Marginal Mentoring: The Effects of Type of Mentor, Quality of Relationship, and Program Design on Work and Career Attitudes," *Academy of Management Journal* 43 (2000): 1177–94; Scandura and Williams, "An Investigation."

66. See Noe, "Women and Mentoring."

67. See Ragins and Cotton, "Mentor Functions."

68. Michael B. Arthur and Denise M. Rousseau, eds., *The Boundaryless Career: A New Employment Principle for a New Organizational Era* (New York: Oxford University Press, 1996); Monica C. Higgins, "The More, the Merrier? Multiple Developmental Relationships and Work Satisfaction," *Journal of Management Development* 19 (2000): 277–96; Monica C. Higgins and Kathy E. Kram, "Reconceptualizing Mentoring at Work: A Developmental Network Perspective," *Academy of Management Review* 26 (2001): 264–88; Higgins and Thomas, "Constellations and Careers."

69. Kram, *Mentoring at Work*.

70. See Higgins, "The More, The Merrier"; see Higgins and Thomas, "Constellations and Careers."

71. Monica L. Forret and Thomas W. Dougherty, "Correlates of Networking Behavior for Managerial and Professional Employees," *Group and Organization Management* 26 (2001): 283–311.

72. See Higgins and Kram, "Reconceptualizing Mentoring."

73. Keele, "Mentoring or Networking?"

74. Forret and Sullivan, "A Balanced Scorecard Approach."

75. Robert J. DeFillippi and Michael B. Arthur, "The Boundaryless Career: A Competency-Based Perspective," *Journal of Organizational Behavior* 15 (1994): 307–24; Michael B. Arthur, Kerr Inkson, and Judith K. Pringle, *The New Careers: Individual Action and Economic Change* (London: Sage, 1999).

76. Monica L. Forret and Thomas W. Dougherty, "Networking Behaviors and Career Outcomes: Differences for Men and Women?," *Journal of Organizational Behavior* 25 (2004): 419–37; Fred Luthans, Richard M. Hodgetts, and Stuart A. Rosenkrantz, *Real Managers* (Cambridge, MA: Ballinger, 1988); James Michael and Gary Yukl, "Managerial Level and Subunit Function as Determinants of Networking Behavior in Organizations," *Group and Organization Management* 18 (1993): 328–51; Sam Gould and Larry E. Penley, "Career Strategies and Salary Progression: A Study of Their Relationships in a Municipal Bureaucracy," *Organizational Behavior and Human Performance* 34 (1984): 244–65.

77. Forret and Dougherty, "Correlates of Networking Behavior."

78. See Forret and Dougherty, "Networking Behaviors."

79. Belle Rose Ragins and Eric Sundstrom, "Gender and Power in Organizations: A Longitudinal Perspective," *Psychological Bulletin* 105 (1989): 51–88; Brass, "Men's and Women's Networks"; Ibarra, "Personal Networks of Women and Minorities."

80. See Forret and Dougherty, "Networking Behaviors."

81. See Gould and Penley, "Career Strategies."

82. Forret and Dougherty, "Correlates of Networking Behavior."

83. Arlie Russell Hochschild, *The Second Shift* (New York: Penguin Books, 2003).

84. Douglas T. Hall, *The Career Is Dead—Long Live the Career: A Relational Approach to Careers* (San Francisco: Jossey-Bass, 1996).

85. Ray Friedman, "Defining the Scope and Logic of Minority and Female Network Groups: Can Separation Enhance Integration?," in Gerald R. Ferris, ed., *Research in Personnel and Human Resources Management* (Greenwich, CT: JAI Press, 1996), pp. 14:307–49; Ray Friedman, Melinda Kane, and Daniel B. Cornfield, "Social Support and Career Optimism: Examining the Effectiveness of Network Groups among Black Managers," *Human Relations* 51 (1998): 1155–77.

86. Elizabeth Lesly, "Sticking it Out at Xerox by Sticking Together," *Business Week* (November 29, 1993): 77.

87. Catalyst, *Creating Women's Networks: A How-To Guide for Women and Companies* (San Francisco: Jossey-Bass, 1999).

88. Ibid.

89. See Friedman, "Defining the Scope."

90. Ibid.

91. See Friedman, Kane, and Cornfield, "Social Support."

92. Catalyst, *Creating Women's Networks.*

93. See Friedman, "Defining the Scope."

94. Catalyst, *Creating Women's Networks.*

95. Ibid.

96. Don Cohen and Laurence Prusak, *In Good Company: How Social Capital Makes Organizations Work* (Boston: Harvard Business School Press, 2001).

97. Rob Cross, Andrew Parker, Laurence Prusack, and Stephen P. Borgatti, "Knowing What We Know: Supporting Knowledge Creating and Sharing in Networks," *Organizational Dynamics* 30 (2001): 100–120.

98. Baker, *Achieving Success through Social Capital.*

99. Meyerson and Fletcher, "A Modest Manifesto."

100. Diane Brady, "The Glass Ceiling's Iron Girders," *Business Week Online* (March 28, 2005), web24.epnet.com (assessed July 4, 2005).

101. Patricia Sellers, "By the Numbers," *Fortune* (February 2, 2004): 22.

9

Women Are on the Same Team...and Other Important Business Rules

Gail Evans

I am forced to begin this chapter with an admonition. Did you know that men fill a room from the center to the front and women from the center to the back? In an office setting, unless they have an assigned seat at the table, women tend to take chairs on the periphery. Then they have a great idea, and they're sitting in outer space; the boss is sitting at the table. The action is happening among the people at the table. A woman has something to say and begins, "This may be an idea we have tried before, *but*..." We know 1,001 things to say before the word *but*. Then the woman quietly explains her idea, preceded by a conditional phrase. She knows she achieved her current position because she is "perfect" and does not want to speak up in the meeting unless her comments are perfect. She says something quite intelligent; others at the table murmur, and the meeting continues.

Ten minutes later, a smart young man lower in rank than the woman but sitting at the table even though he doesn't necessarily belong there, rephrases her idea. He says, "We should—" and suddenly, the power structure says, "That's a great idea!" As people leave the room, the man and the boss discuss the idea, and the woman walks out with a female friend discussing the fact that the man stole her idea. Actually, she gave it away! A real friend doesn't say, "Yes, he stole your idea." She says, "You said it, but he's actually the only one at the table who really heard you. You need to speak more powerfully and own your idea, rather than being so concerned about whether it is perfect.

So I begin by getting angry at all of you and saying, "You don't have to be perfect." If you're always at the meeting table and others say what you wanted to say, maybe you think, "I thought of that three weeks ago," or "I was about to say that." None of that counts. Learn that nobody ever got fired for saying something stupid. Actually practice. Say something stupid at a meeting once, and discover that you don't get fired. The boss only hears and discusses the smart ideas, never the stupid things; that's why that person's the boss.

"Good morning everyone; have you got it?" I'm tough. I'm determined you're all going to be more successful than you ever dreamed you were.

WELCOME TO THE GOLF GAME!

Something I've noticed when speaking to crowds of women—corporate, entrepreneurial, or women who have any kind of business—is that the first question after I finish speaking is, "Do I have to play golf?" My answer is "no." Play golf if you think it is fun, if you have the time to get out there and really have a game, or if you're willing to make a fool of yourself at least once or twice a week. But don't play golf because someone said you must to get ahead in business.

In the 1960s and 1970s, we were told that we were going to succeed. We were supposed to wear navy blue suits with tiny pinstripes and floppy navy blue ribbon ties. We were to succeed by becoming junior men and were expected to be meaner and tougher than any male in the office. In reality, that strategy was ridiculous! It was ineffective and not very empowering.

Golf is today's reinvention of those navy blue suits. It is not a great strategy for most women, but some love it. If so, I encourage them to play. On the other hand, women should not force themselves to play golf simply to emulate men if they dislike the game.

After I gave a speech to a national association of school superintendents, a woman came up and said, "Your comments about golf were amazing to me. I'm actually the first female in modern history who's the school superintendent in my state. When I applied for my job, I was told that there were 88 applicants in two categories. I asked the secretary, 'What two categories?' and she said, 'Eighty-seven men and you.'"

This woman got the job, and shortly thereafter realized that to be part of the fraternity of school superintendents in her state, she had to learn to play golf. So she joined a country club and hired a pro. After she heard me speaking, she realized that for four years she had been perfecting her golf game to become good enough to be able to play with someone. Golf will never be a strategy for her; she wants to do it "just right." Golf is about being at ease with mistakes and bad shots, and players must be comfortable laughing at themselves. Anyway, the players make the deal in the locker room, and women are never going there.

So what do we do if we can't play golf? I've talked over the years about women's need to understand the unwritten rules of business. We don't always have to play by them, but we need to know when we don't. We need to know when we break the rules before we do it. I break them all the time, but I'm aware ahead of time in a business context when I break the rules and know that I will shake people up. They ask, "What's going on with Gail today? Why did she say that?" That is fine, because I've decided in advance that I'm going to do it in this moment. Then I do something an hour later that makes everybody comfortable, and they really hear what I did when I broke the rules.

But if we learn and study the rules, we feel as if we know about speaking up and speaking out, doing our own public relations, and similar activities. As I talked around the country and the world, I realized that we, as women, missed one rule, and that is that we were all born on the same team—the women's team—and we have to start playing there. What the guys understand about this game is about team, and what we don't understand yet is about team.

Playing on the same team is very important. Some readers are probably thinking, "This is going to be one really feminist [bad-word-for-a-lot-of-people] rant, and she is going to set it up as 'us versus them.'" I did not get where I did in this world of business through strategies that pit "us versus them." Women are in television and all over up front looking pretty. Very few executives in the news business are—or have been—female. It is very disturbing that there are actually four of us at the four major news operations, and we have been doing panels together for thirty years. I've retired, and I'm still doing news panels. I keep asking when we'll be replaced. So this isn't about "us versus them." I love the guys. I love to play with the guys, and they love to play with me.

Women need to step out of the world of "us versus *us*." I'm not concerned about the guys; from my perspective they're doing very well! I'm happy for them; it's wonderful. We as women are trying to make our careers work better, and we must learn to start playing together. We all have been taught or teach, "I can do it. If I work hard enough, study hard enough, get smart enough, or have the right breaks, I can do it." As women, we need to change the mantra from "I can do it" to "*we* can do it." Many women have had an isolated success; what we need is collective success.

Whenever I am introduced as "the first" or "the only," I always think it's ridiculous. As long as women have been in the pipeline and active in business, we should not still be celebrating firsts and onlys. One person can do—or change—only so much. It is fun to be the one and only sometimes, but it can be very lonely. It is not a very effective way to create change.

I jokingly say my first book should have been called *Fourteen Men and Me*. I'm a counter; I always count the minorities or women in the room. It just seemed as though I would look around and see fourteen men and me. My other working title for the book was *All I Ever Needed to Learn about Business I Learned from Driving a Nine-Passenger Station Wagon*. That is true. Learning the skills needed to be an executive in business school is great, but women must also learn helpful skills in their personal lives that transfer to business. If nine children want to sit next to the window in a car, and only four windows are available, it's similar to some situations that occur in an office.

So what do we do? How do we join the team? How can we move women ahead collectively? Seriously, one person can create some change; two people can make a little more; real change takes at least three. In most places, we're still worrying about getting one powerful woman in the room. At the current rate of progress, parity on corporate boards may not occur until 2067 according to some studies. When women represent 48.9 percent of the workforce, thinking that we'll reach parity in corporate boards in 2067 means we are not getting anywhere very fast. The tiny steps we make each year are what I call creeping incrementalism. We must take—and be architects of—a bigger step.

I was very interested in listening to Bill Cosby's remarks to the African American community, because although they are controversial, they're very important. What Cosby said in essence to the African American community is exactly what I am saying to women. We need to be responsible for fixing the system—for having it the way we want it. We all know what is wrong and what needs to be changed; that's all about history. Now is the moment to begin to take collective action, because we are powerful enough to do it.

So I want to spend time talking about what we can do to effect change, make the women's team more powerful, and make it work. The first topic is mentoring.

MENTORING

Everyone's reaction is, "They always talk about mentoring, mentoring, mentoring!" I understand that. Part of the problem is that we discuss mentoring as if it were in a tiny, isolated box. We think mentoring happens only when a powerful person leads the way for someone who is weak. That is traditional, "old-time" mentoring. Those who have very powerful mentors should use them; that's terrific. They also must be aware, however, that women tend to look at powerful mentors and say, "Wow; this is great for me for safety and comfort; this person will help keep my career safe."

Great mentors are about visibility, not protection. So a good mentor, rather than protecting, pushes people out to do things—to take the risks and be visible—even when they are uncomfortable and do not want to do it. Even women who get great mentors use them differently than men. For most women, however, great mentors are not available. Also, for most people, mentors do not exist as one person. They are everywhere, and women must start using mentors in powerful ways.

A very important type of mentoring that women rarely use is peer mentoring. Every woman in this room is a great observer. We know what kind of jewelry every other woman is wearing. We could do a commentary on the women's apparel and their style. We have this knowledge because we are brilliant observers. This comes with being female, but we do not use this information to be mentors to each other.

I love the woman who spends months preparing and then reads the audience her PowerPoint presentation. Then she wonders why the boss's eyeballs are rolling and no one seems enthusiastic. She worked hard on that presentation, knows the facts from top to bottom, and is determined to tell everyone in the meeting everything she learned about the subject. The power structure of the meeting is interested in three or four basic points; powerful people care about the bottom line. As you leave the room after seeing her fail, you say to her friend, "It's a shame; Janet worked really hard," but she sure will not get credit for it because everyone was so bored. You need to talk to Janet; you need to have a relationship with her so you can tell her what she needs to know. Mentor her. Take a risk. Don't spend your energy telling someone else why she failed. Tell her what she needs to know to be successful.

I'm going to share a favorite story with a good lesson for everyone. About twenty years ago, I worked in a company with a young woman who was very smart—a real up-and-comer. Clearly, she had the brains to make it big, but she wore tiny white shoes with small heels all year long. She came from California, and I don't want to disparage that state, but I later learned white shoes were more accepted there. Every other woman in the United States knows about the Labor Day and Memorial Day rule, but unbelievably, no one ever told this woman about it. She always wore white shoes, and I noticed them because they looked ridiculous. One day I walked down the hall and noticed two secretaries who were deep in conversation. They were talking and laughing about the woman's white shoes, because it was the middle of December.

At that point, I realized that her white shoes *were* a business issue. Someone needed to tell her that they were distracting from her brains, talent, and ability. I thought to myself, "How can I tell somebody to lose her favorite piece of clothing?" I went through an argument with myself before realizing that if I cared about her and her success, I needed to tell her. So I developed the courage. We went to lunch, and I talked about the white shoes and thought of all the things I could say without being insulting. She understood and lost the white shoes.

Much later, this woman became president of a very large company in New York. She called me and said, "I'm being honored in a big industry dinner in about six months and would love it if you could attend because you really guided me in the years when I was struggling in my career." I said I'd be delighted and went to the dinner. In the ballroom with about a thousand people, when she was up on the dais accepting the award, she told the white shoes story. But she told it a little differently. She said another woman she worked with cared enough about her career and success to take the risk to tell her something she needed to know. At that moment, she was struggling about whether she had the courage, power, and brains to push to the next level or whether she would be happy where she was. She had a nice job and was doing well. At that point, she realized that another woman cared about her success and that she could do it. For her, it was about changing her confidence level, not losing her white shoes. It was about being supported.

This is a wonderful story for me, but its real importance is that we have no idea the effect we have on someone else if we make even a small contribution to them. We know when somebody missteps, and we watch them continue to repeat their mistakes. As women, we learn to be nice and sweet and to avoid criticizing people. They might not like us; it might be uncomfortable; or it might not turn out beautifully. Well, we're smart enough; we know when and how to speak and to whom. We don't coach each other, so we keep repeating the same mistakes. Women somehow believe that each generation of women must learn the same things by experiencing them. We need to share with each other to avoid having to rediscover it each time. If you see a smart woman you care about who is doing something that is not helping her career, there are ways to serve as her mentor. She doesn't need to be twelve steps below you. If you are a peer, you can talk about it. After a meeting, discuss why you weren't heard or why a project wasn't adopted. We can do huge things as peers; we don't have to rely only on important, strategic people to move our careers ahead.

The other part of mentoring is that the minute women are promoted for the first time they must ask themselves, "Am I mentoring a younger woman?" It is your obligation. And if you are a woman of color, mentoring another woman of color is your obligation. Part of the way women will get ahead is by helping each other. Because for every woman who succeeds, I succeed a little, and for every woman who fails, I fail a little.

All the time, I hear from young women who say that the older women make it tougher for them. The older women say, "You know it was really tough for me. I had to give up this or do that. These young women expect to have everything. It's all about entitlement, so we're out there teaching them a lesson." To the extent they do this, older women must stop. They should ensure the success of younger women by teaching them what they have learned. Each generation should not have to experience the same problems.

We need to be there for each other; we know the answers. If two women get together after a meeting, they know every dynamic—everybody who spoke smartly or didn't and everybody who gained and lost. We need to start being there for each other so we can see our collective, not just our individual, success. We look at the big business pie and spend our lives competing in the one tiny sliver we think is open to us. The whole pie is open to us; we are half the workforce! More than one of us can succeed; four can succeed at the same time. We need to ensure that, so we need to look at mentoring in a new, more holistic way, stop waiting for the perfect mentor, and realize that they are all around us. We must be there for each other.

NETWORKING

We also need to think about networking. I'm going to give you a new twist on networking: no one networks like women. It is unbelievable that networking is an issue for women. We know how to network; it's a natural part of us. We have no shame when it comes to personal networking. I had a purse that everybody liked. If I gave a speech to 2,000 women, 10 would come up afterward to ask me where I bought the purse. Three would ask what it cost, because they didn't want to invest in finding it if it was too expensive. When it comes to finding the right school, apartment, or pair of shoes, we will ask anyone anything. We network in our personal lives as the men dream they could network.

Suddenly, when it involves our business lives, we go from "net," the part of the word we love, to "work." We turn networking into work. Networking becomes drudgery and is seen as distributing business cards. One result is that women hand out business cards at networking events they don't want to attend. If they can't figure out how to be there and enjoy it, they shouldn't go. But they distribute forty-five business cards and wonder why they didn't get any business. Networking is not about the number of people contacted; it's about the quality of the relationships. We somehow think networking is only about us and the other person—that it works when somebody gets business in a one-on-one relationship.

Brilliant networkers are clear; networking is about putting two people together. Very successful businesspeople meet person A and remember having heard about a need from person C. They put A and C together, and then, after years of networking, people whom they helped are employed in every place where they do business. So they don't have to network; it's already done. These people remember who assisted them. So networking is much more about building a tight net of people worldwide whom you once assisted in some way. This is fun; it's not an awful thing.

It's a great feeling to put two people together. We love fixing people up. Networking is about fixing people up; it's just doing so in business. It's not about having to meet somebody to make the ask; that's only a small part. We somehow put a box around business networking and have rules about what would or wouldn't be right and whom you could or couldn't ask. We need to loosen it and understand that all the people in our lives, starting with those who were our classmates in kindergarten, are in our network. And we need to be able to use them comfortably.

Use is not a bad or pejorative word. Part of what's happened is that we have tried too hard to separate our personal and business lives. Well, guess what? They meet every day, and the idea that they don't is a fallacy we made up to protect ourselves from being very successful. They always meet. We spend more active time in our lives at work than anywhere else. So the notion of a cutoff doesn't match the way it works, and the two can't be separated. In spite of this, we have that dividing line, and we're safe on the personal side, but it's all risky on the business side.

I was getting on the train at the Atlanta airport two months ago, and two women, probably in their thirties or forties, landed way out at terminal D. (From there, it takes about six minutes to go to baggage claim.) None of us knew each other. The women were both carrying laptops, so I assumed they were businesswomen. They were standing and I was sitting on the train. The first woman looked at the second and asked, "When's the baby due?" To women, that is not a personal question. In the next six minutes, these two women exchanged more information about their lives than any four guys who've been in a golf game together for ten years. One was from Boston; she had three children and was divorced. What I learned about these two women's lives was all of the most intimate details.

Guess what I didn't learn. I have no idea where either worked or what either did for a living. Somehow, the question, "When's the baby due?" is not an invasion of privacy, but their work was so much not a part of them that they didn't share it. I'm not saying that women shouldn't discuss personal matters. In addition, however, they need a good one-line sentence that they've practiced about their identity and role in business or in the workforce that rolls off the tongue in the same way that "The baby's due in October" or "I'm married and have three children" does. Women fear that the other woman they meet might not be employed or might feel insulted. They also worry that they might be more powerful than she is. That's the big dynamic; we don't like to be more powerful than anybody else. This is ridiculous! Work is an integral part of who we are, and we need to make it so. If being asked, "What do you do?" makes you uncomfortable, and you answer with something like "I support IT" or "I help," "I work for," then learn a one-line sentence that says who you are and what you do.

I was talking about this in a speech at an annual convention of a major insurance company. A woman came up afterward, and said, "Gail, I want to tell you something. I am president of a division of this company. Until you talked this morning, I have never introduced myself that way. I have never used the word 'president'; others use it all the time but it never feels comfortable for me to say it. I'm going to go home tonight and practice it with my children." That shows how extreme this is. It shows that we are uncomfortable, so if you're not a president, know that people in high positions also are uncomfortable. We have to learn how to do that, even if it means practicing with our kids or dog or in front of the mirror until the sentence rolls off of our tongues.

One problem we have is that we don't feel as powerful as we can be, and part of that is because we don't present ourselves as being powerful. I'm sure most people who don't know that a woman is a division president assume she is a mid-level executive. Seventy-five percent of the time, I am introduced as former vice president of CNN. Vice president is a nice title, but a vice president is not the same as a senior or an executive vice president. I have reached the point now where I find a humorous way to correct people. It kills me, but I do it because we do not know we are powerful; we spend much time and energy telling ourselves and everyone else that we're not that powerful. We will feel better when those of us who have achieved begin to acknowledge it and not make someone else do it.

Recently, a Fortune 200 firm brought together its 100 top-ranking women from around the world for a luncheon. Before I began speaking to the group, the women introduced themselves. The first woman said she was supporting IT.

I knew no one in the room was below the level of assistant vice president or director, but thirty-five to forty women introduced themselves the same way. Each looked a little less powerful than the woman before her because she didn't want to brag or make anyone uncomfortable.

I stopped and said, "I see this all the time. You are all trying to so hard to be nice to each other that you're looking as if you're a bunch of executive assistants. How will you know whom to network with if you don't actually know who these women really are?" After I said that, we discovered that they were very powerful, and their whole way of connecting with each other changed. So we have to remember that who we are in business is a part of us every day.

I see this happen when I get on airplanes all the time. We get on the airplane, and the guys get on. In ten seconds, the guys say, "This is who I am; this is what I do; is there a deal here?" It's unbelievable! Added to that, if there's not a deal, they either get into a deep conversation about ball scores, or one who does something interesting explains that business to the other. I'm amazed at what I learn when guys are sitting talking to each other on an airplane.

Unless they're very tall, women who get on an airplane like the window seat because they can define their space; no one can be on the other side. They get out the book or the work and send a very loud message saying, "I do not want to be disturbed; this is my moment for peace and quiet. Do not interfere in my space." I understand that; I love the silence of an airplane compared to a busy life. But airplanes are great business places where women can learn how to naturally network. The guys do it totally differently than we do. I'm not saying we're wrong and they're right. I'm just saying that those who want to be good at networking must look at places where it is available and ask, "Am I playing?"

Another thing women do is attend events that are great networking opportunities and sit next to people we know. We walk in the room and know who knows each other and where they are, and this is an opportunity to connect. Making contact with someone we've known for thirty years isn't making a contact. We need to attend these events and connect in new ways with new people. If we leave a two-day event having met five or six people with whom we really have something in common, we have networked brilliantly. Meeting everyone in the room is not necessary; instead, develop a quality relationship with a few people. Then, look at each other, say, "Let's have lunch," and do it.

One way we miss out on networking is by saying wonderful things and then never following through. After I finish speaking, a lot of women come up and give me their business cards, and I think, "That's nice," and never hear from them again. If a man comes up after I speak and gives me his business card, within a week I usually hear from him. He has a request and makes it. We need to remember not to just do the nicety but to follow through. Networking is fun; we need to relax and enjoy it.

Those of you with children notice—and now that I have five grandchildren, I notice—that we're on—or back on—the soccer and T-ball express. I don't have any football grandchildren, but I certainly have soccer, baseball, and T-ball grandchildren, so I get to go to the games again. Somehow, you think missing your children's games is bad, but it's nothing compared to missing your grand-children's. They really care.

At these games, I watch and observe. The guys all stand on one side; it doesn't matter which team their kids are on. They are deep into "Who's here? What do you do? Is there a deal here?" The women are on the other side and have an unwritten rule banning business talk. The only essence of their identity at these social events is that they are the mother of this child, and talking about anything related to business would somehow violate the child.

First, realize that stay-at-home and working moms are exactly the same species. We're all women. Most women live on a continuum; we're in and out of the workforce at various times in our lives. To make it easier for everyone, we need to support each other, not talk judgmentally about the other one.

We need to remember that there all sorts of places to network. I am not recommending going to your child's soccer game with the sole intent of making a business deal. But you are allowed to talk about the other part of your life when it is appropriate, and you don't need to cut yourself in two. Many different networking opportunities exist; we need to relax, learn to enjoy the process, and engage in networking in ways that can make us more powerful.

CONSIDER A WOMAN

Now the next, and most important part of this talk, is to consider a woman. I do not mean to *favor* a woman. I want to make sure nobody leaves this room and says, "She told us we were supposed to favor a woman." It *is* your obliga-tion, though, to enter the world of considering other women. What do I mean by that? I'm going to start in your personal lives. When you get ready to hire the photographer for the wedding, a lawyer to draw up the will, or a contractor to build the addition to your house, do you do the work to find a woman, a woman-owned business, or a woman salesperson who is eminently qualified to compete for the business? I said, "*compete* for the business"; I don't care whether you give her the business. I care that you have done the work to allow her to compete, because that's how women will go from about 13 or 14 percent to about one-third of real power in this country.

Women sign 80 percent of the checks and are responsible for about 89 percent of the buying and financial decisions. So why do we represent only 13 or 14 percent of those with real power? One reason is because we've allowed the "old Rolodex of life" to rule us. We go to the same places—usually white, male places—because that's how it always has been done. Women and minorities can change things by seeking people like ourselves and helping them succeed by allowing them to compete.

People always say to me, "I want the best." I want all of you to have the best; if you do the hard work, you most likely will find another woman who is best at least one-third of the time. It takes work; we actually don't know all those names. When we buy coffee mugs for the office, we always buy from the same place we've bought them for thirty-seven years. Instead, why not find out if a female-owned business or a female salesperson might compete for that business. Get her on the minority vendors list. There are all sorts of business implications to this. It's easiest to look at in our personal lives, but we also must ask, "Did I consider another woman? Did I give a woman a chance to compete for this job?" Your obligation is not to get her the job, and if she obtains it and doesn't perform brilliantly, it's not the end of your career. It's just another vendor or employee who wasn't perfect. It happens all the time. But we're terrified to do this, because we somehow think if we suggested someone who doesn't measure up, it ends up back on us. If you didn't make the actual hiring decision, it doesn't end up back on you. If you made the decision, just be smart enough to cut your losses and move on quickly. We're not going to increase our power and numbers unless we start breaking through the old Rolodexes and bringing new people into the equation.

Usually when I'm speaking at a major corporation, five or six top ranking men in the company, sometimes including the chairman, president, or chief financial officer (CFO), are sitting in the back row. They want to hear what I'm telling the women. They laugh louder and harder than we do at most of it, and when everyone gets nervous and uncomfortable what I hear from them is, "Wait a second; she's talking about teamwork. We love teamwork!" They don't hear the whole feminine part of it; they hear good teamwork and good business.

So I would suggest that considering a woman or minority is important because we've exhausted the old places to do business; the opportunities to grow will come from new communities. Everyone has the inroads to the old construction firm which has been here for ten generations. Women and minorities have the ability to move into new communities and find people who are beginning businesses that will grow and become clients for current employers. So there is a very good business reason for all of this, besides the fact that we need to do it to take care of ourselves. Our companies don't mind this; they will only grow. We really must ask ourselves if we're doing the work to consider a woman. Those who don't will get stuck and will be amazed by how limited their Rolodexes are.

I was preparing to put an addition on my house, which was built in 1923 and is in one of Atlanta's historic areas. In Atlanta, 1923 is pretty historic; as many of you know from *Gone with the Wind*, most of it went away. And I said, "Okay, Gail, you're out here talking about all this. You need to find a female contractor and architect to bid on this project." I knew tons of male contractors, but no female contractors. Somebody said, "Oh I know someone." I met her, and she was nice. She made a bid, but this woman was not really competing. Putting her on the list was not fair, because there was no chance I would give her the project. Every time I talked in Atlanta at meetings I would tell people that I was looking for a good female contractor and architect. I delayed the project six or seven months because I wanted to get someone who could compete.

Finally, one night I was talking, and afterward a woman came up to me following a board of directors event and said, "I know exactly who you are looking for." That female-owned contracting firm bid and competed. I gave that firm the project, not just because women owned it but because they understood what I wanted to do. It took work; it wasn't simple and easy.

We also must do the work to find the vendors and, within our own companies, to consider women and minorities for vacancies and promotions. I have been inside the executive committee rooms in major companies. I know the discussion is, "I'd like to put a woman in this job or a minority in that job." The same discussion occurs six weeks later when the company is hiring somebody whom everyone in the executive committee has known for years. Then the committee members say, "I really wanted to put a woman there" or "I really wanted to put a minority there, but I was not comfortable with any who came to compete." It's not that the intentions aren't good; many times we just go to the same places with the same contacts.

When there is an opening, find a woman who genuinely can compete for it and offer her name. You will meet many women; remember who they are and that they are good and smart. Ten months from now, when you hear of an opportunity, say, "Let me talk to her; let me suggest this name." We need to do the work to ensure that more women and minority names are available. We can find them. When we do, we won't be labeled as a woman who favors women.

Most males understand the notion of taking care of self very well. Rather than looking disparagingly on women who take care of other women, most successful men wonder why we don't do a better job at it, but they don't see it as anything negative. When I talk about this, the men who have worked for me over the years always say, "Gail, you present this as if you never mentored, helped, or advanced men, but you've helped tons of guys." I say, "Yes, but I'm talking to women." There's nothing wrong with being known as a person who takes care of herself. Those in the power structure usually assume that if you're taking care of yourself, you're also taking care of business. People who always give themselves away are not comfortable people to be around in a business context. Because if they are willing to give themselves away, the fundamental unstated belief is that they will give the business away too. The important thing, though, is not about being angry or resentful or letting things build up until you blow up. It's about taking care of business daily so it becomes part of the way you live and doing it with a smile and a little humor.

My biggest piece of advice to women is that no one likes to play on a team with a person who anguishes constantly and thinks everything is impossible or dwells on mistakes made before work. We need to drop the anguish, anger, and frustration. We need to tend to the small stuff.

I love to play with my business school class about the small things that happen in business. I always hear, "Well, I didn't take care of that," or "It didn't really matter; it was small; I saved my power and energy for the big stuff." I challenged the business school class to give me an example of something that was big, because the big stuff is the small stuff that no one took care of.

Small mistakes occur all the time; for example, someone's name is mispronounced. One boss repeatedly mispronounces a person's name and keeps going. Some may think, "It doesn't matter," or "It's all right as long as I get a good review." It's not all right; if it were, nobody would know about it. Some say they're saving their power for something important. Well, part of the reason we get angry and frustrated is because we didn't tend to the little things.

We will be more respected if we take care of each other. We need to remember that it's about taking care of ourselves and other women and making them more powerful in the marketplace. So in the back of your mind, whenever you're getting ready to do something, remember to ask, "Did I consider a woman?" This does not mean to favor a woman but to simply give her a chance to compete.

SHARING INFORMATION

The importance of beginning to share information is the next topic. Most women love perfection, but realistically, the last time anything was perfect was in the fourth-grade spelling bee. Business is about a lot of things, but perfection is not one of them. It's about smart, good judgment. But we need to share information; instead, we become isolated experts. Many women love having jobs that are small. I don't mean nonintellectual; I mean jobs in one isolated area about which they know more than anybody else. Then they can be called in as the expert, and no one will challenge them. This strategy keeps women in the small picture; we always know a lot about our little area. The guys, though, always seem interested in the big picture.

Statistics show that women get promoted based on performance. We get the next job after we've been doing it for a year or five. We get the next job because our performance on the old job was perfect. We did a great job; we knew it perfectly and got promoted to the next place. Men get promoted based on possibility and potential—because someone thinks, "This guy is really smart; he can do that." They can get the job and say to themselves, "I really don't know how to do this, but the boss wouldn't have put me here if he or she didn't think I could do, so I guess I can." We get a job that we have been doing for five years, and all we know how to do is anguish about everything we don't know how to do while still holding on to the old job because we still want that to be perfect. Then we wonder why we get overwhelmed.

We need to loosen up about this and understand that performance is only part of it. We still must be good performers, but perfect performance is not the way to the top, it's only a small part. Often, perfection causes trouble, because it gets us focused on isolated, irrelevant information. But I say we need to share information, so what do we need to do?

Those of us who are smart in isolated areas need to go to lunch together regularly. At that lunch, talk about business at least half the time. Discuss anything during the other half. You will begin to develop a bigger picture of what you do and what is happening at the company because one person is in accounting, another is in customer sales, and a third is in development. As a result, you will look smarter, and your decisions will look bigger.

A great byproduct is that as you begin to talk to each other and share stories, you will discover you're not crazy. As you start to tell what you think is the most bizarre story anyone ever heard, everyone else at the table may say, "That happens to me all the time." This is a great way to develop strategies.

After I spoke to a group of women in a major health care businesswomen's association, the five top-ranking women at a major pharmaceutical house in the United States went to dinner together for the first time. They sat down at the table and said, "Gail says we need to do all these things; let's play the game." One said, "All right, let's each talk about our most complicated, most difficult issue and see if we can be supportive of each other." So the first said, "The biggest issue in this company that never changes is about getting heard." The second one was astonished and said, "That's my biggest issue, too." As they went around the table, all five senior vice presidents in a Fortune 500 firm agreed. They all struggled with being heard and developed a plan to deal with that problem. Most of the time, two or three were in the same meetings. If at least two were present, they made a pact that if one spoke and wasn't heard, any others in the group who were in the room would say, after a minute or two elapsed, "I want to get back to Carolyn's point." It didn't matter if she agreed with Carolyn or not. Her work was to make sure Carolyn was heard. The women agreed to continue to force the conversation back until the person was heard. It took them seven months of doing this before the culture began to change. Mysteriously, they noticed that when one of them spoke everybody actually paid attention, even though they were still speaking the same way they had before. This story shows that there are things we can do.

I told that story in a recent speech at another Fortune 500 firm. A woman who is CFO of the company in the United States and the woman who is president of the same firm in Mexico attended. One said that she and the other woman had been using that strategy for ten years. They had agreed that when one spoke in a meeting and wasn't heard, the other would ensure she got heard. It may not always be about being heard, but we all know what the issues are. We can be there for each other, share information to get the bigger picture, and support each other in issues like getting heard.

If we begin sharing information, we will find out what is possible. One of the biggest issues I hear from women is, "I went in for a raise and got it, so I guess it wasn't enough of an 'ask.'" We don't talk about all these things. Granted, a lot of people lie, but women need to ask, "What can I do; what's the arrangement I can have? What's the flextime arrangement, the salary, the perks?" Many of us work in companies where we're told not to discuss these things; confidentiality is part of the human resources rules. Too bad—the guys talk about it all the time. How will you know what's possible if you can't ask anyone? If you can't find out from the person who had the job ten years ago or three years ago, or who is working down the hall, how will you know what to ask for? Women earn about seventy-eight cents to each dollar a man makes. Much of the reason for that is because we don't know how much to ask for. Unless we start sharing information, we'll never know.

In my first book, I told a funny story about negotiating a contract at CNN. We finished the big negotiations, and I was tying things up with our new general counsel. He asked, "By the way, Gail, do you get the big or the small car allowance?" I thought, "Car allowance?" I had never heard of car allowances. I was smart enough to figure I hadn't gotten it for years, so I smiled and said, "The big one." I told that story in my first book, and for the next three years, every woman who negotiated a contract with me asked for a car allowance. Some were entitled to it and got it; to others, I said, "No, you aren't on that level yet." I then looked at one and said, "What amazes me is that I revealed the car allowance; think of what I didn't reveal. None of you has even moved beyond the car allowance."

We don't know what's possible unless we talk to each other and find out. We must be clear that there is information to be gleaned, and we need to get it from each other. We may not get everything, but we'll have a better idea of what's available by sharing information. So it doesn't matter if it's about perks or salaries; it's about the content of what we do. We must start talking to each other about business and not think everything is confidential. Because nothing is confidential any more; we all know that.

The final thing I'm going to say very seriously is that we all need to learn to be a little quieter about each other. What do I mean by this when I just said to share information? We need to begin to make it fashionable for the world to think that women are good to each other. I'm about to write an editorial about the television show *The Apprentice*. It's good, entertaining television, and I usually don't take light things very seriously. It's so detrimental to the way women perform in the marketplace and to businesswomen and unbelievably harmful to African American women. The stereotyping and what the women have done on the job reinforce all the negative things about us.

If you have never seen *The Apprentice*, it's all about how mean and nasty women are to each other. That's supposed to be funny, except it's not, and we need to recapture the territory. We need to make it fashionable to be known as a woman who is good and caring to other women, and we need to teach our daughters and granddaughters the value of that. We need to teach them that even the person who becomes most popular must still be nice and caring. In all honesty, the guys get a kick out of the nasty fights that go on. We need to stop it and ask if we are being caring or good to each other.

I often hear stories from other women that the most difficult thing in the workplace is other women. Women tell me how some woman harmed them fourteen years ago, and they still won't go to meetings or work on a project with her. That's ridiculous.

Guys generally understand that a team is only as good as its weakest players. We see the little boy who's the hero and best batter out after practice with the kid who strikes out, and we all think, "He's such a nice little boy." He may be, but being nice has nothing to do with it. He's clear that this kid always strikes out. We get two outs in that inning instead of three, and he's going to teach this kid how to see the balls and swing the bat, because that's how to win.

What do we do when another woman or someone else on the team doesn't work as hard or care as much? We want to get rid of her. Instead, we must learn to be there to support the weak parts, not just the strong parts. We need to make being known as nice and decent to each other an important of who we are. That doesn't mean we can't compete, but it means that there are different ways of competing with each other. I received an email message from a woman in a major investment banking house in New York who had read my white shoes story. She wanted to invite me to her company until she got to the part about being quiet. When she got to the point about not talking about other women, she said something like, "Damn it. She's not doing as good a job. If she's not as good, I won't support her, and I'm happy to be known as the person who talked about her." This woman told me:

> I was really furious. I felt as if you were telling me I should support somebody good, bad, or indifferent just because she was a woman. Then, suddenly, my company, which has a woman as senior vice president, appointed a second female executive vice president. The person who got the job was not somebody I would've chosen; she wasn't someone I liked or had much of a relationship with. She was a chief competitor. The morning after the appointment, I walked down the hall toward my office, and four guys at my level were standing in the hall, deep in conversation. As I approached, it was clear that they were waiting for me. The minute I arrived, one looked up with a great smile and said, 'What do you think about Susanne's promotion?' I was dying to tell them what I thought, but I kept hearing you in the back of my mind. I stopped, looked at them, and said, 'It's about time a corporation of this size has a second female executive vice president.' It was over; there was no game to play anymore. If I wouldn't fan the flames with what I had to say, it was done. I realized I bought this woman two or three weeks to move into the new position. I understood that the fact that she got it ultimately was good for me, even though at the time I didn't like it, and I didn't like her.

So we need to understand for every woman who succeeds, we succeed a little, and for every woman who fails, we fail a little. Women are viewed as a group, so being good to each other is important. Being known as women who are supportive of each other is positive for all of us.

I'll leave you with the new first question I am asked the most, which is no longer "Do I have to play golf?" but "When are we going to have a female president of the United States?" The answer is that we will have a female president when the women of the United States decide they want one.

NOTE

Adapted from Gail Evans, "Straight Talk from the Author of *She Wins, You Win: The Most Important Rule Every Businesswoman Needs to Know.*" Keynote address at the Women's Executive Leadership Summit, Madison, WI, October 7, 2004. Sponsored by the University of Wisconsin–Madison School of Business Executive Education Program.

10

Double Jeopardy Survival: Insights and Lessons Learned in Organizational Battlefields

Michele V. Gee

Double jeopardy in the U.S. workplace has also been referred to as double tokenism, double discrimination, and double or twin disadvantage. These terms primarily refer to the disadvantaged work status of individuals who suffer from the confounding effects of both race and gender in the United States. Simultaneously being a woman and a member of a minority group tends to increase discrimination and hostilities that may be experienced in American employment. This chapter focuses on important lessons learned by this African American female. Survival strategies are proposed for double-jeopardy workers in contemporary U.S. society. Insights gleaned from more than two decades of corporate and academic experiences are shared.

DOUBLE JEOPARDY AND THE DUAL EFFECTS OF RACISM AND SEXISM

Racism and sexism, unfortunately, still exist in places of employment in the United States. Although the Civil Rights Act of 1964 was passed more than forty years ago, race still matters in American employment, and so does gender.

Minority women tend to face the greatest disadvantages and discrimination, especially those who were originally brought to the United States involuntarily by force or conquered, enslaved, and forced into labor. These groups are referred to as colonized, involuntary minorities and include African Americans, Native Americans, Mexican Americans (original settlers in the Southwest United States), Native Hawaiians, Alaskan Natives, and Puerto Rican Americans.[1]

Many women encounter sexism on the job; immigrant women of color who voluntarily came to the United States also experience racism and sexism. However, evidence indicates that colonized, involuntary minorities, that is, nonimmigrant minorities, who are also female tend to face the most discrimination and have the lowest status in American society.[2] For example, African American women in management have been found to be confronted with dual low status resulting from the intersection of race and gender.[3] Similarly, several studies have revealed the combined effects of being an African American and a woman manager. A study of African American women firefighters, for example, found that they had to deal with the double bind caused by the convergence of race and gender.[4] The dissimilar lower status and heightened discrimination against African American versus white women is a prime example of what is meant by double jeopardy due to the negative, interactive effect of race coupled with gender. Although female workers share many workplace concerns, women of color face additional disparate challenges. Differences between African American and white women are particularly notable.[5]

In general, women of color experience what has been referred to as gendered racism in the workplace.[6] A recent U.S. Equal Opportunity Commission (EEOC) report on glass ceilings describes the status of all women managers and officials in the private sector.[7] This report found that collectively, women represent 48 percent of all employees but only 36.4 percent of managers and officials. The EEOC report concludes that gender discrimination varies by industry, and influencing variables include headquarters versus field locations, blue- versus white-collar positions, and service versus manufacturing industries.

The EEOC also has reported private sector employment statistics pertaining to women of color indicating that their employment has risen significantly, but many minority women remain in lower occupational categories and are still concentrated in certain industries.[8] Furthermore, of all women of color, African American women made the smallest gains in higher level positions and overall employment. Hispanic and Asian women far surpassed African American women in employment gains.

The Institute for Women's Policy Research has documented a significantly wider gender wage gap for women of color: Hispanic women earned fifty-three cents, and African American women earned sixty-three cents for each dollar earned by white men, and white women earned seventy-six cents.[9] Obviously, much more progress is needed in eliminating the gender wage gap that persists in the United States more than four decades after passage of the Equal Pay Act of 1963.

SURVIVAL AND SUCCESS IN SPITE OF RACISM AND SEXISM

I have experienced and learned much during more than two decades of double-jeopardy status in corporate America and academic institutions. As a highly educated African American woman, I have worked as a marketing professional and manager in Fortune 500 corporations and as a professor of business management and administrator in academe. It still amazes me, when reading and reflecting on current literature, that although considerable progress has been made, so much remains the same. Many workplace challenges are as relevant in the first part of the twenty-first century as they were during the last two decades of the twentieth century. Indeed, it is paradoxical that dynamic changes are coupled with relative stagnation.

As it was over twenty years ago, double jeopardy remains a relevant term in the contemporary U.S. workplace. Unfortunately, racism, sexism, and discrimination persist in the work world despite many laws banning such behavior. Considerable meaning and urgency are still attached to terms and conditions such as the oppressed and marginalized, the disadvantaged, academic achievement gaps, the digital divide, major disparities in housing and health care, and the widening gap between the rich and the poor in the United States.

Many urban ghettos across the country have increasing high school dropout rates. Unemployment, violence, crime, and incarceration are also growing at staggering rates in many urban, minority ghettos nationwide. For example, the 2005 National Urban League (NUL) Equality Index, which measures equality gaps still separating African Americans from whites, assessed the ratio of the status of blacks to whites to be at 0.73. In other words, the overall status of African Americans in 2005 is only 73 percent of that of white Americans.[10]

The NUL Equality Index is a statistical measurement that considers factors such as economics, social justice, education, health, and civic engagement. The biggest gap in living conditions between whites and blacks in the United States is economic. A dramatic racial wealth gap exists: one in every four African American and Hispanic families has no liquid financial assets. In contrast, only 6 percent of white families are without liquid financial assets.[11] Black unemployment in 2005 held at 10.8 percent, which was 2.3 times higher than that of whites, whose unemployment decreased to 4.7 percent.

There are also considerable race- and ethnic-based disparities in health and health care, criminal justice, and education. The life expectancy for blacks is seventy-two years, whereas white Americans can expect to live for seventy-eight years on average.[12] African Americans at every stage of life are twice as likely, on average, to die from accident, disease, behavior, and homicide. With respect to social justice, African Americans are three times more likely than whites to be convicted and incarcerated once arrested. The average jail sentence for blacks, for the same crime, is six months longer than that of whites.[13] In minority-dominated schools across the country, there are twice as many inexperienced teachers who have been in the occupation for fewer than three years.[14]

Slow progress is indicated by these statistics. Much more needs to be done to bring African Americans and other minorities to parity with fellow white citizens. Racial and ethnic inequalities result in the loss of considerable human potential, for which society suffers. Many talented individuals remain trapped in poverty, still reeling from the effects of centuries of oppression and institutionalized racist and sexist practices. Some policies of the majority culture serve to maintain their privileges and the status quo.

At the same time that racial, ethnic, and gender inequalities persist, an alarming proportion of corporate managers exhibit unethical behavior. Financial and other crises have occurred in many businesses due to major lapses in corporate ethics. Enron, WorldCom, Arthur Andersen, Tyco, and Merrill Lynch are just a few examples of businesses that have been implicated in ethically questionable behavior. Several now cease to exist as a consequence of their unethical business activities.

Business executives are going to prison in record numbers due to ethical and illegal activities. For example, the $11 billion WorldCom scandal, the largest accounting fraud in U.S. history, resulted in the sentencing of five former top WorldCom executives to federal prison terms by summer 2005. The executives sentenced include the ex-CEO of WorldCom, who received a sentence of twenty-five years in federal prison for his role in the debacle.

The Sarbanes-Oxley Act of 2002 was enacted in the United States on the heels of the series of corporate scandals involving allegedly corrupt actions of executives in major firms. The Sarbanes-Oxley Act applies to public companies and increases the culpability of business executives for misstatements concerning financial information. In addition, Sarbanes-Oxley addresses corporate governance issues, organizational structure, and protection for whistle-blowers. The law requires certifications for financial statements and various disclosures, and new corporate regulations are being enforced with failure to comply resulting in serious penalties. Provisions in the act also restrict the control of corporations by their executives, auditing committees, accounting firms, and attorneys.[15]

Another result of mushrooming corporate scandals has been a call for renewed emphasis on ethics, integrity, and concern for others in all levels of education. For example, the Association to Advance Collegiate Schools of Business (AACSB International), the premier accrediting organization for business schools, issued new guidelines in 2004 concerning the need for integration of business ethics and governance into management education. Furthermore, many companies now provide ethics training for employees and take corporate social responsibility seriously.

Success in the contemporary workplace can involve complex challenges, particularly for women of color. Serious issues abound concerning the double-jeopardy status of minority American workers. Proposed survival strategies and insights shared in this essay address these issues. Recommendations include the importance of developing self-knowledge and the ability to reflect; successful juggling of multiple roles and responsibilities; coping with workplace racism and sexism through tempered radicalism and appropriate choices related to activism versus silence on the job; and avoiding corporate and academic minefields. Before discussing each of these survival strategies, the changing workplace will be considered because it provides the context in which viable strategies and insights are needed not only to survive but to succeed.

THE CHANGING WORKPLACE

The work world is continuously evolving demographically, geographically, technologically, politically, socially, and economically. More women are entering the workforce; minorities and immigrants are a larger percentage of net new entrants; and the average age of many workforces is rising (particularly in more advanced economies).

Many countries have workforces that are increasingly diverse. In addition, the global marketplace and world economy are inherently multicultural. Considerable cultural diversity exists in the customer/client bases of many organizations as operations expand across national borders. Thus, multiculturalism is a prime characteristic of significant markets for a wide range of organizations.

The employment of women of color in the United States has increased dramatically, as previously indicated.[16] Yet although minorities and women are needed to fuel the world's economies, race and gender discrimination persist. This is another paradoxical aspect of the modern workplace.

The most astute employers understand the implications of demographic changes in the composition of new entrants into the U.S. labor force. The classic empirical work in 1987, *Workforce 2000*, first brought dramatic demographic changes to the attention of many American businesses.[17] This Hudson Institute report indicated that white males would make up a small percentage of net new entrants to the U.S. labor force. American businesses were urged to adopt diversity initiatives to maintain a competitive, productive workforce allowing them to survive, grow, and prosper.

The sequel to the Hudson Institute's landmark study was published a decade later. Titled *Workforce 2020*, the sequel further discussed work and workers in the twenty-first century.[18] Ethnic diversification was predicted to continue among U.S. employees, but at a relatively slow pace. White non-Hispanics entering America's labor force are merely projected to replace exiting white workers during the early part of the twenty-first century, and slightly more than half of all net new workforce entrants will be minorities. (The total number of white male newcomers to the U.S. labor force, however, remains dominant.)

Economies and workplaces of the twenty-first century are complex in structure and challenges. Hypercompetition, across and within nations' borders, has become the norm. The competitive landscape is increasingly global and multicultural for American businesses and industries. The need for successful labor participation of minorities and women is critical. Consequently, managers face critical operational considerations and issues in the world of work. International businesses, governments, nonprofit organizations, and other enterprises need competent leaders who understand that cultural differences can be viewed as assets if effectively managed in the global arena.

Higher skill levels are required in the new information age and the knowledge-based world economy. Yet workforce skill deficiencies and labor shortages in many organizations, industries, and nations remain pervasive.

Several workforce studies identify the skills gap as an issue that managers of diverse employees must address.[19] Strategically, effective management of diverse employees is increasingly important because competition for skilled, productive workers is intensifying globally. Ethnocentrism, the belief that one's own culture is superior to others, is a notoriously unsuccessful approach for contemporary managers.

All employees, especially minority females experiencing double jeopardy, have workplace challenges that can be successfully addressed irrespective of organizational behavior and managerial actions concerning multiculturalism. In particular, self-knowledge, reflection, and networking are critical for workers affected by double jeopardy to thrive in the contemporary workplace.

SELF-KNOWLEDGE, REFLECTION, AND NETWORKING

Knowing oneself—one's background, goals, dreams, and priorities—is critical to personal survival, growth, and success. Reflection, which should be a constructive activity, is important. It differs markedly from excess worry, which leads to anxiety and increased stress.

Graduate and undergraduate students in my business strategy course must conduct resource-based assessments of firms and analyze their strengths, weaknesses, opportunities, and threats. (This SWOT analysis is in addition to other assignments analyzing the industries in which firms operate.) Strengths and weaknesses are internal to the firm, whereas opportunities and threats exist outside of the organization.

Similarly, developing a SWOT analysis of oneself as an individual navigating through life and seeking career advancement can also be strategically effective. When analyzing personal strengths and weaknesses and environmental opportunities and threats, one should consider feedback from others. These others could be mentor(s) or corporate sponsors, trusted colleagues, friends, or family members. After completing a personal SWOT analysis, one should develop and then evaluate strategic alternatives or options. What course of action makes the most sense, at this time, given one's circumstances? For continuous self-development, personal SWOT analyses and strategies should be revised as situations and priorities change.

Self-reflection and analysis are therefore quite important. It is also critical to understand the challenges posed by juggling multiple roles and responsibilities and balance them during various life stages while gainfully employed.

MULTIPLE ROLES, PHASES, AND CHOICES

Workers generally, and female employees in particular, must often perform multiple roles that change during different life stages. Work-family balance can be quite problematic. Regardless of whether one is married or single, working toward career advancement in the midst of workplace challenges, hostilities, and discrimination is highly stressful, especially when simultaneously caring for children or elders. Thus, effectively coping with considerable stress is essential.

Juggling multiple responsibilities is complex but doable. Prioritizing what is most important in life and acting accordingly are critical tasks. The challenge then becomes finding the optimum work situation, given personal and professional goals.

Some women neither marry nor have children, others wait a long time before doing one or the other. They may complete their higher education and begin careers before committing to marriage or family. Others may marry young and start a family while simultaneously developing their careers. Still others are single mothers who must work to support their families. Regardless of the particulars of all possible scenarios, assessing one's personal situation, establishing priorities, and progressing toward short- and long-term goals are crucial.

Goals, responsibilities, roles, and priorities can and do change. Success often is positively related to the ability to multitask and be flexible, adaptable, and open to change in the modern workplace. The world, people's lives, and professions constantly evolve. The dynamic times in which we function may be confusing, exciting, or both.

TEMPERED RADICALISM

What about specific responses to racist and sexist behavior, policies, and practices encountered on the job? Tempered radicalism is one strategy for dealing with rage against workplace inequalities.[20] Tempered radicals identify with a cause or ideology, and choose to work within the system to effect change without upsetting it too much. That is, their rage is tempered at the same time it is acted on to influence change in the status quo.

Some women may choose not to make a highly visible, vocal response to workplace injustice. These individuals, however, are not necessarily silent. Rather, they could be working behind the scene to influence or implement needed change.

Whether a response to a situation involves apparent silence or public voice is not always clear. What may appear as silence may actually be voice exercised in certain venues and visible only to select others. For example, in various managerial roles I have exercised voice aggressively with top management team members (policy makers) behind closed doors. Progressive changes were made, and needed initiatives were implemented. Some inequities were prevented or remedied. Yet it may not be politically wise or expedient to publicly articulate what one has influenced, said, and done. Too much publicly visible voice at this level could undermine the greater good to be accomplished.

Thus, receiving public credit for one's activism or being highly visible is not necessary to act as a successful change agent. Integrity and principles can be maintained. For example, people who interact with me basically understand my perspective on diversity and workplace equity. I engage in dialogue, make presentations, and provide compelling arguments concerning diversity formally and informally, one on one, and in groups. Yet in accordance with my deceased father's wise counsel, I have learned to "choose battles carefully, remain aware of the end goal, stay positive, persevere with dignity, and avoid burning bridges." Different workplace equity issues encountered during various phases of one's career may be addressed in varying forms of voice and activism.

DOUBLE JEOPARDY AND ISOLATION

Many women of color feel quite isolated. My experience, which includes double-token, double-jeopardy status countless times, is a case in point. Often, I have been the first and only African American and/or minority female in a range of situations, including in my academic department, corporate branch, hierarchical position, at professional conferences, committee meetings, in my neighborhood, and so on. And I am not the exception. Over the years, I have heard and read accounts of many other minority women who have had similar experiences. Nonetheless, many women of color continue to forge ahead in U.S. workplaces. As kindred souls working toward common goals, we periodically reach out and encounter each other at conferences, via email, and by reading our publications.

Too often I felt isolated in corporate and academic positions. I have yet to enjoy the luxury and comfort of working with a critical mass of other colonized minority group members in a majority-dominated workplace. Consequently, with varying degrees of success, I have developed and maintained vital links to similar others to counter the isolation experienced in majority-dominated environments.

MAJORITY-DOMINATED VERSUS MINORITY-DOMINATED ENVIRONMENTS

A marked difference exists between majority- and minority-dominated academic settings and workplaces. My bachelor of science degree was from a historically black university: Central State University in Wilberforce, Ohio (my father's alma mater). Wilberforce is a former Underground Railroad site for runaway slaves fleeing to freedom before the Emancipation Proclamation was signed.

My first professional job as a college graduate was with the Chicago Urban League, a minority-dominated organization addressing the needs of the urban disadvantaged. To a great extent, working in environments where African Americans were most of the top managers, served as role models, and functioned as peers and colleagues was wonderful. Minority-dominated organizations were welcoming, and working for them was very comfortable.

Subsequently, for graduate study, I attended a prestigious, private university: the University of Chicago. Ironically, I did not feel highly discriminated against while studying there because my perspective as a graduate School of Business student was that all of us were treated as lowly underlings by the highly esteemed faculty. Most important, the graduate business degree from an elite institution certainly advanced my career.

I worked in professional marketing and managerial positions for IBM and AT&T following completion of my MBA. These were enlightening experiences, and good and bad situations were encountered. I observed the revolving door, which refers to high turnover among the few token minorities who were hired at both corporations. My decision to return to academe and earn a doctorate in business was inspired by my desire to better influence American corporations in their diversity efforts.

RUDE AWAKENING IN ACADEME

My experiences in two of the largest multinational American corporations, considered to be among the most progressive, clearly demonstrated that much more progress in terms of diversity was needed. So, my plan was to return as an expert, to advise large corporations in creating needed change. I enrolled and graduated from a large, urban, state university, the University of Wisconsin–Milwaukee, with a Ph.D. in business. While completing my doctorate, I worked as an adjunct teaching business strategy, marketing, and management courses at two private institutions of higher education, Marquette University and Alverno College, as well as at the public University of Wisconsin–Milwaukee.

After earning my doctorate, I was hired at another campus in the University of Wisconsin System. As I progressed through the tenure process, I had a rude awakening. At this majority-dominated institution of higher learning, I learned that those who have earned a Ph.D. are not all necessarily enlightened, open-minded, or appreciative of diversity. Unfortunately, some faculty members acted exactly the opposite and engaged in exclusion, not inclusion. What an eye-opener this was for an African American female reared by her parents to believe that education was the best means to enlightenment, success, acceptance, and inclusion!

Important lessons have been learned and insights gained as a result of my academic and corporate experiences. Hopefully, sharing these insights will be of value to many readers of this chapter, whether they are women of color, their mentors, top managers, or others.

AVOIDING MINEFIELDS IN CORPORATE AMERICA AND ACADEME

The valuable lessons learned from my varied experiences in several American workplaces are summarized here. Although I did not enjoy every situation, each contributed to the base of wisdom I am still acquiring. Lessons and important insights include the following:

- Be prepared. Continuously develop and improve marketable work skills and competencies.
- Maintain a sense of humor; do not take yourself or others too seriously.
- Believe in yourself and your dreams, and set high goals.
- Network, network, network! Contacts can be developed in many ways, in many different venues, internal and external to the organization.
- Develop strategic alliances, and recognize that these may change over time or in different circumstances.
- Note that allies and enemies can be the same people depending on the cause or issue. The nature of the relationship between you and others, particularly in the workplace, can and often does change over time for many reasons. Changes in structure, leadership, responsibility, experience, maturity, life stage, ideology, legislative mandates, corporate policies, and politics can all result in shifting mutual interests and coalitions.
- Learn to distinguish between supporters and nonsupporters. An ally today may be an adversary tomorrow, and vice versa. Indeed, some people will swing back and forth.
- Try not to judge others or berate yourself. All people have positive and negative qualities, so strive to bring out the good and avoid the bad.
- Balance personal and work life; both are important.
- Market yourself: toot your horn. You are your best advocate.
- Constrain your ego; do not believe the hype as you become more successful. Runaway egos have been the downfall of too many highly talented people.
- Pace yourself in life, be flexible, and learn to go with the flow. Rigidity can be injurious and destructive.
- Learn to engage in distraction appropriately. Sometimes you need a break or need to deflect others!
- Help others as they journey in the work world. Appreciate the fact that your achievements have been made possible by direct or indirect assistance from others and historical gains made by other people of color in the workplace.
- Have no regrets, for they serve no useful purpose. Make the best, most informed decisions at each step, and keep moving forward.
- It is not personal, even if it appears to be! As my teenage son likes to say, "People have issues." Don't allow others' negative, personal issues to infiltrate your being. Avoid being defensive and overly sensitive.

- Practice discretion; this is critical to avoid self-destruction. Words often can be taken out of context, and careless verbalization may have unintended results.
- Be careful using email. If you do not want an email message forwarded around the world, do not send it.
- Do not sweat the small stuff, and it is all small stuff when viewed in the context of unlimited alternatives, choices, and opportunities.
- Understand politics, and become politically savvy.
- Learn to get along with people, including diverse others. Good social interaction skills go a long way.
- Diversity can be defined in terms broader than race, gender, and ethnicity.
- Diverse others in the workplace may include multiple generations working together, for example, returning retirees and older seniors, aging baby boomers, Generation X, and Generation Y.
- Diversity can also include sexual orientation, physical ability, socioeconomic status, and educational attainment.
- Avoid labeling others. People are not always as they appear on the surface.
- Learn to say "no." Double-token, double-jeopardy workers often are asked to serve on committees and work on many projects because diverse representation is needed.
- Do not spread yourself so thin across multiple work activities that you cannot accomplish your goals.
- Remember to allow time to breathe!
- Persevere.

CONCLUDING THOUGHTS

It should be clearly recognized that women and people of color lack the power to totally eliminate racism and sexism, even by engaging in effective activism. Women of color with double-jeopardy status, however, can control their own thoughts, beliefs, attitudes, and behavior. The way life is viewed greatly affects the way it is perceived. For that reason, try to see and appreciate the good in life. Much of the bad that triggers worry and lost sleep may never materialize. As a former mentor, a retired dean of a business school (who happened to be a white male of privilege) said, "Life is good; you just encounter a few speed bumps along the way."

As suggested previously, all workers, especially women of color, need to believe in themselves and their abilities. It is quite helpful to laugh each day and maintain a good sense of humor. In addition, trust your inner instincts, and consider belief in a higher power.

Without a doubt, racism and sexism are alive and well in the U.S. workplace. Double-jeopardy status persists. This chapter, however, has attempted to focus on positive strategies and insights to help minority women (particularly colonized, involuntary, minority women) survive and succeed. Years ago, many people of color in the United States said frequently, "Keep the faith." This is still a good plan.

I urge readers to reflect on this advice within the context of their personal belief systems, personalities, philosophies, and goals and use what seems most effective. Engaging in dialogue with mentor(s), colleagues, family, and friends about insights, strategies, and tactics proposed herein can be quite constructive. Seeking multiple, diverse perspectives can be beneficial for all involved.

NOTES

1. JoAnn Moody, *Faculty Diversity: Problems and Solutions* (New York: Rout-ledgeFalmer, 2004).

2. Ibid.

3. Gwendolyn M. Combs, "The Duality of Race and Gender for Managerial African American Women: Implications of Informal Social Networks on Career Advancement," *Human Resource Development Review* 2(4) (2003): 385–405.

4. J. D. Yoder, and A. Aniakudo, "Outsider within the Firehouse: Subordination and Difference in the Social Interactions of African American Women Firefighters," *Gender and Society* 11(3) (1997): 324–41.

5. Ella Bell, L. J. Edmondson, and Stella Nkomo, *Our Separate Ways: Black and White Women and the Struggle for Professional Identity* (Boston: Harvard Business School Press, 2001).

6. P. Essed, *Understanding Everyday Racism: An Interdisciplinary Theory* (Newbury Park, CA: Sage, 1991).

7. U.S. Equal Employment Opportunity Commission, *Glass Ceilings: The status of Women as Officials and Managers in the Private Sector* (Washington, DC: EEOC, 2004).

8. U.S. Equal Employment Opportunity Commission, *Women of Color: Their Employment in the Private Sector* (Washington, DC: EEOC, 2003).

9. Amy Caiazza, April Shaw, and Misha Werschkul, *Women's Economic Status in the States: Wide Disparities by Race, Ethnicity, and Region (Report)* (Washington, DC: Institute for Women's Policy Research, April 2004).

10. Marc H. Morial, "From the President's Desk [and the Equality Index]," in *The State of Black America 2005: Prescriptions for Change* (New York: National Urban League, 2005).

11. Thomas M. Shapiro, "The Racial Wealth Gap," in *The State of Black America 2005: Prescriptions for Change* (New York: National Urban League, 2005).

12. Annabelle B. Primm and Marisela B. Gomez, "The Impact of Mental Health on Chronic Disease," in *The State of Black America 2005: Prescriptions for Change* (New York: National Urban League, 2005).

13. National Urban League, *The State of Black America 2005: Prescriptions for Change* (New York: National Urban League, 2005).

14. Ibid.

15. John A. Pearce II and Richard B. Robinson Jr., *Formulation, Implementation, and Control of Competitive Strategy*, 9th ed. (New York: McGraw-Hill Irwin, 2005).

16. EEOC, *Women of Color.*

17. William B. Johnston and Arnold H. Packer, *Workforce 2000: Work and Workers in the 21st Century* (Indianapolis, IN: Hudson Institute, 1987).

18. Richard W. Judy and Carol D'Amico, *Workforce 2020: Work and Workers in the 21st Century* (Indianapolis, IN: Hudson Institute, 1997).

19. Ibid.; Johnston and Packer, *Workforce 2000.*

20. Ella Bell, L. J. Edmondson, Debra Meyerson, Stella Nkomo, and Maureen Scully, "Interpreting Silence and Voice in the Workplace: A Conversation about Tempered Radicalism among Black and White Women Researchers," *Journal of Applied Behavioral Science* 2(4) (2003): 381–414.

SUGGESTED FURTHER READING

Cross, E. Y., Katz, J. H., Miller, F. A., & Seashore, E. W., Eds. (1994). *The promise of diversity: Over 40 voices discuss strategies for eliminating discrimination in organizations.* Chicago, IL: Irwin Professional Publishing.

Davis, G., & Watson, G. (1982). *Black life in corporate America: Swimming in the mainstream.* Garden City, NY: Anchor Press/Doubleday.

Deresky, H. (2003). *International management.* New York: Prentice Hall.

Gee, M. V. (2003). Empirical exploration of pedagogical approaches to international management education. In Hans Klein (Ed.), *Interactive innovative teaching and training including distance and continuing education: Case method and other techniques.* Madison, WI: Omni Press.

Hale, F. W. Jr., Ed. (2004). *What makes racial diversity work in higher education: Academic leaders present successful policies and strategies.* Sterling, VA: Stylus Publishing.

Harris, P. R., Moran, R. T., & Moran, S. V. (2004). *Managing cultural differences: Global leadership strategies for the twenty-first century* (6th ed.). Burlington, MA: Elsevier Butterworth-Heinemann.

Hartman, L. P. (2005). *Perspectives in business ethics* (3rd ed.). Boston: McGraw-Hill.

McCuiston, V. E., Wooldridge, B. R., & Pierce, C. K. (2004). Leading the diverse workforce. *Leadership and Organization Development Journal, 25*(1/2), 73–92.

Meyerson, D. E., & Scully, M. A. (1995). Tempered radicalism and the politics of ambivalence and change. *Organization Science, 6,* 585–600.

Oakley, J. G. (2000). Gender-based barriers to senior management positions: Understanding the scarcity of female CEOs. *Journal of Business Ethics, 27*(4), 321–335.

11

Developing Men and Women Leaders: The Influence of Personal Life Experiences

Laura M. Graves, Patricia J. Ohlott, and Marian N. Ruderman

One key mechanism for leadership development is learning from experience.[1] To date, researchers and organizations have focused on the learning opportunities inherent in challenging on-the-job experiences, such as tackling unfamiliar tasks, creating change, or assuming high levels of responsibility. Little attention has been paid to the developmental opportunities inherent in managers' personal life experiences—ordinary experiences in nonwork roles such as spouse or significant other, parent, friend, or community volunteer.[2] In fact, the commonly accepted wisdom is that personal life experiences interfere with managers' work performance and impede their career advancement.

Although we do not deny that personal life experiences are sometimes detrimental to managers' work, we believe that they are an important means of leader development. Interests, roles, and responsibilities outside of work strengthen psychological well-being, afford access to supportive personal relationships, and provide opportunities for developing leadership skills, all of which can enhance leader effectiveness.[3] Thus, ordinary nonwork activities such as pursuing a hobby, organizing a fundraising event, or coaching a youth sports team can actually facilitate leader development.

In this chapter, we discuss the effects of personal life experiences on leader development. We also explore gender differences in the effects of these experiences on leader development. Gender continues to have a substantial impact on individuals' personal and work lives.[4] Furthermore, gender differences in personal life roles are associated with differences in women's and men's career patterns and development opportunities. Thus, it is important to consider gender differences in the effects of personal life experiences on leader development. Finally, we offer actions that organizations and individuals can take to ensure that women's and men's personal life experiences facilitate, rather than impede, their development as leaders.

EFFECTS OF PERSONAL LIFE EXPERIENCES
ON LEADER DEVELOPMENT

As noted, managers' personal life experiences may have both negative and positive influences on the development of their leadership talents. The idea that personal life experiences are detrimental to leader development is grounded in the notion that individuals have a fixed pool of physical and psychological resources.[5] Personal life experiences are presumed to deplete this pool of resources, thereby reducing the resources available for work and creating conflict between the personal and work roles. Researchers have documented the existence of conflict between the personal and work roles, and demonstrated its detrimental effects on psychological well-being, life satisfaction, and job satisfaction.[6] Conflict between the personal and work roles is also presumed to reduce performance, although this effect remains relatively untested.

The negative effects of personal life experiences on work outcomes are presumed to be particularly detrimental for managers. Managerial work is extremely demanding, and individuals who expend their resources on personal life roles are believed to have insufficient resources available for effective performance of their managerial roles. Thus, organizations typically assume that involvement in personal life roles reduces leader effectiveness and are thus reluctant to develop the leadership talents of individuals who are involved in these roles.[7]

The idea that personal life experiences contribute to leader development is grounded in the notion that individuals' resources are expandable, not fixed, and can be transferred between the personal and work spheres.[8] According to this view, investment of time and energy in personal life roles expands, rather than depletes, an individual's resources. Examples of resources that might be generated in personal life roles include new skills, knowledge, and ways of perceiving; enhanced physical and psychological well-being; and expanded support networks.

The expansion of resources should increase managers' effectiveness at work by increasing goal-directed behavior.[9] Individuals' expectancies regarding the likelihood of attaining their goals are based in part on the resources available to them. When individuals have more extensive resources, their expectancies of success are higher, and they are more likely to engage in behaviors that will help them achieve their goals. Thus, managers who generate additional resources in their personal life roles may be more motivated to take steps to attain their goals at work.

Having more resources also increases the likelihood that managers will possess the resources needed to address specific problems or challenges.[10] Furthermore, it may make it easier for them to assign appropriate resources to a particular problem; individuals who have extensive resources can be discriminating in their use, identifying and applying the resources that fit the situation.

An in-depth qualitative study of women managers and executives conducted by researchers at the Center for Creative Leadership (CCL) suggests that many of the resources derived from personal life roles are directly relevant to the leader role, and, thus, are especially likely to contribute to leader effectiveness and development.[11] In particular, personal life experiences offer interpersonal skills, psychological benefits, emotional support and advice, multitasking skills, leveraging of personal interests and background, and leadership practice.

Interpersonal Skills

Interpersonal skills developed because parents, spouses, friends, and community volunteers are directly relevant to performance in today's collaborative business environment. For example, community volunteer experiences in which individuals have no formal authority over their partners can teach leaders the skills needed to get work done in the team-based settings that are common in today's organizations. Parenting experiences may increase an individual's awareness of others' needs and perspectives, and create an ethic of caring for others,[12] thereby increasing his or her ability to relate to work colleagues. As any parent will attest, raising children creates opportunities to learn how to develop others, bargain, and resolve conflict. Other family relationships such as those with in-laws can provide managers the occasion to learn how to deal with significant stakeholders when making decisions.

Psychological Benefits

Having a rich personal life also contributes to psychological strength.[13] Successfully coping with challenges in the personal sphere may increase individuals' feelings of self-esteem and confidence, thereby giving them the psychological resources to conquer challenges at work. Furthermore, activities outside of work may provide a source of gratification and pleasure that buffers the stress and pressure that are typically associated with leadership positions.

Emotional Support and Advice

Individuals' personal life experiences provide them with access to a support network of family, friends, neighbors, and community partners. These network relationships provide them with access to valuable work advice and contacts and a forum for venting emotions concerning stressful work situations.[14] For managers, the knowledge that family and friends are supporting them can be reassuring as they tackle new assignments or thorny challenges at work.

Multitasking Skills

Nonwork experiences also can teach leaders how to better handle multiple tasks. Extra responsibilities at home, for example, can force leaders to sharpen their skills in setting priorities, managing time, and delegating. In such situations, leaders might enlist the help of others or pay for outside assistance. They may also learn to clarify their priorities and be resourceful in handling competing demands. The skills and tactics managers develop by managing multiple tasks in their nonwork lives improve their ability to move projects forward in the workplace.

Leveraging Personal Interests and Background

Hobbies, travel, and consumer experiences sometimes provide valuable knowledge or insights that are directly relevant at work. For example, managers who vacation by immersing themselves in new cultures may gain knowledge that enables them to better handle global responsibilities at work. Managers' personal experiences as consumers may provide them with an awareness of the competitive environment and the marketplace.

Leadership Practice

Involvement in volunteer projects, charitable organizations, and community and religious groups provides managers with a laboratory for testing skills in such areas as influencing others, building teams, managing change, decision making, and other key leadership competencies. Managers may develop leadership skills from such experiences and then apply them at work.

Subsequent research conducted at CCL confirms the positive effects of personal life experiences on individuals' work experiences. A survey-based study of 276 executive and managerial women found that women who were committed to personal roles such as spouse, parent, friend, and community volunteer had higher levels of self-worth and satisfaction with life than those who were not.[15] Moreover, women who were committed to roles outside of work were rated by their colleagues as having better management skills in both the task and interpersonal arenas.

Another study of 346 executive and managerial men and women found that those who were more committed to family roles (i.e., parental role, marital role) gained more work-related resources from their personal lives, experienced higher levels of life and career satisfaction, and were rated as more effective performers by their work colleagues.[16] Research by other scholars also suggests that involvement in parenting, recreational, and community roles generates resources that strengthen work outcomes.[17] Thus, personal life experiences can provide fertile ground for the development of leadership skills.

GENDER DIFFERENCES

Although today's gender roles are less rigid than in the past, the conventional homemaker and breadwinner roles continue to influence gender-role socialization and subsequent experiences in the personal and work domains.[18]

Stereotypical differences in the importance attached to the work and family roles persist; men are more likely than women to value work over family, and women are more likely than men to value family over work.[19] In addition, men and women tend to have different views of family.[20] Among men, the family role is often synonymous with providing financial security for one's partner and children. In contrast, women typically view the family role as ensuring the family's emotional well-being, including being available to family members and aware of their needs.

As a result of these different views of family, women allocate more time and energy to the family domain than do men.[21] Women are also less likely than men to psychologically segment or separate the personal and work domains.[22] Women consider family needs in determining their work roles (e.g., work hours) and may be psychologically (e.g., thinking about family) or behaviorally involved (e.g., talking with a family member) in the family role while working. This blurring of the boundary between family and work allows working women to meet the demands of the traditional homemaker role. In contrast, men's breadwinner role does not require them to make themselves available to their families at work or alter their work schedules to meet family demands. Thus, men tend to psychologically segment or separate the family and work roles, and create a relatively impermeable boundary between the two domains.[23]

Gender differences in family responsibilities are reflected in men's and women's career decisions.[24] Men typically make independent decisions about their careers based on their goals. They pursue linear career paths, following the conventional wisdom of working without interruption in a series of progressively more complex and responsible jobs in one industry.

In contrast, women's career decisions are based on a desire to blend their work and personal lives.[25] Women consider not only available opportunities but also the needs of those around them. As a result, their careers are nonlinear and unpredictable. Early in their careers (first twelve years or so), women are more likely than men to experience employment gaps, or periods of time without employment, typically for childrearing.[26] Women are more likely to work part-time, take voluntary leaves of absence, or retire early to care for family members.[27] These career choices lead to reduced income and lower levels of advancement in the managerial ranks.

Differences in men's and women's family responsibilities also lead to differences in evaluations of their competence in organizations. The low status attached to motherhood and other caregiving roles in society sometimes leads to a devaluation of mothers' social status in organizations, evoking doubts about their competence and suitability for positions of authority.[28] Furthermore, working mothers may be stereotyped as incompetent housewives rather than competent businesswomen. Working fathers, however, are not seen as less competent as a result of the fatherhood role.[29] In fact, a sense of responsibility or maturity is attributed to fathers, leading them to be viewed more favorably than single, childless men.

As a result of gender differences in family responsibilities, career patterns, and perceived competence, women often have less access to developmental opportunities in organizations than men.[30] Women are less likely to receive challenging stretch assignments, job relocations, and international postings that will help them develop their leadership talents. They also have less access to formal training programs and off-site activities, and they receive less financial support for outside educational programs. This lack of access to developmental opportunities assignments inhibits women's advancement in the management ranks.

The discussion highlights the negative repercussions of women's personal life experiences for their development as leaders. Yet earlier we argued that personal life experiences are beneficial for leadership development. Moreover, the women leaders who participated in CCL's research benefited from their personal life experiences. How does gender influence the career-related benefits of personal life experiences? Might personal life experiences be a vehicle for women, who are sometimes denied access to leadership development opportunities at work, to develop their leadership skills?

Research evidence on gender differences in the career-related benefits of personal life experiences is limited and inconclusive.[31] Some scholars have suggested, however, that women derive such benefits more readily than men.[32] In particular, women's greater investment of resources in the family role increases the likelihood that their family experiences will generate resources that enhance leader effectiveness. For example, women's greater responsibilities at home (e.g., household chores, childcare) may compel them to improve their multitasking skills. Extensive involvement in childrearing may also boost women's skills in developing others.

In addition, women's tendency to blur the boundaries between family and work may facilitate the transfer of resources from their personal lives to their work lives.[33] The lack of a psychological barrier between the family and work domains may make it easier for women to bring psychological assets (e.g., sense of gratification, self-confidence), knowledge, and skills gained from family experiences to the work role. In contrast, men's tendency to segment work and family may impede the transfer of resources.

Thus the way women approach the family role may strengthen their ability to turn personal life experiences into leadership lessons that enhance their effectiveness at work. We cannot definitively conclude, however, that managerial women benefit from leadership development opportunities inherent in personal life experiences to a greater extent than managerial men. Not all managerial men and women choose to pursue traditional gender roles.[34] Furthermore, the traditional gender roles described herein do not apply across all racial and ethnic groups. For instance, due to cultural and economic factors, black women and men in the United States have historically played less traditional roles, with women sharing breadwinning responsibilities and men sharing childcare responsibilities.[35] Moreover, managers can develop leadership talents from personal life experiences outside of their family roles—roles where gender may be less relevant. Additional research on gender differences in the benefits of personal life experiences for leader development is needed.

In sum, differences in men's and women's personal life experiences lead to gender differences in leader development. In particular, women's family responsibilities restrict the choices they make about their careers, as well as the development and advancement opportunities available to them in organizations. However, women's family responsibilities may also provide opportunities and challenges that contribute to the development of their leadership talents.

IMPLICATIONS FOR ORGANIZATIONS AND INDIVIDUALS

In an ideal world, there would be no gender differences in the effects of personal life experiences on leadership development—at or outside of work. Furthermore, the negative influence of personal life experiences on leadership development would be minimized and the positive influence maximized for individuals of both sexes. In this section, we describe the steps that organizations and individuals can take to ensure that women's and men's personal life experiences facilitate (rather than inhibit) their development as leaders.

Organizational Actions

Organizations need to adopt a new approach to leadership development that respects the whole person and recognizes the benefits of personal life roles for leader development.[36] Several components are critical to this new approach including work-life programs, management behaviors, workplace norms, and career development practices. These components will help create an organizational culture that acknowledges, values, and supports individuals' personal life roles.[37] Such a culture benefits all employees, not just managers seeking to develop their leadership talents.

Work-life balance programs, such as flexible work arrangements (e.g., flextime, telework, part-time work, paid leaves, unpaid leaves, job sharing) and dependent care assistance (e.g., day care facilities or vouchers, elder-care referrals), are a necessary first step. Such programs are beneficial to all employees, improving not only their ability to take care of their families and overall quality of life but also their career satisfaction and commitment to their employers.[38]

Although many organizations tout their work-life programs, the implementation of these programs leaves a great deal to be desired.[39] Bosses are often unwilling to offer flexible work arrangements to employees, particularly critical employees. Moreover, managers are hesitant to take advantage of such offerings because they fear that doing so will jeopardize their career advancement. Organizations must ensure that managers and employees alike have access to and are encouraged to use work-life programs.

Supportive supervisors are a particularly critical link in creating an environment that values the whole person and encourages use of work life programs.[40] Organizations need to educate supervisors about the importance of valuing the whole person and the skill development opportunities inherent in personal life experiences, such as managing a household or parenting. Supervisors should also be knowledgeable about work-life programs and should be provided with incentives and resources (e.g., equipment or systems needed for telecommuting arrangements) to implement these programs. In addition, organizations need to encourage supervisors to be creative in developing flexible ways of working that meet the needs of the individual and the organization.

Senior executives are another important link in creating a culture that respects managers' personal lives. In particular, senior executives need demonstrate through their own behaviors that the whole person is important. They should also model usage of work-life programs so that it will be clear that these programs are valued and that there will be no retribution against those who use them.[41] For instance, CEOs who leave work to attend their children's soccer games and limit weekend work hours to spend time with family signal that the whole person is important and that use of work-life programs is acceptable. Unfortunately, many organizations have been run by workaholic male executives who sacrificed family and outside interests to meet business needs.[42] There is anecdotal evidence, however, that some of today's senior executives are interested in maintaining a life outside of work.[43]

Organizations also need to consider workplace norms, particularly regarding work hours.[44] In this era of downsizing, restructuring, and focusing on short-term results, managers and employees are expected to work long hours. In many organizations, working long hours has become a badge of honor, and rewards are based on hours worked, not actual performance. Excessive working hours make it difficult for individuals to meet the demands of their personal lives and ignore the developmental benefits inherent in personal life experiences. They also may reduce (rather than enhance) productivity. Organizations should set fair standards concerning the numbers of hours that individuals will work. Moreover, decisions about managers' compensation, development, and advancement must be based on actual performance, not hours worked.

In addition, organizations need to scrap outmoded career development practices.[45] Organizations that define a successful managerial career as an uninterrupted upward sequence of promotions or assume that requests to take time out from career for family reasons reflect a lack of career commitment signal that the whole person is unimportant and discourage individuals from taking advantage of work-life programs. They also make it difficult for individuals to benefit from development opportunities outside of work. Organizations that want to facilitate leader development must develop a new definition of successful managerial career. This definition must recognize that a successful managerial career is not a rigid sequence of promotions but instead may include gaps, interruptions, sabbaticals, or periods of part-time work. Moreover, they should not deny individuals access to developmental opportunities because their careers have included such features.

Development planning processes and leadership training programs must also be reconfigured to recognize the whole person.[46] In development planning, individuals should review all possible sources of leadership development, both at work and outside of work. Furthermore, development plans should allow sufficient time for the individual to pursue learning experiences outside of work, not just those formally associated with their work roles. In leadership training programs, organizations can educate participants on the benefits of wholeness and the leadership development opportunities inherent in their personal life experiences. Participants can be asked thoughtful questions about the learning opportunities available to them outside of work. They also can be asked to engage in goal setting exercises that place career goals in the relation to other personal and family goals. Health-related, family-oriented, volunteer-oriented, and other personal goals should be considered at the same time as work-related goals.

Creating an organizational culture that values the whole person and ensures that women's and men's personal life experiences facilitate rather than inhibit their development as leaders requires extensive commitment by organizations. All of the steps outlined in the preceding paragraphs are necessary. They are designed to help managers meet their family needs, eliminate the career penalties associated with nonlinear career paths and use of work-life programs, and identify and capitalize on the leadership development opportunities inherent in their personal life experiences. Moreover, they are also intended to reduce gender differences in leadership development opportunities that stem from differences in women's and men's personal life experiences and career patterns.

Individual Actions

Although organizational actions are critical, individuals can also take steps to minimize the negative and maximize the positive effects of their personal life experiences on their development as leaders. Of course, individuals must acknowledge their whole selves.[47] They must develop respect for roles outside of work, including those related to the family and community. Deriving leadership benefits from personal life roles is difficult unless one sees value in them.

Individuals also need to clarify what is important to them by prioritizing their roles.[48] Doing so allows them to identify the appropriate mix of personal and work commitments. Individuals can then attempt to create personal and work lives that mirror their priorities. For instance, men and women can seek employers and work environments where the value attached to personal and work activities is consistent with their own priorities. In such settings, leadership development opportunities are less likely to be restricted by mismatches between individual and organizational values.

Furthermore, individuals must recognize that leadership development occurs in their personal lives as well as at work and create development plans that acknowledge both of these sources of leadership development.[49] As a first step, individuals should identify their development needs by comparing their portfolios of skills and experiences to those needed in target jobs or in present and future assignments. Once the skills and capabilities to be developed have been identified, individuals can review both their personal and work roles and experiences for potential learning experiences. It may be helpful to work with a mentor, trusted advisor or friend, or a coach to help identify both development needs and potential sources of learning. Work-related development opportunities may be obvious, but opportunities outside of work can be identified with careful consideration. For example, an individual who needs skills in developing others or team building might consider coaching a youth sports team. A person who would like to practice leadership skills in a relatively low-risk setting might consider a leadership experience in a community organization. Individuals can then create and implement action plans including both on- and off-the-job activities for developing their leadership talents.

To maximize the leadership development opportunities inherent in personal life experiences, individuals need to build support networks in both their personal and work lives.[50] Relationships with supportive others are critical in providing individuals with the flexibility needed to manage both domains. For instance, supportive partners may reduce the burden of family responsibilities, and supportive supervisors or co-workers may allow individuals to engage in flexible ways of working. Throughout the leadership development process, supporters in and outside of work can act as coaches, give feedback, provide encouragement, serve as sounding boards, and otherwise contribute to leadership development efforts.

Finally, people should also serve as role models for others.[51] Individuals who recognize the whole person, seek work situations that match their priorities, engage in development planning processes that consider their personal and work lives, and build networks of supporters will expand their opportunities to develop their leadership talents. To the extent that they share their experiences with others, they can serve as valuable role models—demonstrating the benefits of being a whole person and showing how personal life experiences expand leadership talents.

In conclusion, personal life experiences offer important opportunities for leadership development. However, organizations (and individuals) seeking to develop leadership talent often pay little attention to the development opportunities inherent in individuals' personal life roles. In fact, many view involvement in personal life roles as detrimental to leadership development. This view restricts the leadership development opportunities available to women, who are often highly engaged in family roles. To remedy these shortcomings, we advocate a new approach to leader development that values the whole person and draws on the leadership development opportunities inherent in personal life experiences.

NOTES

1. M. W. McCall Jr., M. M. Lombardo, and A. M. Morrison, *The Lessons of Experience: How Successful Executives Develop on the Job* (Lexington, MA: Lexington, 1988); P. J. Ohlott, "Job Assignments," in C. McCauley and E. Van Velsor, eds., *CCL Handbook of Leadership Development*, 2nd ed. (San Francisco: Jossey-Bass, 2004), pp. 151–82.

2. M. N. Ruderman, P. J. Ohlott, K. Panzer, and S. N. King, "Benefits of Multiple Roles for Managerial Women," *Academy of Management Journal* 45 (2002): 369–86.

3. M. N. Ruderman and P. J. Ohlott, *Learning from Life: Turning Life's Lessons into Leadership Experience* (Greensboro, NC: Center for Creative Leadership, 2000).

4. S. D. Friedman and J. H. Greenhaus, *Work and Family—Allies or Enemies? What Happens When Business Professionals Confront Life Choices* (New York: Oxford University Press, 2000); G. N. Powell and L. M. Graves, *Women and Men in Management*, 3rd ed. (Thousand Oaks, CA: Sage, 2003); L. A. Mainiero and S. E. Sullivan, "Kaleidoscope Careers: An Alternative Explanation for the 'Opt-Out' Revolution," *Academy of Management Executive* 18(1) (2005): 106–23.

5. W. J. Goode, "A Theory of Role Strain," *American Sociological Review* 25 (1960): 483–96.

6. E. E. Kossek and C. Ozeki, "Work-Family Conflict, Policies, and the Job-Life Satisfaction Relationship: A Review and Directions for Organizational Behavior-Human Resources Research," *Journal of Applied Psychology* 83 (1998): 139–49; S. Parasuraman and J. H. Greenhaus, "Toward Reducing Some Critical Gaps in Work-Family Research," *Human Resource Management Review* 103 (2002): 1–15; M. R. Frone, "Work-Family Conflict and Employee Psychiatric Disorders: The National Comorbidity Study," *Journal of Applied Psychology* 85 (2000): 888–95.

7. J. R. Kofodimos, "Why Executives Lose Their Balance," *Organizational Dynamics* 19(1) (1990): 58–73.

8. Ruderman et al., "Benefits of Multiple Roles"; J. H. Greenhaus and G. N. Powell, "When Work and Family Are Allies: A Theory of Work-Family Enrichment," *Academy of Management Review* (in press); S. E. Hobfoll, "Social and Psychological Resources and Adaptation," *Review of General Psychology* 6 (2002): 307–24.

9. Hobfoll, "Social and Psychological Resources and Adaptation."

10. Ibid.

11. Ruderman et al., "Benefits of Multiple Roles"; M. N. Ruderman and P. J. Ohlott, *Standing at the Crossroads: Next Steps for High Achieving Women* (San Francisco: Jossey-Bass, 2002); M. N. Ruderman, "Learning Off the Job," *Personal Excellence* 8(4) (2003): 47.

12. R. Palkovitz, "Parenting as a Generator of Adult Development: Conceptual Issues and Implications," *Journal of Social and Personal Relationships* 13 (1996): 571–92; R. Palkovitz, M. A. Copes, and T. N. Woolfolk, " 'It's Like You Discover a New Sense of Being': Involved Fathering as an Evoker of Adult Development," *Men and Masculinities* 4 (2001): 49–69.

13. Ruderman et al., "Benefits of Multiple Roles."

14. Ibid.; Greenhaus and Powell, "When Work and Family Are Allies."

15. Ruderman et al., "Benefits of Multiple Roles."

16. L. M. Graves, P. J. Ohlott, and M. N. Ruderman, "Commitment to Family Roles: Effects on Managers' Work Attitudes and Performance," Paper presented at the meeting of the Academy of Management. New Orleans, LA, 2004.

17. C. Kirchmeyer, "Nonwork Participation and Work Attitudes: A Test of Scarcity vs. Expansion Models of Personal Resources," *Human Relations* 45 (1992): 775–95; C. Kirchmeyer, "Perceptions of Nonwork-to-Work Spillover: Challenging the View of Conflict-Ridden Domain Relationships," *Basic and Applied Social Psychology* 13 (1992): 231–49; C. Kirchmeyer, "Nonwork-to-Work Spillover: A More Balanced View of the Experiences and Coping of Professional Women and Men," *Sex Roles* 28 (1993): 531–52; G. A. Adams, L. A. King, and D. W. King, "Relationships of Job and Family Involvement, Family Social Support, and Work-Family Conflict with Job and Life Satisfaction," *Journal of Applied Psychology* 81 (1996): 411–20.

18. A. H. Eagly, W. Wood, and A. B. Diekman, "Social Role Theory of Sex Differences and Similarities: A Current Appraisal," in T. Eckes and H. M. Tratner, eds., *The Developmental Social Psychology of Gender* (Mahwah, NJ: Lawrence Erlbaum Associates, 2000), pp. 123–74; N. P. Rothbard, "Enriching or Depleting: The Dynamics of Engagement in Work and Family Roles," *Administrative Science Quarterly* 46 (2001): 655–84.

19. Friedman and Greenhaus, *Work and Family—Allies or Enemies?*; R. G. Cinamon and Y. Rich, "Gender Differences in the Importance of Work and Family Roles: Implications for Work-Family Conflict," *Sex Roles* 47 (2002): 531–41.

20. Friedman and Greenhaus, *Work and Family—Allies or Enemies?*

21. Ibid.; J. T. Bond with C. Thompson, E. Galinsky, and D. Prottas, *Highlights of the National Study of the Changing Workforce* (no. 3) (New York: Families and Work Institute, 2003).

22. A. Andrews and L. Bailyn, "Segmentation and Synergy: Two Models of Linking Work and Family," in J. C. Hood, ed., *Men, Work, and Family* (Newbury Park, CA: Sage, 1993), pp. 262–75; B. E. Ashforth, G. E. Kreiner, and M. Fugate, "All in a Day's Work: Boundaries and Micro Role Transitions," *Academy of Management Review* 25 (2000): 472–911 Rothbard. "Enriching or Depleting?"; Friedman and Greenhaus, *Work and Family—Allies or Enemies?*

23. Andrews and Bailyn, "Segmentation and Synergy."

24. Mainiero and Sullivan, "Kaleidoscope Careers"; M. N. Ruderman, "Developing Women Leaders." in R. Burke and C. Cooper, eds., *Inspiring Leaders* (London: Taylor and Francis, in press).

25. Mainiero and Sullivan, "Kaleidoscope Careers"; Ruderman, " Developing Women Leaders."

26. J. A. Schneer and F. Reitman, "The Interrupted Managerial Career Path: A Longitudinal Study of MBAs," *Journal of Vocational Behavior* 51 (1997): 411–34.

27. Graves and Powell, *Women and Men in Management*; P. Bollé, "Part-Time Work: Solution or Trap?" in M. R. Loutfi, ed., *Women, Gender, and Work: What Is Equality and How Do We Get There?* (Geneva: International Labor Office, 2001), pp. 215–38; M. K. Judiesch and K. S. Lyness, "Left Behind? The Impact of Leaves of Absence on Managers' Career Success," *Academy of Management Journal* 42 (1999): 641–51; J. A. Talaga and T. A. Beehr, "Are There Gender Differences in Predicting Retirement Decisions?" *Journal of Applied Psychology* 80 (1995): 16–28; Friedman and Greenhaus, *Work and Family—Allies or Enemies?*

28. C. L. Ridgeway and S. J. Cornell, "Motherhood as a Status Characteristic," *Journal of Social Issues* 60 (2004): 683–700; A. J. C. Cuddy, S. T. Fiske, and P. Glick, "When Professionals Become Mothers, Warmth Doesn't Cut the Ice," *Journal of Social Issues* 60 (2004): 701–18.

29. Cuddy et al., "When Professionals Become Mothers"; Friedman and Greenhaus, *Work and Family—Allies or Enemies?*

30. Powell and Graves, *Women and Men in Management*; P. J. Ohlott, M. N. Ruderman, and C. D. McCauley, "Gender Differences in Managers' Developmental Job Experiences," *Academy of Management Journal* 37 (1994): 46–67; L. T. Eby, T. D. Allen, and S. S. Douthitt, "The Role of Nonperformance Factors on Job-Related Relocation Opportunities," *Organizational Behavior and Human Decision Processes* 79 (1999): 29–55; Catalyst, *Passport to Opportunity: U.S. Women in Global Business* (New York: Catalyst, 2000); M. Linehan, *Senior Female International Managers: Why So Few?* (Aldershot, UK: Ashgate, 2000); T. J. Keaveny and E. J. Inderrieden, "Gender Differences in Employer-Supported Training and Education," *Journal of Vocational Behavior* 54 (1999): 71–81; Friedman and Greenhaus, *Work and Family—Allies or Enemies?*

31. Rothbard, "Enriching or Depleting?"; Kirchmeyer, "Nonwork-to-Work Spillover"; Graves et al., "Commitment to Family Roles."

32. Rothbard, "Enriching or Depleting?"

33. Ibid.; Andrews and Bailyn, "Segmentation and Synergy"; Ashforth et al., "All in a Day's Work."

34. K. Gerson, *No Man's Land: Men's Changing Commitments to Family and Work* (New York: Basic Books, 1993); K. S. Lyness and D. E. Thompson, "Above the Glass Ceiling? A Comparison of Matched Samples of Female and Male Executives," *Journal of Applied Psychology* 82 (1997): 359–75; C. Kirchmeyer, "Determinants of Managerial Career Success: Evidence and Explanation of Male/Female Differences." *Journal of Vocational Behavior* 24 (1998): 673–92; Friedman and Greenhaus, *Work and Family—Allies or Enemies?*

35. S. D. Toliver, *Black Families in Corporate America* (Thousand Oaks, CA: Sage, 1998).

36. Ruderman, "Developing Women Leaders"; Friedman and Greenhaus, *Work and Family—Allies or Enemies?*

37. D. T. Hall and J. Richter, "Balancing Work Life and Home Life: What Can Organizations Do to Help?" *Academy of Management Executive* 3 (1988): 213–23; C. Kirchmeyer, "Managing the Work-Nonwork Boundary: An Assessment of Organizational Responses," *Human Relations* 48 (1995): 515–36.

38. Bond et al., *Highlights of the National Study*; Powell and Graves, *Women and Men in Management*; Friedman and Greenhaus. *Work and Family—Allies or Enemies?*; L. T. Thomas and D. C. Ganster, "Impact of Family-Supportive Work Variables on Work-Family Conflict and Strain: A Control Perspective," *Journal of Applied Psychology* 80 (1995): 6–15.

39. G. N. Powell and L. A. Mainiero, "Managerial Decision Making Regarding Alternative Work Arrangements," *Journal of Occupational and Organizational Psychology* 72 (1999): 41–56; Ruderman, "Developing Women Leaders."

40. Powell and Graves, *Women and Men in Management*; Friedman and Greenhaus, *Work and Family—Allies or Enemies?*

41. M. N. Ruderman and P. J. Ohlott, "What Women Leaders Want," *Leader to Leader* 31 (Winter 2004): 41–47.

42. Kofodimos, "Why Executives Lose Their Balance."

43. C. Hymowitz, "Working Fewer Hours Is Hard for Most CEOs but Some Find a Way," *Wall Street Journal* (July 12, 2005), p. B1.

44. U.S. Department of Labor, "Hours of Work," *Report on the American Workforce 1999* (Washington, DC: U.S. Department of Labor, 1999), pp. 80–109; Bond et al., *Highlights of the National Study*; P. J. Ohlott, A. Bhandary, and J. Tavares, "What Women Want: Comparing Leadership Challenges in Europe and the U.S.," *Leadership in Action* 23(3) (2003): 14–19; Mainiero and Sullivan, "Kaleidoscope Careers"; C. Hein, *Reconciling Work and Family Responsibilities: Practical Ideas from Global Experience* (Geneva: International Labour Office, 2005); Powell and Graves, *Women and Men in Management*.

45. Mainiero and Sullivan, "Kaleidoscope Careers"; Ruderman, "Developing Women Leaders"; Powell and Graves, *Women and Men in Management*.

46. Ruderman, "Developing Women Leaders."

47. Friedman and Greenhaus, *Work and Family—Allies or Enemies?*; Ruderman and Ohlott, *Learning from Life*.

48. Friedman and Greenhaus, *Work and Family—Allies or Enemies?*

49. Ruderman and Ohlott, *Learning from Life*.

50. Ibid.; Friedman and Greenhaus, *Work and Family—Allies or Enemies?*; Graves and Powell, *Women and Men in Management*.

51. Ruderman and Ohlott, *Learning from Life*.

12

Interrupting the Persistence of Gender Inequities in Loosely Coupled Systems: Effective Management Processes to Address the Lack of Institutional Support for Work/Life Issues in Academic Careers

Louise F. Root-Robbins

It has been well documented that progress toward gender equity in most work-places has not occurred at the pace expected or desired given women's rate of participation in the workforce. However, relatively little has been written regarding effective organization development and change strategies that contribute to progress toward more equitable workplaces. Most workplaces have been established by men for men. Yet fundamentally, men and women differ and have divergent life experiences. Lottie Bailyn claims that just *allowing* women to meet success criteria, on terms that men define representing *their* life experiences, does not ensure equity.[1] Equity requires integrating nonwork life experiences into policies, practices, and procedures to change existing norms and behaviors that disadvantage women. Equal opportunities and equal constraints create the potential for producing more equitable work environments.[2]

Psychologist Karl E. Weick states that intention and action are often at odds within organizations.[3] He explains that conventional images of organizations as tightly connected, responsive, and with large effects that ramify swiftly do not accurately depict how most organizations typically function. Depending on the tightness of the coupling among their parts, organizations have delays, lags, unpredictability, and erratic guidance due to unstable equilibrium and un-trustworthy feedback.[4] These characteristics contribute to a lack of effective responses to cues for change. In addition, they partially explain why faddish management ideas, strategic planning, and change efforts that do not consider these aspects are frequently unsuccessful.[5]

Achieving gender equity requires that organizations become more responsive at every level to the needs of all of their employees. An improved, more comprehensive approach by management is required. Such an approach would integrate organizational change and development skills that have been informed by the need to address not only the rational or tightly coupled aspects of an organization but also those aspects that are loosely coupled and seemingly inscrutable.[6]

This chapter uses examples from higher education institutions to explore concepts and theories related to loosely coupled systems. Academia provides a wealth of opportunities to learn about these aspects of organizations. The findings from these studies should be applicable to many other settings. Slow response to internal and external pressures to change, a feature of loosely coupled systems, also characterizes academia. For example, many social scientists and others have documented that the slow pace of women's progress in higher education has persisted, in spite of steady increases in the number of women students, faculty, and staff over the past several decades.[7] This chapter explores the organizational factors of loosely coupled systems that contribute to the persistence of gender inequities and offers recommendations to improve management processes.

DEFINING LOOSELY COUPLED SYSTEMS: CHARACTERISTICS AND FUNCTIONS

More than being a precise definition of a specific quality of organizational structure, the phrase "loosely coupled system" summarizes a way to think about aspects of organizations.[8] Predicting and activating the cause-and-effect relationship are particularly difficult for members of these systems because connections are intermittent, lagged, dampened, slow, abrupt, and mediated.[9] In this chapter, the phrase "loosely coupled system" refers not to structural looseness but to process looseness, insofar as organizational events unfold unevenly, discontinuously, sporadically, or unpredictably, if they unfold at all.[10]

Weick's description of the characteristics and functions of loosely coupled systems suggests possible ways to increase gender equity.[11] *Loose coupling* is a relative term that refers to numbers, patterns, and strengths of the connections and relationships among the organizational subsystems that are joined by few or weak common variables.[12] Loosely coupled systems have the potential to preserve many independent sensing devices and therefore know their environments better than do more tightly coupled systems, which have fewer independent, externally constrained elements.[13] However, loosely coupled systems are limited and slow in responding to disturbances and influences; therefore, subsystems, once established, tend to be relatively stable.[14] This characteristic of a loosely coupled system allows some parts of the organization to persist and lowers the probability that the organization will have to—or be able to—respond to each change in the environment as it occurs.[15]

Loose coupling also carries connotations of impermanence, dissolvability, and tacitness, all of which are potentially crucial properties of the glue holding organizations together.[16] Weak connections achieve both stability and adaptation with less interdependence, consensus, and mutual responsiveness than are usually assumed.[17] According to Weick, in loosely coupled systems several means can produce the same result; influence spreads slowly or is weak; coordination throughout the system is lacking or dampened; regulations are absent; observers have poor observational capabilities; feedback through connected networks is slow or nonexistent; there is causal independence of the various subsystems; and planned unresponsiveness exists.[18]

Like other types of organizations, loosely coupled systems must be managed properly, giving consideration to their nature and inherent challenges to achieve desired outcomes. Weick describes loosely coupled systems as having seven functions. First, persistence as an outcome of loosely coupled systems is evident in the reduced responsiveness of an organization.[19] Therefore, both archaic traditions and innovative ideas may persevere.[20] Glassman's basic argument is that loose coupling allows some portions of the organization to persist but is not selective in what is perpetuated.[21] In higher education institutions, for example, a dramatic and significant change in the academic workforce has resulted in more instructional staff, who are ineligible for tenure due to the nature of their positions, and increasing numbers of women.[22] However, higher education has neither actively responded nor articulated how it will integrate or incorporate what has become the majority of its workforce. Archaic policies and procedures defining the terms for pursuing and advancing an academic career have persisted in the face of overwhelming pressures for change.[23]

Second, a loosely coupled system may provide a sensitive sensing mechanism.[24] According to the perceptual theory of things and mediums, perception is most accurate when a medium senses something and contains many independent elements that can be externally constrained.[25] But when elements in a medium become either fewer in number, more internally constrained, or more interdependent, their ability to represent some remote thing decreases. Loosely coupled systems, when functioning well, may preserve many independent sensing elements and therefore "know" their environments better than do more tightly coupled systems, which have fewer externally constrained, independent elements. Therefore, mechanisms must be in place to gather cues for change, and the organization must be responsive to create sustainable change.

Third, loosely coupled systems adapt locally.[26] One element can adjust to and modify a local, unique contingency without affecting the whole system. Local adaptations can be swift, economical, and substantial. Thus they can result, for better or worse, in less standardization. This function is readily observed at the academic department level, where some departments integrate women and minorities well and others do not.

Fourth, loosely coupled systems tend to preserve identity, uniqueness, and separateness of organizational elements. Therefore, they create the potential for retaining a greater number of permutations and novel solutions.[27] However, that very uniqueness and separateness can also prevent good ideas from spreading. For example, effective methods for recruiting and retaining women may not be disseminated because mechanisms are not in place to share best practices.

Fifth, a breakdown in one part of a loosely coupled system can be sealed off, but this can make prompt repair difficult.[28] Tenure decisions and search and screen committees that eliminate women and minorities demonstrate how decisions made at the subsystem level can have an impact on the entire organization. Because it is difficult, if not impossible, to gain knowledge regarding these decision-making processes, it is difficult to work toward changing the outcomes.

Sixth, the more room there is for individual self-determination and autonomy, the greater the self-efficacy; however, this also increases resistance and shortens the chain of consequences.[29] For example, units and departments function autonomously; this self-determination fosters self-efficacy and control but can also lead to resistance to change.

Seventh, loosely coupled systems require less coordination.[30] For example, fund allocation in such a system is implicit and therefore unspecifiable, unmodifiable, and incapable of being used as means of change. Most faculty and staff function autonomously and do not receive or require close supervision or evaluation that is linked to their compensation. Decisions related to compensation are not transparent or consistently applied. This loosely coupled arrangement can contribute to the persistence of pay discrepancies.

CONSEQUENCES OF LOOSELY COUPLED SYSTEMS RELATED TO GENDER INEQUITIES

Persistence refers to stability, resistance to change, and continued operations—common outcomes of loose coupling. Persistence is a consequence of loosely coupled systems, along with buffering, adaptability, satisfaction, and effectiveness.[31] Each of these consequences might be construed as an organizational advantage or disadvantage, depending on one's perspective and desired outcomes. As indicated earlier, loose coupling fosters perseverance, but it is not selective in what is perpetuated; therefore, archaic traditions as well as innovative improvisations may be perpetuated.[32]

The reduced responsiveness of loosely coupled systems, a manifestation of persistence, makes them less conducive to systemwide change than those that are more tightly coupled.[33] Persistence could be perceived as an advantage if the status quo is considered satisfactory and maintaining it is preferred.

Orton and Weick suggest that persistence and buffering imply adaptation to change by neutralizing its impact.[34] Perhaps, given the persistence of gender discrepancies in academia, the slow rate of women's career advancement is an example of an organization neutralizing the impact of the influx of women into the academic workforce.[35] The lack of an effective organizational response to the well-documented trend toward escalating numbers of nontenure instructional staff and decreasing numbers of tenure track faculty positions throughout higher education is another example of negative consequences of persistence and buffering in a loosely coupled system.[36]

GENDERED NATURE OF ACADEMIA

The number of women entering the academic workforce has risen over the past several decades.[37] However, the fact that women's increased numbers have not resulted in the expected shift in the composition of the academic workforce highlights the persistence of gender inequities.[38] For example, women earn nearly half of the doctorates awarded in the United States and enter the tenure track in nearly equal numbers to men. Nonetheless, the percentage of women who hold tenured positions remains low relative to male counterparts. Women are not advancing to the upper ranks of the professoriate or to top leadership positions at the same rate as men.[39] Growing evidence reveals that women who advance in academia make personal sacrifices that men are not expected to make, which are often related to children and marriage.[40] In addition, the established norms conflict dramatically with the typical life cycle of women. Problems associated with this conflict are documented by the Mapping Project, a study of 5,087 faculty members at 507 universities and colleges.[41] For example, in higher percentages than men, women faculty reported having fewer children than they wanted, avoiding asking for reduced teaching loads when needed, and neglecting meeting family commitments that would hurt their careers.[42]

In addition, the salary advantage of male compared to female faculty members exists at all ranks and institutional types. The salary gap is largest at the rank of full professor, where, for all institutional types combined, women are paid on average only 88 percent of their male colleagues' compensation.[43]

Although women's participation in academia overall has improved, the increase comes at a time when opportunities for full-time tenured positions are declining.[44] The American Association of University Professors (AAUP) 2003 annual salary survey reported that only 48 percent of full-time female faculty members are tenured compared to 68 percent of their full-time male counterparts. As of 1998, 48 percent of all part-time faculty (but only 36 percent of all full-time faculty) were women. Females without full-time positions hold 57 percent of nontenure track lecturer and instructor positions, which provide little opportunity for tenure. As of 2000, women made up 55 percent of lecturers, 58 percent of instructors, 46 percent of assistant professors, 36 percent of associate professors, and only 21 percent of full professors.[45]

Women remain significantly underrepresented at research institutions but are heavily represented at community colleges. The proportion of full-time women faculty at two-year institutions rose from 38 percent in 1987 to approximately 50 percent in 1998. At the same time, among full professors at doctoral-granting institutions, the proportion of female faculty members was only 19 percent.[46]

EQUITY VERSUS EQUALITY

Bailyn,[47] while acknowledging the importance of protecting one's legal rights to equal pay, having freedom from harassment, and having equal access to opportunities to enter and advance in an occupation, states that equality differs from equity. Equal opportunity, even if it exists, is not equitable if constraints are unequal. She further distinguishes between equality and equity by explaining that the notion that the two concepts are the same assumes the workplace is separate from the rest of life and ignores people's lives outside of work. This notion perpetuates the myth that the workplace is gender-neutral. This myth ignores different life experiences of women and men and promotes the male model, in which work takes priority over nonwork interests and responsibilities, as the ideal academic norm. Bailyn adds that the assumptions that women can follow this model as easily as men and that they will be as successful as male colleagues if they do are false. She argues that fairness (rather than equality) is at issue and that equality should not be limited to the workplace; integration rather than separation of work and nonwork spheres is the goal. Bailyn claims equity will be impossible if one group, for example, those with caregiving responsibilities, is systematically unable to meet the requirements of the ideal worker.[48]

CUES FOR CHANGE

Documented gender inequities in academia have deleterious effects both for individuals and for higher education as an organization.[49] The future direction of higher education should not be determined by default in response to current budget pressures or to maintain the status quo.[50] Theories, models, and processes for organizational development and change management that fit with the current realities of higher education institutions are needed.[51] They must be generated, experimented with, and integrated into the core of higher education to create organizations that are equitable, flexible, responsive, and more readily adaptive to the needs of the students, employees, and society they are intended to serve.[52]

The American Association of University Professors (AAUP), American Council for Education (ACE), National Education Association (NEA), and many individual researchers have issued statements of concern regarding changes in the professoriate, specifically those related to the significant increase in nontenure track appointments and women's overrepresentation in these frequently part-time positions.[53] Over one-half of full-time instructional staff members are employed in nontenure track appointments, and a majority of university and college tenure track and nontenure track teaching faculty and staff are part-time. Academia has not heeded the dire warnings of the consequences of this shift. In fact, tenure track positions continue to decline at an alarming rate, while nontenure track appointments are dramatically rising.[54]

According to the 2003 AAUP Policy Statement *Contingent Appointments and the Academic Profession*, the minimal institutional commitment and relatively rapid turnover that characterize appointments of part-time and full-time nontenure track instructional staff mean that the faculty as a whole is less stable. Fewer members are available to support key academic activities: long-term institutional and curricular planning, mentoring newer faculty, and other collegial responsibilities, such as peer reviews of scholarship and evaluations for reappointment and tenure. In addition, growing evidence shows that the increase in nontenure track positions is resulting in negative outcomes for students.[55] It may also contribute to the decreasing number of individuals seeking doctoral degrees, as academic job possibilities appear bleak.[56] The most frequently cited explanation for the rise in nontenure track positions and decrease in tenure track positions is the need generated by the increased student enrollment at a time when funding for public higher education has steadily declined. This has resulted in hiring greater numbers of lower paid, more flexible nontenure track instructional staff.[57] However, there has been very little analysis of the cost or benefits of these trends to the academy as an organization, to the professoriate, to individuals' career options, to student outcomes, or to society. This lack of analysis has obstructed the development of innovative responses to changes in the academic workforce.

LACK OF ALIGNMENT BETWEEN WORKFORCE AND WORKPLACE NEEDS

The misalignment between the current human resource practices of academic institutions and the needs of the workforce is becoming critical. Unfortunately, the unique nature of academic institutions and the academic labor market constrains them from implementing some responses that nonacademic organizations use to address work and nonwork issues.[58] A mismatch exists between the current work environment and terms of employment on one hand and the professional and personal needs of faculty and staff members on the other.[59] This is particularly true for the new generation arriving at the academic workplace with an attitude that quality-of-life issues are as essential as tenure and salary.[60] Tenure obviously remains important but, according to *The Project on Faculty Appointments at Harvard University*, an institution's location (which also relates to the quality of life) and the ability to integrate professional and personal life are the most important factors in deciding where to accept employment.[61]

Currently, most faculty members are part of dual-career couples, and it is increasingly difficult to meet the demands of full-time work while being responsible family members and active citizens.[62] If higher education institutions do not become more nimble, creative, and adept at responding to change, these issues will become even more acute as unprecedented numbers of tenured faculty retire.[63]

As state budget allocations shrink, public higher education institutions struggle with recruiting and retaining a well-qualified, talented, diverse workforce.[64] An academic career offers few guarantees of returns on the time and financial investment in obtaining a doctoral degree.[65] Limited, relatively inflexible options exist for faculty to define the terms for achieving their career goals (i.e., tenure and promotion), and nontenure track instructional staff have nearly no flexibility to define the terms of their work.[66] Although oversimplified, enduring options in academia are to seek tenure and have a consuming career or to be nontenured and have a contingent job with limited security, compensation, and status. Neither option ensures that one's work and nonwork life will be easily integrated due to the lack of institutional support for nonwork responsibilities.[67]

New and potential scholars are migrating away from academia and looking elsewhere for career possibilities.[68] Some report making alternative career choices based on their observations of the increased number of nontenure track staff as indicated by decreasing numbers of doctoral degrees being granted.[69] There must be a better fit between the needs of the academic workforce and the workplace. Increased flexibility and more manageable workloads are most frequently cited as issues that would create greater alignment.[70]

WORK/LIFE ISSUES

Well-documented trends, such as the increased number of employed women and dual-income and single-parent families, increased hours worked, and competitive pressures have made it necessary for employees to conduct business while in the nonwork domain and vice versa.[71] Technological advances have made this overlap between work and personal life more possible. The result for many individuals, particularly those with caregiving responsibilities, has been heightened conflict or incompatible demands between work and personal commitments.[72] Role conflict is a stressor that contributes to parental overload and poor family performance.[73] It is also negatively associated with work and personal outcomes, such as lowered productivity and dissatisfaction.[74] Effective management of work and nonwork issues has significant implications for the success of individuals' careers and for the employing organizations.[75]

According to Thomas Kochan, co-director of the MIT Workplace Center and MIT Institute for Work and Employment Research, U.S. workers are confronting two major issues.[76] The first and most obvious is that the majority are working harder and longer but not achieving as much as they expected. As a result, many U.S. workers are unsatisfied and stressed.[77] The second issue is that although we are experiencing a transition from an old industrial economy to a knowledge economy, most U.S. industries, policies, and institutions continue to behave as though society has not changed. Consequently, many individuals and their families are caught in an untenable bind between the escalating demands of work and the lack of support for a personal life—a mismatch between the workplace and the workforce.[78]

This lack of alignment has been well documented.[79] Consider the following findings from the Families and Work Institute (FWI) related to today's workplaces:[80]

- Men (at 51 percent) and women (at 49 percent) participate almost equally in the workforce.
- The workplace is increasingly knowledge- and service-based, and technology driven; it is global, fast-paced, and 24/7.
- The job for life has been replaced with growing mobility and job insecurity.
- The workday is no longer 9 a.m. to 5 p.m.—men work 48.2 hours on average, and women (including the 24 percent who work part-time) average 41.4 hours per week.
- Approximately 26 percent of employees in the United States regularly work at least one weekend day.
- 56 percent of U.S. employees are 40 or older versus 38 percent in 1977.
- Technologies (e.g., voicemail, email, pagers, hand-held computers, and wireless networks) are blurring the lines between when people are work and when they are off; 46 percent report they are regularly contacted about their jobs outside of work hours.
- *Time famine*, a term coined by Leslie Perlow, is used to describe people's sense of lack of control over their time. Sixty-seven percent of employed parents say they don't have enough time with their children; 63 percent report that they don't have enough time with their spouse; and 55 percent indicate they do not have enough time for themselves.

The FWI in its 2002 report on the national study of the changing workforce proposed the following six criteria for creating an effective workplace and maximizing employees' contributions, with consideration for people's lives outside of work:

1. provide job autonomy;
2. create learning opportunities and challenges on the job;
3. develop environments where supervisors support employees' success;
4. develop environments where co-workers support each others' success;
5. involve employees in decision making; and
6. create flexible workplaces.[81]

Kochan asserts we need organizational change that is focused on encouraging community groups, labor organizations, business, and government officials to collaborate on addressing these problems.[82] In other words, we need large-scale change that incorporates a strategy to empower those closest to the problems to invent the solutions that work for them.[83] Once new workable solutions are discovered and agreed on, they can be institutionalized by transferring them into policies, structures, and operations that create responsive, flexible organizations.

INSTITUTIONAL RESPONSE

Academic workforce development is complex; decisions depend on programmatic needs, fluctuating demands, availability of qualified faculty, and budgets. Given both the likely continued employment of nontenure track staff and the long-range concerns—including preserving quality of instruction and academic freedom—ideas for institutional change need to be proposed, implemented, and studied to ensure that the contributions of this significant portion of higher education's human resources are captured, cultivated, and supported.[84]

Institutional responses to the accelerating demands and the consequent implications for the academy of the resulting changes in the workforce are not entirely clear and therefore warrant thorough exploration.[85] A thoughtful examination of the changes in the academic workforce and their impact on higher education needs to occur. The accumulating shifts in the dynamics and structure of the academic workplace and workforce have the potential to revolutionize the academy—for better or for worse.[86]

Shrinking budget allocations and diminished public support for higher education affect public and private colleges and universities nationwide. We must gain more understanding and expertise in creating academic institutions that maximize the contributions of all employees and are responsive, adaptable, and flexible in meeting workforce needs.[87] The stakes are too high not to do so; we can no longer afford to operate colleges and universities as if the world and society were the same as when higher education began.[88]

In the midst of all the changes in demographics and division of labor, two things have not changed: (1) faculty still have rigorous selection and promotion processes, and (2) faculty still bear primary responsibility for the academic and educational enterprise. Some feel that these two traditions are at the heart of the resistance to granting privileges or more prestigious titles to women and nontenured academic staff or to sharing decision making with them.[89]

ORGANIZATION DEVELOPMENT AND CHANGE

All organizations must adapt; otherwise, they risk obsolescence and atrophy.[90] Institutions of higher education have been bombarded with many irreversible internal and external changes that have had dramatic effects and that demand creative responses. However, the academy, in many ways, continues to behave as though the world is the same as it was 100 years ago. For example, it reproduces and reinforces the gendered nature of the academic workplace.[91]

Peter Eckel reported that three fundamental tasks are involved in changing higher educational institutions.[92] His analysis is based on his experience with the ACE Project on Leadership and Institutional Transformation and the Kellogg Forum on Higher Education, a collaborative project to explore and better understand institutional change and transformation. These tasks are (1) creating momentum institution-wide (and within academic units), (2) reducing barriers and factors that contribute to maintaining the status quo, and (3) facilitating different ways of thinking.

Most efforts to address issues related to the academic workplace have paid too much attention to what to change and not enough to how.[93] Interventions from the outside, or from the top down, have little chance of success. Better prospects lie in an inclusive, interactive approach in which the interventions emerge from a process of dynamic and engaged dialogue that allows for representation of all the affected groups.

Robert Blake and Jane Mouton concluded that the academy must develop an organizational model that fits universities' unique mission to "spur creativity, commitment, and convictions essential for the pursuit of excellence."[94] They did not discover an ideal or consensus model of how a college or university should operate. Instead they found contradictory images of the academy that include but are not limited to political organization, bureaucracy, quasi-informational gatherings of colleagues, input-throughput-output systems, and institutions that maintained a quasi-stationary equilibrium with their constituents.

Now, more than two decades later, the discussion continues. The issues are even more acute than when Blake and Mouton first advocated cultivating a model of excellence. They developed their model by diagnosing and describing how universities actually function and how they might operate if they were clear about their standards of excellence. They argued that the academy does not function as an organism but as a loose collection of independent units that are so free that the university resists management, administration, or supervision.

To create more equitable workplaces, organizational change must occur and management processes must be implemented to effectively address the underlying attitudes and norms. A *system* is a collection of interrelated parts, or subsystems, that interact and affect each other to varying degrees to function as a whole.[95] A systems framework for organizational development and change involves both examining relationship patterns within and among the subsystems and ways in which the organization functions in the context of these interactions and identifying points for intervention.[96] Organizations may have some rational elements, but in most, many parts are neither logical nor predictable and are not amenable to rational assumptions.[97] Frequently, members participate in functions, activities, and interactions that do not seem to be in the organization's best interest.[98] Organization development and change require understanding all aspects of an organization and noticing and questioning its less coordinated aspects—the loosely coupled parts of organizations.[99]

MANAGEMENT OF LOOSELY COUPLED SYSTEMS

Interactions among organizational members as they work to make sense of information produce a dynamic feedback loop that enables change to occur.[100] This process resembles double-loop learning and Model II theory-in-use, espoused by Argyris, which require alteration in the governing rules. In other words, it requires a new theory-in-use to address the causes of problems and to challenge established organizational patterns. Sharing accurate data promotes movement from single-loop learning, which at best attempts to solve the presenting problems but not the causes, to double-loop learning to prevent reoccurrence of the same problems. Through this exchange, organizational members begin to form new ways to think about significant organizational issues, rather than accepting the status quo.[101]

The management of loosely coupled systems has been most pronounced in the educational administration literature because in the context of educational systems, researchers typically indicate that "loose coupling is an unsatisfactory condition that should be reversed." The three most recurrent managerial strategies for managing loosely coupled systems are:

1. enhanced but subtle leadership,
2. focused effort, and
3. shared values.[102]

SENSE-MAKING AS A METHOD OF MANAGING

Sense-making involves turning a set of circumstances into a situation that is clearly understood and inspires action. Weick states that sense making fills important gaps in organizational theory and is a way to deal with ambiguity and interpret meaning in an organization. Sense-making is about the interplay of action and interpretation, rather than the influence of evaluation on choice.[103]

Data provide only a single point of information about an organization. A multitude of variables are represented in and contribute to a particular data point. Weick, Sutcliffe, and Obstfeld contend that sense-making offers a way to consider and interpret our experiences within an organization along with the complex information we observe, collect, and analyze by "materializing meanings that inform and constrain identity and action." When Weick states that meanings materialize, he means that sense-making is primarily an issue of language and communication. Organizations are constructed and "talked into existence and circumstances are turned into a situation that is comprehended explicitly in words and that serves as a springboard to action."[104]

Most universities do not employ a top-down managerial system. The faculty, academic staff, and students participate actively in a strong tradition of shared governance. Policy development depends on shared governance. Most public higher education institutions must comply with state laws and campus policies and procedures for faculty and for staff. However, most of those in management positions have not been adequately prepared for these important leadership roles and responsibilities.[105]

Efforts to address some of academia's challenges or even attempts to better understand their implications have been met with resistance and criticism. Frequently, recommended policy and procedural changes are inconsistently implemented. The inertia that must be overcome is founded in out-of-date attitudes. A major barrier to overcoming this inertia is lack of dedicated staff, time, and leadership.

Thus, any change strategies must involve modifying attitudes of those who are deeply attached to "doing things the way they have always been done." However, shared governance structure must be viewed and used as a strength and conduit for change, not opposed or circumvented. People tend to over-rationalize their behavior and attribute greater meaning, predictability, and coupling among activities. This overrationalizing makes it difficult to determine what is actually loosely or tightly coupled, adding to the challenge of implementing organizational change in academic settings.[106]

According to Dannemiller, who has integrated Kurt Lewin's action research theories into whole-system-change work, organizational change occurs as people share information, learn about one another's perspectives, determine potential answers to questions, and engage in their common vision for the future. Based on the conviction that all organizational members, not just the experts or leaders, can contribute to the wisdom necessary for success, all parts of the organization should be represented.[107]

However, the continuous response to change and adaptability that is the potential state of loosely coupled systems will not necessarily be achieved either with more contact among organizational members or with improved communication.[108] "Prevailing thinking about organizations places a disproportionate emphasis on interaction, interpersonal relations, and being together. Loose coupling imagery suggests that people get by far longer, on less thick socializing, with less pathology, and more energy and creativity than we presumed."[109]

Accordingly, simply increasing or even improving communication will not necessarily improve equity or increase flexibility in academic workplaces. Countering the negative aspects of persistence in loosely coupled systems requires mechanisms to capture what people are experiencing throughout the organization and connect those discoveries to powerful organizational leaders who make resource allocation decisions. Sense-making can potentially contribute to identifying ways to interrupt the negative consequences of persistence.

Sense-making enables people to learn about organizational realities by increasing the members' attentiveness to the events in a loosely coupled system that might otherwise go unnoticed. Members can then question which organizational events have significance, why, and how they connect. Sense-making can also contribute to taking stock of what and why organizational events do or do not occur, where connections happen and where they do not, and what is apparent and what is less transparent.[110]

According to Argyris, intervention research focuses on conducting experiments to change the status quo and assumes that organizational learning or change cannot occur without challenging an organization's routines.[111] Weick explains that sense-making involves seven properties of the workplace environment that influence the members' efforts to make sense of their situation. These properties affect individuals' initial sense of a situation and the extent to which they are willing to form a new sense of a situation that might be a better fit when confronted with specific or new information. To summarize, these environmental properties are:

1. social context—others influencing one's sense-making;
2. personal identity—one's sense of self influencing sense-making;
3. retrospect—the past influencing what is perceived as present;
4. salient cues—small details stimulating the recall of entire scenarios;
5. ongoing projects—experiences being bounded to make sense of them;
6. plausibility—events being believable and credible; and
7. enactment—that part of self being reflected in what ones sees in any moment of sense making.[112]

CONCLUSION

Organizations that excel discover how to tap the commitment and capacity of individuals at all levels to learn.[113] It is ironic that as the U.S. workforce moves toward a knowledge-based economy, dramatic changes and budgetary restrictions are threatening the core functions of the educational institutions charged with producing the next generation of workers.[114] Adding to this irony is the lack of curiosity that institutions of higher education display in regarding themselves as learning organizations and in applying knowledge related to organizational theory—mostly generated at universities—to themselves.[115]

The combination of the loosely coupled and gendered nature of academic workplaces predisposes the organization to persistence—even when what is being perpetuated has harmful consequences for the organization and its members. The persistent lack of effective organizational responses to the misalignment between workplace needs and the workforce is an issue of national significance, not just for academia but for most organizations.[116]

The best way to change a system is to engage the whole system in fostering inclusion, soliciting genuine input, and actively involving members of the organization.[117] Taking action multiplies the data available from which meaning can be constructed.[118] To review, three recurrent managerial strategies for managing loosely coupled systems should be incorporated into designed change:

1. enhanced but subtle leadership,
2. focused effort, and
3. shared values.[119]

One approach to managing such systems is double-loop learning, in which the system learns to learn. Two ways to facilitate such learning are to provide opportunities for the participants to participate in sense-making and to create a double feedback loop.[120] Such a loop requires a system to question its own underlying assumptions and values and thus risk fundamentally changing the terms of its own organizing.[121] For example, department chairs might be provided current information regarding how their department compares with all other departments on campus in recruiting and retaining women faculty and staff. If this information were regularly reviewed at faculty meetings, undoubtedly questions related to positive and negative trends in this particular department would arise, dialogue would occur, and sense making would commence. From this dialogue the department members create the opportunity to learn together what contributes to promoting gender equity.

People can contribute powerfully to organizational change when they have enough accurate information and are invited to do so.[122] Forming organizational microcosms (i.e., groups of people who represent basically the same mix of knowledge, yearnings, fears, hopes, functions, levels, wisdom, and attitudes that would be found in the larger group) provides efficient and effective access to the whole organization. According to Dannemiller's whole-scale change model, once a microcosm of an organization has a common database, this shared information is the key to creating change. This database allows participants to identify what needs to be different and to effect change in real time.[123]

Fostering dialogue about and interaction with these persistent trends and issues allows for each step of the change process to inform the next.[124] More attention must be placed on incorporating an understanding of the importance and relationship of power and authority in determining which cues for change are recognized and acted on in loosely coupled systems, such as institutions of higher education. Attention should especially focus on how power and authority relate to change associated with gender, race, and rank.

Persistence as a consequence of a loosely coupled system is an example of how important issues can be overlooked if the coupling is so loose that connections don't exist or if mechanisms are not in place to ensure optimal connections. Persistence contributes to inequities if adequate management mechanisms are not established and maintained. Excessive looseness combined with the lack of effective management mechanisms have contributed to the lack of effective organizational responses to the growing numbers of nontenure academic staff and the increasing numbers of women in these ranks. When the coupling is excessively loose and the organization does not or will not recognize cues for change, the organization can sustain negative consequences.

To achieve change in a loosely coupled system, rational, linear theories must be altered. Instead, a more sensitized approach is required to create organizational change that integrates both the rationalized, tightly coupled aspects of academia and the parts that are intractable to analysis through rational assumptions.[125]

We need to instill more mindfulness in organizations and capture people's experiences to create systems that collect, track, and respond to cues for change. We need to interact with and hold leaders and people with power and authority to make decisions accountable for creating more equitable workplaces.

NOTES

1. L. Bailyn, "Academic Careers and Gender Equity: Lessons Learned from MIT," *Gender, Work, and Organization* 10(2) (2003): pp. 137–53.

2. L. Bailyn, *Breaking the Mold: Women, Men, and Time in the New Corporate World* (New York: Free Press, 1993); R. Rapoport, L. Bailyn, J. K. Fletcher, and B. H. Pruitt, *(Beyond Work-Family Balance: Advancing Gender Equity and Workplace Performance* (San Francisco: Jossey-Bass, 2002).

3. K. E. Weick, "Educational Organizations as Loosely Coupled Systems," *Administrative Science Quarterly* 21 (1976): 1–19.

4. K. E. Weick, *Making Sense of the Organization* (Oxford: Blackwell Publishers, 2001), pp. 384–85.

5. C. Argyris, *Overcoming Organizational Defenses: Facilitating Organizational Learning* (Boston: Allyn and Bacon, 1990); T. G. Cummings, *Systems Theory for Organization Development* (New York: Wiley, 1980); H. Mintzberg, "The Design School: Reconsidering the Basic Premises of Strategic Management," *Strategic Management Journal* 11 (1990): 171–95; J. B. Quinn, H. Mintzberg, and R. M. James, *The Strategy Process: Concepts, Contexts, and Cases* (Englewood Cliffs, NJ: Prentice Hall, 1991).

6. Weick, "Educational Organizations."

7. Bailyn, "Academic Careers and Gender Equity"; L. S. Hornig, ed., *Equal Rites, Unequal Outcomes: Women in American Research Universities* (New York: Kluwer Academic/Plenum Publishers, 2003); J. R. Martin, *Coming of Age in Academe: Rekindling Women's Hopes and Reforming the Academy* (New York: Routledge, 2000); C. A. Trower and J. L. Bleak, *Study of New Scholars, Gender: Statistical Report [Universities]* (Cambridge, MA: Harvard Graduate School of Education, 2004); V. Valian, *Why So Slow? The Advancement of Women* (Cambridge, MA: MIT Press, 1998).

8. Weick, *Making Sense of the Organization*, p. 43.

9. Ibid., pp. 400–401.

10. Ibid., p. 384.

11. Weick, "Educational Organizations,", pp. 5–9.

12. K. E. Weick, *The Social Psychology of Organizing* (New York: McGraw-Hill, 1969), p. 111.

13. Weick, "Educational Organizations,", p. 6.

14. Weick, *Social Psychology of Organizing*, p. 112.

15. Weick, "Educational Organizations,", p. 6.

16. Ibid., p. 3.

17. Weick, *Social Psychology of Organizing*, p. 110.

18. Weick, "Educational Organizations,", p. 5.

19. J. D. Orton and K. E. Weick, "Loosely Coupled Systems: A Reconceptualization," *Academy of Management Review* 15(2) (1990): 203–23.

20. Weick, "Educational Organizations."

21. R. B. Glassman, "Persistence and Loose Coupling in Living Systems," *Behavioral Science* 18 (1973): 83–98.

22. Nontenure track faculty refers to adjunct, instructional academic staff and other instructional positions that are often contingent, temporary, or of limited contractual length and frequently with no certainty of renewal. At most higher education institutions, a mechanism exists for transferring to the tenure track, but it is difficult to accomplish and rarely achieved, particularly at research institutions.

23. Bailyn, "Academic Careers and Gender Equity"; T. H. Davenport and L. Prusak, *Working Knowledge: How Organizations Manage What They Know* (Boston: Harvard Business School Press, 1998).

24. Weick, "Educational Organizations."

25. F. Heider, "Thing and Medium," *Psychological Issues* 1(3) (1959): 1–34; K. Lewin, F. Heider, and G. M. Heider, *Principles of Topological Psychology* (New York: McGraw-Hill, 1936).

26. Weick, "Educational Organizations."

27. Ibid.

28. Ibid.

29. Ibid.

30. Ibid.

31. Weick, "Educational Organizations"; Orton and Weick, "Loosely Coupled Systems."

32. Orton and Weick, "Loosely Coupled Systems," p. 213; Weick, "Educational Organizations," p. 6.

33. Orton and Weick, "Loosely Coupled Systems," p. 213.

34. Ibid.

35. Bailyn, "Academic Careers and Gender Equity"; Hornig, *Equal Rites, Unequal Outcomes*; Martin, *Coming of Age in Academe*; Trower and Bleak, *Study of New Scholars*; Valian, *Why So Slow?*

36. American Association of University Professors (AAUP), *Contingent Appointments and the Academic Profession* (Washington, DC: AAUP, 2003).

37. AAUP, *Don't Blame Faculty for High Tuition: Annual Report on the Economic Status of the Profession* (Washington, DC: AAUP, 2004); A. R. Hoschschild, "Inside the

Clockwork of Male Careers," in K. P. Meadow-Orlans and R. A. Wallace, eds., *Gender and the Academic Experience* (Lincoln: University of Nebraska Press, 1994).

38. AAUP, "Balancing Faculty Careers and Family Work," *Academe* 90(6) (2004); American Association of University Women (AAUW), *Tenure Denied: Cases of Sex Discrimination in Academia* (AAUW Educational Foundation and Legal Advocacy Fund, 2004); AAUW, *Women at Work* (AAUW Educational Foundation, 2003); E. Benjamin, *Disparities in the Salaries and Appointments of Academic Women and Men* (Washington, DC: AAUP position paper, 2000); M. Heilman, "Description and Prescription: How Gender Stereotypes Prevent Women's Ascent up the Organizational Ladder," *Social Issues* 57 (2001): 657–74; M. Heilman, "Sex Stereotypes and Their Effects in the Workplace: What We Know and What We Don't Know," Gender and the Workplace: A Special Issue of *Journal of Social Behavior and Personality* 10 (1995): 3–26; Hornig, *Equal Rites, Unequal Outcomes*; J. A. Jacobs and S. Winslow, "Faculty Working Time and Gender Inequality," Paper presented at the 2003 Annual meeting of the College and University Work/Family Association in Philadelphia, PA (2003); M. A. Mason and M. Goulden, "Do Babies Matter? The Effect of Family Formation on the Lifelong Careers of Academic Men and Women," *Academe* 88(6) (2003): 21–27; M. A. Mason and M. Goulden, "Do Babies Matter (part II)? Closing the Baby Gap," Bulletin of the American Association of University Professors. Balancing Faculty Careers and Family Work, *Academe* 90(6) (2004): 3–7; M. A. Mason, and M. Goulden, "Marriage and Baby Blues: Re-Defining Gender Equity in the Academy," *Annals of the American Academy of Political and Social Science* 596 (2004): 86–103; Trower and Bleak, *Study of New Scholars*; Valian, *Why So Slow?*

39. American Council on Education (ACE), *An Agenda for Excellence: Creating Flexibility in Tenure-Track Faculty Careers* (Washington, DC: ACE: Office of Women in Higher Education, 2005); AAUP, *Statement of Principles on Family Responsibilities and Academic Work* (Washington, DC: AAUP, 2001); AAUP, *Contingent Appointments, Don't Blame Faculty for High Tuition*; R. J. Ely and D. E. Meyerson, "Theories of Gender in Organizations: A New Approach to Organizational Analysis and Change," in B. M. Staw and R. L. Sutton, eds., *Research in Organizational Behavior* (New York, JAI Press, 2000).

40. Bailyn, "Academic Careers and Gender Equity"; Mason and Goulden, "Marriage and Baby Blues."

41. R. Drago and C, Colbeck, "The Mapping Project: Exploring the Terrain of U.S. Colleges and Universities for Faculty and Families," Final Report for the Alfred P. Sloan Foundation (2003).

42. Mason and Goulden, "Do Babies Matter?" Part II; J. W. Williams and G. M. Alliger, "Role Stressors, Mood Spillover, and Perceptions of Work-Family Conflict in Employed Parents," *Academy of Management Journal* 37(4) (1994): 837–68.

43. AAUP, *Statement of Principles, Contingent Appointments*.

44. Bailyn, "Academic Careers and Gender Equity"; Hornig, *Equal Rites, Unequal Outcomes*.

45. AAUP, *Contingent Appointments*.

46. Ibid.

47. Bailyn, "Academic Careers and Gender Equity."

48. J. Williams, *Unbending Gender: Why Work and Family Conflict and What to Do about It* (Oxford: Oxford University Press, 1999).

49. Bailyn, "Academic Careers and Gender Equity."

50. M. J. Finkelstein and J. H. Schuster, "Assessing the Silent Revolution: How Changing Demographics Are Reshaping the Academic Profession," *AAHE Bulletin of the American Association for Higher Education* 54(2) (2001): 3–7.

51. Carnegie Foundation for the Advancement of Teaching, *The Condition of the Professoriate: Attitudes and Trends* (Princeton, NJ: Princeton University Press, 1989).

52. L. E. Coate, *Beyond Re-Engineering: Changing the Organizational Paradigm. Organizational Paradigm Shifts* (Washington, DC: National Association of College and University Business Officers, 1996); A. E. Guskin and M. Marcy, "Dealing with the Future Now: Principles for Creating a Vital Campus in a Climate of Restricted Resources," *Change* 35(4) (2003): 10–21.

53. AAUP, "Report on the Status of Non-Tenure-Track Faculty," *Academe* 78 (1992): 39–48; AAUP, *Contingent Appointments*; American Council on Education Center for Policy Analysis, *The New Professoriate* (Washington, DC: ACE, 2002); National Center for Education Statistics (NCES), *A Profile of Part-Time Faculty* (Washington, DC: U.S. Department of Education, Fall/October 2002); NEA Higher Education Research Center, "Part-Time Faculty," *NEA Update* 7(4) (2001); R. G. Baldwin and J. L. Chronister, *Teaching without Tenure: Policies and Practices for a New Era* (Baltimore, MD: Johns Hopkins University Press, 2001); R. G. Ehrenberg and L. Zhang, "The Changing Nature of Faculty Employment," Presented at the TIAA-CREF Institute Conference on Retirement, Retention and Recruitment, New York (April 1–2, 2004); Finkelstein and Schuster, "Assessing the Silent Revolution"; J. M. Gappa, and D. W. Leslie, *The Invisible Faculty: Improving the Status of Part-Timers in Higher Education* (San Francisco: Jossey-Bass, 1993); Jacobs and Winslow, "Faculty Working Time and Gender Inequality"; R. E. Rice, M. D. Sorcinelli, and A. E. Austin, "Heeding New Voices: Academic Careers for a New Generation," New Pathways Working Papers Series, No. 7, Washington, DC: American Association for Higher Education (AAHE) (2000).

54. AAUP, *Don't Blame Faculty for High Tuition*; D. W. Leslie, ed., *The Growing Use of Part-Time Faculty: Understanding Causes and Effects*, New Directions for Higher Education, 104 (San Francisco: Jossey-Bass, 1998).

55. AAUP, *Contingent Appointments*; E. Benjamin, "How Over Reliance on Contingent Appointments Diminishes Faculty Involvement in Student Learning," *Peer Review* (February 2002): 4–10; R. G. Ehrenberg, ed., *The American University: National Treasure or Endangered Species?* (Ithaca, NY: Cornell University Press, 1997).

56. Finkelstein and Schuster, "Assessing the Silent Revolution"; J. H. Levine, "Through Their Eyes: Undergraduate Perceptions of the Career of College Teaching," *College Student Journal* 30 (1996): 232–37; C. A. Trower, "Your Faculty, Reluctantly," *Trusteeship* 8 (2000): 8–12.

57. AAUP, *Contingent Appointments*.

58. M. D. Sorcinelli, and J. P. Near, "Relations between Work and Life away from Work among University Faculty," *Journal of Higher Education* 60 (1989): 59–81.

59. AAUP, *Statement of Principles*; Jacobs and Winslow, "Faculty Working Time and Gender Inequality."

60. C. A. Trower, "Alleviating the Torture of the Tenure Track: All It Takes Is a Little Show & Tell," *Department Chair: A Newsletter for Academic Administrators* 9(4) (1999).

61. J. Bleak, H. Neiman, C. Sternman, and C. Trower, *Faculty Recruitment Study: Statistical Analysis Report. Project on Faculty Appointments* (Cambridge, MA: Harvard Graduate School of Education, 2000); Trower and Bleak, *Study of New Scholars.*

62. Jacobs and Winslow, "Faculty Working Time and Gender Inequality"; J. A. Jacobs and K. Gerson, "Overworked Individuals or Overworked Families: Explaining Trends in Work, Leisure, and Family Time," *Work and Occupations* 28(1) (1998): 40–63; B. Probert, B. "'I Just Couldn't Fit it In': Gender and Unequal Outcomes in Academic Careers," *Gender, Work, and Organization* 12(1) (2005): 50–72.

63. D. W. Leslie, "Renewing Higher Education's Social Contracts: Transparency out of Chaos," *Educational Considerations* 30(1) (2002): 10–13.

64. M. J. Finkelstein, R. K. Seal, and J. H. Schuster, *The New Academic Generation: A Profession in Transformation* (Baltimore, MD: Johns Hopkins University Press, 1998); B. D. Ruben, ed., *Pursuing Excellence in Higher Education: Eight Fundamental Challenges* (San Francisco: Jossey-Bass, 2004).

65. R. G. Baldwin and J. L. Chronister, *Policies and Practices for a New Era* (Baltimore: Johns Hopkins University Press, 2001); *Teaching without Tenure.*

66. Baldwin and Chronister, *Teaching without Tenure*; C. A. Trower, "Your Faculty, Reluctantly," Trusteeship 8(4) (July–August 2000): 8–12; C. A. Trower, "Negotiating the Non-Tenure Track," *Chronicle of Higher Education* (July 6, 2001).

67. E. Benjamin, ed., *Exploring the Role of Contingent Instructional Staff in Undergraduate Learning*, New Directions for Higher Education 123 (San Francisco: Jossey-Bass, 2003); E. Benjamin, "Reappraisal and Implications for Policy and Research," in Benjamin, ed., *Exploring the Role* (2003), pp. 79–113; Levine, "Through Their Eyes."

68. Baldwin and Chronister, *Teaching without Tenure*; Rice et al., "Heeding New Voices."

69. AAUP, *Don't Blame Faculty for High Tuition.*

70. J. T. Bond, E. Galinsky, and E. J. Hill, *When Work Works: Summary of Families and Work Institute Research Findings* (New York: Families and Work Institute, 2004); J. T. Bond, C. Thompson, E. Galinsky, and D. Protas, *The 2002 National Study of the Changing Workforce* (New York: Families and Work Institute, 2003).

71. Bond et al., *The 2002 National Study*; L. A. Perlow, "The Time Famine: Toward a Sociology of Work Time," *Administrative Science Quarterly* 44 (1999): 57–81; J. B. Schor, *Overworked American: The Unexpected Decline of Leisure* (New York: Basic Books, 1992); R. M. Kanter, *Men and Women of the Corporation* (New York: Basic Books, 1977).

72. L. Bailyn, T. Kochan, and R. Drago, "Integrating Work and Family: A Holistic Approach," Sloan Work-Family Policy Network Report, Cambridge, MA (2001); A. Bookman, *Starting in Our Own Backyards: How Working Families Can Build Community and Survive the New Economy* (New York: Routledge, 2004); P. Moen, ed., *It's about Time: Couples and Careers* (Ithaca, NY: ILR Press—Sage House, Cornell University, 2003).

73. Moen, *It's about Time*; Schor, *Overworked American*; Bookman, *Starting in Our Own Backyards*; Jacobs and Gerson, "Overworked Individuals."

74. E. E. Kossek and C. Ozeki, "Bridging the Work-Family Policy and Productivity Gap: A Literature Review," *Community, Work and Family* 2 (1999): 7–32; Moen, *It's about Time.*

75. E. Galinsky, S. Kim, and J. Bond, *Feeling Overworked: When Work Becomes too Much* (New York: Families and Work Institute, 2001); Rapoport et al., *Beyond Work-Family Balance.*

76. T. A. Kochan, *Regaining Control of Our Destiny: A Working Families' Agenda for America* (Cambridge, MA: MIT Workplace Center, 2004).

77. J. Smithson and E. H. Stokoe, "Discourses of Work-Life Balance: Negotiating 'Genderblind' Terms in Organizations," *Gender, Work, and Organization* 12(2) (2005): 147–68; Schor, *Overworked American.*

78. P. Moen and P. Roehling, *The Career Mystique: Cracks in the American Dream* (Lanham, MD: Rowman and Littlefield, 2005); Smithson and Stokoe, "Discourses of Work-Life Balance."

79. J. Heyman, *Can Working Families Ever Win?*, J. Cohen and J. Rogers, eds. (Boston: Beacon Press, 2002).

80. Bond et al., *When Work Works.*

81. Bond et al., *The 2002 National Study.*

82. Kochan, *Regaining Control of Our Destiny.*

83. K. Lewin, *Field Theory in Social Science*, D. Cartwright, ed. (New York: Harper and Row, 1951); R. Beckhard and R. Harris, *Organizational Transitions: Managing Complex Change* (Reading, MA: Addison-Wesley, 1987); M. Weisbord, *Discovering Common Ground* (San Francisco: Berrett-Koehler, 1992); J. Surowiecki, *The Wisdom of Crowds: Why the Many Are Smarter than the Few and How Collective Wisdom Shapes Business, Economics, Societies, and Nations* (New York: Doubleday, 2004).

84. NEA Higher Education Research Center, "Part-Time Faculty," *NEA Update* 7(4) (2001).

85. Ehrenberg, *The American University.*

86. Finkelstein and Schuster, "Assessing the Silent Revolution"; J. M. Gappa and D. W. Leslie, "Two Faculties or One: The Conundrum of Part-Timers in a Bifurcated Work Force," New Pathways Project (commissioned paper),Washington, DC, American Association for Higher Education (1997).

87. Guskin and Marcy, "Dealing with the Future Now."

88. Ruben, *Pursuing Excellence in Higher Education.*

89. Bailyn, "Academic Careers and Gender Equity"; L. S. Hornig, *Equal Rites, Unequal Outcomes: Women in American Research Universities* (New York: Kluwer Academic/Plenum Publishers, 2003).

90. Ruben, *Pursuing Excellence in Higher Education.*

91. Bailyn, "Academic Careers and Gender Equity"; P. Bourdieu and J. Passeron, *Reproduction in Education, Society and Culture* (Beverly Hills: Sage, 1977); G. DeSole and M. A. Butler, "Building an Effective Model for Institutional Change: Academic Women as Catalyst," *Initiatives* 53 (1990): 1–10; E. Pajak and A. Green, "Loosely Coupled Organizations, Misrecognition, and Social Reproduction," *International Journal of Leadership in Education* 6(4) (2003): 393–413; Valian, *Why So Slow?*; Williams, *Unbending Gender.*

92. P. Eckel, "Institutional Transformation and Change: Insights for Faculty Developers," in D. Lieberman and C. Wehlburg, eds. *To Improve the Academy: Vol. 20. Resources for Faculty, Instructional, and Organizational Development* (Bolton, MA: Anker, 2002).

93. Eckel, "Institutional Transformation and Change."

94. R. Blake, J. Mouton, and M. Williams, *The Academic Administrator Grid: A Guide to Developing Effective Management Teams* (San Francisco: Jossey-Bass, 1981).

95. M. J. Hatch, *Organization Theory: Modern Symbolic and Postmodern Perspectives* (Oxford: Oxford University Press, 1997), p. 35.

96. D. Katz, R. L. Kahn, and J. S. Adams, eds., *The Study of Organizations* (San Francisco: Jossey-Bass, 1980); D. Katz and R. L. Kahn, *The Social Psychology of Organizations*, 2nd ed. (New York: Wiley, 1978).

97. Weick, "Educational Organizations."

98. Argyris, *Overcoming Organizational Defenses*; R. L. Kuhn, ed., *Generating Creativity and Innovation in Large Bureaucracies* (London: Quorum Books, 1993).

99. Weick, "Educational Organizations."

100. Dannemiller Tyson Associates, *Whole-Scale Change: Unleashing the Magic in Organizations* (San Francisco: Berrett-Koehler Publishers, 2000).

101. Argyris, *Overcoming Organizational Defenses*, pp. 92–95; J. G. March and H. A. Simon, *Organizations* (New York: Wiley, 1958).

102. Orton and Weick, "Loosely Coupled Systems," pp. 211–13.

103. K. E. Weick, K. M. Sutcliffe, and D. Obstfeld, *Organizing and the Process of Sensemaking* (in press).

104. Ibid., pp. 3–4.

105. A. F. Lucas, *Strengthening Departmental Leadership: A Team-Building Guide for Chairs in Colleges and Universities* (San Francisco: Jossey-Bass, 1994); A. F. Lucas, *Leading Academic Change: Essential Roles for Department Chairs* (San Francisco: Jossey-Bass, 2000).

106. Weick, "Educational Organizations"; Weick et al., *Organizing and the Process of Sensemaking*.

107. Argyris, *Overcoming Organizational Defenses*; Dannemiller, 2000; M. Weisbord, *Productive Workplaces Revisited: Dignity, Meaning, and Community in the 21st Century* (San Francisco: Jossey-Bass, 2004); Surowiecki, *The Wisdom of Crowds*.

108. Katz et al., *The Study of Organizations*.

109. Weick, *Making Sense of the Organization*, p. 391.

110. K. E. Weick and K. M. Sutcliffe, *Managing the Unexpected: Assuring High Performance in an Age of Complexity* (San Francisco: Jossey-Bass, 2001); Weick et al., *Organizing and the Process of Sensemaking*; K. E. Weick and K. H. Roberts, "Collective Mind in Organizations: Heedful Interrelating on Flight Decks," *Administrative Science Quarterly* 38 (1993): 357–438.

111. C. Argyris, "Unrecognized Defenses of Scholars: Impact on Theory and Research," *Organizational Science* 25(1) (1996): 79–87.

112. Weick, *Making Sense of the Organization*, pp. 460–63.

113. P. M. Senge, *The Fifth Discipline: The Art and Practice of the Learning Organization* (New York: Currency Doubleday, 1990), pp. 150–55; W. G. Tierney, ed., *The Responsive University: Restructuring for High Performance* (Baltimore, MD: Johns Hopkins University Press, 1998).

114. Guskin and Marcy, "Dealing with the Future Now"; Ehrenberg and Zhang, "The Changing Nature of Faculty Employment"; Finkelstein and Schuster, "Assessing the Silent Revolution."

115. D. Ward, "Strategic Planning at the American Council on Education (ACE): Guiding a Venerable Institution Forward into a New Century," *Presidency* 6(1) (Winter

2003); D. M. Kolb and J. M. Bartunek, *Hidden Conflicts in Organizations: Uncovering Behind-the-Scenes Disputes* (Newbury Park, CA: Sage, 1992); Ruben, *Pursuing Excellence in Higher Education*.

116. AAUP, "The Role of the Faculty in Budgetary and Salary Matters," in *Policy Documents and Reports*, 9th ed. (Washington, DC: AAUP, 2001), pp. 232–35; Bailyn, Kochan, & Drago, "Integrating Work and Family"; F. Bartolome and P. A. Evans, "Must Success Cost so Much?" in *Harvard Business Review on Work and Life Balance* (Boston: Harvard Business School Press, 2000), pp. 31–60; R. Drago and J. Williams, "A Half-Time Tenure Track Proposal," *Change* 32 (2000): 46–51; Galinsky et al., *Feeling Overworked*; P. Moen and Y. Yu, "Effective Work/Life Strategies: Working Couples, Work Conditions, Gender and Life Quality," *Social Problems* 47(3) (2000): 291–326.

117. W. Burke, *Organization Development: A Process of Learning and Changing*, 2nd ed. (Reading, MA: Addison-Wesley, 1992); Dannemiller, 2000; Eckel, "Institutional Transformation and Change"; Katz and Kahn, *Social Psychology of Organizations*; A. H. Van de Ven and D. Polley, "Learning while Innovating," *Organization Science* 3 (1992): 92–116.

118. Weick, *Making Sense of the Organization*.

119. Orton and Weick, "Loosely Coupled Systems," pp. 211–13.

120. K. E. Weick, "What Theory is Not, Theorizing Is," *Administrative Science Quarterly* 40 (1995): 385–90; C. Argyris and D. A. Schon, *Organizational Learning: A Theory of Action Perspective* (Reading, MA: Addison-Wesley, 1978).

121. Hatch, *Organization Theory*, p. 372.

122. C. Argyris, *Organizational Development* (New York: McGraw-Hill, 1971); Lewin, *Field Theory in Social Science*; Surowiecki, *The Wisdom of Crowds*; Weick, *Making Sense of the Organization*; Weisbord, *Productive Workplaces Revisited*.

123. Dannemiller, 2000; R. C. Norvall, *The Process of Change in Higher Education* (Washington DC: American Association for Higher Education, 1982); P. C. Ritterbush, ed., *Talent Waste: How Institutions of Learning Misdirect Human Resources* (Washington, DC: Acropolis Books, 1972); I. S. Rubin, "Loose Structure, Retrenchment, and Adaptability in the University," *Sociology of Education* 52 (October 1979): 211–222.

124. P. Reason and H. Bradbury, eds., *Handbook of Action Research: Participative Inquiry and Practice* (London: Sage, 2001); K E. Weick, "Organizational Culture as a Source of High Reliability," *California Management Review* 29(2) (1987): 112–28.

125. K. E. Weick, "Management of Organizational Change among Loosely Coupled Elements," in P. S. Goodman, ed., *Change in Organizations: New Perspectives on Theory, Research, and Practice* (San Francisco: Jossey-Bass, 1982), pp. 375–408; Weick, "Organizational Culture as a Source."

13

Managerial Women, Minorities, and Stress: Causes and Consequences

Margaret Foegen Karsten

This chapter explains each part of a straightforward yet complex model that tries to clarify ways in which work- and nonwork-related stressors and those related to work/life interface lead to perceived stress. Individual and organizational consequences of perceived stress and effective methods to cope with it will be described. Stress-related issues relevant to ethnic and racial minorities and women will be integrated in the discussion whenever possible. Definitions of distress, eustress, and stress and a summary of monetary costs associated with dysfunctional stress begin the chapter.

Stress has a huge impact on women, men, and people of color in the workplace. The main focus has been on *distress*, its negative effects, but *eustress*, its beneficial effects, can improve work performance. Though an individual's optimal stress level varies based on personality and other factors, peak task performance typically occurs at moderate levels. Boredom can occur when stress is low; people feel overwhelmed when it is too high.

Stress is defined here as "a physiological, emotional, and mental state that occurs in response to special demands of an event, situation, or action, moderated by individual differences."[1] Events or actions provoking stress are *stressors*. Supposedly, "only significant or unusual situations, rather than the day-to-day minor adjustments of life, can really be said to produce stress."[2] Perhaps repeated, chronic minor irritations might rise to the level of special demands in this definition.

The high costs of stress in monetary and human terms are indisputable. Costs that can be reduced to dollar amounts have been estimated at $300 billion per year.[3] According to the National Institute of Occupational Safety and Health (NIOSH), the percent of stress-related absences among blacks and non-Hispanic whites is lower than their representation in private sector workplaces with 100 or more employees.[4] The same is not true for Hispanic and Asian Americans, however. Hispanic employees account for 21 percent of stress-related absences, though only 11 percent of private sector employees working for organizations employing at least 100 are Hispanic. Comparable figures for Asian Americans are 5 percent and 4 percent. Absenteeism due to stress among Native Americans and Alaskan Natives in the private labor force is less than 1 percent.[5]

A MULTIPURPOSE STRESS MODEL

The details and assumed interrelationships of variables in stress models differ, but most follow a similar format. Stressors are related to tasks, roles, relationships, the physical environment, careers, and organizational structure, culture, or practices. They may be categorized, more generally, as work- and nonwork-related. Their effects are moderated by individual or environmental factors to produce perceived stress, which leads to positive or negative outcomes for individuals and organizations. Primary appraisals, which assess "what's at stake"[6] to decide whether a situation poses a threat, could lead to loss or harm, is irrelevant, or is a positive challenge,[7] and secondary appraisals, which evaluate resources available to reduce a situation's threat potential,[8] affect stress perceptions.

Most research focuses on negative individual or organizational stress outcomes. Individual outcomes can be classified as physiological, psychological, and behavioral, and organizational outcomes relate to commitment, performance, and withdrawal behaviors, but they may be interrelated. Individual coping mechanisms vary based on the nature, intensity, duration, and time of onset of stressors, and the nature of moderating factors. They are generally categorized as problem- or emotion-focused approaches. Stressors related to the job, organizational culture, or work environment that seem to result in adverse consequences may indicate a need for serious, long-term organizational change. Figure 13.1 is a general model of the causes and consequences of perceived stress.

The model's straightforwardness should not obscure its complexity. The same factors may be both moderating variables and stressors. Stressors may interact with each other, as may moderating variables, to worsen or lessen perceived stress. Coping methods also may serve as moderating variables, and social support may be either a coping mechanism or a moderating variable.

Stressors

Stressors may be related to gender, race/ethnicity, or both. Some stressors seem to affect most managers, regardless of gender or race/ethnicity. For example, black and white managerial women in Davidson's study both rank work overload as the top stressor.[9] Women may be more likely than men to perceive organizational politics as a stressor.[10] Minorities and females experience the glass or concrete ceiling, harassment, tokenism, isolation, stereotypes, work-family

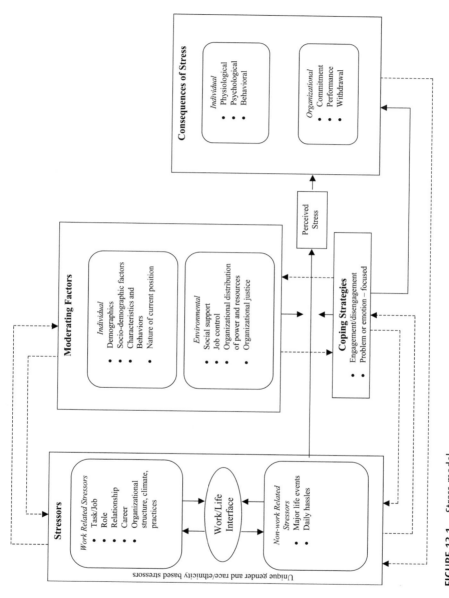

FIGURE 13.1. Stress model.

conflict, the "maternal wall," and prejudice and discrimination, thoroughly discussed by Karsten, as stressors.[11]

Work-family conflict and the maternal wall seem more problematic to whites than blacks. Ironically, due to the slavery legacy, which denied autonomy to black males and females alike, black couples may have more egalitarian relationships, and black women may view the provider role as integral to their role as parents. The *maternal wall* is a manifestation of stereotypical attitudes toward women with children, who are assumed to be more committed to their children than careers. That assumption causes them to receive fewer development opportunities than they otherwise might.[12] Failing to equally consider qualified women and men for positions is illegal, but proving that gender was the underlying reason may be difficult. White (but not black) women experience a "wage penalty" of 6 to 7 percent of income per child.[13] For that reason, the maternal wall may be a greater obstacle for white women.

Single-parent managerial women face special stressors. Compared to those with spouses or partners, they may have greater work overload, less social support, and more financial strain.[14] Their career advancement opportunities and job choice may be limited due to difficulties arranging for child care when attending evening functions, working extended hours, or traveling overnight is necessary. Executives may be expected to attend evening meetings and be able to travel. Single-parent managerial women believe they are sometimes excluded from events because other women view them as a threat.[15] This perception of executive women who are single parents represents their reality, but the extent to which it reflects a stereotype is unknown.

Compared to two-career couples, male and female single parents have less discretionary income. They must spend a larger percentage of total household income on such necessities as housing, utilities, and food. A child's illness is stressful for any parent, but single parents may not have another adult available to help care for the sick child. Extended family members may not live nearby or may be unavailable to help. Care centers that accept mildly ill children are relatively rare and may not exist in rural areas.

Male, single-parent managers face similar challenges but may be less likely to be excluded from social groups due to marital status. They still must cover basic expenses from one income, but that income may be higher than that of similarly situated women due to the persistence of a gender-based wage gap. Anecdotes indicate that those who believe the stereotype that parenting is easier for women due to nurturing abilities considered innate may have higher regard for male single-parent managers than their female counterparts.

Individual and institutional racism, prejudice, and discrimination are particularly relevant stressors for minority managers. All subjects in a study of blacks experienced racial discrimination at some point in their lives; 98 percent had encountered it within the previous year.[16] Seventy-five percent of a sample of 156 African Americans had experienced racial stress as compared to 44 percent of a sample of 376 U.S. citizens of Western European descent.[17] Of the one-third of survey respondents who reported having dealt with discrimination in another study, 61 percent said it was "moderate" or "severe."[18] Examples include inequities in pay, promotion, or job assignments; denial of housing; and refusal of service.

Though many experience everyday unfair treatment regardless of their race/ethnicity, it also may be a manifestation of individual racism. For example, blacks report receiving poorer service in stores and restaurants, less courteous treatment than others, and being followed in stores due to a suspicion of shoplifting.[19] Cornel West, a noted Princeton scholar who formerly taught at Harvard, recounts being unable to hail a taxi in New York City. Though he acknowledges that this incident is minor compared to experiences of other blacks, West says, "the memories cut like a merciless knife at my soul as I waited on that godforsaken corner."[20]

Institutional racism is defined as "policies that exclude [minority group members] from full participation in the benefits offered to other members of society."[21] It may entail imposing harsher penalties on illegal activities when engaged in by minority than majority group members. For example, Utsey and colleagues cite federal drug laws that apply a less onerous penalty for possession of powdered cocaine, which whites are more likely to use, than crack cocaine, which is more available to blacks.[22] Though severe penalties for *any* type of cocaine possession are justifiable in this author's opinion, they should be applied uniformly, not in a way that may create race-based adverse impact. In addition, the root cause of the higher job loss rate among blacks than whites may relate to underlying institutional racism.

More than those of Chinese or Korean descent, Asian Americans of Japanese and Filipino ancestry are likely to think that a double standard in law enforcement results in punishment of a greater percent of Asian Americans than whites who violate the law.[23] All four groups agree that Asian Americans with identical qualifications hold worse positions than whites and that Asians must perform better than whites to succeed.[24]

Other stressors unique to racial/ethnic minorities, including biculturalism, acculturation, and minority status, will be presented next. Then, stressors that occur for those who are doubly disadvantaged based on race/ethnicity and gender will be discussed.

"Soul wound" and "historical trauma" are stressors for Native Americans and other minority groups that have encountered racism and discrimination.[25] Forced migration to urban areas, seizure of land (often without proper compensation), and stays at boarding schools designed to indoctrinate them in the majority culture have contributed to trauma among Native Americans. Another example of an action causing soul wound is the involuntarily sterilization of 40 percent of their women of childbearing age in the 1970s,[26] carried out under the direction of the Indian Health Service. Forced internment of Japanese Americans during World War II also may qualify as historical trauma. Forced splitting of families, physical abuse, and rape of black women by white plantation owners most likely wounded and traumatized blacks even more, but debating which group's pain was worse is futile. Rather, taking steps to root out racial and ethnic intolerance and its negative consequences wherever it occurs is more productive.

Violence is a stressor for targets, bystanders, and perpetrators, and Native Americans have experienced more than their share. They are 2.5 times more likely to be victims of violent crime than the average U.S. citizen. At 98 per 1,000, the violent crime rate among Native American women is greater than for females of any other ethnic group. They are affected by violence at a rate nearly 50 percent higher than that which affects black men.[27]

Women and minorities both deal with social isolation, but its effects may be more pronounced for minorities, particularly blacks. Those who relocate to areas without a strong black community may experience isolation in their neighborhoods as well as their workplaces.[28]

Biculturalism occurs when people feel they must behave, dress, speak, and act differently on the job than at home due to their race or ethnicity. It creates stress for minorities in a majority-dominant work culture. Toliver identifies a positive side of biculturalism in her study of black managers.[29] She maintains that it may be beneficial for blacks to be able to draw on the strengths of two different communities on and off the job. Furthermore, she suggests that marginalization, rather than being a stressor, encouraged the sample she studied to believe that they were part of an elite group while growing up. They had advantages that others of similar ethnic and racial backgrounds lacked, and they were expected to succeed in future careers and in life.

Native Americans typically do not view biculturalism as an advantage. Colonization forced them to adapt to a majority culture that espoused values conflicting with their own. Though the cultures of specific tribal nations differ, they invariably emphasize cooperation, group identification, responsibility for friends and extended family members, and tradition.[30] These characteristics contrast with the majority culture's emphasis on competition, individual achievement, and consumerism.

Acculturation is the process through which people, particularly immigrants or racial/ethnic minorities, adapt to the dominant culture or choose not to do so. *Assimilation* is an acculturation strategy involving immersion in and acceptance of the mainstream culture. *Integration* means being immersed in both the dominant and minority cultures; *marginalization*, linked with the highest stress levels, implies a rejection of both. As an acculturation strategy, *separation* focuses on the minority culture and rejects the majority culture.[31]

Whether or not the acculturation process is a stressor has been debated. It seems to be for Mexican American women, who risk losing support of their ethnic group, and for Native American women. According to Zambrana and colleagues,[32] "risky health behaviors, stress levels, and medical risks all seemed to increase with greater acculturation and decreases in social support of the Hispanic community." LaFromboise, Heyle, and Ozer report that acculturation has led some Native American males to try to dominate females, thereby eroding the previously existing complementary relationship between the sexes.[33] Other studies, however, show more stress among less acculturated individuals.[34] Native American women seem to deal with acculturation better than their male peers. LaFromboise, Heyle, and Ozer suggest this is due to their traditionally greater role flexibility, which made them willing to assume roles that Native American men would have spurned.[35]

Minority status is a social stressor for Asian American refugees and immigrants, but little research has systematically analyzed its impact.[36] Racial/ethnic minority and socioeconomic status combine with institutional role expectations to form a social stratification system, or hierarchical pecking order in which having low status is a stressor.[37]

"Negative synergy" may explain why stressors associated with being female and a member of a racial/ethnic minority group may be more harmful than an additive model implies. It may place their career progress in double jeopardy. Few studies have been done on such individuals, but Davidson's comparison of black and white managerial women shows that both groups rank being undervalued or underutilized among their top three stressors.[38] Beyond that, stressors differ between the two groups. In addition to work overload, mentioned earlier, performance pressure, powerlessness, and a need to be three times as qualified to get the same job as whites complete the top five stressors for executive black women. For their white counterparts, the top five stressors included being the boss, having to acquire and use managerial styles considered masculine, and being assertive and confident.

Some work- and nonwork-related stressors, such as the threat of terrorism and workplace violence and the effects of immigration on racial/ethnic minorities, are beyond the scope of this chapter. They are real concerns, but because volumes could be written about either, they will not be addressed here.

Work-Related Stressors

Work-related stressors appear in Figure 13.1. Change and resulting lack of control may be overriding factors that affect each category of stressor.[39] Job stressors may be quantitative, such as work overload or underload, or qualitative. Either a lack of skills to accomplish a task or repetitive, boring work could be qualitative stressors. The quality of the job experience, not just the quantity of work, helps determine whether it challenges incumbents or provokes strain. Jobs featuring energizing work on diverse tasks, an opportunity to learn, a sense of achievement, and a match between the incumbent's interests and abilities and job requirements have beneficial effects on women's health.[40] Similarly, women who perform "substantively complex" jobs independently and feel valued have "the highest levels of well-being."[41]

Decision latitude and psychological demands influence whether jobs are considered challenging or too taxing. *Skill discretion*, the opportunity to use different skills on the job, and *task authority*, the ability to make decisions affecting one's work, compose decision latitude.[42] Jobs can be placed in one of four quadrants of a grid based on whether psychological demands and decision latitude are relatively low or high. Those featuring both high psychological demands and control, such as those of attorneys and accountants, are of "average" stress; some speculate that higher level managerial jobs also could be placed in this quadrant.[43] Jobs characterized by high psychological demands but low control are most stressful. Lower level managers, mail carriers, administrative assistants or secretaries, teachers, nurses, and restaurant servers fit in this quadrant.[44]

Inter- or intrarole conflict, ambiguity, and role incongruity are examples of role demands. *Interrole conflict* occurs when demands of two different roles clash. For example, if the job requires attendance at a reception outside normal working hours at the same time an employee plans to have dinner with her daughter to celebrate a special occasion, that employee may experience interrole conflict between the roles of parent and employee. *Intrarole conflict* may occur when competing priorities exist at work and synergy is impossible. Spending time on one priority makes less available to devote to the other. *Ambiguity* means uncertainty about tasks to be accomplished or the best ways to complete them. First-time managers typically deal with much ambiguity.

Because the percentage of women and men in management, overall, is nearly equal in the United States, women in leadership roles should no longer be viewed as incongruous. Nevertheless, those who have rigid notions of pre-scribed and proscribed gender-related stereotypes still may perceive role incongruity when they see women in top leadership roles.[45] They also may perceive role incongruity among men whose active involvement with their families necessitates leaving work early or being unavailable for work-related travel.

Challenges associated with maintaining relationships with bosses, co-workers, and subordinates are interpersonal stressors. Harassment is an extreme example of a maladaptive approach to such sources of stress and has been discussed elsewhere.[46] Managers, by definition, must get things done through others, so their jobs are susceptible to relationship stressors. They must reward, motivate, discipline, and gain cooperation from employees; listen to their concerns; mediate disagreements; and evaluate performance. Interpersonal or personality conflicts may occur during any of those activities. If they are *functional conflicts*, in which people ultimately resolve differences, they may be productive. *Dysfunctional conflicts*, the goal of which is to attack and discredit those with opposing views, are counterproductive and create distress.[47]

Conflicts with supervisors tend to induce more distress than those with co-workers,[48] and women may be more upset than men by interpersonal conflict.[49] However, this tendency may not exist for managerial women who have adopted leadership styles similar to those of male peers. Managers' relationships with colleagues may induce stress, and peers may create tension by exerting group pressure to punish workplace nonconformists.

Many advantages of diversity management exist, but if a diverse workforce is not handled appropriately, relationships may become strained. Then *diversity stress*, defined as difficulty caused by uncertainty about the nature of a multicultural situation and suitable responses,[50] may occur.

Stressors associated with the physical environment on the job are self-explanatory. They include inadequate ventilation, extreme temperatures, and noise.[51] Hazards from malfunctioning equipment, potential dangers due to lax security measures, and problems associated with new technology use also fit in this category. Technological change and use of new equipment may lead to negative consequences in some; others will react positively. Proper ergonomic techniques help people avoid strain; proper lighting and periodic exercise may prevent physical strain associated with overuse of video display terminals.

Common career stressors are job insecurity, obsolescence, lack of promotion, and inadequate mobility. Fear of losing one's job is visceral, but in the labor market of the early twenty-first century, lifelong learning is the best guarantee of future employability. Though career ladders are much shorter than they were in the mid-twentieth century, some still mistakenly equate success with vertical movement or number of promotions received. With such a mindset, disappointment is inevitable. Employees should be urged to adopt a more realistic view of career progress and may need to broaden their concept of success.

Aspects of an organization's structure, culture, and practices may become stressors. For example, spreading responsibility for accomplishment of a major project to many units without ensuring coordination could be a structural stressor.[52] A closed, authoritarian culture would be a stressor for many. Failure to define performance criteria, development of vague criteria after an evaluation period ends, rather than at the outset, or distribution of rewards based on "politics" or "popularity" rather than on clear contributions to the organization's goals also are stressors.[53]

Work/Life Interface

The work/life interface is labeled as such to emphasize the fact that boundaries exist between work and home regardless of whether employees currently have obligations to members of a nuclear or extended family. Single employees who live alone may have parents, step-parents, or other relatives who will need their assistance in the future. As Boyar and colleagues state, "All employees have the potential to experience work-family conflict and should not be excluded because they are unmarried, do not have children living at home, or their spouse [assuming they have one] does not work."[54]

This section will focus on conflict that occurs at the work-life or work-family interface. Two distinct variables have been identified: *work-family* and *family-work* conflict. Both are types of interrole conflict that occur when demands of one role make fulfilling requirements of the other difficult.[55] In the

1990s, 25–50 percent of individuals in the United States from ages 25 to 54 who did not live alone and were employed at least 20 hours per week faced work-family conflict (WFC). In contrast, only about 10–14 percent experienced family-work conflict (FWC).[56]

Two features of work-family boundaries, namely, flexibility and permeability, affect conflict and integration levels and ease of transition in either direction. Those working from home have greater *boundary flexibility*, which means they have more discretion regarding where and when they work. *Permeability* refers to the degree to which work interferes with personal or family life and vice versa.[57] Flexibility and permeability promote integration and ease work-home transitions (and vice versa) but also may be associated with increased conflict. Employees retain some control over boundary permeability, however. Those working at home can establish rules to minimize interruptions from other household members while they are engaged in job-related tasks.

Interestingly, WFC relates positively to FWC, but the latter is inversely related to the former.[58] Perhaps this is because family boundaries are easier than work boundaries to infiltrate. When work prevents employees from performing family roles adequately, a spillover of negativity may result. Conflict originating in the family is less likely to spill over to work because "employees make adjustments in their home lives rather than their work lives, since the immediate effect is less damaging to [their] livelihood."[59]

Certain factors increase the odds of WFC, FWC, or both, and others have a protective effect. Negative affectivity, list-making, and use of avoidance or resignation as coping techniques are linked to WFC and FWC. It seems reasonable that negative moods and perceptions and passive responses could increase these types of conflict, but their association with list-making seems counterintuitive initially. People habitually underestimate the amount of time it will take to complete tasks, however.[60] When they see many remaining tasks on to-do lists, they feel as if they have lost control, which may increase perceptions of WFC or vice versa.[61] A preference for being organized negatively associates with WFC and FWC.[62] Preoccupied attachment styles, in which people think of one domain while they are physically in the other, increase the chance of FWC, as do marital tension,[63] number of children, a lack of childcare, and criticisms or burdens family members impose.[64]

Psychological involvement in the job, low levels of supervisory support for those who are highly involved with their work, job dissatisfaction, and work overload increase the risk of WFC.[65] Factors such as "hardiness," supervisory support, and "informal accommodation of work to family" reduce the risk of WFC.[66] Conscientiousness lessens the chances of FWC as do perceptions of instrumental and emotional support.[67]

Among other criticisms of studies on WFC and FWC, Boyar and colleagues lament that "measurement of family responsibility has been deficient."[68] They propose examining the number of people residing in a household rather than number of children to avoid underestimating the effects of providing in-home care for an elderly relative or the children of a sibling.[69] Perhaps extent of physical and/or mental disabilities of those living in the home also should be considered.

Little evidence supports the role of gender as a mediating variable between predictors and outcomes of WFC or FWC in the United States.[70] A study of over 12,000 employees in the Netherlands, however, shows that predictors of WFC differ by gender. Overtime, amount of commuting time, physical demands, and the presence of dependent children increase the likelihood of WFC for women there. Job insecurity, shift work, full responsibility for household duties, and accountability for the care of a chronically ill child in the home predict WFC for men.[71]

Joint outcomes of FWC and WFC are marked with an asterisk on Table 13.1. In addition, WFC is negatively related to organizational commitment;[72] FWC is inversely related to self-reported performance and positively linked to absenteeism.[73]

The last work-life interface issue to be addressed is *stress contagion*, or crossover. Unlike spillover, in which one person's distress in a role, such as work, causes his or her stress associated with personal or family roles to rise, *crossover* occurs when increased distress in one spouse or partner leads to higher distress in the other.[74] For example, a managerial woman whose spouse is a health care professional experiences distress when her husband is called to the hospital where he is employed after normal working hours to assist in life-threatening situations.

Westman indicates that crossover is somewhat more likely to go from husband to wife than vice versa, perhaps because women are more likely to provide social support and to empathize with their husbands' stress.[75] Suggesting that women who have been socialized to accept the "feminine" gender role and have internalized gender stereotypes might be more susceptible to stress contagion is premature, but future research on this idea might be productive.

Nonwork-Related Stressors

Categorizing major life events and daily hassles as nonwork-related stressors may be inaccurate, because some of each may be job-related. This section, however, will focus primarily on life events and daily irritations that occur off the job.

Major life events that are stressors are typically evaluated on checklists or scales. One example is the Holmes and Rahe Social Readjustment Rating Scale (SRRS), developed more than thirty-five years ago to assess the amount of life stress in a year. Most stressors listed in the SRRS relate to personal (not organizational) factors. Items include a spouse's death, a major personal accomplishment, or the birth or adoption of a child. Unlike some checklists, the SRRS

TABLE 13.1.   Adverse Consequences of Stress

To the Individual	To the Organization
Physical	*Withdrawal*
Elevated blood pressure—6,7,11	Increased absenteeism
Coronary heart disease—7,11	Increased tardiness
Headaches—10	Increased voluntary turnover
Psychogenic disorders—12	
Relatively short menstrual cycles—12	*Commitment*
Physical illness (skin disease, cancer)—3	Reduced loyalty (hindrance-related stress)
Raised risk of miscarriage, pre-eclampsia during pregnancy—2	Increased job search (hindrance-related stress)
Low energy levels—9	Increased intent to quit* (hindrance-related stress)
Decline in physical health*	Decreased job involvement
Psychological/emotional	Decreased organizational commitment
Depression—3,5,6,8,10,11*	
Anxiety—3,5,10,11*	*Performance quality and quantity*
Anger/frustration—3,10,11	Reduced productivity
Sleep disturbances—3,10,11	Increased accident rate
Exhaustion—3	Increased error rate
Mental fatigue—11	
Disappointment—10	
Increased psychological distress*	
Reduction in mental well-being*	
Suicidal thoughts—3	
Job dissatisfaction—3*	
Reduced morale—2	
Changes in personality characteristics—9	
Worsened existing personality problems—9	
Weakened emotional and moral constraints—9	
Decline in interest and enthusiasm—9	
Increased cynicism about clients, colleagues—9	
Life dissatisfaction*	
Decreased family satisfaction*	
Cognitive—9	
Decreased concentration	
Increased distractibility	
New information is ignored	
Deterioration of long- and short-term memory	
Deterioration of long term planning ability	

(*continued*)

TABLE 13.1. (Continued)

To the Individual	To the Organization
Behavioral	*Legal and medical costs*
Increased substance abuse — 4,11*	Increased health care consumption
Increased conflict — 4	Increased workers' compensation claims
Eating disorders — 12	Increased number of lawsuits
Smoking — 2	*Other*
Increased shifting of responsibility to others — 9	Increased employee theft
"Bizarre" behavior patterns — 9	Increased aggression
	Increased workplace violence

*Outcomes of Family-Work and Work-Family Conflict
Key

1 = Managers	7 = Blacks
2 = Executive women	8 = Filipino Americans
3 = Black executive women	9 = Source Fontana (1989) [may not be empirically based]
4 = Native Americans	10 = Asian Americans
5 = Native American women	11 = Nonmanagerial employees
6 = Women of color	12 = Employed women

assigns a weight to each event. For example, a speeding ticket counts 11; a spouse's death counts 100.[76]

Items including responsibility for preparation for major holidays were added to the SRRS in the late 1980s or early 1990s to reflect the fact that some stressors may affect women and men differently.[77] Until recently, women typically got ready for holidays by making special foods, buying gifts, and preparing to entertain, regardless of their employment status. Such duties can be time-consuming for anyone who assumes them. Other stressors added to the SRRS to reflect the changing times were single parenthood, crime victim status, chemical dependence, and the process of parenting teens.

The likelihood of becoming ill or injured in the next two years is linked to the overall SRRS score if people do not alter their stress responses. Those who score at least 300 have an 80 percent chance of becoming seriously ill in the future if they continue their current response pattern to stressors. If effective coping mechanisms are used, high SRRS scores may not necessarily result in sickness or injury, however.[78]

The adequacy of major life events checklists in measuring stressors has been debated since the 1970s.[79] After acknowledging that the massive stress literature supports a connection between social stress, as evaluated by a major life events checklist, and mental problems, Turner and Avison question whether results would differ based on gender, race/ethnicity, and socioeconomic status.

Their examination of recent life events, chronic stressors, total lifetime major events, daily discrimination, and total stress in a sample of 900 young black and white males and females shows that reliance on "recent life events systematically and dramatically underestimates the significance of social stress for the mental health of young adults" and that "checklist scores yield substantially biased estimates of total stress exposure across gender, race/ethnicity, and socioeconomic status."[80]

Measuring exposure to recent life events alone without considering chronic stressors may lead to the conclusion that men experience slightly more total stress,[81] but this may not be true. Stress components tend to offset one another. For example, though men witness more violence and are more likely to report exposure to traumatic events, they seem to have less social stress than women. Because women are more likely than men to be affected by stressful events that happen to friends, co-workers, and relatives, they tend to report more strain-producing major and recent life events and more deaths on the SRRS.[82]

In Turner and Avison's study, blacks' reported levels of nearly every type of stress analyzed exceeded those of whites. An inverse relationship occurred between reported stress and socioeconomic status. Respondents in the lowest third based on socioeconomic status showed higher levels of every stress measure than those in the middle or top third.[83] Thus, "limiting stress measurement to a checklist of recent events significantly overestimates total stress exposure among women relative to men and systematically underestimates such exposure among African Americans relative to whites and among persons of lower socioeconomic status relative to their more advantaged counterparts," according to Turner and Avison.[84]

Those disagreeing with the notion that major life events are the most crucial determinants of dysfunctional stress contend that the cumulative effect of small, repeated irritations such as traffic congestion or minor disagreements can be more harmful.[85] Consistent with this view are the ideas that the "mental health effect of chronic stress can be stronger than acute stress,"[86] and minor instances of racial discrimination may "have greater effects on health outcomes than their magnitude may suggest."[87] Furthermore, Meyer notes that many researchers refuse to use scales measuring daily annoyances because they may be influenced by people's moods at the time. Perceptions of daily hassles as stressors may differ based on race/ethnicity. Nonmanagerial Asian American women report higher levels than people of any other ethnic group.[88]

MODERATING FACTORS

Characteristics and behaviors that may moderate the effect of stressors on perceived stress and its consequences to be discussed are agentic and instrumental characteristics, self-efficacy and self-esteem, ethnic identity, hardiness, locus of control, negative affectivity, perfectionism, Type A behavior, and workaholism. Available literature will be summarized, but readers are cautioned that imprecise definitions may lead to overlap or confounding of moderating factors. Also, the literature has many gaps. A few studies examine effects of individual characteristics and behaviors on stress among managers; some look at the impact on employees in general. Research on stress and managerial women has typically focused on white women; research on executive women of color related to factors that buffer the impact of stressors on perceived stress is rare.

Agentic and instrumental characteristics are similar and are related to efficacy. Optimism, self-efficacy, and instrumentality have been called "agentic traits."[89] One definition of *instrumentality* is "agency or means"; assertiveness and confidence are examples of instrumental characteristics according to Portello and Long.[90] Efficacy is the power to produce a desired effect; *self-efficacy* is one's belief that he or she can carry out a task or behavior successfully.[91] All three terms imply action and accomplishment. Managerial women have stronger agentic qualities than female clerical workers, according to Long.[92] Such characteristics are associated with more positive views of the work environment and fewer reported daily annoyances.[93]

Contrary to expectations, Portello and Long indicate that executive women scoring high on instrumental qualities evaluate interpersonal conflict as more troubling than those scoring lower after effects of *negative affectivity*, or negative moods, are removed.[94] This may stem from a belief that as managers, they should be able to deal effectively with interpersonal relations and frustration when doing so is difficult.[95]

The impact of self-efficacy as a moderating variable is mixed. It reduces effects of role overload on anxiety and tension among military staff but does not mitigate the effects of stressors on strain among educational employees.[96]

Self-esteem, the extent to which people value and like themselves, decreases the chance that stressors will result in distress. Low self-esteem is linked to anxiety, depression,[97] reduced self-efficacy, and an increased desire to please others.[98] Compared to men in the workforce, employed women are more likely to believe that others hold them in high regard. Because managerial women typically occupy lower ranked positions than male peers and get relatively little recognition, however, they may have lower self-assessments and therefore may not benefit from the buffering effect of high self-esteem to the same degree that men do.[99]

Racial discrimination affects self-esteem, especially among African Americans. In a study of nonmanagerial African Americans, Simpson and Yinger show a negative relationship between discrimination and both self-esteem and life satisfaction.[100] Nonetheless, 60 percent of Davidson's female executive interviewees seem satisfied with their levels of self-confidence.[101]

The situation differs for Chinese nonmanagerial women in Toronto who have experienced discrimination. They are more likely to have reduced self-esteem compared to Chinese women who have not encountered discrimination. Interestingly, weak evidence indicates that Chinese men who have been discriminated against have higher self-esteem than those who have not.[102]

For Filipino Americans,[103] urban Native American women,[104] and perhaps other groups, a strong ethnic identity buffers the effects of racial discrimination and prejudice on negative outcomes, such as depression. *Ethnic identity* is a high degree of commitment and strong connection to one's ethnic group, as evidenced by knowledge of and pride in its heritage and significant participation in its cultural events and practices.[105] Mossakowski suggests that it may be difficult for discrimination to affect the self-esteem of those with a strong ethnic identity because they immediately dismiss negative racial stereotypes as false. *Enculturation*, or the process through which minorities develop ethnic identity, helps Native American women avert depression and avoid psychological distress and alcoholism while enhancing their self-esteem.[106]

Hardiness, a characteristic attributed to managers, views change as a positive challenge and involves resilience and stress resistance. Because it entails a sense of control over one's life, hardiness may be confounded with locus of control, to be discussed next. It includes a commitment to an important goal or activity.[107] Evidence about whether hardiness mitigates the effects of stressors on strain is mixed, however.

Locus (literally "place") of control may be internal or external and is on a continuum. People with *an internal locus of control* believe their efforts affect outcomes. They are achievement-oriented, responsible individuals who take the initiative to accomplish tasks.[108] Those with an *external locus* believe they lack influence; events that are beyond their control simply occur. Managers are more likely than nonsupervisory employees to have an internal locus of control.[109] As a result, they experience fewer psychological complaints.[110] Managerial women are less likely to have an internal locus of control than male counterparts, which puts them at heightened risk of developing psychological maladies.[111] Studies of managerial women that produced these results are based mainly on white women and may or may not generalize to women of color. In addition, executive women do not seem to have higher anxiety, hostility, or depression than nonmanagerial employees.[112]

Negative affectivity is a tendency to view events pessimistically and is characterized by anger, anxiety, and depression. It colors perceptions of stressors and strain and is linked to frequent use of ineffective coping techniques among white executive women.[113] Whether negative affectivity is a moderator that should be factored out of studies analyzing the relationship between stressors and strains or a variable whose impact on strain is mediated by stressors is being debated. Removing it may only be appropriate if people with high negative affectivity report higher stress levels than those that actually exist.[114] Determining when this occurs seems nearly impossible because self-reported perceptions of strain are subjective. Another unresolved question regarding negative affectivity that is measured via self-reports is whether those who have a high degree perceive additional stressors that others fail to see or choose work environments characterized by above average stress levels.[115]

Women generally have more negative affectivity than men, but women in positions of low control are especially susceptible.[116] This may indicate that negative affectivity has less impact on executive females than on other female employees because management positions, particularly at higher levels, are characterized by a high degree of control.

Several studies show gender differences in depression and unhappiness with women reporting higher levels than men.[117] These are based primarily on whites in various occupations and may or may not generalize to women and men in management. Perhaps women report more negative affectivity because it is more socially acceptable in the United States for women than men to have and openly express intense emotions.[118] Though executive women may differ from the norm, women, with some exceptions, tend to mull over negative emotions and events more than men do, and rumination prolongs depressed moods.[119] This inclination also may contribute to higher reported negative affectivity.

The next three moderating factors—perfectionism, Type A behavior, and workaholism—have similarities. An inner compulsion to avoid error or accomplish as much as possible may be at the root of each.

Perfectionism tolerates no mistakes. Women are more likely than men to have self-imposed standards of perfectionism,[120] but whether this finding generalizes to managerial women and men of various ethnicities is unknown.

Type A behavior has been described as time-conscious, competitive, aggressive, and hard-driving. The "free-floating hostility" associated with Type A behavior may be its most damaging characteristic; that part has been linked to increased coronary heart disease.[121]

Some studies show that women in management exhibit higher levels of Type A behavior than men,[122] but this may reflect differences in organizational environments. Environmental stressors and challenges that managerial women often face in environments numerically dominated by men may precipitate Type A behavior.[123]

The coping method used moderates the effects of Type A behavior on strain. Executive women who employ *problem-focused styles*, in which they attempt to resolve the difficulty directly and actively, reduce symptoms of strain. Those resorting to emotional approaches, in which they vent feelings, seek social support, and blame themselves, have more strain.[124]

Three components characterizing *workaholics* are an inner compulsion to work and high involvement in and low enjoyment of work. In a study of primarily white female MBAs, Burke compares workaholics to "work enthusiasts," formerly dubbed "extra-effort people," and "enthusiastic workaholics."[125] *Work enthusiasts* have high involvement and joy in work but do not feel driven; *enthusiastic workaholics* rate high on all three dimensions. Workaholic managerial women are less optimistic about future careers and less satisfied with their communities and friends than their counterparts who are work enthusiasts;

they have less job, career, and family satisfaction than either work enthusiasts or enthusiastic workaholics.[126] A direct relationship exists between feelings of being driven to work and poor physical and emotional well-being and between work enjoyment and positive well-being.[127]

Enactment of multiple roles simultaneously may buffer the negative effects of stress according to those who believe the *expansion theory*, an idea that human energy is a renewable resource and is not scarce.[128] Instead of draining energy, multiple roles replenish it because people gain resources from each role. When career disappointments occur, employees can draw strength from their relationships. Becoming addicted to work due to personal problems is not recommended, but focusing on work temporarily may provide the perspective needed to objectively evaluate a personal situation.

Other remaining moderating variables include financial resources, management level, and the end of a marriage through death, divorce, or separation.

Portello and Long present evidence that executive women who are married, have children, and have relatively high incomes evaluate stress more positively.[129] How much of the favorable assessment is due to income level and how much is due to additional roles of wife and mother is unknown. Smith reports that stress rises as employees' salaries increase, but other studies contradict this.[130] Female managers with relatively low financial resources who perceive the work environment as more demanding and less supportive are more likely to perceive relationship stressors as threats to their competence.[131]

As executive women are promoted, they are more likely to have jobs that encourage good health and positive environments. Female chief executives seem to have less global job stress than managerial women at lower levels.[132]

Dissolution of a marital relationship may be linked to stress long after it ends. A greater proportion of those who are widowed, separated, or divorced report high stress compared to those who are not.[133] Smith's study does not report stress variations among single (never married), partnered, and currently married individuals.

ENVIRONMENTAL FACTORS

Environmental factors that may moderate the effect of stressors on strain include social support, job control, and organizational justice. The absence of any such factor also may be considered a stressor, and an organization may decide to start providing a specific environmental factor or increase its level to help employees cope with stress. Social support may come from friends or relatives off the job, co-workers, or supervisors. Good supervisors provide task-related, emotional, informational, and appraisal support.[134]

Perceived and actual support may differ. Perceived organizational support is a feeling that that the employer is concerned about workers and appreciates their contributions. This variable is negatively related to role conflict and role ambiguity among individuals with liaison, also known as boundary-spanning, positions.[135]

Black women's strong belief in responsibility to the black community may increase the social support available to aspiring black females. Bell and Nkomo call the "geographic, social, and psychological space where African Americans lived, shared a collective history, and held a common understanding of the way of life in a Black community" their "homeland."[136] Successful black women are expected to "give back" to those in the homeland, and managerial black women's families have done so when they "joined with people in the homeland to give these women unconditional love, armored them to go out into the world and do their best, and told them stories of Black people's painful struggles to achieve racial equality."[137] The families and "homeland" community provided aspiring black women with emotional support that may have been lacking in the workplace.

Emotional support from a supervisor can reduce negative stress consequences that otherwise might result from a job in which employees have little control over the work pace or the way in which tasks are done. This illustrates an interrelationship between two variables, each of which could serve as stressors or moderators depending on the circumstances. In this instance, lack of job control is the stressor, and support is the moderator. A high degree of job control may moderate high job demands to lessen stress. For example, managerial jobs are generally considered less stressful than clerical positions because managers have more job control.

Three types of *organizational justice*, defined as perceived fairness, are distributive, procedural, and interactional. *Distributive justice* refers to perceived equity in the allocation of outcomes, including the organization's resources and power. *Procedural justice* relates to the process through which resources are assigned, and perceived fairness of treatment and information provided in an interpersonal exchange or transaction is *interactional justice*.[138] When low job control is a stressor, perceived organizational justice may cushion its negative impact.[139] When one type of organizational injustice is a stressor, another type may buffer its negative effects. For example, perceived distributional justice may lessen the adverse effects of procedural injustice.

CONSEQUENCES OF STRESS

Though harmful outcomes of stress are widely recognized, some organizational consequences may be positive, especially if the stress is challenge-related rather than hindrance-related. *Challenge-related stress* occurs when individuals perceive a positive net gain from potentially distress-provoking demands, such as work overload or a high degree of responsibility. In *hindrance-related stress*, the net result is negative.

A study of 1,886 primarily male executives in large U.S. firms reveals that challenge-related stress is positively associated with job satisfaction and negatively linked to job search. The association between hindrance-related stress and both job satisfaction and job search are in the opposite directions. An inverse relationship also exists between hindrance-related stress and voluntary turnover.[140] Both types of stress are negatively linked to extroversion and positively associated with neuroticism. The relatively small percentage of women in the sample report more challenge-related stress than the men do.[141]

Another study of over 450 mainly white female nonmanagerial employees at a university again shows that challenge- and hindrance-related stress associate in opposite directions with certain work outcomes. Challenge-related stress is inversely related to job search, intent to quit, and work withdrawal behaviors, such as absenteeism and tardiness. It is positively linked to loyalty. Hindrance-related stress relates negatively to loyalty and positively to work withdrawal behaviors, job search, and voluntary turnover.[142] Both types of stress seem associated with anxiety and emotional exhaustion, two dimensions of psychological strain.[143]

Before research was conducted on challenge- and hindrance-related stress, empirical studies trying to link work stress with negative organizational outcomes, such as job dissatisfaction, intent to quit, and job search, often failed to do so.[144] Cavanaugh and colleagues believe this happened because both challenge- and hindrance-related stress were measured on the same scale.[145] Because they have the opposite impact on work outcomes, they cancel each other out.

Women generally report a higher level of distress than men but have thus far maintained a longevity advantage of nearly eight years.[146] Though they are more willing to say they experience pressure, women do not report worse mental health than men unless they are employed in male-dominated industries and use an interpersonal leadership style.[147] They are, however, two to three times more likely than male peers to report a "history of affective disorders."[148] With some exceptions, women report more chronic maladies; those that men mention tend to be life-threatening. Due to socialization, women may be more willing to report stress symptoms; men may be less likely to discuss health issues.[149]

Stockdale and colleagues reject a biological explanation for varying reactions to work stress among women and men and offer a "structural" explanation instead.[150] They say responses differ due to the extent that women have dissimilar organizational roles. More managerial women than men report stress as a consequence of their experience both on and off the job. When the unpaid "second shift" of domestic and childcare duties,[151] for which women are more likely to be responsible, is considered, women work longer than men. Long work hours affect both mental and physical health. Compared to non-managerial employed women, executive women seem to have better health outcomes, however. The association of multiple roles with a lowered risk of cardiovascular disease is especially strong among females in high status positions but has been noted for all employed women.[152]

Table 13.1 illustrates one possible way to categorize stress outcomes. Some items included may be both individual and organizational consequences; classifying them as one or the other is admittedly arbitrary. For example, an increased number of accidents or errors could have been categorized as an individual behavioral consequence instead of a consequence to the organization pertaining to performance quality and quantity. Similarly, job dissatisfaction could have been considered an organizational, rather than an individual, outcome.

Until relatively recently, most studies of managerial stress were based on white males, and most research on executive females and stress did not consider women of color. For that reason, a shortage of research on outcomes of perceived stress on minorities and women of color exists. Table 13.1 summarizes negative consequences of perceived stress based on studies of various groups, such as managers, employees, female employees, executive women, women of color, and specific minority groups, such as blacks, black executive women, Native American women, and Asian Americans. Unfortunately, empirical studies on stress outcomes are not readily available for each major racial/ethnic group by gender and occupation. For that reason, the summary in Table 13.1 is sketchy. Fontana enumerates negative outcomes commonly attributable to stress but does not cite empirical studies to verify the connection.[153] They are included in Table 13.1, but readers are cautioned that supporting evidence for these consequences may or may not exist.

Notable by their absence from the table are studies pertaining to the effects of stress on Hispanics. A study of Hispanic immigrants was not used because issues they encounter are beyond the scope of this chapter. The few other existing studies are not readily available.

Most items in Table 13.1 are self-explanatory; a few require elaboration, and an explanation is appropriate for some items that have been omitted. For example, *psychogenic disorders*, listed as adverse physical consequences of perceived stress to individuals, are physical illnesses that begin with a psychological problem.[154] Reduced morale is listed as a stress outcome for managerial women in Table 13.1 but is believed to be an adverse consequence for employees generally. So is *burnout*, which does not appear in Table 13.1 but can be defined as extreme physical and mental exhaustion that hinders or may prevent effective job performance. Minor aches and pains, muscle twitches, excess perspiration,[155] and digestive problems,[156] though not listed in Table 13.1, are considered effects of stress on employees.

State workers' compensation laws originally were passed to provide prompt compensation for work-related physical injuries without assigning fault. Their coverage expanded to cover stress-related illness, including emotional distress caused by workplace conditions. Because the number of claims due to on-the-job stress rose by the 1990s, more than thirty states adopted more stringent standards, which led to a reduction in such claims. For example, in Oregon, stress must be the "major contributing cause" of an injury or illness to be compensable.[157] Employee stress from justifiable human resource actions such as performance appraisal and discipline up to and including discharge are not compensable, even if they are handled poorly.[158] To prevail, stress-based workers' compensation claims increasingly must be related to unusual situations. DeFrank and Ivancevich give an example of a female secretary in a major U.S. city who experienced ongoing psychological trauma, but no physical injuries, after a steel beam fell into her office. That was deemed extraordinary enough to warrant compensation.

COPING MECHANISMS

Coping mechanisms are methods to deal with stress at the individual or organizational level or at the interface between the two. This section will discuss positive, rather than dysfunctional, coping mechanisms. The latter may result in increased daily hassles or adverse stress consequences which appear in Table 13.1.[159] *Individual coping* is the management of internal or external demands that are judged to exceed one's resources via cognitive or behavioral means.[160] *Organizational-level coping* methods may include job redesign, adoption of alternative work schedules, or provision of various employee benefits to help workers integrate or balance work and life.[161] Though different coping approaches can be identified, the process is complex, dynamic, and situation-specific.[162] Personality, demographics, other individual characteristics, the context, and a subjective evaluation of the situation greatly affect the effectiveness of the selected method(s). Coping also involves primary and secondary appraisal, described earlier.

As previously indicated, coping methods are commonly classified as problem- or emotion-focused.[163] Stockdale and colleagues add a third category of "appraisal-focused" methods, which others include as a subset of emotion-focused strategies.[164]

Problem-focused methods address the issue directly. They involve planning, thinking positively, seeking information and advice, confronting others, and contacting civil rights organizations if the stressful event entails discrimination. These approaches are considered more effective than emotion-focused coping, but no method is appropriate in all situations. Problem-oriented strategies can be used only when people can take control; if that is impossible, emotion-oriented coping may be the only option. With some exceptions, men seem to use problem-focused strategies more than women.[165] When dealing with racial discrimination, Asian American women are more likely than their male counterparts to use problem-focused coping.[166]

Overall, *emotion-oriented coping*, particularly readjustment of one's thoughts, is a dominant strategy among Asian Americans.[167] When facing discrimination, a majority in Kuo's study believe "things could be worse" and think that Asian Americans "are less victimized" than other minorities.[168]

Use of problem- and emotion-based strategies also differs by nationality and education level among Asian Americans. Chinese Americans are less likely to use problem-oriented approaches than Koreans; Koreans are more likely to use emotion-based approaches than Filipinos, who have a propensity to use problem-oriented strategies. Kuo concludes as follows: "These inter-group differences suggest that despite their common Confucian heritage, ethnicity still has a role in influencing coping choices."[169]

Contrary to popular belief, education, not socioeconomic status, relates to increased problem-focused coping.[170] Among Asian Americans, family income, another component of socioeconomic status, associates negatively with problem oriented strategies.

Ethnic identity is linked to problem-oriented coping among Hispanics. Those with higher levels deal with discrimination by refuting racist stereotypes; those with lower levels try to ignore them.[171]

Emotion-focused coping tries to change emotions arising as a result of stressors. It may include venting (expressing feelings to trusted confidantes as a release), wishful thinking, self-blame, or meditation. Appraisal-oriented coping, defined as a separate category of coping by Stockdale and colleagues but included under emotion-focused methods here, may entail redefining the meaning of the stressful event or situation or avoidance techniques, such as directing energy elsewhere.[172]

As indicated, support-seeking may be either a moderating variable or a coping mechanism in the stress model. When regarded as the latter, it is usually categorized as an emotion-focused strategy. Greenglass identifies two types of support: emotional, which provides a forum for "venting" and empathic reaction to distress; and instrumental, which consists of advice and practical help.[173] The latter seems similar to advice seeking as a problem-focused strategy.

Nelson and Burke maintain that women are at a disadvantage in terms of social support because they experience added challenges finding mentors and role models and being accepted in informal networks.[174] Workplace support seems to reduce work stress for men more than women even when both receive equal amounts.[175] Other research contradicts this finding, however. Studies on federal employees link co-worker support to instrumental and preventive coping among women but not among men. Greenglass,[176] reporting on research with Fiksenbaum, maintains that women's use of negative coping, such as wishful thinking, diminishes when co-workers support them. Single-parent female managers have less support than peers in two-parent households. They are less likely to receive support from ex-spouses or partners and may obtain little from extended families. Nevertheless, they tend to make good use of support they do have, primarily provided by female friends.[177]

Unemployed managerial women engage in activities to provide both emotional and instrumental support to a greater degree than their male counterparts. They are more likely to work for volunteer organizations, which not only provide an outlet but also may lead to valuable contacts to aid the job search process. Unemployed male managers, on the other hand, "tend to actively refuse situations in which they would have access to social support, thereby denying themselves an effective means of coping."[178]

Social support was among the top coping methods female Native American college students used to deal with bicultural conflict in the late 1980s. They also engaged in positive self-talk, worked harder, exercised, obtained professional counseling, and recalled beliefs about spirituality.[179]

Overall, emotion-oriented approaches are linked to increased emotional distress,[180] but specific methods may elicit such a response more than others. Obtaining social support through cultivation of close relationships, discussed here as an emotion-focused strategy, may have positive organizational and personal consequences. Women seek significantly more instrumental and emotional support than men,[181] which may be advantageous in coping with stress. Requesting help also is more consistent with gender role socialization commonly experienced by women.

Approaches that Asian Americans employ to deal with the stress associated with racial discrimination have been discussed. Because of the shortage of easily accessible information on other racial/ethnic groups, only the experiences African Americans have had coping with the stress of discrimination will be mentioned. African Americans rely on different strategies to confront *individual racism*, which affects them personally; *institutional racism*, previously defined as policies that exclude them from full participation in society and enjoyment of societal benefits; or *cultural racism*, the belief in the superiority of the cultural practices of the dominant group.[182]

African American women are more likely than men to seek social support in response to individual racism but prefer avoidance strategies to either problem solving or social support.[183] One study shows that African Americans who have experienced discrimination adopt an avoidance strategy,[184] but other research contradicts this. Feagin indicates that African Americans respond to individual racism with resigned acceptance or verbal counterattack;[185] Lalonde and colleagues suggest that black Canadians' preferred method of dealing with institutional racism is to seek social support.[186]

Why do some African Americans prefer avoidance to more active coping strategies? They and other racial/ethnic minorities find direct confrontation costly in terms of time and energy, even when discrimination is serious. In an individualistic culture such as the United States, which emphasizes competition and personal responsibility for success or failure, gaining support for the idea that a negative outcome was caused by discrimination, rather than a personal shortcoming, is increasingly difficult. Because discrimination is more subtle than it once was, white mid- to upper classes in the United States may be more likely to blame the person alleging discrimination for its existence than to consider the context or other societal factors contributing to the problem.[187]

ORGANIZATIONAL COPING: STRESS
MANAGEMENT INTERVENTIONS

Criticisms of stress management interventions are nearly as widespread as their use. Though they require a commitment of organizational resources and prospective consultants tout their advantages, surprisingly little is known about their effectiveness due to methodological and other problems including inconsistent terminology.[188] Systematic, rigorous evaluation of the effectiveness of stress management is lacking; Arthur indicates that the effectiveness of some interventions remains unknown due to such problems.[189] Dewe and O'Driscoll complain that stress management programs are often administered on an ad hoc basis.[190] Still others say that interventions are too narrow or invite legal liability.[191] Regarding the latter point, Dewe and O'Driscoll ask:

> What thought, for example, has been given to such ethical issues as informed consent, anonymity and confidentiality, potential harm and the individual's right to withdraw or not attend? Where in the intervention process has attention been given to the individual's right to access information collected during the intervention and their right to know how that information may be used, not to mention the legal risks organizations face by failing to pay attention to such issues?[192]

Some organizational interventions, such as equitable development and reward systems, workplace programs to provide social support and networking opportunities, zero tolerance for harassment, and concern for work-life integration, are recommended for organizations wishing to provide a welcoming environment for executive women.[193] These simply reflect good management practice, assuming they result from a needs analysis of a particular workforce and are not instituted as one-size-fits-all measures. Finally, lack of top management support and employees who are unwilling to participate will quickly derail stress management interventions.

Preventive (proactive) or *curative* (reactive) *stress management* interventions may be implemented at the individual, work group, or organizational level. Individual-level techniques are used most often, perhaps because some managers believe that reinforcing the mindset that stress is an individual problem absolves them from responsibility for dealing with it. In the long run, this idea may cause problems because the context seems to influence employees' stress perceptions.[194] Individual-level interventions may be more effective than those implemented organization-wide, however.[195]

Primary preventive approaches are intended to reduce the risks of damage from stressors or eliminate them, whereas *secondary preventive measures* help employees manage their responses to stressors. *Curative interventions* promote healing after strain has harmed employees and have been called tertiary preventive measures.[196] Due to their after-the-fact nature, this seems a misnomer.

Preventive interventions may include one or several of the following: relaxation, physical fitness, exercise, biofeedback, cognitive restructuring, meditation, assertiveness training, and time management. Stress awareness/education is another preventive measure.[197]

Progressive relaxation involves systematically tensing and relaxing muscle groups to obtain a calming response. For high-control employees, cognitive restructuring seems more effective in stress reduction than relaxation, however, according to a meta-analysis of forty-eight studies of stress interventions.[198] Interventions that include relaxation seem to be most effective in combating negative physiological or psychological effects of stress, and ninety-six stress management experts rank relaxation as most practical, easiest to implement, and least costly.[199]

Physical fitness entails monitoring, exercise, and good nutrition to increase cardiovascular and respiratory endurance. Previously mentioned stress management experts rank physical fitness most effective in achieving five of seven objectives, including individual fitness and physiological indices, reduction of negative symptoms, enhancement of psychological well-being, reduction of health care cost, and organizational effectiveness and image.[200] Exercise, which may be considered part of physical fitness or a separate stress management technique, is generally thought to be helpful in reducing stress. For example, Atchiler and Motta show that anxiety levels dropped after one session of aerobic exercise.[201] Even exercise is not recommended in all circumstances, however. In group settings, certain types of exercise can increase competitiveness and aggression, particularly among those with Type A tendencies.[202]

Biofeedback is included in less than 5 percent of stress management programs. It measures physiological changes in muscle and skin to provide information about physical effects of stress interventions and is typically used with relaxation methods.[203]

Cognitive restructuring involves changing perceptions of stress to build resilience. Unwarranted negativity is systematically replaced by more rational thoughts. This strategy seems most effective among individuals whose jobs have a high degree of decision latitude, such as managers.[204] Sixty-seven percent of stress management experts use cognitive restructuring "always," "constantly," or "often" compared to 59 percent who say the same about physical fitness, 56 percent for relaxation, and 35 percent for meditation.[205]

Meditation is focusing on one repetitive stimulus to prevent distraction and induce calmness. It resembles physical relaxation but employs mental exercises to achieve the same end.[206]

Assertiveness training, in which people learn to state their needs openly and honestly while respecting others' needs, is fairly widely used. Nevertheless, stress management experts do not consider it a very effective intervention.[207] In addition, it may clash with the way some Asian Americans and other ethnic groups have been socialized.

Stress awareness/education incorporates preventive techniques, such as relaxation, exercise, and biofeedback. Factual information, such as that presented in this chapter regarding the pervasiveness of stress, its causes, positive and negative consequences, and coping mechanisms, is provided.

Managing time more effectively sounds easy but can be challenging. It also may pose problems for those from ethnic or racial groups that approach time differently than the stereotypical white, non-Hispanic middle- to upper-class male U.S. executive does. After reassessing priorities, those who value the efficient use of time might benefit by asking whether all their current duties are necessary, and if so, whether they could be done less often or delegated to others.

If activities are essential, doing them less frequently saves time. For example, a professor whose department thought it was desirable to publish an alumni newsletter decided to do so twice per year instead of three times, saving time and funds. If work-related duties can be delegated, abandoning perfectionism and assigning them to others is wise. Professionals who can afford to hire help to do household and other chores should do so. The time gained may be well worth the money spent.

Employee assistance programs (EAPs) are invariably part of curative stress interventions. Started to deal with alcohol and drug abuse, EAPs are confidential referral programs led by an in-house coordinator who refers employees with marital, financial, family, or personal problems to appropriate social service agencies for professional counseling or other help. Bento quips that doubt exists about whether EAPs help employers or employees.[208] This is because, due to cost concerns, gatekeepers of EAPs may be reluctant to refer individuals to social workers, psychologists, and psychiatrists, whose help, more than that of professionals with less training, benefits employees experiencing the negative consequences of stress.[209] One of the few studies assessing the effectiveness of EAPs attributes reduced absenteeism, fewer health claims, and savings to their use.[210] In another study, a life insurance company reports $4.23 in claims savings for every dollar invested in an EAP.[211]

So far, stress management interventions have been discussed for employees generally, not necessarily managers, let alone executive women or racial/ethnic minorities in management. Nelson and Burke outline suggestions for executive women who are interested in primary and secondary stress prevention and in curative measures.[212] They suggest cognitive restructuring, self-analysis to identify personal stressors and develop plans for alleviation, and acceptance of positions with high visibility and developmental opportunities to reduce the risk of dysfunctional stress. Palliative measures recommended include meditation, conversations with trusted individuals to reduce the tendency to obsess or ruminate, and daily exercise. As a precaution, Nelson and Burke also urge executive women to develop relationships with physicians, psychologists, and other professionals before their services are needed in the same way they would develop contacts with tax lawyers or accountants on the job.[213]

SUMMARY

The focal point of this chapter is a comprehensive model that attempts to explain the process through which stressors lead to perceived stress, which has many individual and organizational consequences. Moderating factors and coping mechanisms affect perceived stress and may interact to reduce or worsen it. The same factor may be a moderating variable and a coping mechanism; for example, social support can be both. Moderating factors may be individual characteristics and behaviors or organizational variables such as the amount and type of social support, job control, and organizational power. Individual coping methods may be problem-focused or emotion-oriented; organizational coping includes stress management interventions that may be preventive or curative.

Stress-related issues relevant to ethnic and racial minorities and women are integrated throughout the chapter. For example, racism, discrimination, and biculturalism are stressors of particular concern to minorities; racism also may affect self-esteem, a moderating factor. Ethnic identity may buffer the negative effects of stress. Gender issues related to negative affectivity, another moderating variable, are discussed. Managerial women in low- or middle-level positions report more stress than men; executive females at top levels seen to experience less than women at lower levels.

NOTES

The author and publisher gratefully acknowledge permission to reprint an adaptation of Margaret Foeger Karsten, Chapter 11, "Stress and Managerial Women and Minorities," *Management, Gender, and Race in the 21st Century* (Lanham, MD: University Press of America, Inc., 2006): 318–49. Copyright © 2006 by University Press of America, Inc.). Adapted and reprinted with permission of University Press of America, Inc.

1. J. M. Ivancevich and M. T. Matteson, *Organizational Behavior and Management*, 4th ed. (Chicago: Irwin, 1996); M. S. Stockdale, K. P. Murphy, and J. Cleveland et al., *Women and Men in Organizations: Sex and Gender Issues at Work* (Mahwah, NJ: Lawrence Erlbaum Associates, 2000).

2. R. S. DeFrank and J. M. Ivancevich, J.M.,1998. "Stress on the Job: An Executive Update," *Academy of Management Executive* 12(1) (1998): 56.

3. American Institute of Stress, *Job Stress* (New York: American Institute of Stress, 2002).

4. National Institute for Occupational Safety and Health (NIOSH), *Worker Health Chartbook, 2004*, NIOSH Publication 2004-146; available online at www2a.cdc .gov/NIOSH-Chartbook/imagedetail.asp?imgid=47; retrieved November 24, 2004.

5. Ibid.

6. J. V. Portello and B. C. Long, "Appraisals and Coping with Interpersonal Stress: A Model for Women Managers," *Journal of Counseling Psychology* 48(2) (2001).

7. S. O. Utsey, J. G. Ponterotto, A. L. Reynolds, and A. A. Cancelli, "Racial Discrimination, Coping Life Satisfaction, and Self-Esteem among African Americans," *Journal of Counseling and Development* 78(1) (2000).

8. R. S. Lazarus and S. Folkman, *Stress, Appraisal and Coping* (New York: Springer, 1984).

9. M. J. Davidson, *The Black and Ethnic Minority Woman Manager: Cracking the Concrete Ceiling* (London: Chapman, 1997).

10. D. L. Nelson and R. J. Burke, "Women Executives: Health, Stress, and Success," *Academy of Management Executive* 14 (2000): 107–22.

11. M. F. Karsten, *Management, Gender, and Race in the 21st Century* (Lanham, MD: University Press of America Inc., 2006).

12. D. L. Nelson and R. J. Burke, "A Framework for Examining Gender, Work Stress, and Health," in D. L. Nelson and R. J. Burke, eds., *Gender, Work, Stress, and Health* (Washington, DC: American Psychological Association, 2002), pp. 3–14.

13. S. A. Hewlett, "Executive Women and the Myth of Having It All," *Harvard Business Review* 80 (2002): 66–74.

14. S. Gill and M. J. Davidson, "Problems and Pressures Facing Lone Mothers in Management and Professional Occupations—A Pilot Study," *Women in Management Review* 16 (2002): 383–400.

15. Ibid.

16. H. Landrine and E. A. Klonoff, "The Schedule of Racist Events: A Measure of Racial Discrimination and a Study of Its Negative Physical and Mental Health Consequences," *Journal of Black Psychology* 22 (1996): 144–68.

17. D. L. Plummer and S. Slane, "Patterns of Coping Racially Stressful Situations," *Journal of Black Psychology* 22 (1996): 302–15.

18. V. L. Thompson Sanders, "Perceived Experiences of Racism as Stressful Life Events," *Community Mental Health Journal* 32 (1996): 223–33.

19. D. R. Williams, D. I. S. Spencer, and J. Jackson, "Race, Stress, and Physical Health: The Role of Group Identity," in R. J. Contrada and R. D. Ashmore, eds., *Self, Social Identity, and Physical Health: Interdisciplinary Explorations* (London: Oxford University Press, 1999).

20. C. West, *Race Matters* (Boston: Beacon Press, 1993).

21. S. O. Utsey et al., "Racial Discrimination."

22. Ibid.

23. W. H. Kuo, "Coping with Racial Discrimination: The Case of Asian Americans," *Ethnic and Racial Studies* 18 (1995): 109–27.

24. Ibid.

25. K. L. Walters and J. M. Simoni, "Reconceptualizing Native Women's Health: An 'Indigenist' Stress-Coping Model," *American Journal of Public Health* 92 (2002): 520–24.

26. M. A. Jaimes and T. Halsey, "Native American Women," in M. A. Jaimes, ed., *The State of Native America* (Boston: South End Press, 1992), pp. 311–44.

27. Walters and Simoni, "Reconceptualizing Native Women's Health."

28. S. D. Toliver, *Black Families in Corporate America* (Thousand Oaks, CA: Sage, 1998).

29. Ibid.

30. T. D. LaFromboise, A. M. Heyle, and E. J. Ozer, "Changing and Diverse Roles," *Sex Roles* 22 (1990): 455–75.

31. L. Sutton, *Feed a Cold, Starve a Fever: An Exploration into the Relationship between Culture, Belief, and Health*, N.d., online document available at www.members.tripod.com/random_sage/part2b.htm; accessed November 24, 2004.

32. R. E. Zambrana, S. C. M. Scrimshaw, N. Collins, and C. Dunkel-Schetter, "Prenatal Health Behavior and Psychosocial Risk Factors in Pregnant Women of Mexican Origin: The Role of Acculturation," *American Journal of Public Health* 87 (1997): 1022–26.

33. LaFromboise et al., "Changing and Diverse Roles."

34. T. V. Tran, T. Fitzpatrick, W. R. Berg, and R. Wright Jr., "Acculturation, Health, Stress, and Psychological Distress among Elderly Hispanics," *Journal of Cross Cultural Gerontology* 11 (1996): 149–65.

35. LaFromboise et al., "Changing and Diverse Roles."

36. Kuo, "Coping with Racial Discrimination."

37. Ibid.

38. Davidson, *The Black and Ethnic Minority Woman Manager.*

39. Stockdale et al., *Women and Men in Organizations.*

40. R. Barnett and G. Baruch, "Social Roles, Gender, and Psychological Distress," in R. Barnett, L. Biener, and G. Baruch, eds., *Gender and Stress* (New York: Free Press, 1987), pp. 122–41.

41. M. C. Lennon, "Sex Role Orientation, Coping Strategies, and Self-Efficacy of Women in Traditional and Nontraditional Occupations," *Journal of Health and Social Behavior* 28 (1987): 290–305.

42. R. Karasek and T. Theorell, *Healthy Work: Stress, Productivity, and the Reconstruction of Working Life* (New York: Basic Books, 1990).

43. Stockdale et al., *Women and Men in Organizations.*

44. Ibid.; A. Smith, "Perceptions of Stress at Work," *Human Resource Management Journal* 11 (2001): 74–86.

45. D. A. Prentice and E. Carranza, "What Women and Men Should Be, Shouldn't Be, Are Allowed to be, and Don't Have to Be: The Contents of Prescriptive Gender Stereotypes," *Psychology of Women Quarterly* 26 (2002): 269–81.

46. See Karsten, *Management, Gender, and Race in the 21st Century.*

47. M. F. Karsten, *Management and Gender: Issues and Attitudes* (Westport, CT: Greenwood, 1994).

48. E. K. Kelloway, N. Sivanathan, L. Francis, and J. Barling, "Poor Leadership," in J. Barling, E. K. Kellway, and M. R. Frone, eds., *Handbook of Work Stress* (Thousand Oaks, CA: Sage, 2005), pp. 7–34.

49. D. M. Almeida and R. C. Kessler, "Everyday Stressors and Gender Differences in Daily Distress," *Journal of Personality and Social Psychology* 75 (1998).

50. DeFrank and Ivancevich, "Stress on the Job."

51. Karsten, *Management and Gender.*

52. Stockdale et al., *Women and Men in Organizations.*

53. P. Gamse, "Stress for Success," *HR Magazine* 48(7) (2003): 101–4.

54. S. L. Boyar, C. P. Maertz Jr., A. W. Person, and S. Keough, "Work and Family Domain Variables and Turnover Intentions," *Journal of Managerial Issues* 15 (2003).

55. G. M. Bellavia and M. R. Frone, "Work-Family Conflict," in J. Barling, E. K. Kelloway, and M. R. Frone, eds., *Handbook of Work Stress* (Thousand Oaks, CA: Sage, 2005), pp. 113–48.

56. Ibid.

57. S. C. Clark, "Work-Family Border Theory: A New Theory of Work/Family Balance," *Human Relations* 53 (2000): 747–70.

58. Boyar et al., "Work and Family Domain Variables."

59. Ibid., p. 180.

60. R. Buehler, D. Griffin, and M. Ross, "Exploring the 'Planning Fallacy': Why People Underestimate Their Task Completion Times," *Journal of Personality and Social Psychology* 67 (1994): 366–81.

61. G. A. Adams and S. M. Jex, "Relationships between Time Management, Control, Work-Family Conflict, and Strain," *Journal of Occupational Health Psychology* 4 (1999): 72–77.

62. Bellavia and Frone, "Work-Family Conflict."

63. H. C. Sumer and P. Knight, "How Do People with Different Attachment Styles Balance Work and Family? A Personality Perspective on Work-Family Linkage," *Journal of Applied Psychology* 86 (2001): 653–63.

64. J. B. Grzywacz and N. Marks, "Family Work, Work-Family Spillover and Problem Drinking during Midlife," *Journal of Marriage and the Family* 62 (2000): 336–48.

65. Ibid.

66. K. H. Bernas and D. A. Major, "Contributors to Stress Resistance: Testing a Model of Women's Work-Family Conflict," *Psychology of Women Quarterly* 24 (2000): 170–78.

67. Ibid.; C. S. Bruck, and T. D. Allen, "The Relationship between Big Five Personality Traits, Negative Affectivity, Type A Behavior and Work-Family Conflict," *Journal of Vocational Behavior* 63 (2003): 457–72.

68. Boyar et al., "Work and Family Domain Variables."

69. Ibid.

70. Bellavia and Frone, "Work-Family Conflict."

71. M. C. W. Peeters, J. deJonge, Peter P. M. Janssen, and S. van der Linden, "Work-Home Interference, Job Stressors, and Employee Health," *International Journal of Stress Management* 11 (2004).

72. S. E. Anderson, B. S. Coffey, and R. T. Byerly, "Formal Organizational Initiatives and Informal Workplace Practices Links to Work-Family Conflict and Job-Related Outcomes," *Journal of Management* 28 (2002): 787–810.

73. M. P. O'Driscoll, D. R. Ilgen, and K. Hildreth, "Time Devoted to Job and Off-Job Activities, Interrole Conflict, and Affective Experiences," *Journal of Applied Psychology* 77 (1992): 272–79.

74. M. Westman, "Gender Asymmetry in Crossover Research," in D. L. Nelson and R. J. Burke, eds., *Gender, Work, Stress, and Health* (Washington, DC: American Psychological Association, 2002), pp. 129–50.

75. Ibid.

76. Holmes and Rahe (1967), as reported in Karsten, *Management and Gender.*

77. E. Craeger, "Women and Stress," *Wisconsin State Journal* (October 8, 1991).

78. Karsten, *Management and Gender.*

79. R. J. Turner and W. R. Avison, "Status Variations in Stress Exposure: Implications for the Interpretation of Research on Race, Socioeconomic Status, and Gender," *Journal of Health and Social Behavior* 44 (2003): 488–505.

80. Ibid., p. 498.

81. Ibid.

82. R. J. Turner and D. A. Lloyd, "Lifetime Trauma and Mental Health: The Significance of Cumulative Adversity," *Journal of Health and Social Behavior* 36 (1995): 360–75.

83. Turner and Avison, "Status Variations in Stress Exposure."

84. Ibid., p. 496.

85. C. Schaefer, J. Coyne, and R. Lazarus, "The Health-Related Functions of Social Support," *Journal of Behavioral Medicine* 4 (1981): 381–406.

86. K. N. Mossakowski, "Coping with Perceived Discrimination: Does Ethnic Identity Protect Mental Health?" *Journal of Health and Social Behavior* 44 (2003): 318–31.

87. I. H. Meyer, "Prejudice as Stress: Conceptual and Measurement Problems," *American Journal of Public Health* 93 (2003): 262–64.

88. V. L. S. Thompson, "Racism: Perceptions of Distress among African Americans," *Community Mental Health Journal* 38 (2002): 111–19.

89. B. C. Long, "Coping with Workplace Stress: A Multiple Group Comparison of Female Managers and Clerical Workers," *Journal of Counseling Psychology* 45 (1998).

90. Portello and Long, "Appraisals and Coping with Interpersonal Stress."

91. A. Bandura, "Self-Efficacy Mechanism in Human Agency," *American Psychologist* 37 (1982): 122–47.

92. Long, "Coping with Workplace Stress."

93. B. C. Long, S. E. Kahn, and R. W. Schultz, "Causal Model of Stress and Coping: Women in Management," *Journal of Counseling Psychology* 45 (1998).

94. Portello and Long, "Appraisals and Coping with Interpersonal Stress."

95. Ibid.

96. S. M. Jex, P. D. Bliese, S. Buzzell, and J. Primeau, "The Impact of Self-Efficacy on Stressor-Strain Relations: Coping Style as an Explanatory Mechanism," *Journal of Applied Psychology* 86 (2001): 401–9; S. M. Jex and S. M. Gudanowski, "Efficacy Beliefs and Work Stress: An Exploratory Study," *Journal of Organizational Behavior* 13 (1992): 182–91.

97. J. L. Pierce, D. G. Gardner, R. B. Dunham, and L. L. Cummings, "Moderation by Organization-Based Self-Esteem of Role Condition-Employee Response Relationship," *Academy of Management Journal* 36 (1993): 271–88.

98. S. M. Jex, J. Cvetanovski, and S. J. Allen, "Self-Esteem as a Moderator of the Impact of Unemployment," *Journal of Social Behavior and Personality* 9 (1994): 69–80.

99. S. L. Fielden and C. L. Cooper, "Managerial Stress: Are Women More at Risk?" in D. L. Nelson and R. J. Burke, eds., *Gender, Work, Stress, and Health* (Washington, DC: American Psychological Association, 2002), pp. 19–34.

100. G. E. Simpson and J. M. Yinger, *Racial and Cultural Minorities: An Analysis of Prejudice and Discrimination*, 5th ed. (New York: Plenum, 1985).

101. Davidson, *The Black and Ethnic Minority Woman Manager*.

102. A. W. P. Pak, K. L. Dion, and K. K. Dion, "Social Psychological Correlates of Experienced Discrimination: Test of the Double Jeopardy Hypothesis," *International Journal of Intercultural Relations* 15 (1991): 243–54.

103. Mossakowski, "Coping with Perceived Discrimination."

104. Walters and Simoni, "Reconceptualizing Native Women's Health."

105. Mossakowski, "Coping with Perceived Discrimination."

106. Walters and Simoni, "Reconceptualizing Native Women's Health."

107. T. A. Beehr and S. Glazer, "Organizational Role Stress," in J. Barling, E. K. Kelloway, and M. R. Frone, eds., *Handbook of Work Stress* (Thousand Oaks, CA: Sage, 2005), pp. 7–34.

108. D. J. Cherrington, "Needs Theory of Motivation," in R. M. Steers and L. W. Porter, eds., *Motivation and Work Behavior* (New York: McGraw-Hill, 1991).

109. G. M. Kapalka and J. R. Lachenmeyer, "Sex-Role Flexibility, Locus of Control, and Occupational Status," *Sex Roles* 19 (1988): 417–27.

110. W. Weiten, *Psychology Themes and Variations* (Pacific Grove, CA: Brooke/Cole, 1989).

111. W. A. Hochwater, P. L. Perrewe, and M. C. Dawkins, "Gender Differences in Perceptions of Stress-Related Variables. Do the People Make the Place or Does the Place Make the People?" *Journal of Managerial Issues* 7 (1995): 62–74.

112. C. A. Beatty, "The Stress of Managerial and Professional Women: Is the Price Too High?" *Journal of Organizational Behavior* 17 (1996): 233–51.

113. Portello and Long, "Appraisals and Coping with Interpersonal Stress."

114. M. A. Cavanaugh, W. R. Boswell, M. V. Roehling, and J. W. Boudreau, "An Empirical Examination of Self-Reported Work Stress among U.S. Managers," *Journal of Applied Psychology* 85 (2000): 65–74.

115. S. M. Jex, G. M. Adams, M. L. Ehler, "Assessing the Role of Negative Affectivity in Occupational Stress Research: Does Gender Make a Difference?" in D. L. Nelson and R. J. Burke, eds., *Gender, Work, Stress, and Health* (Washington, DC: American Psychological Association, 2002), pp. 71–84.

116. Nelson and Burke, "A Framework for Examining Gender."

117. S. Nolen-Hoeksema, "Sex Differences in Unipolar Depression: Evidence and Theory," *Psychological Bulletin* 101 (1987): 259–82.

118. Jex et al., "Assessing the Role of Negative Affectivity."

119. Almeida and Kessler, "Everyday Stressors and Gender Differences."

120. Nelson and Burke, "A Framework for Examining Gender."

121. N. Adler and K. Matthews, "Health Psychology: Why Do Some People Get Sick and Some Stay Well?" *Annual Review of Psychology* 45 (1994): 229–59.

122. D. Rees and C. L. Cooper, "Occupational Stress in Health Service Workers in the U.K.," *Stress Medicine* 8 (1990): 79–80.

123. Fielden and Cooper, "Managerial Stress: Are Women More at Risk?"

124. Ibid.

125. R. J. Burke, "Workaholism among Women Managers: Work and Life Satisfactions and Psychological Well-Being," *Equal Opportunities International* 18 (1999): 25–35.

126. Ibid.

127. Ibid.

128. Barnett and Baruch, "Social Roles, Gender, and Psychological Distress."

129. Portello and Long, "Appraisals and Coping with Interpersonal Stress."

130. Smith, "Perceptions of Stress at Work."

131. Portello and Long, "Appraisals and Coping with Interpersonal Stress."

132. Nelson and Burke, "Women Executives."

133. Smith, "Perceptions of Stress at Work."

134. Kelloway et al., "Poor Leadership."

135. C. L. Stamper and M. C. Johlke, "The Impact of Perceived Organizational Support on the Relationship between Boundary Spanner Role Stress and Work Outcomes," *Journal of Management* 29 (2003): 569–88.

136. E. Bell and S. Nkomo, *Our Separate Ways: Black and White Women and the Struggle for Professional Identity* (Cambridge, MA: Harvard Business School Press, 2000), p. 183.

137. Ibid.

138. R. Cropanzano, B. M. Goldman, and L. Benson III, "Organizational Justice," in J. Barling, E. K. Kelloway, and M. R. Frone, eds., *Handbook of Work Stress* (Thousand Oaks, CA: Sage, 2005), pp. 63–88.

139. Ibid.

140. Cavanaugh et al., "An Empirical Examination of Self-Reported Work Stress."

141. Ibid.

142. W. R. Boswell, J. B. Olson-Buchanan, and M. A. LePine, "Relations between Stress and Work Outcomes: The Role of Felt Challenge, Job Control, and Psychological Strain," *Journal of Vocational Behavior* 64 (2004): 165–91.

143. Ibid.

144. R. D. Bretz, J. W. Boudreau, and T. A. Judge, "Job Search Behavior of Employed Managers," *Personnel Psychology* 47 (1994): 275–301; C. S. Leong, A. Y. Furnham, and C. L. Cooper, "The Moderating Effect of Organizational Commitment on the Occupational Stress Outcome Relationship," *Human Relations* 49 (1996): 1345–63.

145. Cavanaugh et al., "An Empirical Examination of Self-Reported Work Stress."

146. Nelson and Burke, "Women Executives."

147. M. Gardiner and M. Tiggermann, "Gender Differences in Leadership Style, Job Stress and Mental Health in Male- and Female-Dominated Industries," *Journal of Occupational and Organizational Psychology* 72 (1999): 301–16.

148. Almeida and Kessler, "Everyday Stressors and Gender Differences."

149. Stockdale et al., *Women and Men in Organizations.*

150. Ibid.

151. A. R. Hochschild and A. Machung, *The Second Shift* (New York: Viking, 1989).

152. Nelson and Burke, "Women Executives."

153. D. Fontana, *Managing Stress (Problems in Practice)* (Oxford: British Psychology Society and Routledge, 1989).

154. Stockdale et al., *Women and Men in Organizations.*

155. Beehr and Glazer, "Organizational Role Stress."

156. Stockdale et al., *Women and Men in Organizations.*

157. DeFrank and Ivancevich, "Stress on the Job."

158. Ibid.

159. Portello and Long, "Appraisals and Coping with Interpersonal Stress."

160. Lazarus and Folkman, *Stress, Appraisal, and Coping.*

161. See Karsten, *Management, Gender, and Race in the 21st Century.*

162. Fielden and Cooper, "Managerial Stress: Are Women More at Risk?"

163. A. Billings and R. Moos, "The Role of Coping Responses and Social Resources in Attenuating the Stress of Life Events," *Journal of Behavioral Medicine* 4 (1981): 157–89.

164. Stockdale et al., *Women and Men in Organizations.*

165. A. J. M. Vingerhoets and G. L. Van Heck, "Gender, Coping and Psychosomatic Symptoms," *Psychological Medicine* 20 (1990): 120–35.

166. Kuo, "Coping with Racial Discrimination."

167. Ibid.

168. Ibid.

169. Ibid., p. 124.

170. Ibid.

171. Mossakowski, "Coping with Perceived Discrimination."

172. Stockdale et al., *Women and Men in Organizations*.

173. E. Greenglass, "Work Stress, Coping, and Social Support," in D. Nelson, L. Nelson, and R. J. Burke, eds., *Gender, Work, Stress, and Health* (Washington, DC: American Psychological Association, 2002), pp. 85–114.

174. Nelson and Burke, "Women Executives."

175. Ibid.

176. Greenglass, "Work Stress, Coping, and Social Support."

177. Gill and Davidson, "Problems and Pressures."

178. S. L. Fielden and C. L. Cooper, "Women Managers and Stress: A Critical Analysis," *Equal Opportunities International* 20 (2001): 3–16.

179. LaFromboise et al., "Changing and Diverse Roles."

180. Fielden and Cooper, "Managerial Stress: Are Women More at Risk?"

181. Greenglass, "Work Stress, Coping, and Social Support."

182. J. M. Jones, *Prejudice and Racism*, 2nd ed. (New York: McGraw-Hill, 1997).

183. Utsey et al., "Racial Discrimination."

184. N. Krieger and S. Sidney, "Racial Discrimination and Blood Pressures: The CARDIA Study of Young Black and White Adults," *American Journal of Public Health* 86 (1996): 1370–78.

185. J. R. Feagin, "The Continuing Significance of Race: Anti-Black Discrimination in Public Places," *American Sociological Review* 56 (1991): 101–16.

186. R. N. Lalonde, S. Majumder, and R. D. Parris, "Preferred Responses to Situations of Housing and Employment Discrimination," *Journal of Applied Social Psychology* 25 (1995): 1105–19.

187. Utsey et al., "Racial Discrimination."

188. J. J. Hurrell Jr., "Organizational Stress Interventions," in J. Barling, E. K. Kelloway, and M. R. Frone, eds., *Handbook of Work Stress* (Thousand Oaks, CA: Sage, 2005), pp. 7–34.

189. A. R. Arthur, "Mental Health Problems and British Workers: A Survey of Mental Health Problems in Employees who Receive Counseling from Employee Assistance Programs," *Stress and Health* 18 (2002).

190. P. Dewe and M. P. O'Driscoll, "Stress Management Interventions: What Do Managers Actually Do?" *Personnel Review* 31 (2002): 143–62.

191. C. Bellarosa and P. Y. Chen, "The Effectiveness and Practicality of Occupational Stress Management Interventions: A Survey of Subject Matter Expert Opinions," *Journal of Occupational Health Psychology* 2 (1997).

192. Dewe and O'Driscoll, "Stress Management Interventions."

193. Nelson and Burke, "Women Executives."

194. Long, "Coping with Workplace Stress."

195. J. J. L. Van der Klink, R. W. B. Blonk, A. H. Schene, and F. J. H. Van Dijk, "The Benefits of Interventions for Work-Related Stress," *American Journal of Public Health* 91 (2001): 270–76.

196. Nelson and Burke, "Women Executives."

197. Bellarosa and Chen, "The Effectiveness and Practicality"; S. Cartwright, and C. Cooper, "Individually Targeted Interventions," in J. Barling, E. K. Kelloway, and M. R. Frone, eds., *Handbook of Work Stress* (Thousand Oaks, CA: Sage, 2005), pp. 607–22.

198. Van der Klink et al,, "The Benefits of Interventions."

199. Bellarosa and Chen, "The Effectiveness and Practicality."

200. Ibid.

201. L. Atchiler and R. Motta, "Effects of Aerobic and Non Aerobic Exercise on Anxiety, Absenteeism, and Job Satisfaction," *Journal of Clinical Psychology* 50 (1994): 829–40.

202. S. Cartwright and L. Whatmore, "Stress and Individual Differences: Implications for Stress Management," in A. Antoniou and C. L. Cooper, eds., *New Perspectives in the Area of Occupational Health* (London: Wiley, 2003).

203. Cartwright and Cooper, "Individually Targeted Interventions."

204. Van der Klink et al., "The Benefits of Interventions."

205. Bellarosa and Chen, "The Effectiveness and Practicality."

206. Van der Klink et al., "The Benefits of Interventions."

207. Ibid.

208. R. F. Bento, "On the Other Hand . . . The Paradoxical Nature of Employee Assistance Programs," *Employee Assistance Quarterly* 13 (1997): 83–91.

209. M. E. P. Seligman, "The Effectiveness of Psychotherapy: The Consumer Reports Study," *American Psychologist* 50 (1995): 965–74.

210. F. Landy, J. Quick, and S. Kasl, "Work, Stress, and Well-Being," *International Journal of Stress Management* 1 (1994): 33–73.

211. B. Intindola, "EAPs Still Foreign to Many Small Businesses," *National Underwriter* 95 (1991).

212. Nelson and Burke, "Women Executives."

213. Ibid.

Index

Page numbers followed by f or t indicate figures or tables.

About the Editor and Contributors

Margaret Foegen Karsten is Professor in the Department of Business and Accounting and Coordinator of the Print Business Administration Distance Program at the University of Wisconsin-Platteville, where she teaches management and human resource management courses. She developed a *Management, Gender, and Race* course and has taught it for many years. Her books include *Management, Gender, and Race in the 21st Century* (2005) and *Management and Gender: Issues and Attitudes* (1994), in addition to over twenty other professional publications. She has presented at many national and regional conferences, has received several grants, and has held various administrative positions. Her current research interests include career paths of executive women and the impact of intellectual distance between students and professors on learning.

Claretha H. Banks is Assistant Professor at the University of Arkansas–Fayetteville. Her research interests focus on vocational and adult education/human resource development (HRD), and she teaches courses in those areas. She holds graduate faculty status II and advises graduate students with an interest in vocational and adult education. Claretha has extensive professional experience in business and industry and continues to serve as a consultant to international, national, and state organizations in vocational and adult education and HRD.

Jimmy L. Davis is a doctoral student in the Industrial/Organizational Psychology Program at the University of Georgia (UGA). His research focuses on the psychology of workplace diversity with emphasis on the career and organizational experiences of women and people of color. He is the 2004 recipient of UGA's Fanning Leadership award for leadership among graduate students. Davis has worked on consulting projects for large and small organizations and agencies such as BellSouth, the UGA Accounts Payable Department, United Parcel

Service, the American Cancer Society, the Human Resource Research Organization, and Home Depot.

Suzanne C. de Janasz is Associate Professor of Leadership and Management at the College of Graduate and Professional Studies at the University of Mary Washington. Before earning her doctorate, she was an organization development consultant in the aerospace industry. Her research interests include work-family conflict, careers, mentoring, leadership, and innovative pedagogy, and she has published several articles in journals such as the *Academy of Management Executive, Journal of Organizational Behavior, Career Development International,* and *Journal of Management Education.* De Janasz has made many presentations and has been an invited contributor for a variety of organizations and media outlets. She serves in various leadership roles in the Academy of Management, Organizational Behavior Teaching Society, and the Southern Management Association.

Gail Evans, author of *Play Like a Man, Win Like a Woman* and *She Wins, You Win,* is Visiting Professor at the Dupree School of Management at Georgia Tech. Her previous positions include executive vice president of CNN, where she was employed since its inception, and founding partner of Global Research Services, an Atlanta-based marketing and research firm. Evans's career began in government, and she helped create the President's Committee on Equal Employment Opportunity while working in the Office of the Special Counsel to the President during the Lyndon B. Johnson administration. Evans was elected to the Committee of 200, International Women's Forum, and the Council on Foreign Relations. She is a member of the board of directors for organizations that include the Society for Women's Health Research, the Radio Television News Directors Foundation, the Breman Jewish Heritage Museum, and the Atlanta Girls School.

Monica L. Forret is Associate Professor in the Department of Managerial Studies at St. Ambrose University. She has published articles in *Organizational Dynamics, Journal of Organizational Behavior, Group and Organization Management, Journal of Vocational Behavior, Journal of Business and Psychology,* and *Leadership and Organization Development Journal* primarily in the areas of networking, mentoring, and recruitment processes.

Michele V. Gee has a dual appointment as Assistant to the Provost and Associate Professor of Management in the School of Business and Technology at the University of Wisconsin–Parkside. Her interests include workplace diversity, cross-cultural management, international business, economic development, strategic management, and workforce skills development, and she is currently developing a mentoring program on campus. Gee also provides expertise to the chancellor and campus community in its ongoing strategic planning activities.

She was co-director of the Center for International Studies, co-director of three externally funded regional economic development programs, and has been appointed to many UW System committees/task forces. She is a two-time recipient of the University of Wisconsin System Women of Color Awards and has received several other honors and awards.

Laura M. Graves is Associate Professor of Management at the Graduate School of Management at Clark University. She is a recognized scholar on diversity issues in the workplace. Her work focuses on topics such as balancing work and family, preventing sex bias in employee selection, and managing diverse teams. She recently coauthored *Women and Men in Management* (3rd ed., 2003), which considers how gender influences individuals' experiences in organizations. Her research has appeared in leading academic journals, including *Academy of Management Review, Journal of Applied Psychology, Journal of Organizational Behavior, Human Relations*, and *Personnel Psychology*.

Catherine Kano Kikoski is Professor and Chair of the Graduate Department of Marriage and Family Therapy at St. Joseph College, West Hartford, Connecticut. She is a licensed psychologist and a licensed marriage and family therapist. She and John F. Kikoski have taught, researched, presented, consulted, and published in the field of face-to-face communication with foci on diversity and knowledge creation for over twenty-five years.

John F. Kikoski is Professor of Political Science and Public Administration at Sacred Heart University in Fairfield, Connecticut. He is past president of the section on professional organization and development of the American Society for Public Administration.

Catherine A. Lamboley is Senior Vice President and General Counsel of Houston-based Shell Oil Company, an affiliate of Royal Dutch Shell, the third largest oil and gas group in the world with 112,000 employees and operations in 140 countries. Lamboley joined Shell in 1979 and has spent most of her career in the legal organization. She serves on the Shell Oil Leadership Team. Active in the legal and business communities, she serves on various local and national committees and boards, including the Catalyst Board of Advisors and United Way of the Texas Gulf Coast. She also chairs the Minority Corporate Counsel Association and Houston Area Women's Center Boards

Audrey J. Murrell is Associate Professor of Business Administration at the Katz School of Business at the University of Pittsburgh, where she is also Director of the Program on Women and the Workforce at the University Center for Social and Urban Research. She holds secondary appointments in the Psychology Department and the Graduate School of Public and International Affairs. Murrell has conducted research on positive versus negative effects of career mobility and transition with emphasis on factors affecting careers of women in management, including mentoring, affirmative action, and workplace discrimination. This work has been published widely in management and psychology journals and book chapters. It has been highlighted by the popular media such as the *Wall Street Journal, Black Enterprise,* and *Vida Executive* (in Brazil). Murrell's many recognitions include the Girl Scouts of Southern Pennsylvania's 2002 Women of Distinction award and the Women's Leadership Assembly's Susan B. Anthony Women of Vision award (2001). She is coauthor of *Mentoring Dilemmas: Developmental Relationships within Multicultural Organizations* (1999).

Patricia J. Ohlott is Senior Research Associate at the Greensboro campus of the Center for Creative Leadership. She is coauthor of *Standing at the Crossroads: Next Steps for High-Achieving Women.* Her research focuses on the career development of women and the impact of diversity on management development processes. She has published articles in the *Academy of Management Journal, Journal of Applied Psychology, Human Resource Management, Personnel Psychology, Journal of Management Development,* and *Training and Development.* She coauthored the center's feedback instrument, the Job Challenge Profile, has broad interests in the field of leadership development, and contributed a chapter on the use of assignments for developmental purposes to the center's *Handbook of Leadership Development.* Her work recently received a citation from the American Society of Training and Development for excellence in translating research to practice.

Louise F. Root-Robbins is Honorary Fellow at the Women's Studies Research Center at the University of Wisconsin–Madison. Previously, she served as the University of Wisconsin System Coordinator for the President's Initiative on the Status of Women and was co-director of the UW System Sloan Project for Academic Career Advancement. She has teaching and research experience in the medical and nursing schools at UW–Madison and was a senior administrator at the Wisconsin Department of Public Instruction and Division of Health, where she worked closely with the U.S. Centers for Disease Control to implement statewide HIV/AIDS prevention programs. Root-Robbins is a member of the board of directors of the national organization College and University Work/ Family Association and the Wisconsin Women in Higher Education Leadership. She received the Madison 1993 League of Women Voters Citizen of Distinction Award, the 2003 YWCA Woman of Distinction Award, and the Milwaukee 2003 Margaret Miller Award for distinctive community service on behalf of women's health.

Marian N. Ruderman is Director of Global Leadership and Diversity at the Center for Creative Leadership. Her research focuses on the career development of women and the impact of diversity on leadership development, and she has written widely on these topics. Ruderman is coauthor of *Standing at the Cross-roads: Next Steps for High-Achieving Women* and coeditor of *Diversity in Work Teams: Research Paradigms for a Changing Workplace*. She coauthored the center's feedback instrument, the *Job Challenge Profile*. Her published work has been cited widely in the press and has been applied in the Women's Leadership Program offered by the Center for Creative Leadership. In addition, she speaks frequently to corporate and academic audiences about issues related to the career development of women.

Britain A. Scott is Associate Professor of Psychology at the University of St. Thomas in St. Paul, Minnesota. She has taught social psychology and psychology of women courses for over a decade and currently teaches a seminar called Women IN Their Bodies, in which students learn about theory and research on women's bodily objectification and then engage in experiential physical activities that represent embodied antidotes to the negative psychological effects of living in an objectified body. Several of Scott's publications, presentations, and ongoing research projects address the topic of women's bodily objectification.

Sidney W. Scott is Vice President of Human Resources for Woodward Communications. of Dubuque, Iowa. Previously, Scott held leadership positions in marketing, organization development, and public relations and distribution in three media corporations and was business manager for two physician specialty groups. His firm, Scott Consultants, has assisted organizations with strategic planning, organization development, human resources, and marketing since 1983. Scott's articles have appeared in publications including *Training, Training and Development, Personnel Journal* (now *Workforce*), and *Organization Development Journal*. He has presented for several national organizations, including the Society for Human Resource Management and the American Society of Training and Development. An adjunct faculty member at the University of Wisconsin–Madison Executive Education Center and UW–Platteville, Scott is a Registered Organization Development Consultant and serves on the board of directors of the National Center for Employee Ownership and Monroe Publishing Company. In 2000, he received the Volunteer Leadership Award from the local American Red Cross chapter, and in 2003, Iowa Governor Vilsack selected Scott to serve on the Iowa Health Facilities Council.

Kecia M. Thomas is Associate Professor in the Psychology and African American Studies Departments at the University of Georgia (UGA). She is coordinator for Graduate Education in the Psychology Department. Her research focuses on the psychology of workplace diversity, and over thirty of her articles have appeared in publications, including the *Journal of Applied Psychology, Academy of Management Learning and Education,* and *Journal of Business and Psychology.* She edited an issue of the *Journal of Career Development* on black women's experiences and has written many chapters dealing with diversity. Thomas is author of the first diversity text written by an industrial/organizational psychologist, *Diversity Dynamics in Organizations* and the forthcoming edited volume *Diversity Resistance: Manifestations and Solutions*. She is on the executive committee of the Academy of Management's Gender and Diversity in Organizations Division. The 2004 recipient of UGA's first faculty award for diversity, Thomas has consulted for organizations such as the U.S. Department of Agriculture, BellSouth, and the American Cancer Society.

Thomas J. Zagenczyk is a doctoral candidate within the Organizational Behavior/Human Resources area of the Katz School of Business at the University of Pittsburgh. His research interests include the employer–employee relationship, informal relationships in organizations, and social issues in management.